Patriotism and
First World War Britain

C000262944

Patriotism and Propaganda in First World War Britain

The National War Aims Committee and Civilian Morale

David Monger

LIVERPOOL UNIVERSITY PRESS

First published 2012 by
Liverpool University Press
4 Cambridge Street
Liverpool
L69 7ZU

This paperback version published 2014.

British Library Cataloguing-in-Publication data
A British Library CIP record is available

ISBN 978-1-84631-830-6 *cased*
ISBN 978-1-78138-013-0 *paperback*

Typeset in Sabon by R. J. Footring Ltd, Derby
Printed in Great Britain by CPI Group (UK) Ltd, Croydon CR0 4YY

Contents

Figures and Tables

Tables

Acknowledgements

ANY list of acknowledgements must begin with my parents, who fostered my interest in history, paid substantial parts of the costs of my education, listened to various gripes, whinges and a probably unreasonable share of ill-temper, and did many other things beyond. Thanks.

Further thanks are appropriate to a string of patient and differently inspiring teachers, from Warren Davies and Malcolm Day at William Parker School, to Joanna De Groot, Alan Forrest, Mark Ormrod and Shane O'Rourke at the University of York, each of whom drove my development as a historian and otherwise through their enthusiasm, rigour, good nature and high expectations. Among other debts accumulated at York (social, economic and otherwise) I am delighted to be able to fulfil my part of a bargain with David Mutton with this acknowledgement, unlikely as it seemed at the time. Postgraduate work at King's College London was a stimulating, challenging experience, thanks particularly to Richard Vinen and his dancing eyebrows, along with Bill Philpott and Paul Readman, whose courses drove me towards the subject of this book. My PhD research, of which this book is the product, was the result of timely advice from Adrian Gregory, whose response to an email from an unknown MA student was that the NWAC might be a good topic for someone wanting to study First World War patriotism. Once I had worked out what the NWAC was, I was on my way!

Staff at King's College London ensured I did not rest on my laurels, and I am grateful to Arthur Burns and Richard Vinen for a demanding upgrade viva, which helped to shape my ideas into the form they now take, rather than the somewhat more derivative version of the time, as well as to Bill for generous and supportive help as second supervisor, and to Paul for regular and unstinting attention, encouragement and criticism (as required). I hope that my own attention to students' needs is somewhere approaching the example I was set.

The experience of the PhD was enriched by many other people. I am grateful to Adam Sutcliffe, then the organiser of the departmental seminar, for arranging my first public presentation, though perhaps less grateful for his choice of the second speaker at the seminar (P.J. Marshall), whose presence ensured the largest seminar audience I have yet addressed! The availability of the seminars and other facilities of the Institute of Historical Research were a great boon, and I am grateful for many friendships made or continued there and elsewhere, including Matthew Cragoe, James Dixon, Pieter Francois, Dion Georgiou, Julie Hipperson, Tony Little, Helen McCarthy, Henry Miller, John Price, Roland Quinault, Tim Reinke-Williams, Michael Thompson and Jenny West. Some of these friends have made substantial contributions to my work by reading, listening to or commenting upon various aspects or suggesting further reading, as particularly have Kate Bradley, Stuart Hallifax, Joseph Maslen, Laura Rowe, David Thackeray, Frank Trentmann, and Martha Vandrei. Many, if not all, of these people have ensured sanity through the consumption of food and drink, as has Ian Barrett in his role as fellow MA and PhD traveller, neighbour and all-round good bloke. Ian's mission to the National Archives on my behalf once I had left for New Zealand also enabled me to refine aspects of the book despite my distance from the documents. One of the drawbacks of now living and working on the other side of the world is the inability to spend time in direct contact with these friends.

My ability to spend three years researching a PhD was crucially dependent upon an award from the Arts and Humanities Research Council, and I am grateful for its support. For permission to reproduce the following images from its holdings, I am grateful to the Bodleian Libraries, University of Oxford (Shelfmark: Per. 22281 c.99, no. 5 p. 49; no. 20 p. 235; no. 18 p. 211; no. 16 p. 189; no. 17 p. 198; no. 15 p. 175; no. 16 p. 181; no. 8 p. 85; no. 21 p. 248; no. 21 p. 241; no. 2). For permission to reproduce materials from within their collections I am also grateful to the National Archives and its Image Library, the Parliamentary Archives and the LSE Library.

Aspects of the arguments in this book were presented to audiences at the King's College London departmental seminar, the 'British History, 1815–1945', 'Sport and Leisure History' and 'Women's History' seminars at the IHR, the 'Apéro 14–18' seminar at Christ Church College, Oxford, conferences at Oxford Brookes and Durham Universities, and the History Programme seminar at the University of Canterbury. Further valuable observations were provided by the examiners of my PhD thesis, Jon Lawrence and David Stevenson, the editors and anonymous readers of articles in *Sport in History* and *Cultural and Social History*, as well as those who commented upon my original draft manuscript for Liverpool University Press. I am grateful for all suggestions and, naturally, take all responsibility for remaining shortcomings.

The ability to convert my PhD thesis into this book depended upon embarking upon an academic career. I am thus very grateful to the

History Department and the School of Humanities at the University of Canterbury in Christchurch, New Zealand for gambling upon the potential of a new scholar and providing me with a professional base since 2010. For sustaining me in a bearable condition for the time it took to get that far, I am grateful to King's College London and Queen's University Canada's Bader International Study Centre for teaching fellowships, as well as to Laura Clayton and Maddy Jessop for tolerating my help in the KCL History Department office, and Mark Freeman, Jan Palmowski and Kristina Spohr-Readman.

Cricket remains the one thing that successfully insists upon proper days off. Sanity was retained during the PhD by the scepticism of my research's merits provided by my cricket teams Beaulieu C.C. and Robertsbridge C.C. Happily, scepticism has been retained by members of my new club, Merivale Papanui C.C. Plans to publish this book at an earlier date were stymied by the series of earthquakes in and around Christchurch, beginning on 4 September 2010 and becoming considerably more serious on 22 February 2011. I am grateful to Alison Welsby for her patience, and to students and colleagues for making the last year tolerable. The recent experiences of Carolyn, Alycia and Josh remind me that there is still little to complain about and I hope to remain useful.

List of Abbreviations

ABCUP	Archives of the British Conservative and Unionist Party
Articles database	Database constructed by the author from the ledgers of authors and artists contained in TNA:PRO T102/19 and 21
ASE	Amalgamated Society of Engineers
BEF	British Expeditionary Force
BSP	British Socialist Party
BWL	British Workers' League, see BWNL
BWNL	British Workers' National League. Organisation of ultra-patriotic labour figures led by Victor Fisher, which emerged out of the Socialist National Defence Committee and later changed its name to the British Workers' League (BWL) and then the National Democratic Party (NDP)
Card-index database	Database constructed by the author from the card index contained in TNA:PRO T102/26
CID	Criminal Investigation Department
CCNPO	Central Committee for National Patriotic Organizations
DORA	Defence of the Realm Act
DRR	Defence of the Realm Regulation
FRM	Fight for Right Movement
ILP	Independent Labour Party
IWM	Imperial War Museum, London
LNU	League of Nations Union
LSE	London School of Economics Library
MoL	Ministry of Labour
MoL report	Shortened title for reports headed 'The Labour Situation. Report from the Ministry of Labour'
MP	Member of Parliament
NDP	National Democratic Party, see BWNL
n.p.d.	no publication details

NSFU	National Sailors' and Firemen's Union
NWAC	National War Aims Committee
PA	Parliamentary Archives, London
PDC(5)	Parliamentary Debates (Commons), 5th series
PDL(5)	Parliamentary Debates (Lords), 5th series
PRC	Parliamentary Recruiting Committee
Register database	Database constructed by the author from the meetings register contained in TNA:PRO T102/17
Reports database	Database constructed by the author from the Speakers' Daily Reports contained in TNA:PRO T102/16, 22–26
SDRs	Speakers' Daily Reports
TNA:PRO	The National Archives: Public Record Office, Kew
TUC	Trades Union Congress
UDC	Union of Democratic Control
VC	Victoria Cross
WAC	War Aims Committee
w.e.	week ending
WSPU	Women's Social and Political Union

Introduction

THIS book discusses the National War Aims Committee (NWAC), a cross-party parliamentary organisation established to conduct propaganda within Britain, aimed at maintaining civilian morale in the last and most draining months of the First World War. By July 1917, British civilians had endured three years of disruption to their lives. Alongside anxiety for relatives and friends in the armed forces or other dangerous occupations, civilians had to contend with more intense pressures of work (not only longer hours or changing practices but also ideological associations of all work with the war effort); restrictions or curtailments of leisure; shortages of supplies of all kinds with concomitant economic pressure; and, for the first time in a Continental war, a credible prospect of wartime death or injury at home from enemy action. The new prime minister, David Lloyd George, was convinced by December 1916 that more was required to bolster civilian morale than 'autonomous propaganda' undertaken by the press and voluntary organisations.[1] By the time the NWAC began operations in July 1917, Russia had experienced the first of two revolutions and Britain had witnessed several strikes over working conditions and the advocacy, at a socialist 'convention' at Leeds, of the creation of workers' and soldiers' councils, making the establishment of such an organisation appear all the more urgent. Over the last 15 months of the war, the NWAC held thousands of meetings and distributed over one hundred million publications, propagating a wide-ranging and flexible patriotic message reflective of the total-war environment in which civilians found themselves.[2]

---

1 M.L. Sanders and Philip M. Taylor, *British Propaganda during the First World War, 1914–18*, (London: Macmillan, 1982), pp. 55–57; Niall Ferguson, *The Pity of War* (London: Allen Lane, 1998), pp. 212–30.
2 'Total war' here means a war involving and affecting every member of a society – one which is the pre-eminent issue and activity of that society. It does not suggest that every material and human resource is geared solely to the prosecution of war – such a war is almost certainly an impossible 'ideal type': Stig Förster,

This book is primarily concerned with the representation of patriotism in NWAC propaganda. I consider what relation its patriotic narrative had to pre-war language and imagery, and how the experience of total war affected its presentation. This book thus contributes significantly to the historiographies of both the First World War and patriotism in Britain which, while enormous and ever expanding, still contain significant gaps. A comprehensive history of British patriotism in the war has yet to be written, and this study contributes towards that larger subject.

STUDENTS of the First World War are blessed with an enormous historiography.[3] Numerous general histories demonstrate British experience within wider international contexts.[4] The war's impact on British society has also been well served by both general and more specialist treatments.[5] Specific sections of society – to give two examples, women and soldiers – have also been discussed extensively.[6] Study of patriotism and national identity in Britain has likewise flourished since Hugh Cunningham's 1981 article on the 'language of patriotism'.[7] Such

---

'Introduction', in Roger Chickering and Förster (eds), *Great War, Total War: Combat and Mobilization on the Western Front, 1914–1918* (Cambridge: Cambridge University Press, 2000), pp. 7–9.

3   Jay Winter and Antoine Prost, *The Great War in History: Debates and Controversies, 1914 to the Present* (Cambridge: Cambridge University Press, 2005), p. 1 gives some idea of the scale of historical writing on the subject.

4   E.g. Stéphane Audoin-Rouzeau and Annette Becker, *1914–18: Understanding the Great War*, trans. Catherine Temerson (London: Profile Books, 2002); Hew Strachan, *The First World War*, vol. 1, *To Arms* (paperback edn, Oxford: Oxford University Press, 2003); David Stevenson, *1914–1918: The History of the First World War* (London: Penguin, 2004).

5   E.g. Arthur Marwick, *The Deluge: British Society and the First World War* (Boston: Little Brown, 1965); Trevor Wilson, *The Myriad Faces of War: Britain and the Great War, 1914–1918* (Cambridge: Polity Press, 1986); Gerard J. DeGroot, *Blighty: British Society in the Era of the Great War* (London: Longman, 1996); Adrian Gregory, *The Last Great War: British Society and the First World War* (Cambridge: Cambridge University Press, 2008); Bernard Waites, *A Class Society at War: England, 1914–1918* (Leamington Spa: Berg, 1987); John Turner, *British Politics and the Great War: Coalition and Conflict, 1915–1918* (New Haven: Yale University Press, 1992); Nicoletta F. Gullace, *'The Blood of Our Sons': Men, Women, and the Renegotiation of British Citizenship during the Great War* (Basingstoke: Macmillan, 2002).

6   E.g. Gail Braybon, *Women Workers in the First World War* (London: Routledge, 1989 [1981]); Susan R. Grayzel, *Women's Identities at War: Gender, Motherhood, and Politics in Britain and France during the First World War* (Chapel Hill, NC: University of North Carolina Press, 1999); J.G. Fuller, *Troop Morale and Popular Culture in the British and Dominion Armies, 1914–1918* (Oxford: Clarendon Press, 1991); Helen B. McCartney, *Citizen Soldiers: The Liverpool Territorials in the First World War* (Cambridge: Cambridge University Press, 2005); Michael Roper, *The Secret Battle: Emotional Survival in the Great War* (Manchester: Manchester University Press, 2009).

7   E.g. Hugh Cunningham, 'The Language of Patriotism, 1750–1914', *History Workshop Journal*, 12 (1981); reprinted in Raphael Samuel's important edited collection: *Patriotism, The Making and Unmaking of British National Identity,*

historical scrutiny has become increasingly sophisticated. Historians have recognised that Britain's is a 'four nation' history,[8] and have accordingly either striven to explain (like Linda Colley, for instance) how 'Britishness' encompassed these diverse nations into one polity, or else narrowed their focus to a section of the British Isles. Others have objected to the use of what they consider conflationary terms like 'national identity' or 'patriotism'. Julia Stapleton has made a strong plea for avoiding elision between 'citizenship' and 'patriotism', while Peter Mandler emphasises the importance of 'national character' as a separate analytical category, dismissing 'vague' patriotism as 'a feeling of loyalty to country that does not require a very focused sense of what that nation is or represents'.[9] I subscribe to neither of these last two arguments. I particularly reject the characterisation of patriotism as 'vague'. 'Flexible' or 'diverse' are perhaps better terms, reflecting the purposive nature of patriotism as a form of persuasion.

The study of patriotism and national identity has also been enriched by insights from other disciplines. Benedict Anderson's *Imagined Communities* has been particularly influential. Anderson asserted that the advent of 'print-capitalism' 'laid the bases for national consciousness' by fixing national languages more formally, overcoming differences in vernacular dialects as literacy expanded after the Reformation. Shared print culture enabled individuals who would never meet to feel a sense of commonality. Anderson's 'reflections', like Michael Billig's study of 'banal nationalism', have usefully highlighted the salience of representations of

---

vol. 1, *History and Politics* (3 vols, London: Routledge, 1989); Robert Colls and Philip Dodd (eds), *Englishness: Politics and Culture, 1880–1920* (London: Croom Helm, 1986); J.H. Grainger, *Patriotisms: Britain, 1900–1939* (London: Routledge & Kegan Paul, 1986); Linda Colley, 'Britishness and Otherness: An Argument', *Journal of British Studies*, 31:4 (1992), and *Britons: Forging the Nation, 1707–1837* (London: Pimlico, 2003 [1992]); John Wolffe, *God and Greater Britain: Religion and National Life in Britain and Ireland, 1843–1950* (London: Routledge, 1994); Robert Colls, *Identity of England* (Oxford: Oxford University Press, 2002); Paul Ward, *Britishness since 1870* (London: Routledge, 2004); Paul Readman, 'The Place of the Past in English Culture c.1890–1914', *Past and Present*, 186 (2005); Jonathan Parry, *The Politics of Patriotism: English Liberalism, National Identity and Europe, 1830–1886* (Cambridge: Cambridge University Press, 2006).

8   E.g. J.G.A. Pocock, 'The Limits and Divisions of British History: In Search of the Unknown Subject', *American Historical Review*, 87:2 (1982); Hugh Kearney, *The British Isles: A History of Four Nations* (2nd edn, Cambridge: Cambridge University Press, 2006 [1989]); interesting assessments are offered by Raphael Samuel, 'Four Nations History' and 'Unravelling Britain' (both 1995) in idem, *Island Stories: Unravelling Britain. Theatres of Memory*, vol. II, ed. Alison Light, Sally Alexander and Gareth Stedman Jones (London: Verso, 1998).

9   Julia Stapleton, 'Citizenship versus Patriotism in Twentieth-century England', *Historical Journal*, 48:1 (2005); Peter Mandler, *The English National Character: The History of an Idea from Edmund Burke to Tony Blair* (New Haven: Yale University Press, 2006), p. 7.

national identity in everyday culture and encouraged researchers to seek evidence of patriotic language and imagery there.[10] Finally, Anthony D. Smith's (apparently inexhaustible) considerations of the meanings of 'nation' and 'national identity' offer important insights for historical work. Smith stresses 'the ethnic origins of nations' (as a 1986 work was entitled), describing an ethnic group or community (*ethnie*) as 'a type of cultural collectivity ... that emphasizes the role of myths of descent and historical memories, and that is recognized by one or more cultural differences like religion, customs, language or institutions', usually tied (at least sentimentally) to a specific territorial homeland.[11] In one of his most recent works, Smith offers the following 'ideal-typical' definitions:

> [a nation is] *a named and self-defined human community whose members cultivate shared myths, memories, symbols, values, and traditions, reside in and identify with a historic homeland, create and disseminate a distinctive public culture, and observe shared customs and common laws*. In similar vein, we may also define 'national identity' as *the continuous reproduction and reinterpretation of the pattern of values, symbols, memories, myths, and traditions that compose the distinctive heritage of nations, and the identification of individuals with that pattern and heritage*.[12]

I am particularly concerned with this 'continuous reproduction and re-interpretation', and contend that the ways in which NWAC propagandists represented (or re-presented) familiar themes of patriotic language and imagery in its particular context are significant for wider historical understanding of British patriotism.

Such a project is important because both the history of patriotism and national identity in First World War Britain and of the NWAC are peculiarly ill served by existing work. 'Nothing' in Krishan Kumar's view, 'sustains a nation, or at least nationalism, like war', and yet much exploration of British First World War patriotism and national identity remains to be done.[13] Jay Winter's summary, though interesting, opts almost entirely to discuss the war's post-war consequences for British national identity.[14] Perhaps understandably in a nation dependent upon 'volunteer' soldiers until early 1916, many considerations of First World War patriotism concern themselves predominantly, or exclusively, with the motivations

---

10 Benedict Anderson, *Imagined Communities: Reflections on the Origin and Spread of Nationalism*, (rev. edn, London: Verso, 1991 [1983]), esp. pp. 38–45; Michael Billig, *Banal Nationalism* (London: Sage, 1995).

11 Anthony D. Smith, *National Identity* (London: Penguin, 1991), pp. 20–21.

12 Anthony D. Smith, *The Cultural Foundations of Nations: Hierarchy, Covenant, and Republic* (Oxford: Blackwell, 2008), p. 19; original emphasis.

13 Krishan Kumar, *The Making of English National Identity* (Cambridge: Cambridge University Press, 2003), p. 38.

14 Jay Winter, 'British National Identity and the First World War', in S.J.D. Green and R.C. Whiting (eds), *The Boundaries of the State in Modern Britain* (Cambridge: Cambridge University Press, 1996).

behind voluntary enlistment.[15] Such a focus often betrays an assumption, explicated by W.J. Reader, that such patriotism was 'obsolete' and that the war was an aberrant disjunction after which nothing remained of pre-war society and culture. However, the idea and representation of patriotism did not end in Britain with conscription, and it is troubling that, with some notable exceptions, usually related to studies of gender or the political left,[16] historical discussion of it should do so. Such reticence is less evident in French treatments of the war, where patriotism is linked with the obvious facts of invasion and occupation of the homeland, or in discussions of Germany, where the late activities of the Pan-German League and the emergence of a patriotic Fatherland Party (in September 1917) receive attention.[17]

Even more troubling are simplistic conflations of patriotism with jingoism, like Brock Millman's assertion that 'a "patriot" in wartime Britain was someone willing to employ violence on the home front to silence dissent and maintain national cohesion'.[18] This weak interpretation is contained within Millman's examination of growing war-weariness in Britain, which is also one of the few studies to address the NWAC at any length. It assesses the NWAC's role in opposing dissent, as does Marvin Swartz's work on the Union of Democratic Control, while works by Cate Haste, and M.L. Sanders and Philip M. Taylor consider it as part of more general treatments of British propaganda.[19] Finally, John Horne's excellent, but short, comparative treatment of the NWAC and its French

---

15 E.g. W.J. Reader, *'At Duty's Call': A Study in Obsolete Patriotism* (Manchester: Manchester University Press, 1988); Grainger, *Patriotisms*, pp. 267–318; Robert Wohl, *The Generation of 1914* (London: Weidenfeld and Nicholson, 1980).

16 Especially Gullace, *Blood*; Paul Ward, *Red Flag and Union Jack: Englishness, Patriotism and the British Left, 1881–1924* (Woodbridge: Boydell Press, 1998), esp. pp. 121–48.

17 E.g. Audoin-Rouzeau and Becker, *1914–1918*, pp. 54–64; Jean-Jacques Becker, *The Great War and the French People*, trans. Arnold Pomerans (Oxford: Berg, 1993); Annette Becker, *War and Faith: The Religious Imagination in France, 1914–1930*, trans. Helen McPhail (Oxford: Berg, 1998); David Welch, *Germany, Propaganda and Total War, 1914–1918: The Sins of Omission* (London: Athlone Press, 2000); Matthew Stibbe, *German Anglophobia and the Great War, 1914–1918* (Cambridge: Cambridge University Press, 2001); Roger Chickering, *The Great War and Urban Life in Germany: Freiburg, 1914–1918* (Cambridge: Cambridge University Press, 2007).

18 Brock Millman, *Managing Domestic Dissent in First World War Britain* (London: Frank Cass, 2000), p. 99. Millman has since reiterated this type of definition, coupled with an unsubstantiated assertion that his interpretation reflects common 'first world war parlance': Brock Millman, 'HMG and the War against Dissent, 1914–1918', *Journal of Contemporary History*, 40:3 (2005), p. 416.

19 Marvin Swartz, *The Union of Democratic Control in British Politics during the First World War* (Oxford: Clarendon Press, 1971); Cate Haste, *Keep the Home Fires Burning: Propaganda in the First World War* (London: 1977); Sanders and Taylor, *British Propaganda*.

equivalent discusses the 'remobilisation' of civilians in 1917 and 1918.[20] Other studies, matching Paul Fussell's preoccupation with elite literary attitudes, barely acknowledge the NWAC's propaganda role.[21] No study has yet provided comprehensive discussion of the NWAC's organisational structure and activity (although Sanders and Taylor's work is invaluable for its origins),[22] and Millman's discussion is sometimes seriously misleading.[23] No study offers in-depth consideration of the language and imagery of NWAC propaganda specifically, and certainly not of its broader implications for the study of patriotism. Preoccupation with anti-German rhetoric, particularly atrocity stories, has typified post-war discussion of British First World War propaganda at least since its castigation in 1928 by the wartime dissenting MP Arthur Ponsonby.[24] Harold Lasswell's pioneering work in the 1930s, which noted that the rise of propaganda reflected 'the communization of warfare [and] necessitated the mobilization of the civilian mind', demonstrated a wider-ranging narrative than Ponsonby suggested.[25] Furthermore, considerable atrocities were undoubtedly performed by Germany and its allies, as John Horne and Alan Kramer have demonstrated. Nonetheless, atrocity stories continue to attract most attention, with concomitant assumptions that they were nearly all deliberate lies concocted by journalists or the state – 'black propaganda' – and, by extension, that all propaganda statements were lies.[26] With this focus upon the most sensationalist elements of wartime propaganda, the nuances of the patriotic messages conveyed are

---

20 John Horne, 'Remobilizing for "Total War": France and Britain, 1917–1918', in Horne (ed.), *State, Society and Mobilization in Europe during the First World War* (Cambridge: Cambridge University Press, 1997), 195–211.

21 Paul Fussell, *The Great War and Modern Memory* (London: Oxford University Press, 1975); Katherine Andrews, 'The Necessity to Conform: British Jingoism in the First World War', *Dalhousie Review*, 53:2 (1973); Stuart Wallace, *War and the Image of Germany: British Academics, 1914–1918* (Edinburgh: John Donald, 1988); Peter Buitenhuis, *The Great War of Words: Literature as Propaganda, 1914–18 and after* (London: B.T. Batsford, 1989); Gary Messinger, *British Propaganda and the State in the First World War* (Manchester: Manchester University Press, 1992).

22 Also useful is Stephen Colclough, '"No such bookselling has ever before taken place in this country." Propaganda and the Wartime Distribution Practices of W.H. Smith & Son', in Mary Hammond and Shafquat Towheed (eds), *Publishing in the First World War: Essays in Book History* (Basingstoke: Palgrave MacMillan, 2007).

23 See discussion, pp. 46, 60–61, 244–45 below.

24 Arthur Ponsonby, *Falsehood in War-time: Containing an Assortment of Lies Circulated throughout the Nations during the Great War* (London: Allen & Unwin, 1928).

25 Harold D. Lasswell, *Propaganda Technique in the World War* (2nd edn, London: Kegan Paul, 1938), p. 10.

26 John Horne and Alan Kramer, *German Atrocities, 1914: A History of Denial* (New Haven: Yale University Press, 2001). For the 'shades' of propaganda, see Garth S. Jowett and Victoria O'Donnell, *Propaganda and Persuasion* (4th edn, London: Sage Publications, 2006 [1986]), pp. 16–22.

largely overlooked. However, although atrocity stories continued to play a significant part in NWAC propaganda, they were merely one element of a much broader narrative. Far from mainly using 'black propaganda', moreover, NWAC propagandists' discussions, aimed at civilians, were much more strongly rooted in the realities of everyday experience at home. This book also pays prolonged attention to the reception of NWAC propaganda, something largely missing from other studies.

D ESPITE the extensive historiographies of both the war and British patriotism, therefore, this book addresses substantial lacunae. I consider several key questions. How, and why, was the organisation formed, who was involved with it, and how did it operate? What were its aims, and what significance does this have for the manner in which patriotism was represented? Did the patriotic themes in NWAC propaganda reflect pre-war ideas? If not, how did they differ from this context? If familiar themes were present, were they conveyed in the same manner as before, or did their representation change? How successfully did the NWAC convey its message and did its reception vary between different sections of society? Finally, I seek to answer two questions about the wider meanings of this topic. First, what is the significance of the NWAC's evocation of patriotism for general understandings of patriotism and national identity in Britain? Second, what does the NWAC's story suggest about the war's impact on British society and culture? Was the war really a watershed from which Britain emerged unrecognisable from the nation it had been in 1914 (as so many histories which conveniently end in 1914 or begin in 1918–19 imply)? Alternatively, can continuities in British society and culture be traced through the war and into the 1920s?

To answer these questions, the book is divided into three parts. Part 1 (chapters 1–3) examines the NWAC's establishment, organisation and work. These chapters provide more comprehensive historical treatment of the Committee's day-to-day operations than has previously been available. Chapter 1 examines the wartime situation which prompted its establishment and discusses its links to other organisations like the pre-conscription Parliamentary Recruiting Committee. Chapter 2 assesses the central Committee's work, offering new statistical analysis which suggests that it operated on an under-appreciated scale. Chapter 3, meanwhile, emphasises the importance of the NWAC's local organisational framework based (in England and Wales) upon parliamentary constituencies and the efforts of party political organisers. It demonstrates not only the continuing vitality of locality as a basis for organisation, but that civilian remobilisation varied from place to place.

Part 2 (chapters 4–8) constitutes the book's core. These chapters use the NWAC's published propaganda, together with local press reports of events in thirty constituencies (the organisational unit within which local War Aims Committees – WACs – operated), selected to represent different areas, social composition and levels of activity, to provide a detailed examination of NWAC propagandists' representations of patriotism. I disagree strongly with Niall Ferguson's assertion that the 'content of propaganda need not long detain us'.[27] While his brief catalogue of familiar wartime clichés may have satisfied the purposes of his study, much more comprehensive treatment is required if the wider relevance of the content of wartime propaganda to British history is to be understood.

Chapter 4 summarises the propaganda *in toto*, demonstrating that many themes of pre-war patriotism may clearly be discerned. Extensive reading of NWAC propaganda enables the construction of a wider underlying narrative of patriotic identity. The chapter establishes a model framework of interactive and interdependent 'presentational patriotisms' within which the content of NWAC propaganda can best be understood. These presentational patriotisms constitute broad interpretative categories within which familiar patriotic themes are placed to produce a qualitative rather than quantitative interpretation of patriotic language. These categories are 'presentational' in that their interactions with each other supply a purposive and meaningful narrative. An essential assumption throughout this book is that patriotism is a purposive language. Patriotic rhetoric is deployed in an attempt to persuade people of the necessity for certain types of behaviour. It is not a language that historians should expect to find continually appearing in people's everyday writings (though, of course, some examples can be found), but is one that is deployed to convince people of the need to accept unusual things.

Familiar themes and ideas were used by propagandists to achieve specific things. Most pieces of propaganda combined lengthy discussion of various contextual topics with a core message emphasising civilians' duties to the nation. Considered quantitatively, NWAC propaganda said much more about German iniquity than civilian duty. When both issues are treated as parts of a wider, structured narrative, however, the often brief references to duty become much more significant. Warnings about German misrule provided one of several contextual elements by which demands that war-weary civilians continue to do their duty became not impertinent, but imperative. By placing familiar themes like anti-foreigner sentiment or celebrations of British history within the wider structural categories of presentational patriotisms, therefore, emphasis is placed much more on the purposes served by propagandists' language than on the number of words devoted to each theme. The fact that NWAC propaganda continually condemned German conduct does not mean that wartime patriotism overwhelmingly depended upon fearful or contemptuous negative attitudes, but that such attitudes played an important part

---

27 Ferguson, *Pity*, p. 231.

in highlighting other aspects of British identity. Having established the narrative structure underlying NWAC propaganda, chapter 4 suggests that the narrative categories identified may also be discernible in earlier periods of British history. The chapter also discusses the patriotic role played by religion. As is well documented, most clerics of virtually all denominations embraced the war.[28] The NWAC utilised their assistance at national and local levels, while its rhetoric was tinged with religious and quasi-religious language which ostensibly sanctified Britain's war. The religious edge to the various patriotic categories is discussed further in succeeding chapters.

Chapters 5–8 examine the presentational patriotisms in greater detail. Chapter 5 considers propaganda discussion of numerous 'adversaries' of Britain, both external and internal, and argues for an alternative means of interpreting negative discussions of difference to the familiar 'otherness' paradigm. Chapter 6 also considers difference, in its positive forms, examining NWAC representations of Britain's allies (especially the US, France and the empire). It also posits that British identity was held to repose in several values – liberty, democracy, justice and honour – which, while keys to 'civilisation' and shared by Britain's allies, were also claimed as 'British' creations.

Building on this sense of proprietorship, chapter 7 addresses the core of the NWAC's patriotic narrative, its emphasis on duty, rooted in an extensively developed language of sacrifice. Civilians were reminded of the greater sacrifices of Britain's servicemen and, in combination with other issues, warned of the sacrifices to which future generations would be condemned by a current rejection of duty. The chapter depicts a dualistic evocation of civilian duty which both demanded that Britons, blessed with residence in a nation suffused with the key civilisational values, should accept concomitant obligations to defend them, and celebrated evidence of their ready acceptance of such obligations. Propagandists depicted an expanding community, extending through the family, workplace, locality, nation and beyond, linked by the willing acceptance of duty. One issue that emerges strongly in this book is the close connection between local, national and supranational identities, and chapters 6–7 particularly emphasise this. Finally, chapter 8 considers encouragements to civilians to anticipate the material and civilisational benefits of a new

---

28 E.g. Alan Wilkinson, *The Church of England and the First World War* (London: SPCK, 1978) and *Dissent or Conform? War, Peace and the English Churches 1900–1945* (London: SCM Press, 1981), pp. 21–53; A.J. Hoover, *God, Germany, and Britain in the Great War: A Study in Clerical Nationalism* (New York: Praeger, 1989); Alan Ruston, 'Protestant Nonconformist Attitudes towards the First World War', in Alan P.F. Sell and Anthony R. Cross (eds), *Protestant Nonconformity in the Twentieth Century* (Carlisle: Paternoster Press, 2003); Gregory, *Last Great War*, pp. 152–86.

post-war world, where another such war would be impossible thanks to the League of Nations, and in which Britain, maintaining the increasingly harmonious community established through wartime cooperation, would be a better society. Blended together, these various patriotic strands formed a comprehensive and flexible narrative of civilian experience, modifiable to the requirements of different audiences.

Other studies of patriotism and national identity during the war predominantly address pre-war patriotism and its application immediately after the outbreak of war. Conversely, studies of propaganda consider patriotism too narrowly, discussing its wartime application in isolation, without relating it very greatly or consistently to its pre-war context. The major significance of these chapters is that they both identify how NWAC propaganda was unique, and relate its evocation of patriotism to wider historical discussion. The history of NWAC propaganda therefore becomes not a history 'in parenthesis',[29] but one which may be considered as part of a wider historiography of modern Britain.

Finally, part 3 (chapters 9–10) considers the NWAC's reception. While interesting, the content of NWAC propaganda loses much significance if it had no discernible impact. Chapter 9 examines the reactions of parliament, pressure groups and the national press. Despite an at best sceptical reaction to its existence and activities, the underlying response of these groups was tolerant indifference. Chapter 10 seeks to get closer to public responses to the NWAC. The evidence suggests that the Committee retained a steady if unspectacular presence in the scenery of British life up to the armistice, and was apparently successful in maintaining civilian consent.

As noted above, the book's principal focus is on the ways in which NWAC propaganda adapted patriotic language to specific wartime purposes. As such, I do not devote substantial space to analysing the necessity of the Committee's appointed task of maintaining civilian morale. Assessing the continuing strength of public subscriptions to war loans during the winter of 1917–18, Adrian Gregory suggests that 'popular morale was not as bad as the Government sometimes feared',[30] reflecting a broader perspective within recent research that wartime Britain was much more a place of consent than dissent. This is not a perspective with which I disagree but nor is it one which is within the scope of this book to prove or disprove. To do adequate justice to the state of civilian morale in 1917–18 would require a far larger book and a different focus. Whether or not a propaganda campaign on the scale conducted by the NWAC was entirely necessary, it happened. As the discussion of local agency in chapter 3 demonstrates, some local representatives were certain propaganda was

29 David Jones, *In Parenthesis* (London: Faber & Faber, 1937).
30 Gregory, *Last Great War*, pp. 223–24.

unnecessary in their localities, but others appeared equally persuaded of the need for such efforts. Propagandists used patriotic language to meet the purposes assigned, and apparently continued to obtain audiences and readers – for instance, the Committee's weekly newspaper, *Reality*, boasted that it was requested by over one million people a week in October 1918.[31] In this context, the ways in which NWAC propagandists framed patriotic language deserve extended attention regardless of the strict necessity of each small village meeting.

THIS study provides a much more comprehensive examination of material relating both to the organisation and its propaganda than has previously been available. Organisational and personal papers at the National Archives and Parliamentary Archives are extensively examined to provide fuller information on the NWAC's organisation and work. Its published propaganda (mostly in the National Archives Library, together with assorted material at the Bodleian and British Libraries) is combined with a survey of over one hundred local newspapers covering thirty constituencies. By reading every discovered page of its published propaganda, alongside a wide sample of reported speeches and events within varied localities, a much more detailed and nuanced exploration of NWAC propaganda is possible than via a small sample of pamphlets or of one or two constituencies. Published propaganda and speeches in local settings addressed different audiences and served different purposes. Pamphlets and other written materials were necessarily somewhat standardised to appeal to as wide a range of readers as possible across the nation. Moreover, they were strictly controlled by the NWAC's editorial staff, not least to ensure that one or another political party did not gain an advantage from an officially non-party organisation. By contrast, speeches were more closely tailored to individual communities and sought to explain to local people how their efforts fitted into the wider national picture. They were also more interactive, with possibilities for audience participation through applause, shouted comments or heckling, which, combined with evidence from speakers' reports and public correspondence, provide a richer sense of the impact of the patriotic language deployed by propagandists. This more extensive reading suggests that, rather than simply representing familiar patriotic themes – pride in British history, transnational comparisons and so on – NWAC propaganda contained a more subtle and complex underlying narrative of patriotism than is evident in pamphlets like the crass *Kalendar of Kultur* (a compendium of German atrocities published in September 1917).

---

31 *Reality*, 143, 10/10/18, p. 1 (all abbreviated dates are recorded in the format day/ month/year). See p. 251 below for further discussion.

There are, however, limitations to the source materials. The NWAC's papers, though extensive, are incomplete, having not been considered 'of any great importance' when transferred to the Public Record Office in 1931.[32] Many of the executive Committee's minutes are missing, as seemingly are most of the Meeting Department's, while its meetings register, on which many of the statistics are based, is incomplete after April 1918 – thereafter, only scattered pages remain. Publicity Department reports have also not survived. Moreover, in assessing the NWAC's reception, it has proved particularly difficult to uncover individuals' opinions. While correspondence with the NWAC and, to a limited extent, with newspapers provides some insight into individual attitudes, such evidence may generally be considered the views of those with axes to grind, one way or another (though much NWAC correspondence comprises simple requests for pamphlets or other materials which smack rather less of such committed activism). A survey of civilian diaries and memoirs at the Imperial War Museum, and of working-class autobiographies, unearthed only one direct (and isolated) reference to the organisation, while general allusions to propaganda must be treated cautiously. Similar reticence is manifested in post-war memoirs and reflections of politicians and other influential figures, except for one three-page chapter.[33] Lloyd George found no room in six volumes to mention the organisation which he was most responsible for creating. Even Ponsonby's condemnation of wartime propaganda does not mention it by name. Politicians of all inclinations apparently preferred to forget that a Treasury-funded organisation spent the last 15 months of the war striving to maintain civilian morale. When civil servants began to examine the propaganda systems of the last war in 1938, their attention initially focused on the late activities of the press lords Beaverbrook and Northcliffe, and only slowly identified the NWAC's functions (not helped by the earlier decision to destroy many of its papers).[34] This memoiristic amnesia may also account for the limited historical attention that has since been paid to the NWAC. Despite the highlighting of the NWAC's role by scholars like Horne and Gregory, less attentive discussion of British domestic propaganda in the war's last years still sometimes focuses inaccurately on Beaverbrook's Ministry of Information at the expense of the NWAC.[35] Nonetheless, it remains possible to deduce considerably more general impressions of the NWAC's reception.

Finally, a brief explanation of the chosen local constituencies is necessary (fuller details are available in appendix 1). They comprise only English

---

32 TNA:PRO, PRO17/296, C.T. Flowers to Master of the Rolls, 14/1/31.
33 Sir Harry Brittain, *Pilgrims and Pioneers* (London: Hutchinson, 1945), pp. 164–66.
34 See TNA:PRO INF4/1A.
35 E.g., Lawrence Sondhaus, *World War I: The Global Revolution* (Cambridge: Cambridge University Press, 2011), p. 258.

and Welsh constituencies because the constituency-based organisational structure of the NWAC was implemented only in these parts of Britain. In Scotland, two WACs, for 'West' and 'East' Scotland were established in Glasgow and Edinburgh. The Committee never operated significantly in Ireland – though a NWAC 'cinemotor' (a mobile cinema projector van) toured Ireland very late in 1918 – and the Irish War Aims Committee, established in the summer of 1918, bore no evident relation to the constituency organisations discussed in this book.[36] Nonetheless, I consistently discuss 'Britain' and 'British' patriotism. This does not constitute ignorance of or lack of interest in 'four-nations' history. While Scotland is discussed in certain sections (the effect of NWAC activities on the Clyde, for instance, is discussed in chapter 10), the local perspectives illustrate the 'typical' methods of NWAC propaganda and local organisation, ranging from a very active constituency WAC like Evesham to a virtually inactive one (Dulwich). Furthermore, discussion of 'British' patriotism reflects propagandists' own language. They most often discussed 'Britain' (and generally seemed to mean 'Britain' where they said 'England'), though smaller and larger entities were also regularly discussed in patriotic terms.

THE NWAC deserves greater significance in the history of British wartime society. Its propaganda deployed a complex and flexible narrative of patriotism informed by pre-war patriotic motifs but adapted to the requirements of a war-weary civilian society, which enhances wider understandings of British patriotism. The meaning and representation of wartime patriotism clearly did not die with the New Divisions at Loos or the Somme, and nor should the war be seen as an abrupt end to the 'long nineteenth century'. Histories of Britain's First World War are beginning to pay greater attention to the context of the surrounding years,[37] and this book emphasises the substantial continuities that can be identified with pre-war British society. Much undoubtedly changed, but NWAC propaganda remained a recognisable descendant of the pre-war 'language of patriotism'.

---

36 On the Irish War Aims Committee, see PA, Lloyd George Papers, LG/F/69/2.
37 E.g., recently, Gregory, *Last Great War*; Roper, *Secret Battle*.

PART 1

The National War Aims Committee

CHAPTER 1

The Development of Wartime Propaganda and the Emergence of the NWAC

O N 4 August 1917, the third anniversary of Britain's entry into the First World War, David Lloyd George, the British prime minister, addressed the inaugural meeting of the National War Aims Committee (NWAC) at the Queen's Hall in Westminster. Despite his reservations about the performance of the British Expeditionary Force (BEF) in France and Belgium (and more particularly its commander-in-chief, Sir Douglas Haig), he praised the 'British method of advancing with the least cost in life' which, he said, took time but was 'sure'.

> But whilst the army is fighting so valiantly let the nation behind it be patient, be strong, and, above all, be united … The strain is great on nations and on individuals, and when men get over-strained tempers get ragged, small grievances are exaggerated, and small misunderstandings and mistakes swell into mountains …
> The last reaches of a climb are always the most trying to the nerve and to the heart, but there is a real test of grit, endurance and courage in the last few hundred feet or score of feet in the climb upwards.[1]

By mid-1917, following a revolution in Russia, limited reports of a mutiny in the French Army[2] and a series of strikes in Britain, there was genuine governmental concern that domestic disaffection might make it impossible to continue the war to a successful conclusion. Such concerns had been significant in Lloyd George's attitude to the organisation of the war for a much longer period. On 1 January 1915 he had warned the War Cabinet that there is 'a real danger that the people of Britain and France will sooner or later get tired of long casualty lists … A clear definite victory … will alone satisfy the public that tangible results are

1   PA, Lloyd George Papers, LG/F/160/1/10, 'Report of Proceedings at the Inaugural Meeting of the National War Aims Committee'.
2   David French, 'Who Knew What and When? The French Army Mutinies and the British Decision to Launch the Third Battle of Ypres', in Lawrence Freedman, Paul Hayes and Robert O'Neill (eds), *War, Strategy and International Politics: Essays in Honour of Michael Howard* (Oxford: Clarendon Press, 1992), pp. 145–47.

being achieved',[3] and his support of an 'indirect' strategy reflected this concern. However, public opinion, demonstrated by the initial wave of voluntary enlistment and a continuing electoral and industrial truce, remained strong throughout 1914–16. Even conscription, though decried by some as un-British and 'immoral' – and despite the resignation of the Home Secretary, Sir John Simon, in protest at its introduction – passed relatively serenely through parliament.[4] Nonetheless, by 1917 Lloyd George's government had decided that systematic domestic propaganda was necessary to maintain public assent to the war, and this chapter explores the NWAC's creation to serve this purpose.

IF opposition was to be expressed to the war in its early years, it was most likely to come from 'the left', from the Parliamentary Labour Party, Independent Labour Party (ILP), British Socialist Party (BSP) or the trade unions, as well as some radical elements of the Liberal Party. However, the war brought about abundant employment opportunities,[5] while, according to Paul Ward, the 'anti-war left was a small proportion of the left, and only a tiny minority when compared to the population of the war as a whole'. This was because the pre-war left had 'constructed a radical version of patriotism' endorsing national defence, especially in Britain, 'the natural home of democracy, liberty and free institutions'.[6] With overwhelming evidence of popular support for the war after 4 August 1914, Labour and the Trades Union Congress (TUC) rapidly agreed to electoral and industrial truces. In 1915, following numerous strikes on the Clyde, Labour and the TUC accepted the Treasury Agreement – which introduced dilution (the employment of less-skilled men in jobs previously reserved for skilled workers), 'the suspension of restrictive practices and enforcement of compulsory arbitration' – and the Munitions of War Act – which inaugurated a 'leaving certificate' that prevented workers from changing jobs without their previous employers' permission.[7] This showed, in James Hinton's view, 'a readiness to oblige which went far beyond the minimal requirements of patriotism'.[8]

Indeed, according to Ward, even the majority of the 'anti-war left' (including Ramsay MacDonald and the Union of Democratic Control [UDC], the 'most influential group among opponents of the war') believed the war had to be fought to a successful conclusion, despite

3   David Lloyd George, *War Memoirs of David Lloyd George* (6 vols, 1933–36), I (London: Ivor Nicholson & Watson, 1933), pp. 372–73.
4   Ward, *Red Flag*, pp. 121, 133–40; Millman, *Managing*, pp. 50, 73.
5   Waites, *Class Society*, p. 165.
6   Ward, *Red Flag*, pp. 126, 122. See also Waites, *Class Society*, p. 181.
7   DeGroot, *Blighty*, pp. 113–15.
8   James Hinton, *Labour and Socialism: A History of the British Labour Movement, 1867–1974* (Brighton: Wheatsheaf Books, 1983), p. 99. Cf. DeGroot, *Blighty*, p. 115, on the limitations of the concessions.

vigorously criticising its conduct. The exceptions were 'some absolutist pacifists' and a group around John Maclean on the Clyde who believed the war should become 'a civil war against the British ruling class, and thus supported the idea of revolutionary defeatism', though Adrian Gregory contends that Maclean's revolutionary influence on Clydeside was exaggerated. While the anti-war left reserved the right to criticise the war – doing so, for instance, over conscription on the basis that voluntary enlistment was more patriotic – the majority did so within a framework of underlying belief in the rightness of the cause.[9] Meanwhile, the government preserved the essential image of a liberal state, despite ever-tightening restrictions on civil liberties, demonstrated especially by the Defence of the Realm Act (DORA), by allowing a certain amount of dissenting literature to be published unmolested, so that just 'enough material leaked out, by authors sufficiently well known, to establish the fact that in the UK tolerance for dissenting opinion remained, liberty was preserved and censorship was light'.[10]

By 1917, however, such consensus showed signs of weakening. Following the 1916 Somme campaign, the government had to accept it was running out of men. In January 1917, Germany recommenced unrestricted submarine warfare to starve Britain into submission. And in March, the British learned of the overthrow of the Russian tsar. These issues, directly or indirectly, contributed to the undermining of British public opinion.

'At the beginning of 1917', according to the pacifist and historian Caroline Playne, the majority of the public remained 'concentrated on keeping the war going'. There was also, however, 'a group, small by comparison, consisting of people who had never liked the war and of others who believed in it but now thought the time had come when it should be stopped'.[11] It was those 'others who believed in it' that concerned the government. Bernard Waites contends that there 'was a brutal division in the military character of the war with the death of idealism and voluntarism on the Somme', emulated at home by increasing state controls and the introduction of conscription with 'a coercive apparatus of munitions and military tribunals which dispelled the voluntary character of participation and of the industrial truce'.[12] However, public opinion seemingly held steady during the Somme campaign. It was the campaign's failure to

---

9 Ward, *Red Flag*, pp. 126–29, 138–40; Gregory, *Last Great War*, pp. 188–90, 228. See also F.L. Carsten, *War against War: British and German Radical Movements in the First World War* (London: Batsford Academic and Educational, 1982).

10 Millman, *Managing*, p. 78. For a less sceptical presentation of the same point, see Stephen Badsey, 'Press, Propaganda and Public Perceptions', in Michael Howard (ed.), *A Part of History: Aspects of the British Experience of the First World War* (London: Continuum, 2008), p. 28.

11 Caroline E. Playne, *Britain Holds On: 1917, 1918* (London: George Allen & Unwin, 1933), p. 19.

12 Waites, *Class Society*, p. 184.

achieve the 'clear definite' victory Lloyd George had demanded in 1915 which apparently elicited an actual and (equally importantly) a perceived change of mood. Until the Somme, the 'Kitchener' Armies, composed of those ostensibly enthusiastic patriots of the autumn of 1914, remained largely unused in combat.[13] It seems reasonable to suggest, therefore, that popular tolerance of the war's length accompanied expectations that once the massed ranks of volunteers were unleashed, the war would come to a victorious conclusion. The official film, *The Battle of the Somme*, released on 21 August 1916, produced what Nicholas Reeves describes as an 'intensely emotional response', 'a reverent, almost religious mood of people deeply moved' which may have contributed to the changing mood at the end of 1916.[14] As far as the public knew, many men were dead or wounded who had voluntarily enlisted, and the battle-lines were largely unaltered. Such long-term success as the campaign may have had could hardly have been transparently obvious to the British public – 95 years on, and with access to copious official documentation, a decisive conclusion on its merits has still not been delivered.[15]

The Somme's aftermath also had much more tangible effects at home. Most fundamentally, the government never again had sufficient manpower to meet all the nation's needs. By February 1917, before that year's major campaigns, the army was receiving 50,000 fewer men each month than were needed to maintain its existing strength.[16] Naturally, the high command demanded more men be produced. Lloyd George, while promoting a casualty-saving strategy, nonetheless was compelled to find new sources of manpower for both the armed forces and the most important industries.[17] Initially the Ministry of Munitions sought to increase dilution within the strictures of the recently established trade card scheme, which had allowed the Amalgamated Society of Engineers (ASE) and other 'craft unions' the right to grant their members exemptions from

---

13 For qualifications to such an impression of willing enthusiasm, see Adrian Gregory, 'British "War Enthusiasm" in 1914: A Reassessment', in Gail Braybon (ed.), *Evidence, History and the Great War* (Oxford: Berghahn Books, 2003); David Silbey, *The British Working Class and Enthusiasm for War, 1914–1916* (London: Frank Cass, 2005); Stuart Hallifax, '"Over by Christmas": British Popular Opinion and the Short War in 1914', *First World War Studies*, 1:2 (2010).

14 Nicholas Reeves, *The Power of Film Propaganda: Myth or Reality?* (London: Cassell, 1999), pp. 33, 36.

15 See, e.g., the divergent interpretations in Tim Travers, *The Killing Ground: The British Army, the Western Front & the Emergence of Modern Warfare, 1900–1918* (Barnsley: Pen & Sword, 2003 [1987]), pp. 127–99; Gary Sheffield, *Forgotten Victory: The First World War: Myths and Realities* (London: Review, 2001), pp. 159–89; Robin Prior and Trevor Wilson, *The Somme* (New Haven, CT: Yale University Press, 2005).

16 Brock Millman, *Pessimism and British War Policy, 1916–1918* (London: Frank Cass 2001), p. 83.

17 Waites, *Class Society*, p. 203.

conscription.[18] However, the Cabinet wished to restructure this system. In March it resolved that, because of the strong sentiment against industrial compulsion, it would be 'impossible' to introduce such a scheme without first seeking the necessary manpower and material through 'voluntary enrolment' and the restriction of less important industries.[19] Nevertheless, in early April, several unions, including the important ASE, were told by Arthur Henderson, the Labour party's chairman and chief representative in the coalition War Cabinet, 'that the trade card scheme would have to be replaced by a more selective method of protecting essential workers', a centrally controlled schedule of protected occupations. The ASE executive accepted this arrangement provided skilled men would be called up only after all military-age dilutees, but were ignored by shop stewards, who had already embarked on a series of strikes (discussed below).[20]

Ironically, the less tangible but real success of the Somme campaign also weakened public enthusiasm for the war. The German high command, shaken by their immense and unsustainable casualties, altered their strategy. Specifically, they endorsed the recommencement of unrestricted submarine warfare (previously abandoned in 1916 after protests by the American president, Woodrow Wilson) from 1 February.[21] Consequently, merchant shipping losses rose from 153,512 tons in January to 545,282 tons in April, with concomitant depletion of shipping caused by the reluctance of neutrals to risk the crossing to Britain.[22] This meant Britain's wheat stocks, amounting to 14 weeks'-worth in December 1916, were reduced to less than seven weeks by early May; while at one point, only four days' supply of sugar remained.[23] Although the introduction of measures of greater shipping efficiency in the short term, and the convoy system in the longer term,[24] ensured Britain was never actually threatened with a 'food crisis', the results of these losses were nonetheless extremely significant. In March the cabinet considered that publishing shipping losses might educate 'the British public [which had] not yet realised the seriousness of the situation', but was also concerned that 'the losses might become so serious that we could not publish them without risk of panic'.[25] Much more significant, however, was the effect of such losses on food supplies. Throughout the war public attention – especially working-class opinion – naturally focused on the cost of food. As Waites notes, concerns including 'excess profits, high food prices and

18 Turner, *British Politics*, pp. 165, 167–68; Hinton, *Labour and Socialism*, p. 98.
19 TNA:PRO CAB 23/2/1365-103: War Cabinet 103, 23/3/17.
20 Turner, *British Politics*, p. 168; David French, *The Strategy of the Lloyd George Coalition, 1916–1918* (Oxford: Clarendon Press, 1995), pp. 85–86.
21 Stevenson, *1914–1918*, pp. 101, 171.
22 French, *Strategy*, p. 43; Millman, *Pessimism*, p. 71.
23 French, *Strategy*, pp. 44, 81; DeGroot, *Blighty*, p. 87.
24 French, *Strategy*, pp. 74–81.
25 TNA:PRO CAB 23/2/1365–97: War Cabinet 97, 15/3/17.

inequalities of distribution were affronts to the "moral economy" of the English working class', and food prices were the major factor in a broad dissatisfaction amounting to 'a heightened "them/us" view of the world', particularly since wartime working conditions hindered working-class families from 'shopping around' or buying in bulk. Condemnation of profiteering and high prices also enabled dissenters to emphasise their patriotism.[26] Rationing proved an effective long-term solution, although the ill-considered decision to ration sugar, butter and bacon to districts on the basis of previous consumption – thus providing more food to the more affluent – can hardly have improved feelings of inequality.[27] Gregory contends that the maintenance of unrationed bread, and restoration of supplies in February 1918 to the levels available before February 1917, also played a 'crucial' psychological role in demonstrating the failure of the submarine campaign.[28] In the shorter term, however, food concerns fed public disaffection. In July 1917 the cabinet was informed that the eight Labour Commissions established after the May strikes had each reported high food prices as a major cause of unrest.[29]

The wave of strikes across Britain in April and May was based upon a combination of these issues. While the ostensible reason for most of the strikes related to the removal of the trade card scheme and the extension of dilution beyond war-related production, in Coventry the strike related to 'maldistribution and shortage of food',[30] and a report prepared by the Ministry of Labour (MoL) for the War Cabinet on 24 May 1917 affirmed some discontent at 'undue profits ... being amassed by the middlemen' and a feeling that 'an unfair share of the sacrifices entailed by the War is being borne by the working classes'.[31] Perhaps equally worrisome was the greater understanding of the actual conditions at the front which accompanied veterans' return to industry, another legacy of the post-Somme manpower situation, which Waites suggests 'was particularly important in undermining patriotic zeal'.[32]

One further factor in the weakening consensus on the war was the news in March 1917 of the revolution in Russia. This news was greeted with cautious optimism by many Britons uncomfortable with an alliance with Russian autocracy,[33] particularly the left, since the 'alliance was no longer contrary to British traditions' like 'parliamentarism and political

---

26 Waites, *Class Society*, pp. 222–24; Ward, *Red Flag*, p. 133.
27 Waites, *Class Society*, p. 228.
28 Gregory, *Last Great War*, p. 216.
29 TNA:PRO CAB 23/3/1365-187: War Cabinet 187, 16/7/17.
30 French, *Strategy*, p. 86; Waites, *Class Society*, p. 209; Turner, *British Politics*, p. 168.
31 TNA:PRO CAB24/14, GT832: 'Labour Situation', w.e. 24/5/17.
32 Waites, *Class Society*, pp. 184, 203. However, McCartney, *Citizen Soldiers*, pp. 109–10, suggests civilians were soon well aware of conditions at the front.
33 Playne, *Britain Holds On*, p. 36.

liberty'.[34] Nevertheless, the revolution reinvigorated the dissenting spirit of the left in Britain, which had hitherto been 'shifting to the right'.[35] Dissent grew stronger and more confident in 1917,[36] its most explicit link to the revolution being the Leeds Conference called in June.

While Ward suggests most delegates did not see Leeds 'as the first step in following Russia but as a celebration of the Russian people's taking of the British left's advice to follow Britain' it became a symbol of dissent's growing plausibility for the masses,[37] despite its limited practical effect. Marvin Swartz notes that the anti-war elements of the ILP and BSP were 'both grossly over-represented ... [since] many members had simply abandoned both parties for the [ultra-patriotic] BWNL [British Workers' National League]', so that delegates voted nearly two to one in favour of a negotiated peace at Leeds, compared to a vote of more than five to one in favour of continuing the war to victory at the January Labour Party Conference.[38] The most unusual resolution called for the formation of workers' and soldiers' councils, which the MoL felt was 'an earnest' of 'widespread pacifist agitation deliberately based on the Russian model ... initiated with the intention to embarrass authority'. However, the ministry considered that

> Mr. Robert Smillie [Miners' Federation of Great Britain] and Mr. Robert Williams [National Transport Workers' Federation] were present in their pacifist and revolutionary capacity respectively, rather than as representative of the unions to which they belong, and it may be accepted that the same remarks apply to the very large majority of the 580 quasi-labour delegates.

Further, it believed the workers' and soldiers' councils would face too many rivals to succeed. Nevertheless, though the conference:

> was in no sense competent to voice the opinions and demands of Labour, but was rather a political [vehicle for] the discontented and disgruntled of various parties ... it would be a mistake ... to dismiss it from consideration as negligible.

---

34 Ward, *Red Flag*, p. 143.
35 Ross McKibbin, *The Evolution of the Labour Party, 1910–1924* (3rd edn, Oxford: Clarendon Press, 1986 [1974]), p. 91.
36 Millman, *Managing*, p. 206.
37 Ward, *Red Flag*, p. 144; Millman, *Managing*, p. 209.
38 Swartz, *Union of Democratic Control*, p. 159; Millman, *Managing*, p. 208. The BWNL was an organisation of ultra-patriotic labour figures, led by Victor Fisher, which emerged from the Socialist National Defence Committee formed in April 1915 by G.H. Roberts, George Barnes, George Wardle (all later coalition Cabinet members and Barnes a President of the NWAC), Fisher, Robert Blatchford, Stephen Walsh and H.G. Wells. It later changed its name to the British Workers' League (BWL) and fought the 1918 general election as the National Democratic Party (NDP): Ward, *Red Flag*, p. 124; J.O. Stubbs, 'Lord Milner and Patriotic Labour, 1914–1918', *English Historical Review*, 87:345 (1972); Roy Douglas, 'The National Democratic Party and the British Workers' League', *Historical Journal*, 15:3 (1972).

It was necessary instead for 'authoritative representatives of Labour [to] make it quite clear to the world that the views of the conference are not the views of organised Labour'.[39] Furthermore, while not itself a serious revolutionary event, the Leeds Conference, occurring around the same time that news of the French mutinies began to reach governmental ears, significantly affected some of the War Cabinet (as will be discussed below), while the revolution meant for some that 'it could no longer be claimed that Britain was the freest country in the world'.[40]

THESE issues during the first half of 1917 alerted the government to the need to maintain public enthusiasm for, or at least acceptance of, the war. In Lloyd George's case, however, his preoccupation with public opinion ensured that he apprehended the need for an extensive propaganda campaign well before the events of 1917. At his first War Cabinet as prime minister, Lloyd George highlighted propaganda for urgent attention. Before his accession, propaganda was organised by the Foreign Office, and domestic propaganda (once the Parliamentary Recruiting Committee's role ended with the introduction of conscription) was carried out only by unofficial organisations – like the Central Committee for National Patriotic Organizations (CCNPO – supposedly confined to propaganda in the empire), the Navy League, the Victoria League and the Fight for Right Movement (FRM) – whose principal merit, in the opinion of official foreign propagandists like Charles Masterman, was in distributing their literature, thus enabling them to keep a low profile.

Masterman, a writer and Liberal MP heavily involved with publicising the government's national insurance scheme since 1911, had been instructed by the prime minister, Herbert Asquith, to develop propaganda for Dominion and neutral audiences in 1914. He thus established the War Propaganda Bureau at Wellington House (which became a short-hand name for the organisation).[41] A conference in September 1914 secured the assistance of many prominent literary figures as Britain, like Germany and France, undertook the 'mobilisation of intellect' in support of the war. Writers like G.K. Chesterton enthusiastically wielded their pens in publications discreetly circulated by Wellington House, but also produced self-motivated propaganda such as Chesterton's weekly columns in the *Illustrated London News* in which (again like German and French writers) he mused on warfare between civilisation and barbarism.[42] Such

39 TNA:PRO CAB24/16, GT1034: 'Report on the Labour Situation', w.e. 6/6/17; Waites, *Class Society*, p. 226; Chris Wrigley, 'The State and the Challenge of Labour in Britain, 1917–20', in idem (ed.), *Challenges of Labour: Central and Western Europe, 1917–1920* (London: Routledge, 1993), p. 264.
40 Ward, *Red Flag*, p. 144.
41 For extended discussion, see Sanders and Taylor, *British Propaganda*, pp. 15–54.
42 Sanders and Taylor, *British Propaganda*, pp. 39, 111; Julia Stapleton, *Christianity,*

independently generated propaganda assisted people like Masterman by obscuring official activities, but it also meant that only limited control could be maintained over the presentation of the war to the public. Masterman reported in 1915 that Wellington House propaganda was conducted on the basis of 'facts and general arguments based upon those facts', rather than imaginative inventions or appeals.[43] However, provided authors did not transgress military censorship rules by revealing sensitive information, there was little beyond individual conscience to inhibit more outlandish interpretations elsewhere. While DORA included substantial options for suppressing unwelcome publications,[44] these were relatively sparingly used, and in any case more likely to be wielded against the war's critics than its over-enthusiasts. The rational output promoted by Masterman, therefore, always competed with private propaganda efforts.

Despite its foreign propaganda remit, Wellington House also generated some material for home consumption, in part disseminated through bodies like the CCNPO. During 1915, permission was sought from the Treasury to extend operations within Britain, and copies of the anti-German cartoons of the Dutch artist Louis Raemaekers were distributed at a trade union conference in Bristol.[45] Further dissemination of visual propaganda in Britain was established at the end of 1916 through Masterman's commissioning of war artists like Muirhead Bone and C.R.W. Nevinson. Continuing his commitment to 'truthful' propaganda, Masterman, according to Nevinson, placed no restrictions on what the artists could paint, though the censorship of Nevinson's *Paths of Glory* (depicting dead British soldiers) demonstrated that limits to artistic freedom existed in practice. Nonetheless, the publication by Wellington House (before its eventual absorption into the Ministry of Information) of four volumes of *British Artists at the Front*, reproducing works by Nevinson, John Lavery, Paul Nash and Eric Kennington, somewhat affirmed its continuing commitment to honest depictions of the war, incorporating such works as Nash's image of a desolate battlefield with the seemingly ironic title *We Are Making a New World*.[46]

Patriotism and Nationhood: The England of G.K. Chesterton (Lanham: Lexington Books, 2009), pp. 152–53 and ff. On the mobilisation of intellect and the war between civilisation and barbarism, see, e.g., Martha Hanna, *The Mobilization of Intellect: French Scholars and Writers during the Great War* (Cambridge, MA: Harvard University Press, 1996); Audoin-Rouzeau and Becker, *1914–1918*, chapter 5; Wallace, *War and the Image*; Welch, *Germany, Propaganda*; Stibbe, *German Anglophobia*, and parts of chapters 4–6 below.

43 TNA:PRO INF4/5, 'Report of the Work of the Bureau established for the purpose of laying before neutral nations and the Dominions the case of Great Britain and her allies', 15/6/15, p. 2.

44 Millman, 'HMG', p. 422, succinctly lists the available regulations.

45 Sue Malvern, *Modern Art, Britain and the Great War: Witnessing, Testimony and Remembrance* (New Haven: Yale University Press, 2004), p. 17.

46 On the war artists generally, see Malvern, *Modern Art*, esp. chapters 1–2; Sanders

Further material for home consumption was supplied by the military from 1916 through MI7(b), a branch of the Directorate of Military Intelligence, which prepared and distributed military information for publication. During 1916 MI7(b) also circularised home forces, seeking officers with literary experience who, together with some civilian writers, had voluntarily produced nearly a thousand articles for publication by the end of the year.[47]

This jumble of functions, direction and dissemination was unacceptable to Lloyd George, who sought to wrest control of propaganda away from any existing ministry. In early January 1917 he commissioned the *Daily Chronicle*'s editor, Robert Donald, to report on British propaganda arrangements.[48] Donald recommended replacing the existing arrangements with a central propaganda organisation directed by a single individual. This prompted the creation of the Department of Information under the control of the novelist and FRM member John Buchan in February 1917.[49] According to Donald, no MP was willing to accept the job, suggesting antipathy towards 'a somewhat distasteful, albeit necessary, evil'.[50] Though intended to be entirely independent, the department remained significantly linked to the Foreign Office, and its organisation into four sections by Buchan (administration, intelligence, art and literature, press and cinema) perhaps for this reason omitted a specific home propaganda section, despite Buchan's avowed intention to attend to British opinion 'when direction is needed'.[51] Despite this, the new organisation was accepted by the Cabinet on 20 February.

Nevertheless, growing evidence of war-weariness in the early months of 1917 meant domestic propaganda continued to occupy governmental minds. On 30 March, War Cabinet disapproval of the Department of Information's efforts was revealed by the suggestion that it 'should, if necessary, organise a special branch' to 'educate' British public opinion about 'the history and potentialities of the countries, such as Mesopotamia or Palestine, where victories have been or are likely to be achieved'.[52]

---

and Taylor, *British Propaganda*, pp. 122–23; Paul Gough, *A Terrible Beauty: British Artists in the First World War* (Bristol: Sansom & Company, 2010). On Masterman's expectations and Nash's work, see Malvern, *Modern Art*, pp. 49–50, 18–21. My knowledge of war art has been greatly assisted by supervising Leeann Potter's Honours dissertation on British war artists and propaganda (University of Canterbury, 2010).

47 TNA:PRO INF4/1B, 'Military Press Control: A History of the work of MI7' (1920), pp. 9–10.

48 This account of the development of British propaganda up to the establishment of the Department of Information follows Sanders and Taylor, *British Propaganda*, pp. 55–65.

49 DeGroot, *Blighty*, p. 175.

50 Sanders and Taylor, *British Propaganda*, p. 63.

51 Sanders and Taylor, *British Propaganda*, pp. 64–65.

52 TNA:PRO CAB23/2/1365–109: War Cabinet 109, 30/3/17. Note the reflection

Similarly, at a conference on 15 April between the Home and War offices, Munitions and Labour ministries, and the Admiralty Shipyard Labour and National Service departments to establish the production of weekly reports on the 'labour situation', it was decided that the MoL should 'indicate the directions in which they are of the opinion that propaganda on behalf of the Government is desirable' beyond explanations of labour-related Departmental activities.[53] In the first of the resultant weekly reports, David Shackleton, the permanent secretary of the MoL and former Labour MP, warned of 'widespread hints of suspicion on the part of the workmen as to the intentions of the Government and as to the effect of the measures at present in contemplation'.

> Further, the essential aims and causes of the war have tended to become obscured and forgotten ... not only has the significance of the German atrocities been to some extent forgotten, but their very heinousness has been palliated by the blunting of susceptibilities due to their constant repetition.

Shackleton concluded that

> The chief need ... is for a better education of the working-classes as to the actual military situation and needs, the aims of the Allies so far as it is possible to define them, and the results that would inevitably follow from an inconclusive peace. In order to bring points of this kind home, press propaganda, and even speeches delivered in London are not sufficient ...
> What is really wanted ... is an organized effort to create a right atmosphere throughout the country. This could be done if Members of Parliament – and particularly Labour Members – were to speak regularly in industrial centres, but it is of almost greater importance that there should be a local orator representing the orthodox element in the trade unions ...
> In peace time propaganda of this nature is carried out on a large scale by the Party machines and it is suggested that the same machines might now be used ...[54]

By this time, Buchan had begun to establish domestic propaganda officially. On 18 May he submitted a memorandum to the War Cabinet, acknowledging that although 'no provision' was made in February for domestic propaganda, 'a considerable amount of propaganda in Britain

---

of Lloyd George's taste for both 'Eastern', or indirect, strategy, and for morale-boosting victories of any kind. On a further purpose of such work (laying foundations for imperial expansion), see James Renton, 'Changing Languages of Empire and the Orient: Britain and the Invention of the Middle East, 1917–1918', *Historical Journal*, 50:3 (2007).

53 TNA:PRO CAB23/13, GT 733: 'Labour Intelligence', 15/4/17.
54 TNA:PRO CAB24/14, GT832: 'Labour situation', w.e. 24/5/17. The 'need for extensive propaganda ... to revive the early enthusiasm' was recapitulated in the report for the week in which the Leeds Conference was held: TNA:PRO CAB24/16, GT1034: 'Report on the Labour Situation', w.e. 6/6/17.

itself' was now necessary since newspapers were so small, owing to paper shortages, and because of the 'almost entire cessation of public speaking'. Buchan was 'anxious' to arrange 'direct propaganda' in 'all the chief centres' of Britain. He noted that 'Labour Deputations' had been sent to visit 're-occupied territories' and felt they should 'lecture in their own districts … with our official films and slides' and also wanted MPs to involve themselves in propaganda work, with the department's 'assistance in the way of information, illustrations and booklets'. Buchan suggested that cabinet approval was required for Treasury subsidy.[55] Four days later, the War Cabinet approved his proposal 'in principle' and instructed him to contact the Treasury regarding funds.[56] When they decided, following the Leeds Conference, that 'the time had come to undertake an active campaign to counteract the pacifist movement, which at present had the field to itself', preparations were probably already underway to establish the National War Aims Committee.[57] Certainly by mid-June, negotiations had begun between the four party groups (Coalition Liberal, Asquithian Liberal, Conservative, Labour) on the subject. Robert Sanders, a Conservative whip and the future Vice-Chairman of the NWAC, wrote on 15 June of 'a scheme on foot for holding a series of meetings in the country to counteract the pacifist and syndicalist propaganda. Edmund [Talbot, the Conservative chief whip] wants me to represent the party on the executive committee. Freddy Guest [Lloyd George's chief whip and the NWAC's Chairman-in-waiting] is very keen' while J.W. Gulland, chief whip of ex-prime minister Asquith's faction of the Liberals and the man in overall charge of Liberal party machinery, was believed willing to help.[58] On 7 July, an account worth £5500 was opened for the NWAC at the London City & Midland Bank.[59] Presumably around this time, Guest reported to Lloyd George that his 'Propaganda Committee' – consisting of himself; Sanders; the Coalition Liberal, Sir Hamar Greenwood; Robert Tootill, a Labour MP and vice-President of the BWNL; and the Liberal Whip and 'Gullandite', A.H. Marshall – had met at Downing Street.[60]

---

55 TNA:PRO CAB 24/13, GT774: 'Propaganda at Home. Memorandum by the Director, Department of Information', 18/5/17.
56 TNA:PRO CAB 23/2/1365-142: War Cabinet 142, 22/5/17.
57 TNA:PRO CAB23/3/1365-154: War Cabinet 154, 5/6/17.
58 Sanders Diary, 15/6/17, in John Ramsden (ed.), *Real Old Tory Politics: The Political Diaries of Sir Robert Sanders, Lord Bayford, 1910–35* (London: The Historians' Press, 1984), p. 87. Note the very specific motivations for propaganda recorded by Sanders.
59 TNA:PRO T102/7, J.A. Jutsom (London City & Midland Bank) to Sanders, 7/7/17.
60 PA, Lloyd George Papers, LG/F/21/2/2, Guest to Lloyd George, n.d. The note is filed between a letter of May and another of early June, but Sanders's diary suggests this is too early. On Tootill's BWNL connections, see Stubbs, 'Milner and Patriotic Labour', p. 733, n. 1; Douglas, 'National Democratic Party', p. 536.

However, the involvement of Asquith's Liberals was problematic. On 12 July Sanders complained that 'Gulland has been making difficulties as to joining the propaganda campaign now being organised … It looks rather as if his party is now out for blood' owing to the government's perceived unpopularity. Despite its avowed non-party status, an element of party politicking continued to characterise the NWAC's administration throughout 1917–18. On this occasion, however, a change of attitude apparently rapidly occurred, with Gulland soon 'quite friendly as regards our speaking committee'.[61] On 18 July the Committee asked the Marquess of Crewe (Lord Lieutenant of London, chairman of the London County Council and a former member of Asquith's cabinet) to chair the planned inaugural meeting.[62] The next day, the manager of Queen's Hall was approached, and the inaugural meeting (and existence) of the NWAC was announced in *The Times* on 24 July, with details of its presidents: Lloyd George, Asquith, the Conservative leader and Chancellor of the Exchequer Andrew Bonar Law and the Labour cabinet member, George Barnes, who had filled Arthur Henderson's War Cabinet role while the latter was away in Russia, and would soon replace him altogether following Henderson's resignation in early August over the proposed socialist conference in Stockholm.[63]

Alongside Sanders's suspicion that they were 'out for blood', the problems experienced with Gulland (and, by association, Asquith) may have reflected a similar discomfort with propaganda to that which necessitated Buchan's appointment as director of the Department of Information. When later asked by the NWAC for party funds, Gulland wrote that there 'seems to be great objection that any Government should use public money for the formation of public opinion at home – which secretly uses public funds'.[64] This was an attitude indicated by some MPs when the NWAC sought Treasury funding for their work (see chapter 9). On 31 August, Sanders recorded that 'Asquith and Gulland have stopped [all attempts to get public money] up to now'.[65] Whatever motivated their obstructionism, whether a feeling that such activities were un-British, or because it was bad politics to fund Lloyd George's brainchild with 'Asquith's' money, by late July the NWAC's work was underway.

---

61 Sanders Diary, 12/7/17, 20/7/17, in Ramsden, *Tory Politics*, pp. 87–88.
62 TNA:PRO T102/2, letter, unsigned to Crewe, 18/7/17.
63 TNA:PRO T102/11, Thomas Cox (NWAC General Secretary) to Robert Humphreys, 19/7/17; 'Mr Lloyd George and War Aims: A New Committee', *Times* (24/7/17), p. 7.
64 Letter by J.W. Gulland, read by Sir Edward Carson, Parliamentary Debates, House of Commons, fifth series (PDC(5)), 99 (13/11/17), col. 315.
65 Sanders Diary, 31/8/17, in Ramsden, *Tory Politics*, p. 89.

EMBRACING Shackleton's suggestion of May, organisation of the NWAC was turned over to the Conservative, Liberal and Labour party machines, confirming that 'when politicians needed means of communication and organization ... it was to the parties [not] the state that they turned for the machinery and expertise'.[66] In this the NWAC followed in the footsteps of a previous, though unlike the NWAC, 'officially official' domestic propaganda organisation, the PRC.[67] At all levels there were parallels in personnel and organisation. The PRC had been an all-party organisation with Asquith, Bonar Law and Henderson as presidents. At least one member of its executive committee, the Labour MP (and chief whip during 1917) James Parker, eventually served on the NWAC's executive Committee (joining in October to maintain the political balance when extra MPs Ronald McNeill, Walter Rea and W.H. Cowan took seats as heads of sub-committees). Two of the PRC's honorary secretaries, Sir John Boraston and Arthur Peters, took the same roles in the NWAC, alongside the Liberal officials G. Wallace Carter and G.W. Thompson, while like Carter and Peters, Thomas Cox and Sidney Vesey put their past experience in the PRC meetings sub-department to good use in the NWAC, Cox as general secretary, and Vesey as the Unionist organiser in the Meetings Department.[68] Some of these administrators had pre-war experience in similar organisations (in the same way that several Wellington House officials followed Masterman from the National Insurance Commission).[69] In 1911 Sir Arthur Steel-Maitland had criticised Cox's organisation of the National Union's speaking department, complaining to Bonar Law that his 'system is wooden and rigid ... Thus, if a constituency will not take the individual speaker he sends, it can go without altogether ... His wares are to be taken or left. They ought to be adapted and pushed.' By contrast, Boraston, Conservative principal agent from 1912, was part of a 'team of experts, all of sufficient status to deal with politicians'.[70] Shortly before the war, Wallace Carter, as secretary of the Central Land and Housing Council and chief organiser of Lloyd George's land campaign, had recruited 80 full-time and 150 volunteer speakers, supervising a campaign in which, Ian Packer notes,

---

66 John Ramsden, *A History of the Conservative Party*, vol. 3, *The Age of Balfour and Baldwin, 1902–1940* (London: Longman, 1978), p. 125.

67 Cf. Millman's description of the NWAC in *Managing*, p. 229.

68 TNA:PRO WO106/367, 'The Work of the Parliamentary Req Cte [*sic*]'; 'Parliamentary Recruiting Committee. Meetings Sub-Department Report'; T102/16, 'National War Aims Committee. Minutes of Meeting held at the House of Commons, S.W., 24th October, 1917'; T102/18, personnel list; Speech of Captain Guest, PDC(5), 99 (13/11/17), cols 288–89.

69 Sanders and Taylor, *British Propaganda*, p. 40.

70 Steel-Maitland to Bonar Law, December 1911, cited in Ramsden, *Balfour and Baldwin*, p. 47 (cf. Cox's treatment of complainants in chapter 10); on Boraston, p. 68.

'not only were 90–120 meetings occurring each day, but 1.45 million booklets and 1.5 million leaflets had been distributed on rural matters alone'.[71] Peters, meanwhile, had been the Labour party's national agent since 1908 and was, in Ross McKibbin's words, 'a diligent, if uninspired officer ... both Wesleyan and teetotal, and rather oversubscribed to that fund of piety at Head Office which those who were neither Wesleyan nor teetotal found irritating'.[72]

The NWAC's organisational model was also heavily indebted to the PRC, establishing Meetings and Publications Departments. To spread recruiting propaganda across the nation, the 'speaking staff of the three great parties were placed at the disposal' of the PRC, while

> Local Joint Parliamentary Committees consisting of active members of the three great parties in the constituencies created an official organisation in almost every area throughout England and Wales ... In nearly every case the political agents of the three great parties were appointed Joint Hon. Secretaries of the Local Committees ... gentlemen ... not only experienced in every phase of propaganda work, but with whom the members of the Sub-Department had been personally associated in important public activities previous to the war.[73]

Many of the NWAC's officers learnt these lessons first-hand, establishing local War Aims Committees (WACs), using the same agents and providing speakers frequently drawn from the party speaking staffs. Before August, letters were circulated to Conservative and Liberal political agents and whatever local representatives of the labour movement existed. By the commencement of the NWAC's inaugural meeting on 4 August, 23 WACs were already established, beginning with South Dorset on 28 July, and including several centres of unrest like Swansea, Leicester, Jarrow, Huddersfield and Coventry (table 1).[74] Of these, only one (St Helens) definitely had a Labour secretary, reflecting the generally problematic relationship with Labour experienced by the NWAC (which had not afflicted the PRC). These issues, however, are discussed in subsequent chapters.

The presence of constituencies like Southport, Wells and Great Yarmouth as early formed WACs probably reflects the early plans of the NWAC, explained in a circular letter to speakers as being 'mainly

---

71 Ian Packer, *Lloyd George, Liberalism and the Land: The Land Issue and Party Politics in England, 1906–1914* (London: Boydell Press, 2001), p. 125.

72 McKibbin, *Evolution*, p. 4.

73 TNA:PRO WO106/367, 'Parliamentary Recruiting Committee. Meetings Sub-Department. Report'.

74 TNA:PRO T102/26. These statistics derive from a database constructed from the NWAC's card index of WACs (henceforth noted as card-index database). A full copy of this and all databases referred to is contained in David Monger, 'The National War Aims Committee and British Patriotism during the First World War' (PhD dissertation, King's College London, 2009).

Table 1 WACs formed by 4 August 1917

Established	Constituency	Secretaries/contacts
28/07/17	South Dorset	Col. G.F. Symes M.V.O. (L); F.W. Powell (U)
30/07/17	Swansea	W.J. Crocker (L); B. Bottomley (U)
30/07/17	Isle of Thanet	Revd B.J. Salomons (L); H.W.M. Morris (U)
31/07/17	Leicester	Chas E. Clark (U); T.W. Smith (L); W.J. Arculus (U)
02/08/17	Huddersfield	James W. Morrison (L); E. Clarkson (U)
02/08/17	Great Yarmouth	Wm Wade (U); W.J. Oldman (L) Address: 'Joint Secs ...'
02/08/17	Jarrow	Jack Raine (L); George Clarkson (U)
02/08/17	St Helens	A. Valentine (L); R. Waring (La); P.A. Twist (U)
02/08/17	Wells	C.H. Poole (L); R.J. Cooke (U)
02/08/17	Hackney Central	Stanley Barton (U); Arthur S. Brown (L)
03/08/17	Horncastle	A. Julian (L); A.H. Beeton (U)
03/08/17	Lewes	Harry Courtney (L); Thomas Grave (U)
03/08/17	Bristol West	Vincent Thompson (U)
03/08/17	Carlisle	Henry K. Campbell (L); B.L. Hilton (U: resigned according to note)
03/08/17	Hull Central	A.T. Hallmark (U)
03/08/17	Hull East	David Harrison (L)
03/08/17	Southport	R. Standring (U); A. Keith Durham (L)
04/08/17	Wirral	F. Harrison (L); A. Birkett (U)
04/08/17	Rugby	J.R. Almond (U); F.M. Burton (L: deleted); J.J. Scrivener (L)
04/08/17	Harwich	J.A. Bolton (L); T. Ablewhite (U)
04/08/17	West Bromwich	Will G. Bastable (L); Alfred Curtis (U)
04/08/17	Rotherhithe	F.H. Benson (L); W. Queen (U); W.T. Hook (U: deleted)
04/08/17	Coventry	Leonard Walsh (U); Karl L. Spencer (L)

confined to open-air meetings at the various seaside resorts throughout the country'. This early campaign resulted in 1298 meetings in 54 'holiday resorts' by 25 September.[75] Before August, arrangements were made between the NWAC and the CCNPO regarding the cessation of the latter's propaganda work. On 27 July, Guest wrote to Sir William Grey Wilson, secretary of the CCNPO, that the NWAC was 'preparing

75 TNA:PRO T102/2, letter, unsigned to Councillor C.G.B. Ellison, J.P. (Barrow in Furness), 20/8/17; see also identical letters of same date to J. Beard (Birmingham), T102/1 and J. Cuthbertson (Birmingham), T102/2; T102/16, 'National War Aims Committee: Meetings Department Report', 25/9/17. The NWAC's work is examined in chapter 2.

to undertake a continuous and vigorous educational campaign during the ensuing months', and that since its aims coincided with the CCNPO's, it was 'thought advisable' that 'all future meetings on these patriotic lines should be held under one name only' and that the CCNPO should, therefore, cease operations. Grey Wilson subsequently told a CCNPO organiser that although he believed the CCNPO 'as a private institution has a far freer field than [the NWAC] can possibly hope to have', there was no alternative but to be 'swallowed as far as our war aims activities are concerned'.[76]

By the time Lloyd George stepped onto the Queen's Hall platform, therefore, the NWAC had begun to establish a nation-wide network of WACs, intended to be the local executives responsible for assisting the national Committee in attaining six aims:

1. Generally to strengthen the national morals and consolidate the national war aims as outlined by the executive Government and endorsed by the great majority of the people.
2. To counteract, and, if possible, render nugatory the insidious and specious propaganda of pacifist publications.
3. To indicate, and, where possible, specifically define, the advantages of an Entente Peace, especially in relation to its effect on the daily lives of the people, to dwell on the democratic development and improvement in the lot of the working class which State control and other war changes have already secured; to suggest the prospect of further improvement and greater freedom when the war is over; generally, to envisage the rewards of success.
4. To explain and emphasise the meaning of a German Peace – its political, commercial, economic and social consequences – and to call up and employ that vast reserve of moral courage and determination which lies dormant in the nation.
5. To inspire all war workers at home, especially those hidden from view, with a living sense of their responsibility and share in the great task; to give them tangible proof of the Government's appreciation; so to brace and hearten them that, however long the war may last, its crusading character may be their dominating thought.
6. To encourage unity and stifle party and class dissensions by dwelling insistently on the momentous issues at stake, on the gravity of the crisis, on the spontaneous co-operation of Oversea Dominions, on the moral and material support of America[,] on the fact that the cohesion and resolution of the Allies depend very largely on the example and inspiration of this country, and on the records of history which make it impossible to conceive that the people of this country will waver in their fixed purpose.[77]

These guidelines were evident in the speeches made at the NWAC's inaugural meeting. On 4 August *The Times* announced that prominent

---

76 TNA:PRO T102/3, Guest to Grey Wilson, 27/7/17; Grey Wilson to N. Grattan Doyle, 2/8/17.
77 TNA:PRO T102/16 '(Confidential) Aims of Home Publicity', n.d.

clergymen, including the Archbishop of Canterbury and the most senior British Catholic, Cardinal Bourne, would attend, alongside over one hundred MPs, twenty cabinet-members, and London and provincial mayors and councillors.[78] Speeches reflected all four political groups' perspectives. The Marquess of Crewe, in the chair, was a member of both Asquith's wartime cabinets, but not Lloyd George's ministry,[79] while Lloyd George, Sanders and Tootill spoke on behalf of their respective groups. Also present were the Italian foreign minister, Baron Sonnino, and the Serbian prime minister, while Crewe read a supportive message from General Botha in South Africa, J.C. Smuts having refused to speak at an event on 'the saddest anniversary in the story of man'.[80] Thus the meeting heralded political unity both inside the country and with Britain's imperial and external allies.

Crewe insisted that

> there is no change in our general aims as they were originally announced by Mr. Asquith in the Autumn of 1914 ... Those aims are, in two words, Reparation [for France, Belgium, Serbia, Poland, Romania and Armenia] and Security ... based ... on the foundation of race, or on the avowed preference of the inhabitants of each area ... [and] not only against military attack, but against all aggression ... however it may be disguised.[81]

Crewe's short speech reflected the NWAC's first and third aims, and he concluded, 'We believe in our cause, and our goal is the liberty of the world.' Sonnino, unsurprisingly, emphasised the sixth aim, describing the 'brotherly covenant' of Britain and Italy, and stressed the allies' need to 'lend each other mutual support ... for the triumph of the common cause'. However, Sonnino also touched on the third aim, proclaiming Italy's goal as 'the liberation of our brethren from ... cruel oppression' while stressing the desire to ensure a Wilsonian 'better general organisa-tion of the Comity of Nations'.

The main event was the prime minister's speech, which touched on the first, second, fourth, fifth and sixth aims of the NWAC. Lloyd George emphasised the danger of German victory, referring to Serbians as 'vic-tims of Teutonic barbarity' and declaring that Britain fought to 'defeat the most dangerous conspiracy ever plotted against the liberty of nations

---

78 'The Prime Minister at Queen's Hall', *Times* 4/8/17, p. 9.
79 Frank P. Chambers, *The War behind the War, 1914–1918: A History of the Political and Civilian Fronts* (New York: Arno Press, 1972 [1939]), pp. 587–90.
80 Smuts to M.C. Gillett, 6/8/17, in W.K. Hancock and Jean Van der Poel (eds), *Selections from the Smuts Papers*, vol. 3, *June 1910-November 1918* (7 vols, Cambridge: Cambridge University Press, 1966), p. 536.
81 The following discussion draws upon the transcript of F. Primrose Stevenson's short-hand notes: PA, Lloyd George Papers, LG/F/160/1/10, 'Report of Proceeding at the Inaugural Meeting of the National War Aims Committee'.

... carefully, skilfully, insidiously, clandestinely planned in every detail with ruthless cynical determination'. Without Britain's contribution, he maintained, the situation would have been even worse. 'It would have been the subjugation of Europe ... in servitude ... at the mercy of this great cruel Power.' He stressed that 'a bad peace goes on and on', and that there

> must be no next time. It is far better in spite of all the cost, yea, and all the sorrow, and all the tragedy of it, to have done with it ... Let us be the generation that manfully, courageously and resolutely eliminates war from amongst the tragedies of human life.

He scornfully acknowledged that

> There are people in this country who would introduce ... disintegrating methods to direct the conduct of the war (laughter). The nation has chosen its own Workmen's and Soldier's Committee (cheers), and that is the House of Commons ... We cannot allow sectional organisations to direct the war, nor to dictate the peace (cheers).

He exhorted the nation to bear the strain and see the war through to victory, declaring, 'Anyone who promotes national distrust or disunion at this moment is helping the enemy and hurting his native land' and promised that 'together we shall reach the summit of our hopes'.

Lloyd George was followed by Sanders, who summarised the NWAC's objects in 'two colloquial phrases ... we want to tell people that we have got to stick it, and for God's sake don't grouse'. Drawing on his wartime military service in the Middle East,[82] he demanded that people consider conditions at the front when complaining about workplace privileges, food prices, beer shortages and air-raids, before moving a resolution (appropriated from the CCNPO) 'to continue to a victorious end the struggle in maintenance of those ideals of Liberty and Justice which are the common and sacred cause of the Allies'.

Tootill, seconding the resolution, rejoiced 'that the vast majority of the more responsible and level-headed leaders and officials and the rank and file of the great Labour movement of this country are firmly convinced and vigorous supporters of ... victory'. He enquired of the anti-war left, 'where do we find any record of any specific public pronouncement directed against the indescribable devastations and inhuman cruelties the Central Powers have delighted to inflict upon weak and defenceless nations?', implying that such groups were 'secretly or openly backing the Germans'. 'A great national duty of incalculable importance rests upon all of us in the present state of the country in relation to the war', Tootill argued, concluding, 'if we were to suffer defeat ... what becomes of our

---

82 See Ramsden, *Tory Politics*, pp. 80–84.

hopes and prospects for future development towards a truer and nobler and more enlightened state?'

Within these speeches were embodied all the declared aims of home publicity. After several months, or years, in the making, Britain had an organisation, though not technically official, dedicated solely to maintaining public patriotism. To what extent it succeeded is the subject of the remainder of this book.

CHAPTER 2

The NWAC at Work

OVER 16 months, the NWAC evolved from a privately funded, un-official organisation, into a publicly funded, quasi-official body. Influential and independent, it represented the primary parliamentary device of domestic patriotic 'education' for the remainder of the war, strong enough to withstand suggestions by Lord Beaverbrook that it should be incorporated within his new Ministry of Information. According to Brock Millman, 'perhaps the most important purpose of the NWAC had nothing to do with propaganda' but was its 'secret repressive agenda'.[1] However, the evidence of this chapter rejects Millman's inaccurate inter-pretation of the NWAC's scope and purposes.

When it began in mid-1917, the NWAC was a small organisation, reliant on private donations, comprising five MPs and based at Conservative Central Office in St Stephen's Chambers. While undoubtedly 'Lloyd George was the guiding political light of the NWAC',[2] he (and his fellow presidents) had little involvement with its operations beyond making the occasional speech and forwarding some correspondence. When a London businessman, W.W. Howard, suggested the necessity of publicly recapitulating 'the facts relating to the beginning of this awful war', since 'memory will fade with the time which has elapsed', offering £500 to assist with expenses, Lloyd George passed this letter to the NWAC. Howard was then informed of their work, which was 'being very rapidly pushed forward'. 'Seeing the work necessarily entails a heavy expenditure', the reply continued, 'this Committee would welcome any donation to its funds which you would like to subscribe'.[3]

However, by then the NWAC's executive, together with Sir Edward Carson, assigned by the War Cabinet to 'assume general supervision over

---

1   Millman, *Managing*, pp. 245, 229.
2   Millman, *Managing*, p. 232.
3   TNA:PRO T102/5, W.W. Howard to Lloyd George, 16/8/17; reply (unsigned), to Howard, 29/8/17.

[domestic] propaganda' on 21 August,[4] had already decided that such
funds were insufficient to effectively run the campaign. On the 30th,
Carson told the War Cabinet the campaign might need

> as much as 100,000*l*. It was understood, however, that there was a good
> deal of opposition to the use of public money for the maintenance of a
> cause to which a certain number (though a small one) of the tax-payers
> were opposed.[5]

This prompted extensive negotiations between the NWAC, the party
central offices and the government. With no likelihood of Conservative or
Liberal purse-strings (controlled respectively by Sir George Younger and
Gulland) loosening significantly, the NWAC resolved on 3 October that,
due to 'the impossibility of financing the work of the Committee from
private subscriptions or Party funds', the Committee thought it essential
'to obtain the requisite money from public funds'.[6] The following day
Carson informed the War Cabinet that the £17,000 of private subscriptions 'were now exhausted', and added that further private investment
might enable 'the Pacifists [to] attribute this support to the capitalist
class'. Consequently, the War Cabinet accepted 'in principle' that the
NWAC should receive Treasury funding.[7]

On 16 October the NWAC submitted an estimate to the Treasury
for the six months ending 31 March 1918, amounting to £113,858
(with another £5000 added for activities in Scotland, apparently as an
afterthought). This comprised £780 respectively for central staff wages
and office supplies; £61,878 for four weeks' campaign each in 345 constituencies;[8] £8015 for staff wages in the Publicity Department (including
£2600 for outside literary contributors); and £42,405 for all the various
items expected to be produced by this department – such as pamphlets,
postcards, cigarette cards, lantern lecture material and posters – including £10,000 towards cinema propaganda.[9] These arrangements were
confirmed by 24 October, when it was reported that the NWAC's private
account had been closed, that the Office of Works and the Stationery
Office had received the 'necessary authority' to provide the relevant
facilities, and that Sanders was assured that 'the ordinary Treasury rules
would not be unreasonably enforced'.[10]

---

4 TNA:PRO CAB 23/3/1365-221: War Cabinet 221, 21/8/17.
5 TNA:PRO CAB 23/3/1365-226: War Cabinet 226, 30/8/17. Sanders recorded
   in his diary a day later that 'Asquith and Gulland have stopped that up to now':
   Sanders Diary, 31/8/17, in Ramsden, *Tory Politics*, p. 89.
6 TNA:PRO T102/16, NWAC minutes, 19/9/17, 3/10/17.
7 TNA:PRO CAB 23/4/1365-245: War Cabinet 245, 4/10/17.
8 Millman erroneously suggests from these estimates that the NWAC intended to
   operate in all 468 constituencies (*Managing*, p. 233).
9 TNA:PRO T102/16, NWAC: 'Statement of Estimated Expenditure for 6 months
   ending March 31st', 1918, 16/10/17.
10 TNA:PRO T102/16, NWAC minutes, 24/10/17.

When parliament was consulted about NWAC funding, however, only £1000 was sought as a token vote in Committee because, according to Guest,

> what the Germans most want to know is the mental attitude of our workers ... and if by a Debate in this House on a Vote for educational purposes they were to ... [think] that we had suddenly had to adopt an active campaign ... either to oppose pacifism or to stiffen the courage of our industrial classes, they would get more satisfaction than I am sure this [Supply] Committee means to give them.[11]

Although the decision to seek a token vote received 'a lot of opposition',[12] and much criticism for the secrecy it entailed, at both the original debate on 13 November and the second reading on 14 December, despite considerable debate of the principles involved in allowing domestic propaganda to be carried out at all (discussed in chapter 9), an amendment seeking to reduce the vote to 'a sum not exceeding £900' was defeated.[13] The warning of the Asquithian Liberal, Timothy Davies, that it 'will be £10,000 in a week's time, £100,000 in two months' time, and £500,000 in six months' time if we allow the £1,000 to-night', was overridden by arguments like Carson's that a rejection would 'allow the country to be a prey to the vilest ... and the most unpatriotic misrepresentations ... which are costing the country life after life at the front'.[14] Ronald McNeill, a Unionist NWAC member, argued that opposition from politicians affiliated with, or sympathetic to, organisations like the UDC – for instance Noel Buxton, Joseph King, Philip Morrell, Robert Outhwaite, Arthur Ponsonby and C.P. Trevelyan, who all spoke against the Token Vote and were six of twenty-two MPs, along with other UDC members like Ramsay MacDonald and Fred Jowett who supported the amendment on 13 November – amounted to 'an attempt here to instil into the public mind drops of poison', for which the NWAC represented a possible antidote.[15]

The NWAC's increased financial requirements reflected the organisation's expansion. The original five MPs were augmented by a further four, representing the four main political groups. Walter Rea, an Asquithian Liberal, became chairman of the Meetings sub-committee on 30 August 1917, while Sir William H. Cowan (Coalition Liberal) was asked to investigate the establishment of a Scottish War Aims Committee. On the same day, McNeill was appointed, with Buchan and Peters, to establish

---

11 PDC(5), 99 (13/11/17), col. 291.
12 Sanders Diary, 17/11/17, in Ramsden, *Tory Politics*, p. 91.
13 PDC(5) 99 (13/11/17), col. 346; vol. 100 (14/12/17), col. 1596.
14 Speeches of Timothy Davies and Sir Edward Carson, PDC(5), 99 (13/11/17), cols 333, 316, 340.
15 Speech of Ronald McNeill, PDC(5), 99 (13/11/17), col. 340. Trevelyan and Ponsonby were founders of the UDC. On the others, see H.M. Swanwick, *Builders of Peace: Being the History of the Union of Democratic Control* (London: Swathmore Press, 1924), p. 180.

the Publicity Department, which he chaired from 25 September. To keep the party balance even, James Parker joined the Committee as a Labour representative on 24 October.[16] By September the acceptance of the sub-committee's report meant the Publicity Department would grow significantly, with salaried staff including a director and assistant-director, and in 1918 the central committee had 46 full-time salaried members of staff (including eight earning more than £500 a year) beyond the MPs and chief political agents who voluntarily made up the core executive.[17] Treasury funding prompted relocation to 25 rooms at 54 Victoria Street.[18] Even this was insufficient space for the growing organisation. In May 1918, with more staff being transferred to the building, Cox asked whether a partition could be 'thrown across' a passage to make another room, and in September further 'developments [had] taken place in one or two directions necessitating the provision of extra room'.[19] Such continuing investment suggests an organisation continuing to enjoy strong government support throughout the remainder of the war.

IN executing its functions the NWAC was initially beset by two significant and interrelated problems: the lack of a definitive governmental statement on war aims and the reluctant involvement of Labour organisations. D.L. Mort, Secretary of the Briton Ferry Trades and Labour Council, in response to the NWAC's invitation to assist locally wrote,

> we consider it a waste of time & money ... all this trouble could be alieviated [sic] if Cabinet Ministers made statements clear and understandable in the House of Commons. If Ministers made a definate [sic] statement, like the Russian declaration, in <u>Workers</u> not in <u>Diplomatic</u> language, everybody would understand.[20]

The point was taken. On 25 September it was acknowledged that 'the need for a definite statement on this subject and directions to our speakers thereupon will become urgent', and on 10 October the Committee added that 'Organised Labour in nearly every constituency declines to co-operate ... on the ground that our aims are not defined ... [T]his reason or excuse should be removed as quickly as possible.'[21] Parliamentary critics of the Committee, like Ponsonby, suggested it was 'useless ... to go on pretending that there is no ground for misunderstanding and misinterpretation of what our war aims are ... Why do you not state your

---

16 TNA:PRO T102/16, NWAC minutes, 30/8/17, 25/9/17, 24/10/17.
17 TNA:PRO INF4/1B, 'Staff of National War Aims Committee'.
18 TNA:PRO T102/3, Carson to Sir Arthur Durrant (Office of Works), 5/10/17.
19 TNA:PRO T102/10, Cox to Durrant, 28/5/18, 6/9/18.
20 TNA:PRO T102/8, D.L. Mort to Peters, 18/8/17 (misrecorded as 18 March, 1917; a reply was sent on 21/8/17). See also T102/3, A.E. Dutton (Secretary, Crewe and District Trades Council) to NWAC, 23/8/17.
21 TNA:PRO T102/16, NWAC Minutes, 25/9/18, 10/10/18.

terms fairly?'[22] The central committee felt handicapped by the continuing absence of a statement, noting its necessity again in December.[23]

While Lloyd George's January 1918 statement at the Caxton Hall alleviated this problem,[24] the reluctance of many Labour groups to take part in war aims work induced Peters' resignation, shortly after the Labour party produced its own war aims statement in December.[25] His resignation, because of Labour's own war aims statement and concerns about some of the propaganda, was announced in January.[26] Although Guest denied in early February that the 'representative of labour' had resigned (presumably because Tootill and Parker both remained NWAC members), Stanley Baldwin, on behalf of Lloyd George, informed the Commons in early June that Peters had resigned 'some six months ago', but rejected Outhwaite's suggestion that Tootill and Parker represented the government rather than Labour.[27] However, their credibility as 'authentic' Labour representatives was limited.

The NWAC's reorganisation in April 1918 shows the large number of participants in the Committee executive. In addition to Guest, Sanders and Cox (who did not attend the sub-committees), the Meetings Committee comprised Rea (as chairman), Greenwood, Tootill, Boraston, Wallace Carter and Thompson; together with Sir Harry Brittain, representing the Anglo-American Committee; Capt. the Rt Hon. Earl of Onslow, representing the War Office; Commander Walcott for the Admiralty; and H.L.M. Bebb as Treasury representative. While Brittain did not sit on the Publicity Committee, its non-MP personnel were otherwise the same, alongside McNeill (as chairman), Cowan, Parker and Marshall.[28] These sub-committees undertook the majority of the NWAC's daily work, though outside assistance was also sometimes sought (for instance, in preparing proposals for a 'War Trophies Exhibition', Brittain canvassed the opinions of staff at the Dorland advertising agency).[29]

JON LAWRENCE emphasises both the 'widespread belief that political legitimacy still rested, at least in part, in the open public meeting', and politicians' belief in, even reliance upon, 'educating' the public which

---

22 Speech of Arthur Ponsonby, PDC(5), 100 (19/12/17), cols 2005–6.
23 TNA:PRO T102/16, NWAC Minutes, 8/12/18.
24 For the factors motivating Lloyd George's statement, including NWAC pressure, see V.H. Rothwell, *British War Aims and Peace Diplomacy, 1914–1918* (Oxford: Clarendon Press, 1971), pp. 143–47; David Stevenson, *The First World War and International Politics* (Oxford: Oxford University Press, 1988), pp. 183–84, 191–93.
25 John N. Horne, *Labour at War: France and Britain, 1914–1918* (Oxford: Clarendon Press, 1991), pp. 309–11.
26 'Political Notes', *Times*, 29/1/18, p. 7.
27 PDC(5), 101 (6/2/18), col. 2241; 106 (6/6/18), cols 1741–42.
28 TNA:PRO T102/16, NWAC Minutes, 4/4/18.
29 London School of Economics Library (LSE), Brittain Papers, BRITTAIN/0010.

continued in Britain until 1914, and it is significant that early discussions regarding a domestic propaganda body revolved specifically around the holding of meetings.[30] Throughout its operations, the NWAC continued to place almost devotional faith in the power and importance of public meetings, irrespective of periodical adverse comments. The presence of the parties' chief agents as secretaries, with their expertise in arranging political meetings, reflects this preoccupation, as does the fact that the (voluntary) central executive and party staffs gave so much of their attention to meetings that the reorganisation of the Meetings Department on the salaried basis of the Publicity Department was not considered necessary until April 1918, when district organisers were appointed to further coordinate meetings campaigns.[31] Moreover, the experience of NWAC staff in the PRC may also have reaffirmed the significance of open-air meetings. According to Kit Good, recruiters had recognised that 'to reach the "street-corner lad" the war had to be brought to the street corner' through public meetings.[32] Between August 1917 and December 1918, at least 115 MPs agreed to speak at NWAC meetings, but only two were recorded as producing original written material for the Publicity Department (though many speeches became NWAC pamphlets).[33] Early Committee discussions were dominated by meetings, with arrangements for the Publicity Department not beginning until 30 August and not confirmed until late September, while an offer to transcribe the inaugural meeting received the response that 'the only report that will be required ... will be that which we ... [can] obtain from the ordinary Press channels'.[34]

Various groups within constituencies were rapidly identified as important audiences by the Committee. While the original emphasis was on meetings in summer holiday destinations, by late September almost as many meetings had been arranged in 'industrial areas' (995 compared to 1298). Plans had also begun to hold meetings 'in or near factories ... in consultation with the Ministry of Munitions', and in London's 'parks and open spaces', where pacifist propaganda was perceived to be 'securing a considerable measure of attention if not support'.[35] This reflected the

30 Jon Lawrence, *Speaking for the People: Party, Language and Popular Politics in England, 1867–1914* (Cambridge: Cambridge University Press, 1998), pp. 164, 178–80; Sanders Diary, 15/6/17, 20/7/17 in Ramsden, *Tory Politics*, pp. 87, 88; n. 12 above.

31 TNA:PRO T102/16, NWAC Minutes, 4/4/18.

32 Kit Good, 'England Goes to War, 1914–15' (PhD dissertation, University of Liverpool, 2002), p. 143.

33 Figures based on two databases compiled from NWAC files: one from the Meetings Register in TNA:PRO T102/17 (henceforth noted as Register Database) and the other from ledgers of articles by outside contributors, and accounts of artists contributions, in T102/19 and 21 (henceforth noted as Articles Database).

34 TNA:PRO T102/13, unsigned (Cox) to F. Primrose Stevenson, 31/7/17.

35 TNA:PRO T102/16, NWAC minutes, 25/9/17; on the wartime contest for parks and other public spaces, see Jon Lawrence, 'Public Space, Political Space', in Jay

'widespread belief', noted by Lawrence, that the symbolism of 'political occupation' and 'physical control of civic space' engendered by public meetings was key to political legitimacy.[36] The NWAC's members were also concerned by the 'appearance ... or prevalence of anti-war views in certain rural districts, the Home Counties and other non-industrial areas' (perhaps areas expected to be more 'reliable', though Gregory also notes the weak commitment of such areas to War Loans at around the same time). Consequently, every constituency was to be consulted about establishing a WAC. The presence of MPs was also considered crucial – 'at least one large meeting should be held in each constituency [with another MP] present in addition to the local member', thus ensuring that national rather than local political legitimacy was upheld, whilst allowing MPs to maintain their reputations in an era when public meetings remained a yardstick of political ability. Finally, military camps were targeted because of evidence of conscripts' 'great ignorance'.[37] By mid-October, women were also specifically targeted since war-weariness was believed by Committee members to be 'prevalent among women'; 'special' meetings were therefore necessary, to be organised with 'the help and co-operation of leading women in their areas'. Thus, women's active involvement in public meetings was perhaps endorsed without their (in Lawrence's words) 'appropriating the rituals of (male) popular politics'.[38] An advertisement for a NWAC lantern lecture on 15 November 1918 reflected this attitude towards female involvement at meetings. The phrase 'Ladies admitted' suggests both that this was still relatively unusual, and, perhaps, that they remained not entirely 'welcome' (although this could reflect the fact that the lecture was to be held in the Hull Soldiers' Club).[39] By late October 1917, the NWAC had also sought out 'Non-conformist Ministers ... prepared to assist ... in speaking at Meetings', presumably having identified nonconformity as a key element of pacifism.[40] Thus, the

---

Winter and Jean-Louis Robert (eds), *Capital Cities at War: Paris, London, Berlin, 1914–1919*, vol. 2, *A Cultural History* (Cambridge: Cambridge University Press, 2007).

36 Lawrence, *Speaking*, pp. 164, 180–88; On the significance of meetings for MPs' reputations, see also H.C.G. Matthew, 'Rhetoric and Politics in Great Britain, 1860–1950', in P.J. Waller (ed.), *Politics and Social Change in Modern Britain: Essays Presented to A.F. Thompson* (Hassocks: Harvester Press, 1987).

37 TNA:PRO T102/16, NWAC minutes, 25/9/17. On the dubious commitment of the Home Counties and rural areas, see Gregory, *Last Great War*, pp. 220–33, esp. pp. 229–30.

38 TNA:PRO T102/16, NWAC minutes, 10/10/17; Lawrence, *Speaking*, p. 190. The dissenting MP Joseph King alleged that NWAC speakers in Portsmouth had refused to answer women's questions in mid-November, suggesting such concerns with political propriety still exercised some minds: PDC(5), 100 (4/12/17), cols 245–46.

39 TNA:PRO T102/7, flyer advertising lantern lecture by F. Kirkwood, Soldiers' Club, Hull, 15/11/18.

40 TNA:PRO T102/16, NWAC minutes, 31/10/17.

NWAC attempted to incorporate as many groups potentially estranged from its messages or usually limited in their access to political meetings as possible – workers and nonconformists especially on one hand, rural populations and women on the other. To what extent these groups were considered 'unreliable' elements is difficult to say. While the NWAC claimed to speak for 'the great majority of the people', they also hoped to reach 'those hidden from view'.[41] Whether or not such groups truly required special attention,[42] what is important is that leading figures in the organisation decided such efforts were necessary and tailored their campaigns accordingly. In the process, the NWAC's target audience came to encompass a very large proportion of the adult civilian population.

Standard campaigns not utilising 'special' speakers – whether MPs or other noted figures – involved two speakers (usually one Conservative and one Liberal), most frequently members of the paid speaking staffs of the parties, giving two meetings daily between Monday and Saturday across a constituency. In December, with no definite war aims statement yet forthcoming, the central committee formulated 'Instructions for Speakers', perhaps responding to criticisms directed at speakers' performances:

(1) The object of the National War Aims Committee is 'to keep before our nation both the causes which have led to this world war and the vital importance to human life and liberty of continuing the struggle until the evil forces which originated this terrible conflict are destroyed for ever'.

(2) The War Aims Committee knows no party and does not support or oppose any party.

(3) War Aims speakers must confine their speeches to an exposition of War Aims. These are set forth in our publications.

(4) War Aims speakers must make no attack upon political opponents ... [nor] refer to any questions of ordinary party controversy.

(5) Where it is desired to put a resolution at a War Aims meeting, the following official form of words should be used:-
'That this meeting thanks ... for his address, and records its inflexible determination to do all in its power to assist in carrying on the war to a victorious conclusion, so that Liberty and Justice may be established and permanent peace secured.'[43]

These instructions clearly emphasised national and patriotic rather than party political ideals and were designed to ensure a level of uniformity among speakers and prevent any party from gaining an advantage via public meetings intended to enhance national unity – an urgent matter when public meetings were still the essence of political legitimacy.

---

41 TNA:PRO T102/16, '(Confidential) Aims of Home Publicity', n.d.

42 For discussion of the enduring patriotism of workers and women, see, e.g., Gregory, *Last Great War*, esp. chapters 5–6; Gullace, *Blood*.

43 TNA:PRO T102/16, 'Report up to 8th December, 1917'. This was quoted in Parliament to allay suspicions of the NWAC's political influence: speech of Captain Guest, PDC(5), 100 (14/12/17), cols 1558–59.

Means of improving speakers' performances were actively sought. In October 1917 the central committee agreed that 'arrangements should be made for the Staff speakers and regular volunteer Speakers to go to France', in groups, to 'gain in effectiveness', and in a War Cabinet memorandum two days later, Carson suggested that since 'an appeal is now being made to Members to address Meetings ... on behalf of the [NWAC] ... facilities should be given to them to witness for themselves what they desire to describe to their audience', along with groups of workers.[44] However, not all proposals were equally welcome. A Rochdale citizen's suggestion that NWAC speakers should address issues like profiteering, beer supplies and trade union conditions drew the haughty response that if someone would

> not support the nation in this crisis from patriotic reasons, I do not think an unlimited supply of beer, or its total prohibition would help matters. We can only appeal to the patriotic impulses of the nation, and it is only for high ideals that people will endure.[45]

While the Meetings Department's operations became more regimented with public funding,[46] the basic campaign format did not apparently change. A database compiled from the Meetings Department Register permits tentative general conclusions.[47] First, regarding the number of days of meetings held by the NWAC (the unit by which the NWAC itself measured performance),[48] the Register suggests that, until the end of April 1918, where records become incomplete, there were 4539 days planned, at an average of 412.7 days per month. Extrapolating from this, an estimate of 6190 days' worth of meetings by the end of October 1918 is possible, equating to an average of 13.5 days of NWAC events each day.[49] That is, on any day between 1 August 1917 and 31 October 1918,

---

44 TNA:PRO T102/16, NWAC minutes, 10/10/17; CAB24/28, GT2268: 'Propaganda. Suggested Visits of Workers and Others to Theatre of War.', 12/10/17.
45 TNA:PRO T102/1, A. Barber to Wallace Carter, 13/11/17; Wallace Carter to Barber, 21/11/17.
46 See, e.g., TNA:PRO T102/16, NWAC minutes, 5/12/17.
47 Though this data is incomplete. For instance, a minute records that between 4 August and 10 October 1917, 3192 meetings were held – TNA:PRO T102/16, NWAC minutes, 10/10/17. Calculations based on the database suggest a total of 1197 days and thus 2394 meetings, assuming 2 meetings per day were held.
48 PDC(5), 101 (18/1/18), col. 610.
49 Extrapolation: (412.65 days × 15 months [August 1917 – October 1918] =) 6189.6 ÷ 457 (days of 15 months) = 13.54. Further, if the general assumption is of two meetings per day, this produces an average of 27.08 meetings per day. By comparison, Guest told Parliament that up to 3 July 1918, 10,665 meetings had been held. See PDC(5), 108 (16/7/18), col. 887. If this is divided by 337 (the number of days between 1 August 1917 and 3 July 1918), a figure of 31.65 is reached as the average daily number of meetings during this period. This suggests the Register Database, though clearly not totally accurate – the absent data for the early summer of 1918 precludes this – allows reasonably reliable estimates.

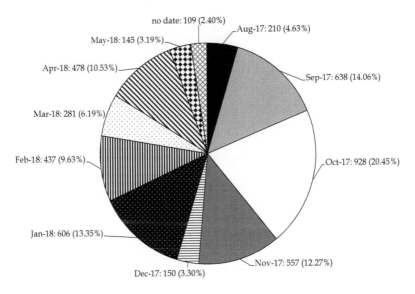

Figure 1. Number of campaign days beginning each month, 1 August 1917–31 May 1918

13 or 14 constituencies could be expected to be holding NWAC events (see figures 1–2). While Millman is correct that David Sweet's figure of 900 NWAC meetings is a considerable underestimation, his own rather cursory examination of the figures leaves much to be desired.[50]

Second, using all available Register records, at least one day of events was arranged in 320 local WACs (usually one per constituency, but also regional organisations such as 'South Wales' or 'Scotland'). On average, these WACs held 17.7 days of events, ranging from a high of 162 days in Coventry to a single day in 51 constituencies (figure 3). That nearly two-thirds of the constituencies holding any events held one to nineteen days' worth (and that over half of these – 109 – held one to four days' worth) suggests either that public opinion was generally not perceived by local organisers to be unduly antagonistic to the war, or that these organisers were too apathetic or overburdened with other work to make much effort (chapter 3 examines this issue). Furthermore, following constituency

---

50 Millman, *Managing*, p. 234. His figure of 3959 meetings arranged between April and October 1918 echoes the number of records in the Meetings Register, the last of which was arranged on a date in late October, although these represent the number of separate campaigns organised (including those cancelled) rather than the number of days or meetings. His curious footnote refers only to NWAC minutes for September and October 1917, which cannot account for 1918's meetings.

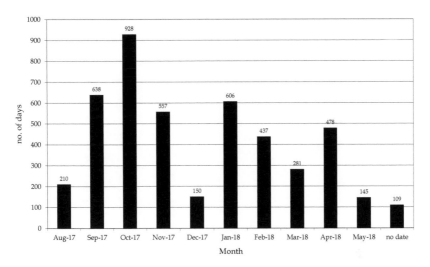

Figure 2. Progression of number of campaign days beginning each month, 1 August 1917–31 May 1918

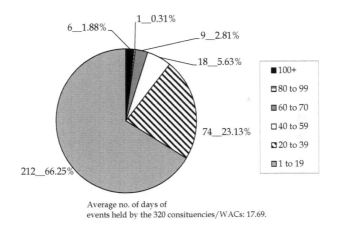

Average no. of days of
events held by the 320 consituencies/WACs: 17.69.

Figure 3. Total days of NWAC events per constituency

classifications established by Neal Blewett and John Turner,[51] it can be suggested that, in terms of holding any events at all, urban constituencies (or their local organisers) were less enthusiastic about holding events, rural constituencies held meetings at a relatively proportionate rate, while constituencies that mixed urban and rural components, and mining constituencies, were more enthusiastic than might be expected. In terms

---

51 Neal Blewett, *The Peers, The Parties and the People: The General Elections of 1910* (London: MacMillan, 1972), pp. 488–94; Turner, *British Politics*, pp. 469–79.

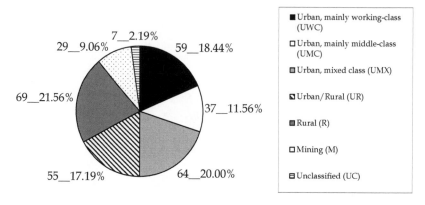

Figure 4. Number and percentage of constituencies holding NWAC events, by classification

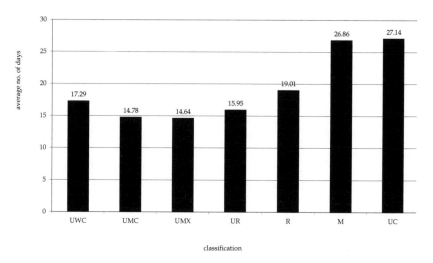

Figure 5. Average number of days per constituency by classification

of average days per constituency, urban middle- and mixed-class and urban/rural constituencies held a below-average number; whereas urban working-class constituencies held about the average; and mining and rural constituencies held an above-average number of days of NWAC events (figures 4–5). It is also noteworthy that each classification was represented by one of the seven most active constituencies (in terms of days of events). This demonstrates that no type of constituency was particularly targeted centrally – although the significantly larger average in mining constituencies must be acknowledged – and (as chapter 3 illustrates) that the impetus for organising meetings lay principally with local WACs.

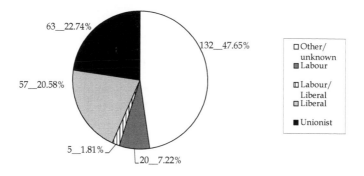

Figure 6. Non-MP/War Cabinet speaker affiliations

Third, and perhaps most interesting, the Register enables conclusions to be drawn about the people acting as speakers at meetings. There were basically four types of speaker employed for NWAC meetings. Sometimes, WACs organised their own speakers, independent of the NWAC. These people were classified as 'local speakers' on the register, and are often virtually impossible to classify further. Most frequently, however, speakers were drawn from the party speaking staffs, especially the Liberals and Conservatives. A third category could be described as 'special speakers', encompassing public figures like the Earl of Denbigh (who was very active on behalf of the NWAC, apparently holding 92 meetings generally with audiences of about one thousand by mid-May 1918),[52] the Archbishop of York, the author Henry Newbolt and various US, French and Belgian speakers. Finally, there were MPs. Figures 6–7 provide statistics of the political affiliations of non-MPs. Unsurprisingly, most of these speakers with known affiliations were Liberals or Unionists, contributing respectively 57 and 63 speakers, and a total of 2688 and 2898 days to NWAC meetings, compared to 1927 by all other contributors.

W.J. Keel was a Liberal speaker, appearing regularly at meetings in London in September and October 1917, and from late July 1918 onwards. P.J. Kelly was a Labour speaker based in Manchester who regularly spoke in Northern areas, while Bryan O'Donnell was a Conservative speaker who appeared throughout the country. Their correspondence with staff at the central committee illuminates the process by which speakers were assigned, and their working conditions. Generally, speakers were booked for meetings anything from a couple of days to a

---

52 PDC(5), 106 (13/5/18), col. 44. Most of these did not appear on the Register as they were locally funded and the Register related to campaigns requiring central investment.

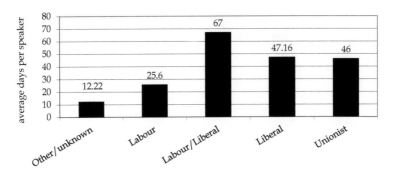

Figure 7. Days per speaker contributed by non-MP/War Cabinet affiliations

fortnight in advance. Keel reported that one meeting in Poplar was 'very good, about 200 present, speeches repeatedly punctuated with applause, but no questions, though apealed for ... Speakers meeting lasting 1¾ hours but watches being checked by several in crowd shewed it was near opening time [*sic*].'[53] Evidently, discussion of patriotic duties could retain interest for only so long.

Appeals for questions re-emphasise the continued existence of a political culture whereby legitimacy rested in an active engagement with the public – a need to talk 'with' rather than 'to' audiences. On another occasion, in Battersea, Keel reported that his meeting was disturbed by 'a peace meeting some distance away <u>broken up by some of our audience</u>', who returned with part of a chair as a souvenir of their efforts. As before the war, apparently, 'the use of physical force remained a central, and widely tolerated, element of popular politics' (though advance warning of such violence could also be used by police as a pretext for cancelling a meeting).[54] However, unlike the pre-war situation, the way a speaker handled the crowd sometimes made little appreciable difference to their reaction. Kelly reported that when a colleague 'could not get a hearing' for his speech from several hundred army-age 'fine strong fellows' in Gower, he instead answered questions for two hours 'in splendid style, which of course they did not like'. There is little suggestion here of the respect for rhetorical skill against heckling that Kathryn Rix suggests was part of the culture of public meetings.[55] Speakers commented on

---

53 TNA:PRO T102/7, Keel to W. Kay Waterson (NWAC London organiser), 17/9/17.
54 TNA:PRO T102/7, Keel to NWAC, 7/10/17. On physical forces, see Lawrence, *Speaking*, p. 181; Lawrence, 'Public Space', pp. 294–96.
55 TNA:PRO T102/7, Kelly to Peters, 3/10/17; Kathryn Rix, '"Go Out into the Highways and the Hedges": The Diary of Michael Sykes, Conservative Political Lecturer, 1895 and 1907–8', *Parliamentary History*, 20:2 (2001), pp. 228–9; cf. Lawrence, *Speaking*, pp. 188–90.

particularly troublesome areas, Kelly remarking that though Harborough was 'a hot bed of pacifists we got very little opposition', while O'Donnell, when instructed to speak at Merthyr, replied he would 'feel much obliged for the donation of a "Tin Hat" and some yards of sticking plaster'.[56] Both Keel and Kelly apparently worked diligently for the standard remuneration (£1.1.0 per day plus third-class rail fares), Keel thanking the NWAC for his engagements, which were 'a great help ... financially and have kept me from thinking too much of my sons death and daughters mental condition [*sic*]'.[57] O'Donnell, by contrast, was seemingly a troublesome speaker. He objected to third-class rail fares 'on <u>principle</u> ... as unbefitting <u>my occupation</u> ... when "very temporary gentlemen", including warrant officers, are <u>compelled</u> by regulations to travel first', and because speakers could not be expected to compose speeches 'in a crowd whose odour is noisier than its voice'.[58] 'Surely', he added, 'the N.W.A.C. does not expect Members and Candidates to travel 3rd class. Why should I ...?' Vesey responded that most MPs sought no remuneration at all. Nevertheless, O'Donnell's persistent complaints finally resulted in his receiving the difference in fares from Boraston, through Conservative Central Office. However, he remained a difficult employee, twice reprimanded for poor performance or attendance.[59]

While party speakers addressed most meetings, MPs were the star attractions. Over one hundred appeared at least once, according to the Register, ranging from frequent speakers like the Rt Hon. W.T. Brace (who contributed 27 days), W. Llewellyn Williams (23), C.A. McCurdy (18) and J.H. Edwards (16); to 55 MPs who appeared only once. Figures 8–10 demonstrate MPs' contributions by political affiliation.[60] Much the largest number of different MPs were Conservatives (almost half), as might be expected from the party that regarded itself as the pre-eminent 'purveyor of patriotism'.[61] However, strikingly, Conservatives provided proportionally the smallest average number of days. The MPs most generous with their time were Coalition Labour MPs, who it was presumably hoped would best inspire workers, followed by Coalition and Asquithian

56 TNA:PRO T102/7, Kelly to Wallace Carter, 28/7/18; T102/10, O'Donnell to Vesey, 13/10/17.
57 TNA:PRO T102/7, Keel to NWAC, 29/10/17.
58 TNA:PRO T102/10, O'Donnell to Vesey, 9/8/17.
59 TNA:PRO T102/10, O'Donnell to Vesey, 12/8/17; Vesey to O'Donnell 13/8/17, 15/8/17; 11/2/18, 14/2/18; Cox to O'Donnell, 16/9/18.
60 Affiliations based upon F.W.S. Craig, *British Parliamentary Election Results, 1918–1949* (rev. edn, Basingstoke: MacMillan Press, 1977); Michael Stenton and Stephen Lees (eds), *Who's Who of British Members of Parliament, A Biographical Dictionary of the House of Commons: Based on Annual Volumes of 'Dods' Parliamentary Companion' and Other Sources,* II (1885–1918) and III (1919–45) (Hassocks: Harvester Press, 1978, 1979).
61 Nigel Keohane, *The Party of Patriotism: The Conservative Party and the First World War* (Farnham: Ashgate, 2010), p. 99.

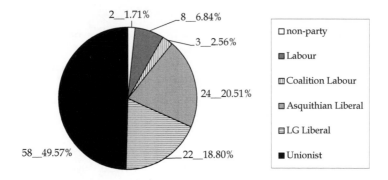

Figure 8. MP/War Cabinet affiliations

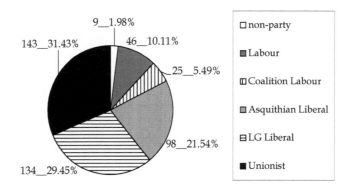

Figure 9. MP/War Cabinet: number of days contributed per affiliation

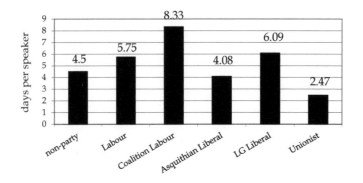

Figure 10. MP/War Cabinet: days per speaker contributed per affiliation

Liberals. These were all new parliamentary groupings who perhaps, particularly in the Liberals' case, saw NWAC meetings as an opportunity to gain wider public recognition and visibility, and convey their message. Despite the NWAC's avowed restriction of party politicking, Sanders told parliament that when 'a Minister comes down to speak on war aims or anything else you cannot bind him down entirely to stick to your war aims', while Guest admitted that 'one must give more latitude to speakers of national importance' when they took NWAC meetings, and trust that 'they will not take undue advantage of the opportunities'.[62] Clearly, despite the NWAC's all-party nature, party political issues were not entirely ignored. Wallace Carter told Rea (both Asquithian Liberals) that for 'obvious reasons we want our own leaders to take their share'.[63]

The Meetings Department also ran mobile cinema ('cinemotor') tours before and after the summer of 1918 (when sunset was early enough to make them practicable). These tours have been cited as one of the NWAC's most innovative contributions to propaganda work,[64] but were not in fact tremendously original. Travelling vans had been used to capture public imagination for propaganda purposes as early as the 1880s, when 'gypsy caravans' with lantern lecture equipment toured the countryside 'educating' rural Britons with a resource 'beyond the means of local associations', while '[a]ppropriate cinematograph war films were shown from two vans' by the PRC in 1915.[65] During 1917, a War Office Cinematograph Committee (WOCC), involving the Canadian press baron (and future Minister of Information) Lord Beaverbrook, the film producer William Jury and Sir Reginald Brade of the War Office, also operated, producing and distributing fortnightly newsreels in collaboration with a film company in which it bought shares, as well as investing in more substantial productions like D.W. Griffiths' film *Hearts of the World*.[66] Cinema was also used by other nations. French newsreels in the early years of the war presented images of the continuation of everyday life despite the war. During 1917, films also began to be circulated between allied nations, leading to increased emphasis on inter-allied cooperation and friendship.[67] A 1916 report by Wellington House regretted

---

62 PDC(5), 100 (14/12/17), cols 1530, 1558.

63 TNA:PRO T102/12, Wallace Carter to Rea, 5/10/17; On Wallace Carter's allegiance: Sanders Diary, 20/12/17, in Ramsden, *Tory Politics*, p. 94.

64 Millman, *Managing*, p. 240; Haste, *Home Fires*, p. 42; Horne, 'Remobilizing', p. 206.

65 Rix, '"Go Out"', pp. 210–12; and 'The Party Agent and English Electoral Culture, 1880–1906 (PhD dissertation, Cambridge, 2001), pp. 209–10; TNA:PRO WO106/367, 'Parliamentary Recruiting Committee. Meetings Sub-Department. Report'.

66 TNA:PRO INF4/1B, first and second 'Reports of the War Office Cinematograph Committee', September 1918 and August 1919.

67 Pierre Sorlin, 'Film and the War', in John Horne (ed.), *A Companion to World War I* (Oxford: Wiley-Blackwell, 2010), pp. 355, 360.

a perceived German advantage in access to neutral cinemas, claiming that Germany had better appreciated the role of cinema as 'a kind of "Bible" for the working classes', who could not be reached by written publications.[68] Suspicion of cinema's social influence also meant that cinemas were much more tightly controlled in Germany than elsewhere in 1914, facilitating their use for propaganda purposes once the German authorities abandoned strict censorship in favour of exploitation in the second half of the war. This culminated in the foundation of the *Universum-Film-Aktiengesellschaft* (Universal Film Company) at the end of 1917 to produce films, without evident government inspiration, to assist efforts at 'patriotic instruction' (with mixed success). During 1917, cinema vans also began to be deployed by the German military to entertain soldiers.[69]

The NWAC, with experienced PRC men heavily involved, expanded upon the PRC's example, using ten Ministry of Information-owned vans originally intended for use in Russia.[70] Nevertheless, the tours were an impressive success. In one week in April 1918, ten tours visited 57 towns and villages, giving shows to audiences averaging over 2600 people (one as large as 15,000) – perhaps 150,000 in total – and the tours were so popular that the Meetings Department had to disappoint WACs asking for the vans to visit their constituency.[71] The cinemotors did not, however, show NWAC-created films. The £10,000 earmarked for cinema was devoted to an abortive 'British National Film' which, having been destroyed by fire upon first completion and re-shot by November 1918, was never shown publicly as it was considered 'so unmistakeably fitted for the particular purpose' for which it was made – that is, depicting German barbarity and tying this to the perils of striking – as to be unworthy of peacetime release.[72] The Ministry of Information supplied films, including such titles as 'Patriotic Porkers', 'Our Naval Air Power', 'With the Forces in Mesopotamia', 'Woolwich Arsenal' and 'With the W.R.A.F.',[73] the NWAC executive having decided not to involve themselves with other

---

68 TNA:PRO INF4/5, 'Second Report on the work conducted on behalf of the government at Wellington House' (1/2/16), p. 6.

69 Welch, *Germany, Propaganda*, pp. 40–56, 215–16; Ute Daniel, *The War from Within: German Working-class Women in the First World War* (Oxford: Berg, 1997), pp. 255–57.

70 Sanders and Taylor, *British Propaganda*, p. 106; PDC(5), 105 (29/4/18), cols 1283–84.

71 TNA:PRO T102/18, 'CINE-MOTOR CAMPAIGN. Report of Attendances for week April 8th to 13th 1918.'; T102/4, letter (unsigned) to Revd G.L. Foster (Cambridge), 17/4/18.

72 TNA:PRO T12519 – file 13904/1920, H.C. Brook Johnson to John Bradbury, 19/5/19; Report, 19/3/20. On the film, see Nicholas Reeves, *Official British Film Propaganda during the First World War* (London: Croom Helm, 1986), pp. 125–30, 215–16; and below, pp. 132–33.

73 TNA:PRO T102/5, J.M.G. ('Green's Film Service') to Barber, 11/10/18, Captain Lord Briscal for G.O.C. Royal Air Force, Blandford to NWAC, 8/10/18.

film production.[74] The Publicity Department confined itself to producing prose, poetry and artwork.

A S discussed, production of printed propaganda material was secondary to the pivotal role assigned to meetings. Sanders told the Commons that pamphlets which 'for some absurd reason we call literature' left him cold, but had some effect, as did speeches (about which he was only slightly more complimentary).[75] This reflected the belief in the political legitimacy conferred by public interaction with voters at meetings, and plans to create a Publicity Department were not begun until 30 August 1917, when McNeill, Buchan and Peters formed an establishing sub-committee. They recommended the appointment of an editorial committee comprising an editor and two assistants to oversee the department. The editor should be 'a thoroughly competent and trained professional journalist ... who is a well-informed politician, versed in public affairs generally', and his assistants experts on the local press and 'a news expert'. These officials should 'establish friendly and confidential relations with as large a section of the Press as possible', and provide material from the Department of Information, War Cabinet and Labour Ministry without Press Bureau (the government's censor) scrutiny to 'a carefully selected list of newspapers'. The sub-committee thought permanent 'salaried writers' unnecessary, as the department could obtain pieces at 'ordinary journalistic rates' from outside contributors. Aside from press material, the sub-committee expected pamphlets, leaflets, cartoons, posters, postcards and (at this point) cinema and lantern lecture material to be produced for distribution by local WACs which 'command[ed] the machinery of the party political organizations in the constituencies, who are accustomed to the distribution of literature'. They noted approvingly W.H. Smith & Sons' offer to

> place at the unreserved disposal of the Government our organization for distributing printed matter throughout the Country; to co-operate with your Local Organizations; to promote the sale of any publication which you may issue ... In short, to augment your publicity organization by the organization of our Firm.[76]

Further, they thought material should be offered to 'Free Libraries, Polytechnics, Mechanics Institutes, and any club willing to ... make them readily available to Members and visitors'. Peters objected that most of this work 'has already been commenced by the existing Literature Committee', adding that the editorial committee was unnecessary and that it was wrong

---

74 TNA:PRO T102/16, NWAC Minutes, 5/12/17.
75 PDC(5), 100 (14/12/17), cols 1528–29.
76 TNA:PRO T102/14, George Tyler to 'The Director of National Information, St. Stephen's Chambers', 22/10/17. On Smiths's propaganda activities, see Colclough, 'No such bookselling', pp. 27–45.

to 'dispense with the services of the staffs of the Literature Departments of the great political parties ... placed freely at our disposal without any cost'.[77] Nevertheless, the report was adopted in late September, with the caveat that the department should work with existing literature departments, and McNeill became chairman. Soon afterwards, Gerard Fiennes, formerly assistant editor at the *Pall Mall Gazette* and *Standard* (both Unionist newspapers), was appointed editor, with E.W. Record, an official of the Liberal Publication Department, as his assistant.[78]

Fiennes was evidently very involved in instructing authors on the appropriate line to take. Asking the Archdeacon of Winchester for an article based on a sermon, he wrote that what he particularly wanted stressed was 'the sense of absolute faith in the righteousness of our cause and the consequent assurance that we may trust the issue to God and, secondly ... that the hero self-consecrated to right is also the saint'.[79] On another occasion, he asked the prominent author Marie Corelli to produce something for 'women and girls ... to combat the sense of war weariness ... which seems to be affecting some of them'. The piece should not be '"preachy" but ... pointing out ... [that we must] endure to the end. Also, of course, the immense influence ... that ... keeping a stiff upper lip at home has on the minds of our fighting men'. Other than this, however, he left the details to the author![80]

Material produced for the Publicity Department had several possible destinations. Much NWAC material appeared in two newspapers. *Reality* was the NWAC's weekly four-page newspaper, available free at W.H. Smith shops and stalls throughout the country. Although the Department of Information printed the paper, the NWAC produced the content.[81] Further, a second illustrated paper, *Welcome*, was, if not officially a NWAC organ, at least substantially composed of NWAC-supplied material, receiving at least 256 pieces between March and November 1918, including 184 pieces of artwork.[82] Other material for that newspaper was supplied by artists and writers attached to MI7(b), including Bruce Bairnsfather and A.A. Milne.[83] The Publicity Department's pieces

---

77 TNA:PRO T102/16, 'Report of Sub-Committee on Publicity Campaign', 25/9/18.
78 TNA:PRO T102/12, Fiennes to Record, 31/10/17.
79 TNA:PRO T102/15, Fiennes to the Archdeacon of Winchester, 11/10/17.
80 TNA:PRO T102/2, Fiennes to Marie Corelli, 23/11/17.
81 TNA:PRO T102/3, letter (unsigned) to Robert Donald (Editor, *Daily Chronicle*), 12/12/17.
82 Statistics of the destinations of Publicity Department material are based upon an Articles Database, based on ledgers and accounts of the Publicity Department, TNA:PRO T102/21 and 19.
83 TNA:PRO INF4/1B, 'Military Press Control: A History of the Work of MI7', pp. 20–21. For extended discussion of NWAC propaganda to soldiers in *Welcome*, see David Monger, 'Sporting Journalism and the Maintenance of Servicemen's Ties to Civilian Life in First World War Propaganda', *Sport in History*, 30:3 (2010); idem, 'Soldiers, Propaganda and Ideas of Home and Community in First

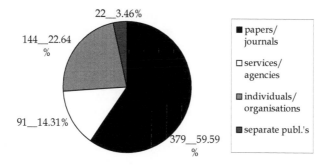

Figure 11. Publicity Department: destination of pieces

were also supplied to three news supply services or agencies, including one run by Cassell's Publishers; to individual newspapers and journals; occasionally to organisations like the Navy League; and some became pamphlets, leaflets and booklets (see figure 11). The newspapers which were supplied directly with NWAC material (rather than via supply services or other routes) – including, in some provincial papers, weekly War Supplements – included national dailies like the *Manchester Guardian*, *Daily Telegraph* and *Daily Mail*; provincial papers like the *Essex Herald*, *Leicester Mercury* and *Aberdeen Journal*; religious papers including the *Church Monthly* and *Jewish Express*; and special interest publications like *Nursing Notes*, the *British Workman*, *Family Friend* and *Our Home*. As this abbreviated list suggests, NWAC pieces ranged across many themes.[84] Of 596 pieces submitted to the NWAC, 331 (55.5 per cent) were accepted for publication by the Publicity Department.

Except, perhaps, for *Reality*, the NWAC's pamphlets were its most obvious and readily accessible form of publication. A set of 15 were advertised in various newspapers, including the *Daily Mail* and the *Church Times*, as being available free on request in September 1917.[85] Included was one of the NWAC's most popular pamphlets, the *Kalendar of Kultur*, which listed various German wartime atrocities.[86] The NWAC produced several series of pamphlets, including the 'German Aims' series, produced by the Liberal MP Charles McCurdy; the 'Message' series,

---

World War Britain', *Cultural and Social History*, 8:3 (2011).

84 Content is extensively discussed in Part 2.

85 See e.g. TNA:PRO T102/3, John Dumphrey to NWAC, 20/9/17, enclosing cutting of advertisement from the *Morning Post*. T102/1, Albert D. Beckwith to NWAC, 20/9/17; Arthur Boutwood to NWAC, 21/9/17; T102/6, Revd H.E. Jones to Cox, 24/9/17.

86 E.g. TNA:PRO T102/3, Revd T.V. Evans to NWAC, 24/9/17; T102/4, Mrs Fulford to NWAC, 22/9/17.

reproducing noted speeches (mostly by political figures, but also Rudyard Kipling); and *Searchlights*, featuring pieces by prominent Labour figures like Ben Tillett and Victor Grayson, popular authors including G.K. Chesterton and speeches by Lloyd George, Woodrow Wilson and others. The Committee were inundated with offers from local citizens to assist in distributing this literature,[87] with varying levels of ingenuity. A Suffolk doctor, for example, having discovered one of the envelopes of NWAC pamphlets distributed in Barclays bank branches, offered to place pamphlets in village post offices, suggesting that since 'the small branches of Banks are now closed ... [t]he Post Offices would be the best centres for [such] distribution'. He received five hundred packages for the purpose, and the NWAC's gratitude.[88] In Cornwall, T.C. Hepp received official endorsement to employ Boy Scouts in distributing NWAC pamphlets, as did the WAC secretary in Plymouth.[89] W.H. Smith & Sons also used Scouts to assist their distribution efforts, as well as dispatching 'large numbers' of pamphlets to breweries for circulation in village inns.[90] However, the offer by Day's Variety Agency to use a wireless-controlled Zeppelin to distribute pamphlets at meetings was declined – though the novelty would undoubtedly represent an attraction, it would also distract audiences from the speeches,[91] which were, after all, considered the ultimate conveyor of political legitimacy.

The pamphlets were certainly widely distributed. Perhaps the most intensively distributed was number 33, *Our United War Aims*, which summarised Lloyd George's January war aims speech. WAC estimates to distribute this pamphlet totalled 2,560,200 between 10 January and 3 March 1918, at a cost of £654.16.0. Liverpool's WAC offered to distribute 130,000 copies without charge. These were enormous figures, contributing to the hundred million NWAC publications which W.H. Smith & Sons was thanked for distributing by November 1918. By comparison, during the year of the 1895 election, the Liberal and Conservative parties each distributed around twenty-five million pamphlets, and only five and two million respectively the year before.[92] While Stephen Colclough rightly

87 E.g. TNA:PRO T102/3, S.A. Earnshaw to NWAC, 5/10/17; T102/5, Sister Mary Julia for the Revd Mother (Community of the Helpers of the Holy Souls) to NWAC, 16/4/18; T102/8, J. Moor (ASE member, Hartlepool) to NWAC, 20/9/17; John Moore to Bartlett, 2/9/17.

88 TNA:PRO T102/1, Dr H.G. Biddle to NWAC, 14/5/18.

89 TNA:PRO T102/5, Hepp to Cox, 9/2/18; T102/1, R. Wherry Anderson, 'Report on Propaganda in Cornwall and Devon', 4/9/18.

90 Colclough, 'No such bookselling', p. 40.

91 TNA:PRO T102/3, correspondence between H. Goodson (Day's Variety Agency) and Vesey, 11, 12 and 15/4/18.

92 Statistics regarding pamphlet no. 33 from Meetings Register database; TNA:PRO T102/13, letter, unsigned (probably Cox) to W.H. Smith & Sons, 14/11/18; Rix, 'Party Agent', p. 205. Cf. also the distribution figures for Lloyd George's land campaign, cited p. 30 above.

emphasises the importance of this activity to reaching 'a truly mass audience', it nonetheless remains the case that the NWAC's activities prioritised public meetings above publications.[93]

ALONGSIDE its creative and distributive roles, the Publicity Department, and the NWAC generally, also served as an instrument of surveillance. Beginning in August 1917, the NWAC examined growing numbers of newspapers, beginning with 'Labour' papers like the *Labour Leader*, *Daily Herald* and *British Citizen and Empire Worker* (the BWNL's journal), followed by various provincial papers from Birmingham, Bristol, Leeds, Leicester, Liverpool, London and Sheffield, and other papers like *Pearson's Weekly*, *Tit Bits*, *Answers* and *Home Notes*.[94] In October, Fiennes asked the *Manchester Daily Despatch*'s editor to send him a copy of a pacifist pamphlet reported in the paper, along with 'any similar pamphlets' which had been seen.[95] In November he went further, contacting both the Director of Military Intelligence and the Home Secretary. He asked General Macdonogh whether MI7b could examine 'smaller provincial papers' for the NWAC, particularly the correspondence pages, 'where the pacifist purpose does not lie on the surface', which the NWAC could not cover, and for which cuttings agencies were insufficiently expert. Any 'matter which points to discontent and disheartenment among the people may be regarded as pacifist intendancy and this notification to us will be materially helpful'. Two days later he asked Sir George Cave to 'give instructions that a copy of everything ... [seized by police] should be sent to the Publication Department', which would be of 'enormous assistance',[96] presumably enabling the NWAC to more accurately address and undermine anti-war material. Contemporaneously, Cox wrote to the Home Office asking that it share its information on 'Pacifist gatherings' with the Committee so that 'we may set our local committee machinery going'.[97] Shortly afterwards, Cox met Basil Thomson, a senior figure in the Metropolitan Police and head of the Criminal Investigation Department (CID), who ran police operations relating to 'Pacifist and Revolutionary Organisations', and agreed that Cox would receive 'early information of any pacifist movement which came to [Thomson's] notice and that he will try and arrange out-door or indoor meetings as a Counter-blast'.[98]

---

93 Colclough, 'No such bookselling', pp. 42–43.
94 TNA:PRO T102/3, correspondence between NWAC and Messrs Everett & Sons, 9/8/17–12/12/17.
95 TNA:PRO T102/8, letter (unsigned), probably Fiennes, to Editor, *Manchester Daily Despatch*, 19/10/17.
96 TNA:PRO T102/8, Fiennes to Macdonogh, 14/11/17; T102/2, Fiennes to Cave, 16/11/17.
97 TNA:PRO HO45/10743/263275/265, Cox to Home Office, 15/11/17.
98 Swartz, *Union of Democratic Control*, pp. 183–84, 190; TNA:PRO HO45/10743/ 263275/265, Minute by Thomson, 26/11/17; C.D. Carew-Robinson to Cox,

The NWAC was evidently undertaking a surveillance role both to better understand the nature and arguments of the organisations it had been established to counteract, and, with the arrangements between Cox and Thomson, to compete directly with such groups (once again, predominantly through meetings). However, this falls far short of Millman's characterisation of the NWAC as 'secret machinery by which dissenters could be intimidated and in the extreme physically suppressed', or his scandalised suggestion that 'patriot excess was not only tolerated, but organized, employed, even manufactured by the government'.[99] As Lawrence has shown, physical force and the 'control of civic space' remained a key element of political legitimacy in 1914,[100] and there is little to suggest this changed with the absence of peace-time political meetings. While speakers like Keel and Kelly expressed no disapproval of the disruption of pacifist meetings, neither did they claim they encouraged it. Nor is it clear that, had the war continued longer, the NWAC would have been empowered to 'refer cases directly' to the Director of Public Prosecutions, for which Millman's only evidence is its suggestion in December 1917 in NWAC minutes. Had this been likely, 11 months was surely long enough to establish the principle.[101] His contention that NWAC surveillance amounted to a sinister and 'gigantic intelligence gathering apparatus', backed by evidence that they examined public reactions to Lord Lansdowne's letter to the *Daily Telegraph* in November 1917 (which called for a restatement of war aims that would remove suggestions that Britain intended to annihilate Germany),[102] is undermined by Sanders's diary. This shows that such steps led Wallace Carter to threaten resignation if he was forced to 'circularise our local agents', since Asquith was uncertain of his response at the time, so that only a press survey was apparently undertaken. This hardly equates with Millman's characterisation of the NWAC as 'Lloyd George's stormtroopers'.[103] And while links existed between the BWNL and the NWAC, it is also true that the NWAC deliberately avoided too close a relationship, for instance denying emphatically that it had lent the BWNL a cinemotor.[104]

L.L. Farrar Jr.'s suggestion that 'the critical issue [of British propaganda] became much more to discourage defeatism than to encourage

28/11/17.

99 Millman, *Managing*, p. 245.

100 Lawrence, *Speaking*, p. 181. See Jon Lawrence's discussion of Millman: 'Review: Brock Millman, *Managing Domestic Dissent in First World War Britain*', *Twentieth Century British History*, 14:1 (2003), pp. 86–88.

101 Millman, *Managing*, p. 247.

102 Turner, *British Politics*, p. 249.

103 Millman, *Managing*, pp. 246, 248; Sanders Diary, 20/12/17, in Ramsden, *Tory Politics*, p. 94; TNA:PRO T102/16, 'Public Opinion of the Lansdowne Letter'.

104 TNA:PRO T102/9, letter (unsigned) to Coun. G. Naylor (Unionist Labour Party), 4/5/18.

aggressive nationalism' is surely correct.[105] Millman refers to 'Scheme L' – a plan to mobilise all armed forces stationed within Britain in the event of a 'doomsday scenario' of civilian unrest, to be followed by a '*levée en masse* of volunteers' (which, incidentally, he only explains means 'The Volunteers', equivalent to the Home Guard, in an endnote).[106] His suggestion that, in the event of the scheme's implementation, cooperation between the NWAC, the police and the military 'was only the logical next step', and that the NWAC itself would mobilise its manpower resources,[107] seems a gross overstatement of its power. Presumably in this event Bryan O'Donnell, constantly beset with leg injuries, fevers and other maladies during his NWAC service,[108] would have hobbled forth with his '"Tin Hat" and ... yards of sticking plaster' to see off the revolutionary workers of Britain, led by Captain Guest and Colonel Sanders. While the NWAC endured unflattering characterisations as both a corrupting political influence and a staggeringly incompetent organisation by Parliamentary critics,[109] none of the UDC MPs (who presumably would have been among the first men rounded up in Millman's doomsday scenario) suggested that it was involved in a sinister plan to create a mass army of 'patriots',[110] the better to trample the last worker and the last British liberties into the ground. It seems much more likely that the NWAC's purpose was, as advertised, 'to resist insidious influences of an unpatriotic character' by keeping 'before the country the causes which had led to the War, and to encourage the country to continue until those causes had been removed forever'.[111] As John Horne suggests, while partially useful, 'heavy reliance on coercion would undermine [the government's] essential democratic legitimacy and prove counter-productive'. Instead, what was required was a 'remobilisation' of public support for the war, based on local judgements of its necessity and voluntary local involvement,[112] and a reliance on the power of patriotic appeals.

---

105 L.L. Farrar Jr, 'Nationalism in Wartime: Critiquing the Conventional Wisdom', in Frans Coetzee and Marilyn Shevin Coetzee (eds), *Authority, Identity and the Social History of the Great War* (Providence: Berghahn Books, 1995), p. 137.
106 Millman, *Managing*, pp. 282–85, 299, n. 37.
107 Millman, *Managing*, p. 294.
108 TNA:PRO T102/10, folder 'Bryan O'Donnell'.
109 Also in Swartz, *Union of Democratic Control*, p. 191.
110 Millman defines a 'patriot' as a middle- or working-class thug determined to use violence to silence dissent. Millman, *Managing*, p. 99; 'HMG', p. 416.
111 Speech of Captain Guest, PDC(5), 99 (13/11/17), cols 286–87.
112 Horne, 'Remobilizing', p. 198 and *passim*.

CHAPTER 3

Local Agency, Local Work:
The Role of Constituency War
Aims Committees

TO ensure a truly national campaign, NWAC activities could only be
organised at a local level. By September 1917, it was judged that all
constituencies required local War Aims Committees, rather than the 200
or so initially targeted.[1] Having decided that the public was war-weary
and in need of patriotic revival, Lloyd George had demanded a domestic
propaganda organisation. Once the NWAC had been established to fulfil
this role, its organisers canvassed local opinion, seeking to discover where
work was required and where local political authorities judged that the
public remained sound. José Harris claims that, politically and culturally,
Britain experienced 'a subterranean shift in the balance of social life away
from the locality to the metropolis and the nation' after 1900,[2] but local
institutions and expertise remained crucial to the successful organisation of any nationwide campaign. Historians have recently asserted
the 'enduring power of the local' in both political and cultural terms,[3]
corroborating Duncan Tanner's contention that, at least until 1918, the
'context of social experience ... was local, not national' and that politics
consequently had to be tailored to non-uniform local expectations.[4]
These assertions are supported by the NWAC's organisational structure,
and the content of its propaganda (on which, see chapter 7). The central
committee could have only very limited knowledge of public opinion
in individual localities. By contrast, party agents, who usually acted as

---

1   TNA:PRO T102/16, Meetings Department Report, 25/9/17.
2   José Harris, *Private Lives, Public Spirit: A Social History of Britain, 1870–1914*
    (Oxford: Oxford University Press, 1993), pp. 18–19. See also Jon Lawrence, 'Class
    and Gender in the Making of Urban Toryism, 1880–1914', *English Historical
    Review*, 108 (1993), esp. pp. 650–51.
3   E.g. Philip Harling, 'The Centrality of Locality: The Local State, Local Democracy,
    and Local Consciousness in Late-Victorian and Edwardian Britain', *Journal of
    Victorian Culture*, 9:2 (2004), p. 218; Paul Readman, 'The Place of the Past in
    English Culture c.1890–1914', *Past and Present*, 186 (2005).
4   Duncan Tanner, *Political Change and the Labour Party, 1900–1918* (Cambridge:
    Cambridge University Press, 1990), citation p. 420.

secretaries and chief organisers of WACs, brought specialist knowledge of their constituency, not only of local political attitudes, but also of the area's human geography and the patterns of everyday lives. In relation to foreign propaganda, Masterman had affirmed in 1915 the importance of avoiding the German example of 'promiscuous dumping of unwanted literature', which served only to irritate 'those who she wishes to win over'.[5] The same possibility applied locally for domestic propaganda – what might be appropriate for one area was not necessarily appropriate for all. By combining central resources with local organisation and expertise the NWAC could offer a more flexible and locally responsive campaign than with a purely central approach. Further, the involvement with, and tacit endorsement of, the NWAC by local figures constituted a significant ideological imperative, offering some appearance of spontaneity and self-mobilisation rather than overarching state-driven propaganda. In principle, local involvement meant that propaganda was imparted to, rather than imposed upon, the public.

A S CHAPTER 1 demonstrated, the NWAC followed the PRC in utilising local party agents as secretaries of constituency WACs (as did other organisations).[6] The NWAC's Meetings Department reported in October 1917 that 'almost every constituency' had a WAC, War Savings Committee, Food Economy Committee, National Service Committee and Munitions Works Committee, with varying personnel, but often the same secretaries.[7] Similarly, the *Conservative Agents' Journal* noted the example of the Conservative and Liberal agents in Bradford who held seven joint honorary secretaryships.[8] The use of political agents had several practical purposes. First, these were men known and trusted by the central organisers, meaning they could carry out work locally without close monitoring. This reliability was assisted by the increasingly homogeneous work done by party agents by 1900, resulting from the mobility between constituencies accompanying their professionalisation.[9] A similar approach could therefore be expected in most areas. Another party-

5   TNA:PRO INF4/5, 'Report of the Work of the Bureau established for the purpose of laying before neutral nations and the Dominions the case of Great Britain and her allies' (15/6/15), introduction by Masterman, p. 2.

6   E.g. the Conservatives' National Union resolution to place agents at the disposal of the National Service Committee: *Archives of the British Conservative & Unionist Party (ABCUP), Series II. Minutes and Reports of the British Conservative Unionist Party* (microfiche ed., Hassocks, 1978) 'Minutes of N.U. Executive Committee: 8 Feb 1917–7 Jun 1917', minute, 13/3/17: 'Parliamentary National Service (Meetings) Committee'.

7   TNA:PRO T102/16, 'Meetings Department Report, 10th October, 1917.'

8   *ABCUP*: 'Conference Reports 1947–1963; Campaign Guides 1951–1974; CAJ 1902–1983', *Conservative Agents' Journal*, 47 (January 1918), p. 14.

9   Rix, 'Party Agent', pp. 98–99.

political advantage in utilising agents in such activities was to ensure that they remained 'essential' workers, exempt from conscription.[10] In 1916 Bonar Law had stressed the importance of maintaining the Conservative party organisation, despite the present absence of organisational work in the wake of coalition government and the cessation of electoral registration.[11] Involving political agents in war aims and other work would, therefore, provide war service while maintaining the carefully cultivated networks of local political influence developed since the 1880s.

Moreover, the NWAC's local organisation depended specifically upon the presence and willing involvement of agents. In the Yorkshire mining constituency, Osgoldcross, the local Conservative chairman, F.S. Hatchard, reported in October 1917 that it was impossible to form a WAC since they had no agent.[12] This represented an organisational difficulty for the NWAC since many agents had enlisted in the armed forces or taken war work elsewhere. *The Conservative Agents' Journal* claimed that over one hundred Conservative agents had enlisted while in Torquay the Liberal W. Blackler informed the NWAC that 'our Agent is in the Army + I am too busy to take up any work', though Torquay's WAC was actually established soon afterwards.[13] The comments of Hatchard and Blackler suggest that the absence of agents inhibited local organisation – Torquay's WAC was seemingly initially established by the Conservative agent, though Liberals were subsequently represented. Other local party notables were apparently unable or disinclined to involve themselves in such (voluntary) organisational work.

In other instances, the weak efforts of local agents were blamed for the lack of organised propaganda. The Conservative Horace Chatterton complained to the central committee that in Norfolk 'the local agents do little or nothing to organize the meetings', with consequent poor attendances.[14] In Elland (the constituency of UDC member Charles Trevelyan), a clergyman asked the central committee in September 1917 to assist him in organising propaganda locally, having already approached the local agents, since 'the politicians do not intend to take the matter up'. However, he was informed that the NWAC was continuing efforts to establish a WAC in Elland, and encouraged to place himself at its disposal thereafter, though nothing was seemingly done until October 1918.[15]

---

10 E.g., TNA:PRO T102/3, Capt. G.R. Donald to Cox, 31/7/17, concerning the request of Coventry's Liberal agent, Karl Spencer, for exemption from military service because of the proposed formation of a WAC.

11 Keohane, *Party of Patriotism*, p. 61.

12 TNA:PRO T102/26 – Osgoldcross card-index entry.

13 *Conservative Agents' Journal*, 46 (October 1917), p. 139; TNA:PRO T102/26 – Torquay card-index entry.

14 TNA:PRO T102/2, Chatterton to Vesey, 25/1/18.

15 TNA:PRO T102/1, Revd Luke Beaumont to NWAC, 14/9/17; NWAC to Beaumont, 18/9/17; T102/26 – Elland card-index entry.

The NWAC's commitment to a constituency-based, agent-led organisation is confirmed by its realignment of some local WACs to conduct NWAC work 'through the new Constituency Organizations as soon as convenient' after the 1918 electoral boundary redistributions.[16] In Wigan, the Conservative agent Thomas Southworth, who had operated a joint-WAC for Wigan and Ince since August 1917, was asked to focus solely on Wigan from June 1918 as the NWAC was 'working on the basis of new Constituencies'.[17] This seemingly inflexible approach perhaps reflected political considerations, given the concerns expressed by some MPs about the NWAC's potential exploitation for electoral advantage. Wigan was represented by a Conservative, whereas Ince had a Labour MP – the NWAC's constituency card index recorded Southworth as the contact for Wigan, but R.T. Phillips (Labour) for Ince, perhaps indicating different approaches in the two constituencies. The central committee's lukewarm response to organisation by non-political figures perhaps suggests concern for accountability, particularly after November 1917 when NWAC finances became Treasury-based. Party agents were trusted, and sufficiently expert, to make and adhere to appropriate estimates for events, whereas individual civilians were an unknown quantity. Whether this assumption was accurate is debatable, given the correspondence between Vesey and Sir J.W. Greenwood of the Stalybridge Conservative and Unionist Association. Greenwood wrote on behalf of the local agent, whose invoice for distributing 16,000 leaflets was rejected by the NWAC because of Treasury instructions to pay for nothing without prior estimates. Greenwood complained that his agent's work throughout the war in Stalybridge had rendered a WAC unnecessary there:

> if he had been less energetic + patriotic he might have arranged a series of meetings + distributions of literature under your auspices + received ten or twenty pounds for himself as other Agents have done. [Instead] he has given his whole time to the war, been paid his usual salary by us + borne the burden of all increased charges himself.[18]

Despite Greenwood's allegation of venality, however, it remained true that central organisers knew more about their own provincial workforce than if they allowed WACs to be administered by private citizens.

A further assumed benefit of agents' involvement was their sway over local politicians. In discussing proposals for an empire-wide commemoration of the anniversary of the declaration of war, the secretary of the CCNPO remarked to Cox that we 'have not in times past found the majority of the Mayors very helpful, but no doubt your agents will

---

16 TNA:PRO T102/13, fragment of letter (n.d.) signed by Boraston, Wallace Carter and Thompson, on reverse of note in correspondence with J. Swithenbank.
17 TNA:PRO T102/13, folder 'S', letter, unsigned to Southworth, 6/6/18.
18 TNA:PRO T102/5, correspondence between Greenwood and Vesey, October 1917–February 1918, citation in letter, 8/11/17.

stimulate many of them into hearty co-operation'.[19] Where agents were unavailable, regional agents sometimes involved themselves. For instance, the Conservative agent W.J. Arculus involved himself in at least 16 constituencies over four counties.[20] In April, when the Meetings Department was reorganised, 'District Organizers' like Arculus were appointed 'to supervise the efforts of local Committees' – perhaps indicating that the NWAC was not satisfied with the work of all local agents.[21] In June, Cox provided Charles Cockburn, the Conservative 'County Organising Agent' for Northumberland, with the names of Northumberland's Unionist and Liberal district organisers, adding that the 'main idea is to see that active [WACs] are established' to ensure 'effective' and widespread propaganda.[22] While local action was preferable, therefore, alternative arrangements would be made where necessary.

Most important, practically, was the agents' local expertise. Agents who had been in their constituencies for a while knew the best places to hold meetings, and the times when sizeable audiences could be obtained. They were familiar to proprietors of halls, schoolmasters and others whose indoor spaces were needed for winter work. This could sometimes be a hindrance, as in Wigan, where Southworth reported that he could not help with the organisation of a nationally planned event commemorating the outbreak of the war since several 'of the Clergy here look with great dis-favour [*sic*] on the efforts of political agents, (outside their own work) & would certainly not respond to the appeal if made by me, as I am so well known'.[23] Generally, however, local knowledge was more help than hindrance. This expertise was perhaps especially important in constituencies that were not entirely urban, where the population was spread widely. The rural constituency of Evesham, for instance, contained three medium-sized towns (Evesham, Droitwich and Pershore) and numerous smaller communities. Between October 1917 and the armistice, meetings were arranged in 77 different parishes, with estimated attendances ranging from 15 at a winter meeting in Pendock (described as 'a real bit of "No man's land"') to 600 at Shipston-on-Stour in August 1918.[24] Without expert local organisation, propagandists would

19 TNA:PRO T102/2, Grey Wilson to Cox, 19/6/18.
20 TNA:PRO T102/26 – Bosworth, Derby, Derby (Mid), East Northamptonshire, Harborough, Ilkeston, Leicester, Loughborough, Melton, Northampton, Nuneaton, Rugby, South Northamptonshire, Stratford-on-Avon, Warwick and Leamington and West Derby card-index entries.
21 TNA:PRO T102/16, NWAC minutes, 4/4/18.
22 TNA:PRO T102/2, Cox to Cockburn, 13/6/18.
23 TNA:PRO T102/13, Southworth to NWAC, 6/7/18.
24 Statistics based on a database constructed by the author from Speakers' Daily Reports, contained within TNA:PRO T102/16, 22–26 (henceforth Reports Database). On Pendock, see T102/23, Speaker's Daily Reports (henceforth SDRs) – John Farnsworth, Evesham (Pendock), 23/1/18.

have found great difficulty in providing opportunities for the whole local population to hear their messages. From their registration work agents also knew what sort of audience speakers might face, enabling them to adjust their remarks accordingly. Furthermore, as Rix notes, it was expected that 'agents should possess not only professional knowledge, but also qualities such as tact, adaptability, courtesy, and an ability to keep in touch with the electorate',[25] all skills invaluable in persuading local dignitaries to participate, making arrangements with local officials or proprietors for the use of public spaces, and smoothing over difficulties.

From a practical viewpoint, the parties' constituency organisations clearly provided 'an unrivalled vehicle of political mobilisation'.[26] But also important in leaving much of the organisation of propaganda in local hands were the social and ideological implications. The involvement of local notables (generally equal representatives of local parties) in a committee of 12 to 30 did not make them 'mere carriers of state-produced propaganda'.[27] Rather local WACs represent part of what Horne calls the '"self-mobilization" of civil society', defined by Pierre Purseigle as

> the set of organized and plural groups that, beyond the domestic and familial spheres, interacted with the State … [and] *established and arranged mediations* of the war experience that imposed restrictions upon the State or offered means, however limited, to resist the State's infringement on rights and liberties.[28]

By leaving the organisation of state propaganda ostensibly in local hands (albeit guided by experienced and partisan political organisers) the NWAC offered communities a sense of autonomous involvement in, rather than subordinate manipulation by, its propaganda. In the same way that, as Keith Grieves shows, national calls for more efficient and extensive food production were more effective for having been 'mediated locally', producing 'a more consensual tillage campaign',[29] so patriotic propaganda meetings could benefit from being arranged and attended by familiar local figures.

Furthermore, the nation was not a homogeneous whole, sharing exactly the same interests and anxieties, but an agglutination of culturally

---

25 Rix, 'Party Agent', p. 103.

26 Horne, 'Remobilizing', p. 201.

27 Pierre Purseigle, 'Beyond and below the Nations: Towards a Comparative History of Local Communities at War', in Jenny Macleod and Purseigle (eds), *Uncovered Fields: Perspectives in First World War Studies* (Leiden: Brill, 2004), p. 98.

28 Horne, 'Remobilizing', p. 195; Pierre Purseigle, 'Introduction: Warfare and Belligerence: Approaches to the First World War', in idem (ed.), *Warfare and Belligerence: Perspectives in First World War Studies* (Leiden: Brill, 2005), p. 25; original emphasis.

29 Keith Grieves, 'War Comes to the Fields: Sacrifice, Localism and Ploughing Up the English Countryside in 1917', in Ian F.W. Beckett (ed.), *1917: Beyond the Western Front* (Leiden: Brill, 2009), p. 167.

and socially diverse regions and localities, connected by certain ideas and institutions, but different from place to place.[30] In allowing local direction of propaganda, the NWAC enhanced the likelihood of public comprehension and acceptance of its messages. With local figures as chairmen, and offering introductions and votes of thanks, a local inflection was added to the necessarily somewhat standardised and delimited words of the centrally provided speakers or NWAC publications – sometimes augmented by including locally specific material in the main speaker's address.[31] Thus 'the voice of authority was clothed in more popular accents', as Horne puts it, assisting what Purseigle describes as the 'appropriation of the national narrative through local cultural codes'.[32] Just as earlier, genuinely self-mobilised propaganda utilised local cultural commonplaces, the NWAC's organisational structure and approach to propaganda suggests awareness that wartime propaganda's 'efficiency' 'depended as much on the taking of local identities into consideration and on the participation of local civil society, as on the potency of the state apparatus'.[33] A memorandum in the NWAC's minutes stressed that

> views expressed in the London Press do not necessarily reflect public opinion outside London. The tone of the provincial press is on the whole more consistent, less materialistic and more representative of solid English opinion. The greater communal spirit which prevails in Provinces ... enables the Provincial Editor to crystallise public opinion in his district more accurately.[34]

Similarly, the NWAC's organisational structure acknowledged that local experts could better gauge local public mood than London-based organisers arranging meetings on the basis of quotas, with little concrete knowledge of their necessity.

From the outset, the organisation of NWAC activities, whether the arrangement of meetings or the distribution of literature, was placed in local hands, except for a few centrally arranged nationwide campaigns. The promotion of Lloyd George's January war aims speech was one example. The central committee actively encouraged the distribution of their short précis. The organisation of cinemotor tours was also centralised, largely because demand outstripped supply.[35] Additionally, two special events, 'France's Day', celebrated on 12 July 1918 (the closest

---

30 Cf. the post-1945 Conservative view of 'local patriotism' and local government, in Matthew Cragoe, '"We Like Local Patriotism": The Conservative Party and the Discourse of Decentralisation, 1947–51', *English Historical Review*, 122:498 (2007), p. 980.
31 See chapter 7.
32 Horne, 'Remobilizing', p. 206; Purseigle, 'Beyond and below', p. 99.
33 Purseigle, 'Beyond and below', p. 101.
34 TNA:PRO T102/16, memorandum, 'The Government and the Press', 20/8/17.
35 See above, pp. 54, 58.

Friday to Bastille Day), and the 'War Anniversary' (4 August) were heavily promoted centrally, and on the latter occasion a message from Lloyd George was distributed to places of public entertainment, to be opened and read at 9 p.m.[36] These events apart, however, local propaganda was arranged locally. The next section offers some statistical analysis of the efficacy of this approach.

IN ALL, 344 WACs were established during the war, from a total of 528 constituencies or regional areas recorded in the NWAC's card index. Just over 65 per cent of constituencies apparently established WACs. However, these statistics possibly understate the real figures, being complicated by the redrawn 1918 electoral boundaries. The card index includes many entries for new constituencies about which nothing is recorded, and it seems likely that existing WACs from old constituencies sometimes continued their operations. Of those constituencies existing before 1918, 304 out of 428 established WACs (71 per cent).[37] Figure 12 demonstrates the rapid establishment of WACs. By 31 October 1917, 228 committees, almost two-thirds of those eventually formed, were already established. Through the winter, a moderate number were added, but in no month in 1918 were more than nine new committees established until September, when the last months of the war saw 41 new committees, perhaps in some cases reflecting the wish by agents or others to demonstrate local activity.[38] It is inaccurate to assume, as historians following Millman's interpretation might, that this reflected increased surveillance and potential coercion of industrial areas at the end of the war. Of 22 new WACs in pre-1918 constituencies after September, only three (East Northamptonshire, Elland and Leigh) were predominantly working-class or mining constituencies. The other 19 included the middle-class London constituency Dulwich, and rural constituencies like Chelmsford and Anglesey, where a desire to appear active seems more likely than a sudden need, after the successful reversal of Germany's spring offensive, to exhort civilians to work harder.

---

36 E.g. '"Hold Fast." The Premier's Message to the Empire', *Norwood Press and Dulwich Advertiser*, 10/8/18, p. 2.

37 Statistics from card-index database.

38 In some cases, these late establishments might reflect missing data or long-standing inertia after an earlier (unrecorded) formation. Others are almost certainly duplicates of existing WACs in former constituencies. For instance, John Horne, utilising the Speakers' Daily Reports in TNA:PRO T102/22–24 refers to extensive activities in Royton in 1918. Horne, 'Remobilizing', pp. 209, 283 n. 61. The only date which the card-index database offers for Royton WAC's establishment is 5 September 1918, probably because Royton was a new constituency in 1918, replacing Middleton (which had a WAC by early-August 1917). The database is, therefore, flawed but, particularly when restricted to the pre-1918 constituencies, still offers useful analytical material.

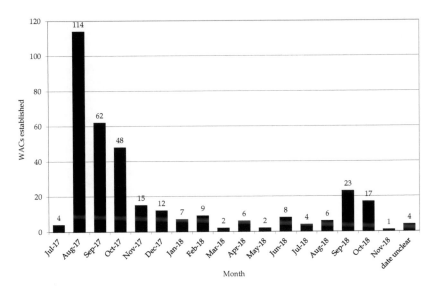

Figure 12. Monthly WAC establishment

While there were particularly active constituencies of all types, there were nevertheless some discrepancies between the classifications. Chapter 2 demonstrated that constituencies of all types were active in arranging NWAC events, although mining constituencies were noticeably more active.[39] In terms of WAC establishment, there were also interesting discrepancies. Tables 2–4 offer a statistical breakdown of WAC establishment by constituency classification. The first table provides figures based upon all records in the NWAC's card index. These suggest that agents and local figureheads in urban, mainly middle-class and rural constituencies were significantly less enthusiastic about forming WACs than in other constituencies, with only slightly over half such constituencies forming a WAC. Most likely to form WACs were urban/rural constituencies like Barnstaple or Ripon, containing both fairly large towns and significant areas of countryside. Nearly three-quarters of such constituencies formed WACs, based on the complete card index. Almost as likely to form WACs were urban, mixed-class constituencies (usually constituencies within large towns and cities),[40] over 70 per cent of which had WACs. Urban, mainly working-class and mining constituencies, meanwhile, formed WACs at a rate of about two in three.

---

39 See above, pp. 46–48.
40 The statistics for these WACs include city-wide WACs like Manchester, Leeds and Birmingham, which subsumed all constituencies into one WAC – discrepancies between working-class and middle-class districts have been resolved by assigning such WACs to urban, mixed-class classifications.

*Table 2 WAC formation by constituency classification**

Type**	Total constituencies	%	No. with WACs	% with WACs	Total % of WACs
UMC	58	11.0	32	55.2	9.3
UMX	99	18.8	71	71.7	20.6
UWC	103	19.5	69	67.0	20.1
UR	79	15.0	58	73.4	16.9
R	118	22.4	68	57.6	19.8
M	57	10.8	38	66.7	11.1
Unclassified	14	2.7	8	57.1	2.3
Totals	528	100	344	65.2	100.1

*Statistics from card-index database.
**UMC: urban, mainly middle-class; UMX: urban, mixed class; UWC: urban, mainly working-class; UR: urban/rural; R: rural; M: mining.

However, like the monthly statistics, these classification figures are distorted by the 1918 boundary redistributions. Table 3, dealing only with constituencies existing before 1918, provides a clearer depiction of the pattern of WAC establishment. Rural and urban, middle-class constituencies remain less likely to form WACs (though rural constituencies in this case were least likely to form a WAC), but in both cases the likelihood of establishment is greater than in the overall statistics. Likewise, the other constituency types also show increased percentages of constituencies with WACs, expanding the overall average of WACs to constituencies from 65.2 to 71.0 per cent. Most significant, however, is the large increase in percentage of mining constituencies with WACs, which become the most frequent establishers of WACs, rather than the fourth most frequent overall. This reflects the fact that most existing mining constituencies formed WACs before 1918. The subsequent redrawing of boundaries and renaming of constituencies created several new mining constituencies, mostly sections of existing larger mining constituencies, thus distorting the picture somewhat.[41]

Table 4 demonstrates the salience of these arguments. Again including only the pre-1918 constituencies it shows the differing rates at which

41 E.g. the pre-1918 Derbyshire mining constituencies, Mid-Derby and Chesterfield, both had WACs. After 1918 they became Belper, Chesterfield and Clay Cross, the last of which was not recorded as having a WAC (and had no records beyond a name card in the card index). Thus, although the two WACs continued as before, statistically the presence of Clay Cross in the card index reduced the apparent percentage of mining constituencies with WACs. Michael Kinnear, *The British Voter: An Atlas and Survey since 1885* (Ithaca, NY: Cornell University Press, 1968), pp. 142–45, provides maps of constituency boundaries before and after 1918.

Table 3 WAC formation by constituency classification (pre-1918 constituencies)

Type	Total constituencies	%	No. with WACs	% with WACs	Total % of WACs
UMC	43	10.1	28	65.1	9.2
UMX	86	20.1	67	77.9	22.0
UWC	87	20.3	63	72.4	20.7
UR	61	14.3	49	80.3	16.1
R	108	25.2	64	59.3	21.1
M	35	8.2	29	82.9	9.5
UNC	8	1.9	4	50.0	1.3
Totals	428	100.1	304	71.0	100

Table 4 WAC formation by constituency classification to 31 October 1917 (pre-1918 constituencies)

Type	No. with WACs, 31/8/17	% of total class. WACs, 31/8/17	No. with WACs, 31/10/17	% of total class. WACs, 31/10/17
UMC	12	42.9	21	75.0
UMX	31	46.3	54	80.6
UWC	29	46.0	54	85.0
UR	13	26.5	26	53.1
R	9	14.1	36	56.3
M	15	68.2	22	75.9
UNC	4	100.0	4	100.0
Totals	113	37.2	217	71.4

local communities remobilised. By 31 August 1917, over 68 per cent of the 22 mining constituency WACs eventually formed were already established. No other classification approached this level of mobilisation. The three exclusively urban types had all reached more than 40 per cent of their final totals, while constituencies with a rural element were considerably slower to mobilise. Though eventually urban/rural constituencies formed a WAC more than 80 per cent of the time, only 13 were formed by 31 August (26.5 per cent of the final number) and only 26, a little over half the eventual number, by 31 October. Rural constituencies were even more sluggish. On 31 August only nine rural WACs existed – less than 15 per cent of the eventual number, and only one in twelve of all pre-1918 rural constituencies. Though this rate increased substantially

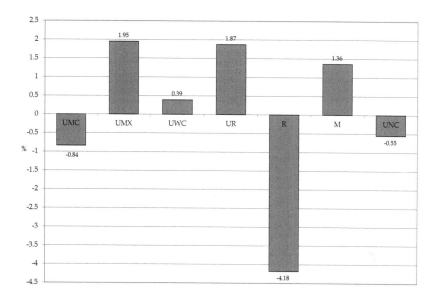

Figure 13. Difference between percentage of pre-1918 constituencies and percentage of WACs

by 31 October, rural constituencies, accounting for over a quarter of all the pre-1918 constituencies in the card index, at this stage still only represented slightly more than three in every twenty established WACs. As figure 13 emphasises, these constituencies never established WACs at a rate proportional to their national proliferation.

These statistics demonstrate the strength of local judgements regarding the value of establishing a WAC. In a mining constituency like Mid-Glamorgan, a committee was formed early in August 1917, the Unionist organiser Thomas Thomas later informing the central committee that the 'I.L.P. are organising meetings in a fortnight's time[. We] have discussed their actions – [the] only way to counteract their influence is to hold open air meetings here every night.' By contrast, rural constituencies repeatedly insisted that WACs were not required. In Cirencester, the Conservative agent T. Davies wrote that he and the Liberal agent had 'carefully considered this matter' before deciding there was 'not the least occasion for anything to be done, there is no anti-war propaganda beyond the usual feeling of war weariness'.[42] Here, local experts clearly made judgements based on the political exigencies of their constituencies. In East Norfolk the Liberal W.E. Keefe explained that he found 'no local

---

42 TNA:PRO T102/26, card index: Mid-Glamorgan, 11/9/17. Cirencester, 12/2/18.

Table 5 Regional distribution of WACs

Region	Total cons. in card index	% cons.	No. with WACs	Regional %	National %
London/South	196	37.1	116	59.2	33.7
Midlands/Wales	186	35.2	120	64.5	34.9
North	146	27.7	108	74.0	31.4
Totals	528	100	344	65.2	100

Table 6 Regional distribution of WACS (pre-1918 constituencies)

Region	Total cons.	% cons.	No. with WACs	Regional %	National %
London/South	156	36.5	103	66.0	33.9
Midlands/Wales	153	35.8	108	70.6	35.5
North	119	27.8	93	78.2	30.6
Totals	428	100	304	71.0	100

opinion favourable to the holding of meetings. My Unionist Colleague has not shown any inclination to take active steps. Think Village meetings are of little value [sic].' Additionally, there were sometimes mitigating circumstances. The Birmingham-based Conservative regional organiser, H. Pratt, reported that there was 'no one working in East Worcester who might take on War Aims work', suggesting that no agents were present, while in Ramsey, Wallis Simpson explained that the Conservative Association saw no benefit in a campaign and the constituency had no Liberal or Labour agents to approach. In North Norfolk, H.M. Upcher (affiliation unknown) wrote that 'our Agent has resigned' and promised to report a decision in due course. Nothing further was recorded.[43]

Complementary to the impact of the social composition of constituencies on WAC establishment was an element of regional difference. Tables 5–6 show the variation in WAC establishment in London and the South; the Midlands and Wales; and the North.[44] Whether considering

---

43 TNA:PRO T102/26, card index: East Norfolk, 2/2/18; East Worcester, 4/2/18; Ramsey, 1/2/18; North Norfolk, 6/2/18. The similarity of the dates suggests the central committee, aware of the limited involvement of rural constituencies, had suggested new WACs and campaigns.

44 Statistics from card-index database. For analytical purposes, the constituencies within these regions consist of *London/South*: constituencies south of the northern borders of Somerset, Wiltshire, Berkshire, Hertfordshire and Essex. *Midlands/*

all records in the card index, or only those relating to pre-1918 constituencies, it is clear that while WAC establishment in the Midlands/ Wales region conformed broadly to the national average, London/South constituencies formed WACs at a disproportionately low rate, whereas northern constituencies formed proportionally more WACs. This cannot be ascribed to the presence of London constituencies which might have been expected to be less locally involved and more centrally directed. Of 53 London boroughs existing before 1918, 35 were recorded as having WACs (66.0 per cent),[45] almost exactly the regional average. Nor is it attributable to the greater proliferation of rural constituencies in the South since, although 15 rural constituencies there did not form WACs, the proportion that did (slightly below 60 per cent) was larger than in the North (54.6 per cent). That mining constituencies, the most frequent establishers of WACs, were entirely absent in the South, but common in the North, skews the statistics somewhat, as does the disproportionate absence of (generally less enthusiastic) urban, middle-class constituencies in the North.[46] Only slightly over half the southern middle-class constituencies, 18 of 33, formed WACs. However, perhaps surprisingly, the other exclusively urban constituencies also proved difficult to motivate in the South. In southern working-class and mixed-class constituencies, WACs were formed, respectively, at a rate of around 65 and 72 per cent, which in regional terms was strong. However, the northern figures for the same classifications were around 76 and 83 per cent. Only in urban/ rural southern constituencies, like Maidstone, Reigate or Camborne, was there something approaching unanimous approval of WAC formation, with 21 of 25 constituencies forming WACs at some point, though even these statistics barely surpassed their northern equivalents, where 13 of 16 urban/rural constituencies had WACs.

Reasons for not forming a WAC were fairly consistent regardless of region. At Ormskirk, the Unionist agent G.W. Carr reported that he had consulted the local Liberal and Conservative party heads, who 'agreed that there is no anti-war campaign going on here'; therefore no committee would be formed. This was echoed in Croydon (which eventually formed a WAC in June 1918) by J. Ledger Keating, who said it was 'not possible' to act; besides, there was 'no pacifist propaganda at present'.[47]

Wales: Welsh constituencies (plus 'South Wales' regional WAC), English constituencies north of southern boundary and south of the southern borders of Cheshire and Yorkshire. *North*: constituencies north of the southern borders of Cheshire and Yorkshire, and also 'Scotland' regional WAC.

45 These and subsequent statistics refer to pre-1918 constituencies only.

46 Already a small minority of northern constituencies, their representation in the card index was further inhibited by city-wide WACs, leading to a classification in the database as urban, mixed-class. Any constituencies (like Sheffield Hallam) that apparently stood aloof from city organisations are noted individually.

47 TNA:PRO T102/26, card index: Ormskirk, 7/9/17; Croydon, 25/8/17.

The Conservative A.P. Hastings's excuse for not forming a committee in Hertford, because 'as long as air raids are on it would be difficult to get meetings up', seems rather implausible, but it is noticeable that mostly rural East Anglian coastal constituencies (Midlands/Wales region), except Great Yarmouth and Lowestoft (neither of which were rural), consistently declined to form WACs, as did several inland constituencies and many of the large suburban constituencies to the east of London. The central organiser, Wallace Carter, informed an American speaker that 'in most of the east coast towns they feel that the German raiders, both by sea and air, provide all that is necessary in stimulating our War Aims so that up to now we have held very few meetings indeed in the Eastern Counties'.[48] One local historian noted that, in Croydon, air raids caused 'a general clenching of teeth and always an increased determination to destroy the power which used these means of war'.[49] Possibly, therefore, raids were influential in such constituencies,[50] but generally the South simply appeared less discontented than the rest of the country. The fact that the Midlands/Wales figures are slightly weaker than the North is mainly attributable to the large number of rural constituencies there (60, of which 60 per cent formed a WAC). Midland mining constituencies actually exceeded northern establishment-rates, and other classifications were broadly comparable. The South, with its smaller industrial workforce, was less affected by the renewed controversies over dilution from the spring of 1917,[51] which was one factor prompting the NWAC's original creation. Consequently, despite concerns expressed about sentiment in the Home Counties and rural areas, there was seemingly less sense of urgency by the central organisation and local administrators about the South.[52]

THE process of establishing a WAC was usually relatively simple. Conservative and Liberal agents were circularised in late July 1917, as were local Labour representatives (either an established agent or

---

48 TNA:PRO T102/26, card index: Hertford, 1/2/18; T102/11, Wallace Carter to Major G.H. Putnam, 7/6/18. On the effectiveness of raids as direct propaganda, see the speech of Commander Bellairs, PDC(5), 99 (13/11/17), col. 322.
49 H. Keatley Moore (ed.), *Croydon and the Great War: The Official History of the War Work of the Borough and Its Citizens from 1914 to 1919, Together with the Croydon Roll of Honour* (Croydon: Corporation of Croydon, 1920), p. 39.
50 Air raids were not solely confined to southern constituencies, but by 1917 were largely confined to the London area and the east coast. Wilson, *Myriad Faces*, pp. 389–93, 508–11.
51 Waites, *Class Society*, pp. 203–08.
52 Based on this statistical analysis, 30 case studies were selected (ten per region; a representative number of each constituency classification; proportions based on establishment dates; other criteria include secretarial affiliations and the number of grants made). Appendix 1 discusses the criteria used and lists the case studies. These 30 WACs form the basis for local consideration of propaganda in Parts 2 and 3. On the issue of rural and southern reliability, see p. 43 above.

figures like trades council secretaries). Those willing to help then called a meeting of local political representatives. In Keighley, an urban, mainly working-class constituency in West Yorkshire, the local WAC was announced on 11 August 1917.[53] Keighley's Liberal MP, Sir Swire Smith, became its president, with three vice-presidents, Sir John Clough, J.E. Haggas and G.W. Pickthorne, representing the Conservatives, Liberals and Labour. The local Conservative and Liberal agents, J.D. Hird and W.E. Foster, became joint secretaries. In all, 28 men were elected to the committee, including the mayor, an alderman, a doctor, a knight and three more Cloughs. Interestingly, there was no attempt to disguise the committee's purpose, which was reported as being to 'hold meetings and engage in general propaganda'. This approach was very different to that of the '[s]trict secrecy' pursued by Charles Masterman's organisation in generating foreign propaganda.[54] This supports Harold Lasswell's assertion in his inter-war study of propaganda that

> As far as the home public is concerned, there is nothing to be gained by concealment, and there is a certain loss of prestige … when secrecy is attempted. The carrying power of ideas is greatly increased when the authority of the government is added to them.[55]

Apparently the combination of governmental authority with local agency was considered sufficient justification for domestic propaganda. Keighley WAC was seemingly quite effective, and unlike some other cases, Labour representation was maintained for most, if not all, of the war. Pickthorne, an ILP veteran, continued to appear (or to be scheduled to appear) on WAC platforms at least until July 1918.[56]

In some instances, local WACs were established after specially arranged regional conferences. The NWAC noted the success of a conference in Newcastle, which remedied many of the 'elements of mistrust which found expression among certain labour sections'. The Meetings Department considered such conferences invaluable as 'suggestions, criticisms and objections can be dealt with on the spot, and the need of securing co-operation of every available local institution can be emphasised'. Alongside planned conferences in Leeds and Manchester, the Meetings Department recommended further conferences in 20 cities across England and Wales.[57]

---

53 'Local News. Keighley. Formation of a War Aims Committee For Keighley', *Keighley News*, 11/8/17, p. 6. See also the summary of Keighley WAC's activities by a local journalist: Keighley Public Library, BK424, H.A. France, notebooks, no. 4.
54 TNA:PRO INF4/5, 'Report of the Work of the Bureau established for the purpose of laying before neutral nations and the Dominions the case of Great Britain and her allies' (15/6/15), introduction by Masterman, p. 2.
55 Lasswell, *Propaganda Technique*, p. 14.
56 'National War Aims. The Campaign in Keighley and District', *Keighley News*, 13/10/17, p. 5; 'France's Day at Keighley', *Keighley News*, 13/7/18, p. 5.
57 TNA:PRO T102/16, 'Meetings Department Report', 25/9/17.

In Liverpool a conference was held with representatives from across South-west Lancashire, presided over by Max Muspratt, the lord mayor. Sanders represented the NWAC. Again there was no attempt to disguise the organisation's purpose. Muspratt explained that the conference would 'consider the best way to promote the work of propaganda which the [NWAC] had undertaken'. Archibald Salvidge, the influential head of the Liverpool Workingmen's Conservative Association, had been troubled at the Liverpool-Abercromby by-election in June 1917 by the behaviour of some civilians in support of a candidate of the Discharged Sailors' and Soldiers' Federation. The 'nasty, strident, undisciplined note' reminded him of 'the disturbing things which are beginning to leak through about Russia'.[58] He suggested, therefore, that 'the chief need of a committee of that description was to act as policemen, and to watch the insidious underground policy adopted ... to mislead the people, and to sow seeds of disaffection and social unrest', confronting orators of 'opposition propaganda' with rival meetings. The general secretary of the National Union of Dock Labour, James Sexton, agreed with Salvidge that such critics 'did not represent one-fifteenth of the working-classes of the city', and called for WACs to be established in every constituency, supported by all parties and labour groups who so desired.[59] According to the NWAC's card index, all constituencies surrounding Liverpool formed WACs by the end of 1917, except Widnes and Ormskirk (which never did).

Conferences could also be arranged for other purposes. In December, Mrs Fletcher in Oldham was approached to speak at a 'War Aims Women's Conference' at Newton-le-Willows. The instructions sent to local committees suggested that it 'may be well to arrange special meetings for women of a social and educational nature' and encouraged WACs to seek the help of local women of 'all classes'. 'These meetings should be of a purely local and friendly nature for mutual encouragement and support, rather than formal public gatherings'.[60] The intention seems similar to the types of activity with which organisations like the Primrose League had been concerned since the late nineteenth century, which allowed women a certain limited role in public and political life.[61] Women were not to be addressed in the same way as men, but to receive more informal 'support', seemingly partially maintaining the gendered distinction between public and private spheres. This suggests some continuation of nineteenth-century ideas of

---

58 Stanley Salvidge, *Salvidge of Liverpool: Behind the Political Scene, 1890–1928* (London: Hodder & Stoughton, 1934), pp. 159–60. On the Abercromby by-election, see Stephen R. Ward, 'The British Veterans' Ticket of 1918', *Journal of British Studies*, 8:1 (1968), pp. 157–58.

59 'Allies' War Aims. Conference in Liverpool', *Liverpool Courier*, 12/10/17, p. 4. On Sexton's use of 'Tory' politics in Liverpool, see Tanner, *Political Change*, p. 141.

60 TNA:PRO T102/4, letter, unsigned, to Mrs Fletcher, 20/12/17.

61 On this see Martin Pugh, *The Tories and the People, 1880–1935* (Oxford: Basil Blackwell, 1985), esp. pp. 43–69.

home and community acting as 'cognitive boundaries, limiting aspirations and ideas about what was possible and desirable'. The idea of a 'purely local' approach in propaganda to women implies that women should be addressed on 'local' rather than 'national' issues, thus continuing to offer what historians of the mid-nineteenth century have described as 'only limited access to alternative conceptions of their "place" from outside'.[62] According to Patricia Hollis, women's accretion of a locally delimited public role via extensive involvement in local government before 1914 was predicated on making this separate-spheres ideology a 'supportive language' allowing women to 'avoid conflicts' between private and public values and work by emphasising the capacity of the 'different attributes and skills' of their 'domestic background' to 'strengthen civic life'.[63] Actually, as subsequent chapters show, propaganda towards women did not entirely retain such inward-looking localness as that outlined in the above instructions, instead demonstrating links between local efforts and national achievements. Nevertheless, these plans suggest that some in authority had yet to appreciate what Nicoletta Gullace labels the wartime 'renegotiation' of citizenship.[64]

Once established, WACs acted with considerable (though limited) autonomy. In Wigan, the NWAC encouraged the formation of a WAC, following a Navy League report warning that 'the pacifists have divided up Lancashire into 13 districts and are working them systematically. It is certainly no time to be shutting down any patriotic efforts.' A joint WAC was established for Wigan and Ince on 21 August 1917, but initially seemed reluctant to hold meetings. A central report noted that 'they stated that it was not advisable to hold an open-air campaign ... at present', prompting the central committee to contact their 'Central District Agents, and [ask] them to persuade the local Committee to hold a campaign'. Shortly thereafter, J.W. Greening, acting agent for the National Unionist Association in Lancashire and Cheshire, reported that Wigan WAC wanted strong speakers because

> audiences at Open air meetings there are extremely critical, and ... only speakers of the first class would be acceptable ... They mention ... [coalition Labour MPs] Mr. Brace, Mr. Roberts, and Mr. Barnes. Failing one of these they thought Mr. Hilare [*sic*] Belloc would be a good substitute. We pointed out the improbability of ... these gentlemen being sent, but pledged ... that you would send first rate men [representative of the three parties].[65]

---

62 Leonore Davidoff, Jeanne L'Esperance and Howard Newby, 'Landscape with Figures: Home and Community in English Society' (1976), in Leonore Davidoff, *Worlds Between: Historical Perspectives on Class and Gender* (Cambridge: Polity Press, 1995), p. 44.

63 Patricia Hollis, *Ladies Elect: Women in English Local Government, 1865–1914* (Oxford: Clarendon Press, 1987), pp. 471–72.

64 Gullace, *Blood*.

65 TNA:PRO T102/13, file S, report (copy), unsigned, 'WIGAN, Lancashire', n.d.

Indeed, none of these speakers appeared, though the Labour MP for Ince, Stephen Walsh, spoke three times in November. Other prominent speakers included the Conservative MPs for Wigan and St Helens, and the Coalition Liberals T.J. Macnamara (a junior Cabinet member) and C.A. McCurdy, a prolific NWAC contributor.[66] The work in November alone cost £55.3.8 in expenses (excluding centrally paid speakers' expenses). In July 1918, Thomas Southworth, now acting for Wigan alone, sent a campaign plan to the central committee, outlining 21-days' meetings at a cost of £24. Southworth defended the unusual arrangement of Sunday meetings to the speakers as necessary 'to counteract the agitation of the Pacificists [*sic*]', which met with central approval.[67]

The Wigan case demonstrates the limits of local independence. A WAC was quickly established, but initially reluctant to launch a campaign. The NWAC, with reports of local unrest, sought to stimulate action through regional organisers – these were presumably familiar to the local secretaries in a professional context while also, ostensibly, one stage removed from central figures demanding action. Having successfully persuaded the WAC to organise meetings, the central committee acceded to the request for prominent speakers of differing affiliations (albeit not those specifically requested), allowing local organisers to feel they were setting the agenda locally. In August 1918, Southworth was also personally sent £10 in recognition of his work in July,[68] a move presumably designed to encourage subsequent diligence. This indicates that the NWAC, though keen to let local figures make arrangements, would not simply defer to local judgements if they believed propaganda was needed. Inevitably there was more concern to mobilise an industrial constituency like Wigan than apparently placid rural constituencies. Nonetheless the NWAC persisted in pursuing activities through a local organisational structure, demonstrating not only a pragmatic recognition of the potentially prohibitive costliness of conducting propaganda without local assistance (organisers would necessarily have been sent to the area, and accommodated throughout the campaign), but also a commitment to local inclusion, and an acknowledgement that without the participation of knowledgeable local activists, propaganda risked alienating people it might otherwise inspire. Although the NWAC was not content to let sleeping dogs lie, it sought to maintain local involvement and at least the appearance of local agency and choice.

Other material in this file suggests this was a Navy League report; 'National War Aims Committee: Report with reference to the position at Wigan, Lancashire', n.d. (c. September 1917); Greening to NWAC, 18/9/17.

66 TNA:PRO T102/17, Meetings register, nos 479–82.
67 TNA:PRO T102/13, file S, 'Wigan and Ince Divisions. National War Aims Committee Campaign. November 1917'; campaign plan, 8-28/7/18; Southworth to speakers, 27/6/18; NWAC to Southworth, 18/6/18.
68 TNA:PRO T102/13, NWAC to Southworth, 14/8/18.

That WACs felt they were agents of their own instruction is partially demonstrated by regular requests for specific speakers. In Watford, for example, organisers requested either J.R. Clynes or J.H. Thomas as speakers in October 1917, but had to settle for another Labour MP, Charles Duncan.[69] The Unionist MP Col. G.R. Lane-Fox received a letter from the Liberal secretary of the Isle of Thanet WAC, offering his 'best thanks' for agreeing to speak at Ramsgate in December, and inviting him to lunch with the mayor. Other MPs were the subject of 'special requests' by WACs.[70] Birkenhead succeeded, along with several Welsh constituencies, in obtaining William Brace, who was seemingly highly regarded as a speaker.[71] Not only MPs were specifically requested, however. The local secretaries at Kingswinford particularly wanted the speakers Harry Walker and A. Beveridge for a campaign, while both Morpeth and West Staffordshire WACs requested the Liberal speaker Thomas Ternent to take meetings in the week beginning 5 November 1917, but were disappointed, as he was already engaged at Middleton.[72] While local WACs could not always be accommodated with their preferred choice of speakers, the fact that they felt their opinions were sufficiently relevant to make requests worthwhile suggests an environment of mutual interaction rather than the NWAC simply sending whomever it chose. Presumably, local WACs asked for specific speakers either because of their reputation or because they already knew their style, and felt they would provide appropriate propaganda for the community. Particularly with MPs, when a specific speaker was unavailable the central committee sought a replacement with a similar outlook (for instance, another Asquithian Liberal). Again, this suggests more than simple gestures towards local autonomy; it seemingly indicates a concerted effort to adhere to local wishes, predicated upon an assumption that such wishes reflected careful judgements of varying attitudes and moods.

THE NWAC relied upon a local organisational structure to deliver its message in an effective, extensive and sensitive manner, both for pragmatic and principled reasons. Only local organisation could hope to efficiently reach large sections of a local population, while the cession of some elements of control to local organisers reduced the appearance of

69 TNA:PRO T102/2, NWAC to Clynes, 15/9[/17]; T102/14, NWAC to Thomas, 18/9/17; T102/17, Meetings register, no. 310.
70 TNA:PRO T102/4, Revd Bernard Salomons to Lane-Fox, 19/11/17. Lane-Fox subsequently cancelled the meeting owing to other obligations; for 'special requests', see T102/5, NWAC to Sir Gordon Hewart, MP, for Salford WAC; T102/12, NWAC to Sir Joseph Compton-Rickett, MP, for Newton WAC.
71 TNA:PRO T102/17, Meetings register, nos 65, 176–8, 663, 982, 987, 1551.
72 TNA:PRO T102/17, Meetings register, nos 904 (Walker and Beveridge), 537, 541, 509.

a monolithic, omnipresent state. Rather than imposing itself on civilians within their own local communities, the involvement of local figures in the arrangement and presentation of propaganda served, if not to conceal the state's presence, at least to dilute its taste. Further, it encouraged communities to think that it was their agency which prompted this remobilisation, rather than state disquiet at civilian reliability. Where local communities proved reluctant 'self-mobilisers', the NWAC was sometimes prepared to intervene, but preferred to maintain a local organisational basis. The rapid formation of WACs in 1917 indicates the local appetite for remobilisation, at least among political and civic elites. Moreover it enabled equally rapid dissemination of a wide-ranging narrative of patriotism, initially through meetings and, by September, through publications.

Patriotism for a Purpose: NWAC Propaganda

CHAPTER 4

Presentational Patriotisms

PART 1 of this book detailed the NWAC's establishment and its organis-ational structure. Part 2 is concerned with the ideological structure of NWAC propaganda. NWAC propaganda used familiar patriotic themes and ideas within a framework of 'presentational patriotisms': broad interactive and interdependent discursive categories which combined to provide a flexible patriotic narrative reflecting civilians' total-war experiences. This narrative revolved around a core message of patriotic duty, contextualised by several other elements which demonstrated the necessity of accepting such obligations. This was not a narrative structure set out by the NWAC for its propagandists to adhere to.[1] Rather, it is a model construct based on a close reading of the NWAC's printed and spoken propaganda (the latter reprinted in the local press). The interaction of the various contextual and core sub-patriotisms with each other within the narrative framework offered a patriotic message adaptable to different audiences and situations.

Setting the propaganda's content within this interpretative framework enables qualitative assessment of the language used, emphasising the purposes behind the rhetoric. Rather than assigning primacy to the most extensively discussed elements within patriotic rhetoric, this approach contends that the interactions of the wider presentational categories gave patriotism its vitality by enabling similar conclusions to be drawn from a range of approaches. Without adequate contextualisation, the NWAC's core appeal to duty may have seemed unreasonable, given the efforts already undertaken by civilians. Hence, using one or more contextual presentational patriotisms, the majority of most discussions explained why the appeal was made. Placing several familiar patriotic ideas and images within a particular presentational patriotism does not overly

---

1 Skeleton lectures were apparently provided by the NWAC, but none survive in the files. A 'model' speech lampooned in *Labour Leader* in February 1918 must be treated cautiously, as the evidence of over 100 local newspapers does not reveal any speech conforming substantially to the content and structure contained. For discussion of the *Labour Leader* article and skeleton speeches, see p. 238 below.

schematise the range of themes and arguments, but recognises that the same rhetorical purpose was served by several alternative arguments. Propagandists had many familiar patriotic themes and ideas at their disposal from which to construct an argument to convince war-weary civilians to continue doing their 'duty'. Interpreting the manner and variety of these constructions may reveal more than merely re-identifying and re-cataloguing those familiar themes.

The core duty message was actually a three-pronged mixture, combining a hortatory 'civic patriotism', suffused with the self-denying rhetoric of 'sacrificial patriotism', with a celebratory evocation of what may be termed a 'concrescent community' growing together through shared sacrifice and acceptance of duty. The various contextual sub-patriotisms explained why such duty was necessary. 'Adversarial patriotism' exploited the identification of negative difference to highlight dangers to British society, whereas 'supranational patriotism' celebrated the differences and similarities between Britain and its major allies. 'Proprietorial patriotism' evoked the ideological bases behind British society, while 'aspirational patriotism' offered civilians a sense of the material and civilisational benefits to be gained by seeing the war through to a victorious end. Adrian Gregory, following several earlier scholars, has recently empha-sised the heavy and heady religiosity of wartime Britain,[2] and the rhetoric contained in all of these categories was also frequently bolstered by the addition of a spiritual patriotic gloss. The language of NWAC propaganda built on foundations laid during the nineteenth and early twentieth centuries. The use of such familiar ideas enabled ready comprehension by civilian audiences, permitting a smoother transmission of the propa-ganda's rhetorical purposes. This chapter establishes the broad narrative framework in which these ideas were used. Detailed analysis of the various presentational sub-patriotisms follows in subsequent chapters.

THERE was nothing greatly original about the types of patriotic ideas and imagery used in NWAC propaganda. Apart from more consistently evoking servicemen as patriots par excellence than was usual in peacetime, many familiar elements of British patriotic ideology are discernible. Most obviously, propagandists readily compared British national characteristics favourably with those of other nations – particularly Germany – but also other enemies and even allies. This comparative instinct, often (though sometimes falsely) referred to as 'othering' in the current historiography of Britain,[3] was rife throughout NWAC propaganda. At Ripon, in November

---

2   Gregory, *Last Great War*, chapter 5.
3   For the antecedents of the historical study of the 'other', see especially Edward W. Said, *Orientalism* ([1978] 5th ed., London: Penguin Books, 2003); Colley, 'British-ness and Otherness' and *Britons*.

1917, Major E.F.L. Wood, the constituency MP, in a speech of remarkable ferocity (particularly since Wood, as Viscount Halifax, later gained a reputation as an arch-appeaser of Germany) told his large audience that Germany's 'violation' of Belgian neutrality, the deportation of Belgian and French civilians to act as 'slave' labour, the resort to 'black piracy on the high seas' and various other immoral transgressions 'proved beyond a shadow of doubt that there was an irreconcilable antagonism between the German outlook on civilisation and [Britain's]'.[4] The NWAC Publications Department seized upon a *Philadelphia Ledger* article entitled 'Lest we Forget the Unboasting British', which insisted that 'when it comes to self-laudation the British are the poorest advertisers the world has seen', reprinting it (rather boastfully) both as a pamphlet and an article in its newspaper, *Reality*.[5] Such concerns also appealed to British insularity, identifying 'unique' characteristics and potential threats to them.

Another traditional patriotic motif was a recourse to history to inspire patriotism in the present generation. At Golborne, Lancashire, Viscount Wolmer, Conservative MP for Newton, encouraged his audience to 'think of the history of their country and the part Englishmen had played in the history of the world',[6] while a cartoon appeared in *Welcome* (a free newspaper for servicemen on leave in Britain) depicting a sailor, watched approvingly by Nelson's ghost, applying the 'Nelson touch' by hitting a German over the head (figure 14). One of the most agreeable areas of historical self-satisfaction related to Britain's heritage of parliamentary democracy. In an anonymous weekly column distributed to local newspapers, 'The War and Westminster', Captain D.D. Sheehan, an independent Irish nationalist MP, emphasised parliament's significance, celebrating 'this palladium of [the British peoples'] liberties and sacred ark of their rights … their stoutest bulwark and protection'.[7] Woodrow Wilson's declared intention to 'make the world safe for democracy' provided a continuing motivation for celebrating Britain's democratic credentials.

If British patriotic rhetoric traditionally included an appreciation of freedom, it was one comprising both rights and responsibilities. Questions of

---

4   'Major the Hon. E. Wood, M.P., and the War', *Ripon Gazette*, 8/11/17, p. 3.
5   *The Unboasting British; An American Tribute* (Searchlight series, 29, [1918]); '"Lest we Forget the Unboasting British." A Tribute from the United States', *Reality. The World's Searchlight on Germany*, 141, 26/9/18, p. 1.
6   'Lord Wolmer, M.P., at Golborne. Why Germany Must be Beaten,', *Wigan Examiner*, 4/12/17, p. 3. On history and identity, see Christopher Hill, 'The Norman Yoke', in *Puritanism and Revolution, Studies in Interpretation of the English Revolution of the 17th Century* (London: Mercury Books, 1962); Peter Mandler, *History and National Life* (London: Profile Books, 2002); Readman, 'Place of the Past'.
7   'The War and Westminster. By a Soldier M.P. Parliament and the People', *North Devon Herald*, 3/10/18, p. 6. On Sheehan's involvement with the NWAC, see p. 187 below.

THE OLD TOUCH.

Figure 14. Roland Hill, 'The Old Touch', Welcome, no. 5, 1/5/18, p. 49

duty and civic service featured prominently in NWAC propaganda, recognising the patriotic duties being performed by servicemen and women, and civilians, but stressing the continuing necessity of fulfilling civic duty at home. 'Your infantryman is a quiet man as a rule', wrote Sergeant H.V. Holmes in one pamphlet. 'Conscious that he is doing his duty, he does not very much worry about those that are not.'[8] Consequently, those at home should also ensure they fulfilled their duty. Miss E.M. Goodman pseudonymously informed female readers in a provincially distributed *War Supplement* that while land girls and others brought in the harvest, women unable to do such work should instead help by undertaking the 'small duty' of domestic work on others' behalf, like baking, cooking or washing. 'This is not new women's work, it is the woman's part time out of mind … [except] now it is England we shall save.'[9]

Pre-war patriotic discussion had consistently referred to religion, and this was mirrored by NWAC attempts to involve clergymen in local committees and individual meetings, and through articles and pamphlets like

8   Sergeant H.V. Holmes (London Scottish), *An Infantryman on Strikes: An Appeal to the Workers of Great Britain* (n.p.d., probably 1918), pp. 8–9.
9   Margaret Osborne (Miss E.M. Goodman), 'The Woman's Part. Help for the Land Worker', in, e.g., *Droitwich Guardian War Supplement*, week ending (w.e.) 13/7/18, p. 2.

the Liberal MP Charles McCurdy's *To Restore the Ten Commandments*,
or the speech (published by the NWAC) of the Archbishop of York,
Cosmo Lang, who said there was 'a moral and religious duty to stand
steadfast'.[10] At a meeting in Lanreath, Cornwall, Revd L.A. Williams
informed his audience that 'England had been especially blessed by God
and used by him in defence of liberty and justice throughout the ages',
and thus was obliged to continue this defence in the present war.[11]

Before the war, religion had been particularly useful in justifying British
imperialism, providing a 'civilising mission' to accompany empire's more
cynical purposes.[12] Empire was another site of patriotic imagery, to the
extent that by the outbreak of war some had added 'British Empire' to
the lexicon of British identities.[13] The poet Edward Thomas, who died
in France not long before the NWAC's formation, wrote in 1909 that
'what with Great Britain, the British Empire, Britons, Britishers, and
the English-speaking world, the choice offered to whomsoever would
be patriotic is embarrassing, and he is fortunate who can find an ideal
England of the past, the present and the future to worship'.[14] Empire
featured frequently in NWAC propaganda, both as part of a larger British
identity, and as a discrete element in itself. An Australian soldier in
Ilfracombe, Devon, stressed that Britain and its (white) Empire were one
since whenever 'an Australian was coming to England he always said he
was "going home." The Australians were [therefore] fighting their own

---

10 Charles A. McCurdy, MP, *To Restore the Ten Commandments: The Basis of a
    Permanent Peace for Europe* (London: Hodder & Stoughton, n.d. [1918]); *Hands
    Across the Atlantic: Personal Impressions of the United States at War by the
    Archbishop of York* (n.d. [1918]), pp. 25–26. See also Dr Fort Newton, *Fighting for
    the Faith* (*Searchlight* series, 10). On the relation between religion and patriotism,
    see, e.g., Wolffe, *God and Greater Britain*; Colley, *Britons*.
11 'British War Aims Campaign in South-East Cornwall', *Cornish Times and General
    Advertiser*, 8/2/18, p. 3.
12 Ronald Hyam, *Britain's Imperial Century, 1815–1914: A Study of Empire and
    Expansion* (3rd edn, Basingstoke: Palgrave MacMillan, 2002), esp. pp. 108–
    23; Catherine Hall, *Civilising Subjects: Metropole and Colony in the English
    Imagination, 1830–1867* (Cambridge: Polity, 2002), esp. pp. 136–39; Brian
    Stanley, 'Church, State, and the Hierarchy of "Civilization": The Making of
    the "Missions and Governments" Report at the World Missionary Conference,
    Edinburgh 1910', in Andrew Porter (ed.), *The Imperial Horizons of British
    Protestant Missions, 1880–1914* (Grand Rapids: William B. Eerdmans, 2003),
    pp. 58–84.
13 See especially Lord Milner, G.C.B., *The Nation and the Empire, Being a Collection
    of Speeches and Addresses* (London: Constable and Company, 1913). The mean-
    ing of empire to British national identity is, however, heavily debated. See, e.g.,
    the varying interpretations in Colley, 'Britishness and Otherness'; Hall, *Civilising
    Subjects*; Bernard Porter, *The Absent-Minded Imperialists: Empire, Society, and
    Culture in Britain* (Oxford: Oxford University Press, 2004); Andrew Thompson,
    *The Empire Strikes Back? The Impact of Imperialism on Britain from the Mid-
    Nineteenth Century* (London: Pearson, 2005), esp. pp. 179–202.
14 Edward Thomas, *The South Country* (London: Everyman and J.M. Dent, 1993
    [1909]), p. 55.

BRITISH VICTORY CALENDAR

FEBRUARY
18, 1916.
BRITISH
OCCUPATION
OF THE
CAMEROONS.

The triumphant capture of this great German dependency, equal in area to Great Britain and Germany combined, was effected by the concerted action of British, French and Belgian troops, powerfully assisted by warships and marines. The completed conquest of all the German Colonies has provided an impressive illustration of the direct and indirect results of British sea power: every part of the Empire co-operated freely in this fine achievement. The ultimate ownership of these territories, which embrace an area of 1,032,280 square miles, must largely depend upon the wishes of their inhabitants.

1918	FEBRUARY				1918
Sunday - -	✠	3	10	17	24
Monday - -	✠	4	11	18	25

Figure 15. NWAC, British Victory Calendar, February 1918

battles',[15] while the February section of the NWAC's 1918 *British Victory Calendar* (figure 15) celebrated the 'occupation of the Cameroons' by depicting African soldiers, a rare image as most imperial references in NWAC propaganda focused on the white Dominions.

As these examples suggest, there was nothing outwardly remarkable about the patriotic imagery invoked by the NWAC; it utilised many staple elements and characters. 'British' lions and bulldogs featured in cartoons and in the title of a pamphlet transcription of a speech by Earl Curzon, *The British Lion's Share*.[16] John Bull's role of disapproving patriot was, understandably, largely superseded by 'Tommy Atkins' (usually soldiers in general rather than a particular character): an over-fed gentleman-farmer was unlikely to engender the same response from disgruntled civilians facing food shortages as the ideological embodiment of loved ones doing

---

15 Speech of Lieutenant P.H. Aspinall, in *Ilfracombe Chronicle*, 3/11/17, p. 3.
16 Earl Curzon of Kedleston, *The British Lion's Share* (*Searchlight* series, 27, [1918]).

their patriotic duty abroad – but this was a wartime exception to general practice.[17] It would be relatively simple to identify these and (depending on perspective) to argue for the continuing strength of earlier ideas, or to criticise the NWAC's attempt to convince people using outdated language. But this would provide a rather superficial account of NWAC propaganda content. Where NWAC propaganda *was* remarkable was in the way it transformed these familiar patriotic motifs into a presentational model of patriotic ideology suitable for a total-war audience. To convince this audience to accept ongoing discomfort and deprivation required a presentational model melding elaborate contextual illustrations of national identity with a core message of patriotic duty to provide a cognisable narrative of civilian experience. Investigating the narrative structure of NWAC propaganda as a whole enables a more qualitative assessment of its content which recognises the purposes behind the language and images rather than simply quantifying the amount of space each element of discussion filled. The next section of this chapter outlines the several presentational sub-patriotisms by which the NWAC message was imparted and (tentatively, given the fluidity of their interactions) the narrative framework by which it was delivered.

BY far the most evident contextual element, both spatially and because of the vituperative language characteristic of much of it, was what may be called *adversarial patriotism*. This conceptualisation seeks to avoid the now rather loaded 'otherness' paradigm.[18] NWAC propagandists identified several adversaries, foreign and domestic, rather than a single, over-arching 'other' against which to test British identity. Chief amongst these, naturally, was Germany, and certainly more ink was spilled and words spat in this direction than towards any other adversary (or sub-patriotism), but adversarial patriotism is not simply a renamed 'otherness'. Linda Colley's seminal explication of British identity contends that, despite political and cultural differences at home, Britons defined themselves 'as a single people ... in reaction to the Other beyond their shores'.[19] This was not the case in NWAC propaganda, where 'the vast majority of' or 'all right-thinking' Britons were encouraged to identify themselves against Germany *and* Germany's allies *and* Bolshevik Russia *and*, most crucially, against other Britons. This last group of adversaries included conscientious objectors and 'pacifists' (by which the

---

17 On the usual importance of John Bull see Miles Taylor, 'John Bull and the Iconography of Public Opinion in England, c. 1712–1929', *Past & Present*, 134 (1992).
18 For some of the arguments relating to the use of 'otherness', see, e.g., the debate on cultural history begun by Peter Mandler in *Cultural and Social History*, 1:1–3 (2004).
19 Colley, *Britons*, p. 6.

NWAC meant both genuine pacifists and anyone advocating negotiated peace, like the UDC or ILP) sometimes, but not usually, accused of being pro-German or German-funded; but it could also include potential strikers and the war-weary, who were treated adversarially (though often quite differently from 'pacifists') as people, generally patriotic and loyal, and suffering from an aberration caused by fatigue or despair. The essential point was to identify an adversary which threatened the British way of life, even (perhaps especially) amongst those broadly considered sound. Since Colley's work, 'otherness' has been adapted conceptually so that multiple 'others', perhaps both negative and positive, external and internal, may contribute to national identity,[20] so that this distinction may not alone justify an alternative concept. Nonetheless, Catherine Hall asserts that we 'can understand the nation only by defining what is not part of it',[21] and, while Hall may not intend to eliminate alternative interpretations, it is this 'only' which crystallises the major difficulty with the paradigm. The fundamental assumption behind a meaningful interpretation of 'otherness' remains that the recognition of difference constitutes the basis of identity. If stripped of this structural function (as it sometimes is in the hands of less scrupulous scholars than Colley and Hall), 'otherness' or 'the other' become reduced to trendy code words for 'difference' or 'enemy/rival'. The concept of adversarial patriotism diverges from 'otherness' most significantly in rejecting this structural premise and making the identification of (negative) difference one of several interactive aspects contributing to national identity.

Another contextual sub-patriotism partially concerned with difference may be labelled *supranational patriotism*. This element transcended a simply 'national' approach to patriotism by comparing Britain, both flatteringly and unflatteringly, with its allies (at least the empire and the other 'great' powers, France and the USA). For instance, the experiences of French civilians were heralded as examples to their British counterparts: despite the privations and dangers of invasion, French civilians continued to work hard, close to the battle zone, and were lauded for their unsurpassed patriotism. Similarly, the American labour leader, Samuel Gompers, was praised for his uncompromising views on the wartime responsibilities of labour. Implicitly, British labour might achieve influence similar to that which Gompers had with Wilson, were it similarly to renounce wartime strikes and work delays. Here difference was used positively to encourage British emulation of foreign virtues and inspire competitive patriotism. It also worked inversely, identifying

---

20 E.g. Marjorie Morgan, *National Identities and Travel in Victorian Britain* (Basingstoke: Palgrave, 2001), esp. pp. 83–118; Pille Petersoo, 'Reconsidering Otherness: Constructing Estonian Identity', *Nations and Nationalism*, 13:1 (2007).

21 Hall, *Civilising Subjects*, p. 9.

virtues allegedly possessed by Britons but not by their allies, like modesty (if not awareness of irony). Alternatively, supranational patriotism could involve locating common virtues and qualities shared by the Allies (especially the 'great' powers), which confirmed the superiority of their cause and their nations. It was from such conceits that much of the enthusiastic propagandising for a League of Nations emerged.

This final aspect of supranational patriotism was linked extremely closely to the third contextual sub-patriotism, designated *proprietorial patriotism*. This sub-patriotism identified several key values – liberty, democracy, justice, honour (in short, the principles of 'civilisation', often combined with Christianity) – which were defended by Britain and its Allies from adversaries, foreign and domestic. Patriotic pride also necessitated that, while acknowledging shared Allied interest in protecting these values, Britain should be identified as either particularly responsible for their inception (as frequently suggested in discussing liberty or democracy) or particularly suffused with them. Honour was especially heralded as peculiarly British – only Britain went to war in 1914 without an ostensible direct threat to its possessions – and propagandists often spent considerable time discussing the causes of the war and Britain's involvement in it.

In providing these key values, proprietorial patriotism not only created criteria against which to judge adversaries and comrades, it also formed the vital bridge between these comparative contextual forms and those sub-patriotisms comprising the core message of duty, particularly two mutually dependent presentational forms: *civic patriotism* and the idea that the war had established a *concrescent community*, that is a community 'growing together' through the shared experiences of the war. These were essentially alternate but reinforcing interpretations of the relationship between individuals and their wider communities. Civic patriotism was the harsher, more demanding side of this relationship, stressing that since individuals were part of a national community which provided cherished rights and values, they must be prepared to do their full patriotic duty when required. In this interpretation, civic patriotism means a sense of the inherent national duties of citizenship, rather than an alternate (and equally valid) sense of municipal identity.[22]

Complementary to this harsh interpretation of the individual–community relationship was the gentler, more encouraging idea that the war had engendered a concrescent community (or communities) of patriotic individuals. This concept held that civilians had largely done their patriotic duty during the war, and insisted that all benefited from this positive acceptance of civic responsibility by their communities growing closer together. This was applied in various ways. Links were

---

22 On which, see, e.g., Matthew Vickers, 'Civic Image and Civic Patriotism in Liverpool, 1880–1914' (DPhil dissertation, University of Oxford, 2000).

frequently drawn between the home- and battlefronts, stressing the equal significance of patriotic duties undertaken by servicemen and civilians. These ideas reinforced local pride. Speakers often tailored speeches to include references to the deeds of a local regiment, encouraging civilians to take pride in its achievements (while the civic side exhorted them to maintain their efforts in order not to let down their fighting brethren), and also sometimes compared the efforts of a particular locality favourably with others. However, praising community efforts also bolstered links between locality and nation – speakers in isolated areas emphasised the links between local experience and the national war effort.[23] More broadly (particularly in published propaganda, addressing a national rather than local audience) such ideas could also combine with elements of supranational patriotism to celebrate the closer ties between Britain and its empire, and between allied nations. Concrescent community rhetoric was essential to NWAC propaganda, providing a determinedly positive interpretation of civilian experience; while other sub-patriotisms included celebratory elements, this concept was the only presentational sub-patriotism solely concerned with praise and celebration.

Linked closely to civic patriotism was the third element of the core duty message, which extended civic patriotism by explicating a specific requirement. This may be called *sacrificial patriotism*. The main purpose of this sub-patriotism was to demand self-sacrifice from civilians as part of their patriotic duty; a willing acceptance of certain sacrifices – food and fuel restrictions, longer working hours – for the good of the community. It conformed strongly with the extensive languages of sacrifice used in Britain and elsewhere throughout the war, including the idea of *l'impôt du sang* (the 'blood tax') highlighted by John Horne for France and Adrian Gregory for Britain.[24] Servicemen and children were particularly used to convince civilians to accept these sacrifices. Many servicemen had made the 'ultimate sacrifice' of death for their country, and those still serving made considerably more daily sacrifices than civilians. Therefore, NWAC propagandists argued, nothing was more unpatriotic than civilians refusing to bear their immeasurably lighter sacrifices. An element of this sacrificial rhetoric was also evident in supranational patriotic discussion of French civilians' harder lives. Sacrificial rhetoric related to children, meanwhile, stressed the necessity to accept further sacrifices so that future generations could continue to live the British way of life. In the brooding menace of various adversaries, propagandists possessed an implicit or explicit image of the consequences of a lack of such patriotic self-sacrifice.

---

23 On the continuing importance of locality in Britain, see chapter 3.

24 John Horne, '"*L'impôt du sang*": Republican Rhetoric and Industrial Warfare in France, 1914–18', *Social History*, 14:2 (1989); Gregory, *Last Great War*, esp. chapter 4.

This emphasis of the need to sacrifice for future generations fed into another contextual sub-patriotism best described as *aspirational patriotism*. This informed civilians of both the material and civilisational benefits to be gained through the fulfilment of patriotic duty. Building on rhetoric celebrating the more cooperative spirit between employers and employed, governors and governed, aspirational patriotism stressed the societal advances already achieved and dwelt upon the need for a 'land fit for heroes' and the likely further benefits accompanying victory (provided Britain retained the unity developed since 1914). Aspirational patriotism also offered a civilisational/ideological aspiration of a 'world without war' where militarism was eradicated and which the League of Nations would preserve. The alternative to the fulfilment of these aspirations, implicitly or explicitly, was a society at the mercy of Britain's adversaries and, by inference, those of civilisation.

To a greater or lesser extent, all of these elements were also contextualised by religious rhetoric that constituted a *spiritual patriotism*. In some instances propaganda included prolonged reflection on the religious meaning of the war, but spiritual patriotism more usually refined and enhanced other sub-patriotisms, creating an interesting mix of religious and secular rhetoric in NWAC propaganda. Hence the values and ideals enshrined by proprietorial patriotism were commonly labelled 'Christian' values of civilisation (shared by Britain's major allies), enabling claims that Britain was fighting a 'holy war' (Britain's enemies, of course, assumed that they, too, were fighting such a war).[25] This, in turn, consecrated the sacrifices made by servicemen on behalf of the nation, and placed the actions of adversaries outside 'Christian' morality, while working for the happiness of future Britons could also be characterised as a religious duty. Anthony D. Smith stresses the idea of a nation as a 'sacred communion', by which he means 'an imagined community of the faithful that unites the dead, the living, and the yet unborn along an upward linear trajectory, but one that lives not just in the imagination ... but equally in the conscious will and mass sentiments.'[26] Furthermore, there was a strong millenarian undertone in much NWAC propaganda. This could be used secularly (especially influencing the concrescent community idea) by speakers claiming that the war had purged Britain of malignant pre-war characteristics like political factionalism. It was also used, however, in a more specifically religious sense, as some clergymen at NWAC events celebrated religion's wartime renaissance in Britain.

25 On the two-sided nature of these claims, see Hoover, *God, Germany, and Britain*; Audoin-Rouzeau and Becker, *1914–1918*, p. 116 and ff.; Alan Kramer, *Dynamic of Destruction: Culture and Mass Killing in the First World War* (Oxford: Oxford University Press, 2007), pp. 175–80.
26 Anthony D. Smith, 'The "Sacred" Dimension of Nationalism', *Millennium – Journal of International Studies*, 29:3, (2000), pp. 802–03.

It is worth dwelling a little further on the spiritual element in NWAC propaganda, not least because some of the interpretation applied across Part 2 is open to terminological challenge. Smith argues that, while 'religion is vital to both the origins and the continuing appeal of both nations and nationalism in the modern world', and although 'nationalism often has a special role for the messianic hero and heroine, and for the idea of a messianic age', it is nonetheless inappropriate to ascribe millen-arian (millennial) impulses to national identity. Smith argues that while 'millennialism' 'wishes to flee a corrupt world' and 'expects imminent supernatural intervention to abolish the existing order', 'nationalism seeks to reform the world in its own image' and 'preach[es] the necessity of human autoemancipation to realize the true spirit and destiny of the nation'. For him, millenarianism and nationalism seek different results. Further,

> The drama of the nation has three climactic moments ... its golden age, its ultimate national destiny, and the sacrifice of its members. But, since the ultimate destiny of the nation can never be known ... all we can be sure of is that it will come about only through the commitment and self-sacrifice of its members, and that is what the nation must continually uphold, remember, and celebrate.[27]

For Smith, although the 'cult of sacrifice' is 'closely linked to the ideal of national regeneration and revival',[28] sacrifice is not tied to millenarian predictions of a future 'golden age', but is the means by which 'ultimate national destiny' may be achieved. Nonetheless, as will be illustrated in subsequent chapters, NWAC propaganda seemed to claim more than that sacrifice was an 'autoemancipatory' contribution to national destiny. Some propagandists directly suggested a return to a more harmonious and cooperative society in language definitely tinged with millenarianism, broadly defined. This does not mean that frequent allusions were made to Christ's second coming, inaugurating a 'thousand-year age of blessed-ness'. Rather there was a more generalised 'belief in a future golden age of peace, justice, and prosperity',[29] what Malcolm B. Hamilton describes as 'a collective ... form of salvation to be experienced and enjoyed by a whole community or the larger part of it', sometimes infused with overtly Christian language. Hamilton maintains that millenarianism 'runs as a current through society, greatly varying in intensity over time, attracting varying numbers of followers ... with varying degrees of influence in their lives and in society generally'.[30] Conceivably, NWAC 'millenarianism'

---

27 Anthony D. Smith, *Chosen Peoples* (Oxford: Oxford University Press, 2003), pp. 15, 218.
28 Smith, *Cultural Foundations*, p. 45.
29 'Millenarianism, *n.*', *Oxford English Dictionary*, http://dictionary.oed.com, accessed 26/7/07.
30 Malcolm B. Hamilton, 'Sociological Dimensions of Christian Millenarianism', in

constituted another 'bold appropriation of the language of popular protest', like the conversion of 'jubilee' – an Old Testament term referring to land redistribution after fifty years to restrict long-term wealth – into a term for state ceremonial, most likely seeking to maintain social cohesion, though it certainly contained a greater element of religiosity than the distinctly secular forms of millenarianism traced by Alan Kramer in relation to expectations in Bolshevik Russia and Italy.[31]

The application of spiritual patriotism to the other sub-patriotisms is highlighted in subsequent chapters. However, one broader application of spiritual patriotism may be profitably addressed here. NWAC propaganda used religious or quasi-religious imagery to provide reassurance that Britain was fighting a holy war, for Christian principles, to achieve a millenarian regeneration of church and society. Such rhetoric was assisted by the frequent presence and involvement of clergymen in NWAC propaganda: as writers, speakers, chairmen or members of the platform party, clerical association with propaganda assisted the infusion of religious language into NWAC rhetoric.

This idea of a holy war was most conveniently exemplified for NWAC propagandists by the campaign in Palestine. In December 1917 the capture of Jerusalem by troops commanded by Sir Edmund Allenby provided the ultimate representation of Britain's holy war. *Reality* quoted the *Daily Express*'s opinion that Muslims would 'welcome General Allenby into the Sacred City with the same fervour as the Christian and the Jew' since the Turks had mistreated everyone, whereas Allenby had walked into the city 'in all appropriate simplicity, bringing peace for all creeds and justice for all races'.[32] The next edition reproduced a *Punch* cartoon showing Richard the Lionheart surveying Jerusalem, with rays of light shining on the city, soon followed by a Spanish cartoon showing Christians bowed down in prayer above the city (figures 16–17). The juxtaposition in the latter cartoon (particularly useful since it came from a neutral state) of modern-day British soldiers marching past seemingly anachronistic pilgrims suggested Britain's capture of Jerusalem was the outcome of a timeless (international) Christian struggle, complementing Bernard Partridge's image of *English* Christian chivalric adventure, consecrating the war through the recapture of the 'Holy City'.[33] With the successful conclusion of the Palestine campaign in October 1918, the Liberal E.W. Record (assistant

---

Stephen Hunt (ed.), *Christian Millenarianism: From the Early Church to Waco* (London: Hurst & Company, 2001), pp. 13, 25.

31 Wolffe, *God and Greater Britain*, p. 156; Kramer, *Dynamic of Destruction*, esp. pp. 294–97. Kramer's version seems closer to what is termed 'aspirational patriotism' here, though this could, of course, relate closely to millenarian rhetoric, as chapter 8 discusses.

32 'Freedom for Palestine', *Reality*, 101, 19/12/17, p. 4.

33 See Allen J. Frantzen, *Bloody Good: Chivalry, Sacrifice, and the Great War* (Chicago and London: University of Chicago Press, 2004), pp. 76–77.

THE LAST CRUSADE.
CŒUR-DE-LION (looking down on the Holy City): "My Dream Comes True!"

*Figure 16. Bernard Partridge, 'The Last Crusade' (reproduced from Punch),
Reality, no. 102, 26/12/17, p. 1*

editor of the NWAC's Publications Department) labelled Richard and
Allenby 'Crusaders Old and New' in his weekly column for local newspapers, urging readers to 'keep [Richard's] uplifted sword ever in mind
until the greatest of all crusades is finally and completely accomplished
and the real Armageddon [rather than Allenby's victory at Megiddo,
the modern site of the biblical Armageddon], the last of battles, fought
and won'.[34] Record's reference to Armageddon implied Allied religious
superiority, suggesting that the Allies were on God's side, fighting Satan's
representatives on earth. In a society in which religious belief continued

---

34 'A Letter from London. By "Thought-Reader" [Record]', *North Devon Herald*,
3/10/18, p. 3. For a recent interpretation suggesting the limited influence of
crusading ideas on the men serving in Palestine, see James E. Kitchen, '"Khaki
Crusaders": Crusading Rhetoric and the British Imperial Soldier during the Egypt
and Palestine Campaigns, 1916–1918', *First World War Studies*, 1:2 (2010).

WHAT SPAIN THINKS OF PALESTINE'S LIBERATION

Figure 17. 'What Spain Thinks of Palestine's Liberation' (reproduced from El Imparcial), Reality, no. 104, 10/1/18, p. 4

to exercise a strong influence, spiritual patriotism could potentially offer an emphatic validation of Britain's war effort, notwithstanding the fact that God was claimed equally by both sides.[35]

WERE there a master narrative of NWAC propaganda, it might be structured like the framework sketched above. Adversarial patriotism would provide one or more adversaries, which threatened the key values of civilisation (particularly important to Britain) represented by proprietorial patriotism. These in turn were defended by nations which shared these values (supranational patriotism). Having identified the key values, and the threat to them, the master narrative might then celebrate civilians' patriotic contributions and increasing unity (concrescent community) and exhort them to continue in their duty (civic patriotism). This exhortation could be augmented by comparing servicemen's sacrifices with those of civilians (sacrificial patriotism) and emphasising Britain's involvement in a 'holy war' (spiritual patriotism), before concluding by summarising those aspirations already met and

---

35 Hoover, *God, Germany, and Britain.*

others for which the war had to continue. However, this was not the case. The model outlined above is a composite image emerging from extensive examination of NWAC propaganda, including meetings held across thirty constituencies. It is extremely unlikely that any contemporary civilian would have been exposed to NWAC propaganda to the same extent. Typically, a piece of NWAC propaganda utilised perhaps two, three or four of these sub-patriotisms. For instance, an article discussing the League of Nations might address supranational, proprietorial, civic and aspirational patriotism, and a standard critique of German atrocities might range across adversarial, proprietorial and civic patriotism. Though some pieces, particularly those presented as 'straight' news might stick to one issue, the usual minimum in any NWAC piece would be a contextual and a core sub-patriotism, even if the core message amounted to only a sentence or two after a long contextual illustration, to emphasise the need for continuing patriotic duty.

Nevertheless, some examples of NWAC propaganda touched upon many of the presentational patriotisms. Probably the best example is the South African War Cabinet member General J.C. Smuts's speech in Tonypandy, in October 1917:

> After three years of the most agonising suffering the heart of dear little Wales beat true, the hammer strokes of fate had not crushed them, but only improved their mettle. (Applause) [significant instances of each sub-patriotism noted: *concrescent community*] ... It had been a war not of armies, but ... of peoples, of nations, of systems and ideals, a war of ultimate principles, and a war of the souls of the people ... [*proprietorial*] the true battlefield was in the souls of the nations. (Applause) ... [*spiritual*]
>
> What was the basis of the British Empire? It was liberty, constitutional government, and freedom (Hear, hear). The real principle on which they existed was that principle of liberty and self-government which had been conceded to almost every part of the British Empire [*proprietorial*] ... [or] would be conceded more and more in the future ... They did not want to be slaves and dictated to by others. They wanted to manage their own affairs, they wanted security, freedom, and self-government in their industrial life in Wales, and he said that those principles, on which the British Empire existed, were principles of universal application [*aspirational, proprietorial, supranational*] ...
>
> In Germany they had no self-government and no liberty ... The whole idea of the German system was devoted to develop power and to making the human individual serve the ends of the State [*adversarial*] ... It was a moral war and a spiritual war. They saw to-day the agonies of a dying world ...
>
> That was God's Providence, and, perhaps, it was better so [*spiritual*], but he asked ... Was the new order going to rise on the principles of liberty and freedom ... or was the foundation going to be laid by this principle of force, of power, and of the will to power for which Germany stood? ... [*proprietorial, adversarial*]
>
> We would not ... allow the young manhood of the nations to be sacrificed to the Moloch of war ... we wanted all our energy and power devoted to exploiting our economic resources, to improving the internal

conditions of the people, and as long as they had militarism and standing armies so long would poor, suffering mankind never see any chance at all. If they wanted a better England and Wales, and a better Tonypandy, they must have victory first. (Applause) [*sacrificial, aspirational, civic*].

... he did not think it necessary to make an appeal to them, but they could leave a record behind for their children which would ... make them remember their fathers with gratitude for answering the call of duty [*aspirational, civic*]. As they had faced their responsibilities in the past, so he knew they, and all the peoples of the British Empire, would continue to respond to the very end, and contribute their all, consider their lives cheap, their efforts cheap ... so long as they knew there would be a chance to live a free and righteous life for the generations to come. [*concrescent community, sacrificial*] (Loud applause).

The NWAC reprinted a considerably longer version of this speech as a pamphlet, which suggests it was representative of their message.[36] The speech demonstrates many of the techniques discussed above, and the fluidity with which the presentational forms could be employed, some (particularly proprietorial and aspirational patriotism) recurring throughout, blending easily with others.

AS already suggested, the interaction of the various elements of NWAC propaganda's patriotic narrative was assisted by the fact that they redeployed existing patriotic rhetoric in a format targeted at a wartime audience. Some evidence of antecedents of the individual patriotic categories outlined above can also be found in pre-war examples, though far more detailed examination of earlier periods would be necessary before it would be possible to suggest that the whole narrative could be replicated elsewhere.

Adversarial patriotism may readily be found in earlier periods. British Napoleonic-era propagandists sought to convince audiences that the French adversary – an 'other' in Stella Cottrell's view, as in Colley's – threatened Britain both materially and ideologically.[37] Cottrell does not demonstrate, however, that British ideals were 'defined' against those of France, but rather tends to show that the French adversary's failings made it a threat to Britain. British values were already in place and remained the same as before. They were threatened and challenged by French aggression, rather than being defined in opposition to the French. It was not the existence of a 'different' France per se, but the assumption that it posed a threat which encouraged civilians to volunteer.

---

36 'General Smuts at Tonypandy', *Mid-Rhondda Gazette*, 3/11/17, p. 1. The pamphlet was *General Smuts's Message to South Wales: Speech Delivered at Tonypandy, Rhondda, On October 29, 1917* (n.p.d.: part of a collection of NWAC pamphlets in National Archives Library).

37 Stella Cottrell, 'The Devil on Two Sticks: Franco-phobia in 1803', in Samuel, *Patriotism*, I, pp. 261–69.

Germany was increasingly identified as a serious threat to Britain in the later nineteenth and early twentieth centuries, as an economic, imperial and military rival.[38] However, such views had earlier precedents. For instance, in the 1870s and 1880s Queen Victoria, because of her familial links, was accused by some radicals of interfering with British policy on Germany's behalf.[39] Germany may have seemed more distant in earlier decades, but was still a possible adversary.

Nineteenth-century anti-Russian sentiments differed somewhat from those of NWAC propagandists, whose criticism concentrated on the Bolsheviks they believed had corrupted Russian democracy and betrayed the allies. In the 1870s and 1880s, anti-Russianism was seemingly based on a perception of Russia's serious strategic threat to Britain (its eastern imperial rival). Adversarial threats could apparently supersede moral (or civilisational) outrage, as in the 1890s when potential disruption of the European balance of power seemed worse than Ottoman transgressions in its treatment of Armenians.[40] By contrast, pogroms against Jews enabled Russia (already a strategic as well as moral threat) to be condemned 'in the name of Christianity, humanity and England', the latter based on England's 'particular and close relationship with liberty'.[41] Here, as in 1917–18, atrocity stories served particular purposes.

Precursors of the NWAC's patriotic critique of internal adversaries are evident, among other examples, in earlier (socialist and non-socialist) criticisms of 'socialism'. In presenting the Labour Party and ILP as 'British', for example, Ramsay MacDonald simultaneously labelled groups representing other, competing forms of socialism as 'un-British'.[42] In all the examples above, as in 1917–18, it was not simply difference, but the apparent threat to Britain or Britishness which provoked feelings of adversarial patriotism.

Supranational tendencies in British discourse are discernible in several elements of pre-war patriotism enunciated across the political spectrum. The close affinity with the Dominions expressed in NWAC propaganda is redolent of the attitudes of Liberal Imperialists like Rosebery, Asquith, Grey and Haldane, as well as the pro-tariff reform inclinations

---

38 Paul M. Kennedy, *The Rise of the Anglo–German Antagonism, 1860–1914* (London: George Allen & Unwin, 1980). On growing anxieties, see also John Ramsden, *Don't Mention the War: The British and the Germans since 1890* (London: Little Brown, 2006), chapter 2.

39 Richard Williams, *The Contentious Crown: Public Discussion of the British Monarchy in the Reign of Queen Victoria* (Aldershot: Ashgate, 1997), p. 167.

40 Peter Marsh, 'Lord Salisbury and the Ottoman Massacres', *Journal of British Studies*, 11:2 (1972); Roy Douglas, 'Britain and the Armenian Question, 1894–7', *Historical Journal*, 19:1 (1976).

41 David Feldman, *Englishmen and Jews: Social Relations and Political Culture, 1840–1914* (New Haven: Yale University Press, 1994), pp. 128–35.

42 Paul Ward, 'Socialists and "True" Patriotism in Britain in the Late 19th and Early 20th Centuries', *National Identities*, 1:2 (1999), p. 184.

of important figures like Joseph Chamberlain or Alfred Milner, who argued that 'over and above [a Briton's] local and racial patriotism, he will recognise that his highest allegiance is to the Empire as a whole'.[43] Chamberlain was similarly prominent in the Anglo–US 'rapprochement' of the 1890s. Reconciliation depended substantially on assumptions of common Anglo-Saxonism, according to Stuart Anderson.[44] This Anglo-Saxonism combined evolutionary theory with the recently established 'Teutonic origins' theory in Anglo–US historiography, which claimed that Britain's (and, therefore, the US's) democratic instincts were forged in ancient Germany and transferred to Britain by Teutonic invaders after the fifth century. This common 'ancestry' supposedly linked the nations in 'a kind of larger patriotism of race'.[45] Further, American imperialism offered the comforting impression of validating Britain's own imperial activities.[46] Anderson suggests that Anglo-Saxonism helped to create assumptions on both sides of the Atlantic that Britain and the US were 'natural allies with a common civilising mission'.[47] Such ideas attracted considerable influential endorsement at the beginning of the twentieth century, including Chamberlain, Rosebery and Arthur Balfour in Britain, and Theodore Roosevelt and Woodrow Wilson in the US, and were reignited after the US declaration of war in 1917.

Both Liberals and socialists in the nineteenth and early twentieth centuries saw 'no contradiction between patriotism and internationalism'; mid-nineteenth-century Liberals assumed British and world interests were the same, namely the 'spread of liberal constitutionalism and free trade', while a little later the ILP 'saw internationalism as a plurality of patriotisms', celebrating internationalism via May Day celebrations imbued with British (or more precisely, English) symbolism.[48] The British approach to foreign nations before 1914 was selective. France under Napoleon III only became an acceptable partner after Napoleon embraced free trade in the 1860 Anglo–French Commercial Treaty, suggesting willingness to accept 'English tutelage'.[49] Similar impulses influenced Lloyd George's 'imitation and rivalry' of German social administration, selecting the

---

43 H.C.G. Matthew, *The Liberal Imperialists: The Ideas and Politics of a Post-Gladstonian Élite* (Oxford: Oxford University Press, 1973), pp. 152–62; Milner, *Nation and Empire*, p. 489.

44 Stuart Anderson, *Race and Rapprochement: Anglo-Saxonism and Anglo–American Relations, 1895–1904* (London: Associated University Presses, 1981), p. 117.

45 Anderson, *Race*, pp. 12, 28–45.

46 Bradford Perkins, *The Great Rapprochement: England and the United States, 1895–1914* (London: Victor Gollancz, 1969), p. 67.

47 Anderson, *Race*, p. 152.

48 Parry, *Politics*, p. 388; Ward, *Red Flag*, p. 114.

49 Parry, *Politics*, pp. 225, 235–36; J.P. Parry, 'The Impact of Napoleon III on British Politics, 1851–1880, *Transactions of the Royal Historical Society*, 6th series, 11 (2001); Robert and Isabelle Tombs, *That Sweet Enemy: The French and the British from the Sun King to the Present* (London: William Heinemann, 2006), pp. 256–65.

admirable organisational elements without the militaristic and compulsive tenets which might offend liberty-loving Britons, while other social
reformers sought inspiration from Britain's white Dominions, especially
Australia and New Zealand.[50]

Peter Mandler has recently discussed the 'civilisational perspective'
which informed English national character during the nineteenth century.
Initially a counterblast to revolutionary French 'democracy', 'civilisation' emphasised 'loyalty to institutions rather than group identification
around a common culture', and for a long time 'portray[ed] an English
way of doing business rather than an English nation or people'.[51] J.P.
Parry has similarly stressed mid-nineteenth-century Liberal emphasis on
'civilisation', together with a constitutional stress on parliament's role in
establishing British freedom and self-government, a democratic tradition
assumed to derive from Anglo-Saxon society, and to have been progressively reclaimed since the Norman Conquest.[52] Proprietorial patriotism
is evident in this understanding of Britishness (and Englishness), and
supranational patriotism followed closely.

Matthew Vickers imbues the term 'civic patriotism' with a narrower,
municipal (though equally valid) sense to that used here. Nevertheless,
he demonstrates a similarly exhortative patriotism in Liverpool between
1880 and 1914, where Liverpool's image revolved around commerce,
its port encouraging residents to consider themselves members of the
'Second City of the Empire', thus enabling local pride to rest on national/
imperial prestige. For Vickers, 'emphasis on the individual's relationship
with the community ... [resolved] the tension between personal freedom
and communal efficiency'. Individuals who 'damaged the city's reputation
could be accused of lacking civic patriotism and adjudged unworthy of
the status and privileges of citizenship'.[53] Around 1900, civic patriotism
is also discernible in responses to the poor physical condition of army
recruits, which provoked increasing state and voluntary intervention in
motherhood, cast as a national duty.[54] Similar concerns influenced calls
for 'citizen training' in organisations like the Scouts, to complement skills
developed at school, home and church.[55]

---

50 E.P. Hennock, *British Social Reform and German Precedents: The Case of Social
    Insurance, 1880–1914* (Oxford: Clarendon Press, 1987), pp. 170–72, 177–
    79; Antoinette Burton, 'New Narratives of Imperial Politics in the Nineteenth
    Century', in Catherine Hall and Sonya O. Rose (eds), *At Home with the Empire:
    Metropolitan Culture and the Imperial World* (Cambridge: Cambridge University
    Press, 2006), pp. 220–27.
51 Mandler, *National Character*, pp. 28–33, 38.
52 Parry, *Politics*, pp. 43–45; Hill, 'Norman Yoke'.
53 Vickers, 'Civic Image and Civic Patriotism', pp. 7, 45, 161.
54 Anna Davin, 'Imperialism and Motherhood', *History Workshop Journal*, 5 (1978).
55 Allen Warren, 'Sir Robert Baden-Powell, the Scout Movement and Citizen Training
    in Great Britain, 1900–1920', *English Historical Review*, 101:399 (1986). Cf. the
    criticisms of John Springhall and Anne Summers in vol. 102 (1987).

It is now a historiographical commonplace that nations are 'imagined communities' of 'deep horizontal comradeship'.[56] In late nineteenth-century Britain, perhaps the most potent community 'imaginations' belonged to Idealists:

> Defining the state as a moral entity and ... casting citizenship as a moral endeavour ... diminished the legalistic, retributive character of the state. Instead they emphasised its positive face, while ... reminding their audience of the duties of moral citizenship.[57]

In this approach to community, outlined by Sandra den Otter, can be seen something akin to interactions between civic patriotism and the concrescent community idea. The NWAC's relationship to idealist thought is seemingly confirmed by the involvement as a speaker of Sir Henry Jones, author of *Idealism as a Practical Creed* (1909), who believed 'rights ought to be considered essential to a liberal society, but only if they coincided with the duty to serve the wider good of society'.[58] This approach extended earlier interpretations of society and community. José Harris contends there was effective 'indifference to notions of community' until around 1870. Thereafter, however, 'there was a shift from viewing society as an aggregation of private individuals to a vision of society as collective, public, evolutionary, and organic'.[59] Whether or not they used the term 'community', however, many people contemplated it throughout the nineteenth century. This is especially evident in interactions between local and national identity, which have recently been the subject of an appeal for greater historical attention.[60] Tom Paine found to his cost that ordinary British radicals in the 1790s would not accept criticism of their local attachments, or denial of the possible evolution of ideas 'from the cottage to the region, the nation and beyond'.[61] While post-1830 reforms derogated some local control over daily life, residence in towns and villages continued to create an 'immediate sense of belonging', public life which

---

56 Anderson, *Imagined Communities*, p. 7.

57 Sandra den Otter, '"Thinking in Communities": Late Nineteenth-Century Liberals, Idealists, and the Retrieval of Community', in E.H.H. Green (ed.), *An Age of Transition: British Politics 1880–1914* (Edinburgh: Edinburgh University Press, 1997), p. 79. See also, idem, *British Idealism and Social Explanation: A Study in Late Victorian Thought* (Oxford: Clarendon Press, 1996), pp. 149–204.

58 Den Otter, 'Thinking in Communities', pp. 71–72. Jones spoke at NWAC events on at least 22 days according to the Meetings Register database. On his propaganda links, see also PA, Lloyd George Papers, LG/F/79/32.

59 José Harris, 'English Ideas about Community: Another Case of "Made in Germany"?', in Rudolf Muhs, Johannes Paulman and Willibald Steinmetz (eds), *Aneignung und Abwehr: Interkultureller Transfer zwischen Deutschland und Großbritannien im 19. Jahrhundert* (Bodenheim: Philo, 1998), p. 148; Harris, *Private Lives*, p. 37.

60 Readman, 'Place of the Past', pp. 176–79.

61 Ian Dyck, 'Local Attachments, National Identities and World Citizenship in the Thought of Thomas Paine', *History Workshop Journal*, 35 (1993), pp. 121–26.

'gave substance to parochial and civic identities'.[62] Furthermore, despite increasingly centralised government, locality still remained critical in mid- to late nineteenth-century Britain, allaying public scepticism based on the 'legacy of Old Corruption … [an] abiding mistrust of the centre' and implying '*popular* sovereignty and control'.[63] By 1900, national identities were increasingly sought in smaller communities and localities, whether by resurrecting local dialects,[64] pageantry[65] or identifying local quintessences of the nation.[66]

In NWAC propaganda, 'sacrifice' was frequently used to describe servicemen's actions, including the 'ultimate sacrifice' of martial death. Such sacrificial rhetoric was common to Britain, particularly in imperial contexts in the later nineteenth and early twentieth centuries, where sacrifice, heroism and (sometimes) chivalry were conflated to demonstrate patriotic values. Max Jones's description of the 'language of sacrifice' used to 'ascribe meaning' to the doomed 1911–12 Antarctic expedition resonates elsewhere. The explorers' deaths 'were redeemed by their contribution to a higher cause', varying to reflect different sets of values, according to inclination. Narratives of the expedition became 'sites for the negotiation of collective identities', from familial to national level, rather than 'instruments of social control'.[67] While imperial 'heroes' like Scott, Henry Havelock and Horatio Nelson represented self-sacrificial embodiments of national prowess, throughout the nineteenth and early twentieth centuries,[68] expanding nineteenth-century concerns with

---

62 David Eastwood, *Government and Community in the English Provinces, 1700–1870* (Basingstoke: MacMillan, 1997), *passim* (p. 91).

63 Philip Harling, 'The Powers of the Victorian State', and J.P. Parry, 'Liberalism and Liberty', both in Peter Mandler (ed.), *Liberty and Authority in Victorian Britain* (Oxford: Oxford University Press, 2006), pp. 46, 86. For examples of the continuing significance of local affinities in later periods, see also K.D.M. Snell, *Parish and Belonging: Community, Identity and Welfare in England and Wales, 1700–1950* (Cambridge: Cambridge University Press, 2006).

64 E.g., Patrick Joyce, *Visions of the People: Industrial England and the Question of Class, 1848–1914* (Cambridge: Cambridge University Press, 1993), esp. pp. 279–304; Philip Howell, 'Industry and Identity: The North–South Divide and the Geography of Belonging, 1830–1918', in Alan R.H. Baker and Mark Billinge (eds), *Geographies of England: The North–South Divide, Material and Imagined* (Cambridge: Cambridge University Press, 2004), pp. 64–87, esp. pp. 82–87.

65 E.g. Vickers, 'Civic Image and Civic Patriotism', pp. 43–75; Readman, 'Place of the Past'.

66 E.g. James Vernon, 'Border Crossings: Cornwall and the English (Imagi)Nation', in Geoffrey Cubitt (ed.), *Imagining Nations* (Manchester: Manchester University Press, 1998); Catherine Brace, 'Finding England Everywhere: Regional Identity and the Construction of National Identity, 1890–1940', *Ecumene*, 6:1 (1999).

67 Max Jones, '"Our King upon his knees": The Public Commemoration of Captain Scott's Last Antarctic Expedition', in Geoffrey Cubitt and Allen Warren (eds), *Heroic Reputations and Exemplary Lives* (Manchester: Manchester University Press, 2000), p. 115; idem, *The Last Great Quest: Captain Scott's Antarctic Sacrifice* (Oxford: Oxford University Press, 2003), pp. 235–36.

68 E.g. John M. Mackenzie, 'Heroic Myths of Empire', in idem (ed.), *Popular*

chivalry and selflessness also associated sacrifice with everyday activities. Both Mark Girouard and Allen Frantzen note the importance of 'muscular Christianity' in further developing chivalry's public significance, imbuing it with the moral purity, self-restraint and self-reliance which permeated works like Samuel Smiles's influential *Self-Help* (1859).[69] Self-sacrifice became both exemplary and mundane.

Sacrificial language was closely linked with religion. John Wolffe demonstrates that, both nationally and locally, the Church's appropriation of sacrificial heroes blended 'a Christian concept of martyrdom' with 'the cause of the nation and the Empire'.[70] According to Jay Winter, increasing wartime interest in spiritualism marked a '[c]ontinuity, not transformation' of existing religious and spiritual attitudes.[71] In broader terms, too, such continuities are evident, and historians have suggested the close bonds between religion and national identity in Britain, which seem to amply demonstrate the long heritage of spiritual patriotism. Colley contends that despite 'other powerful identities', Britain's predominant Protestantism constituted the 'foundation' of British identity in the eighteenth and early nineteenth centuries.[72] Wolffe convincingly argues that, rather than becoming 'secularised' before 1914, Britain saw 'changes in the ways of being religious', with ideas of Christianity, nationality and imperialism interacting in a patriotism with 'absolute spiritual claims which led it to the threshold of ... [equating] the cause of Britain with the cause of God'.[73]

Aspirational patriotism is also discernible in several pre-war contexts. The emergence of 'new Liberal' concerns with social reform reflected interest in a collectivism aiming at 'social harmony which entailed self-sacrifice and altruism'.[74] This collectivism had 'deep roots ... in pressures

---

Imperialism and the Military, 1850–1950 (Manchester: Manchester University Press, 1992); Graham Dawson, *Soldier Heroes: British Adventure, Empire and the Imagining of Masculinities* (London: Routledge, 1994); Cynthia Fansler Behrman, *Victorian Myths of the Sea* (Athens, OH: University of Ohio Press, 1977), pp. 96–98.

69 Mark Girouard, *The Return to Camelot: Chivalry and the English Gentleman* (London: Yale University Press, 1981), pp. 141–4; Frantzen, *Bloody Good*, pp. 137–44; also Olive Anderson, 'The Growth of Christian Militarism in Mid-Victorian Britain', *English Historical Review*, 86:338 (1971).

70 John Wolffe, *Great Deaths: Grieving, Religion and Nationhood in Victorian and Edwardian Britain* (Oxford: Oxford University Press, 2000), pp. 150–52.

71 Jay Winter, 'Spiritualism and the First World War', in R.W. Davis and R.J. Helmstadter (eds), *Religion and Irreligion in Victorian Society: Essays in Honor of R.K. Webb* (London: Routledge, 1992), p. 185.

72 Colley, *Britons*, pp. 53–54. Cf. J.C.D. Clark's argument that 'Protestantism alone was not enough' to forge Britishness: 'Protestantism, Nationalism and National Identity, 1660–1832', *Historical Journal*, 43:1 (2000), p. 274.

73 Wolffe, *God and Greater Britain*, pp. 256–60.

74 Michael Freeden, *The New Liberalism: An Ideology of Social Reform* (Oxford: Clarendon Press, 1978), p. 93.

from below' according to Stuart Hall and Bill Schwarz, and though new
Liberal social reform partly represented a 'politics of containment' in
David Sutton's view,[75] it was presented in patriotic terms to the public as
'a high type of national life' providing those previously excluded with 'a
new and vast stake in the country'.[76]

F.M.L. Thompson's discussion of the limits of 'social control' is a
salutary caution (useful for historians of propaganda) that changing
working-class values between 1800 and 1900 did not simply reflect
'"middle-class values" ... imposed on the workers; they were also
"working-class values" developed through selection and adaptation to
the changing environment'. Thompson's argument that 'the working
class was eminently capable of generating its own cultural evolution and
development in response to [its varied] aspirations and needs'[77] is equally
applicable to NWAC propaganda. Propagandists did not address civilian
aspirations out of simple generosity, but because of evident demand for
material recognition of war-work.

Aspiration and national identity markedly converged in demands by
middle- and working-class men and women for parliamentary reform.
John Garrard emphasises that middle-class men demonstrated their
'political fitness' before the 1832 Reform Act 'by virtue of their attachments to civil society'. Participation with charities, for example, extended
engagement with local communities – middle-class men traded active
acceptance of social and civil responsibilities for enhanced political rights.[78]
Subsequently, working-class political aspirations demanded recognition of
their national contributions through taxation, endorsement of the rule of
law and potential national defence. Additionally, such demands assumed
that working-class voters offered constitutional benefits through 'moral
purification of politics and a disinterestedness of purpose'. The granting
of the franchise was held by some to be the key to class harmonisation.[79]
Women, too, sometimes based claims for citizenship on the different qualities they offered the nation. Suffragists denied that they claimed political
rights self-interestedly, endorsing instead the relation of rights and duties,
and citing their contribution to civil society through philanthropy and

---

75 Stuart Hall and Bill Schwarz, 'State and Society, 1880–1930', and David Sutton,
    'Liberalism, State Collectivism and the Social Relations of Citizenship', both
    in Mary Langan and Bill Schwarz (eds), *Crises in the British State, 1880–1930*
    (London: Hutchinson, 1985), pp. 20, 74.
76 R. Rea, MP, cited in Freeden, *New Liberalism*, p. 166.
77 F.M.L. Thompson, 'Social Control in Victorian Britain', *Economic History Review*,
    34:2 (1981), pp. 207, 196.
78 John A. Garrard, *Democratisation in Britain: Elites, Civil Society and Reform since
    1800* (Basingstoke: Palgrave, 2002), pp. 121–50.
79 Keith McClelland, '"England's Greatness, the Working Man"', in Catherine Hall,
    Keith McClelland and Jane Rendall, *Defining the Victorian Nation: Class, Race,
    Gender and the British Reform Act of 1867* (Cambridge: Cambridge University
    Press, 2000), pp. 92–94.

other activities.[80] Women's claims to an independent political identity also often centred upon their affinities with family and domestic political affairs.[81] In such arguments, an underlying theme was that women's enfranchisement would benefit the nation by broadening its perspectives.

Besides Britain's traditions of anti-militarist sentiment, which had scuppered pre-war attempts to introduce conscription,[82] some antecedents of the less material 'world without war' strand of aspirational patriotism are apparent in internationalism. Late nineteenth-century British political thought contained an element of liberal internationalism which believed 'it was possible to build a just international order on the basis of existing patterns of cooperation between distinct political communities' and advocated 'the development of international law, arbitration, free trade, and multilateralism' and 'supranational structures'.[83] In the early twentieth century, according to P.J. Cain, J.A. Hobson hoped industrial cooperation would unite people 'in community and co-operation at both the national and international level' and render 'external aggression redundant'.[84] A decade later, the pacifist Norman Angell asserted that internationalised credit, industry and communications were leading to economic interdependence and the irrationality of war.[85] Hobson and Angell's internationalist aspirations are particularly interesting as both became UDC members. The NWAC's promotion of a League of Nations appropriated UDC-influenced ideas, trumpeting the aspiration of a world without war and in the process undermining 'pacifist' criticism, as chapter 8 discusses.

As the examples above suggest, the categories contained within the patriotic narrative of NWAC propaganda were rooted in rich pre-war soil. Rather than attempting to plant something entirely new, NWAC propagandists could, through judicious watering, pruning and weeding,

---

80 Jane Rendall, 'The Citizenship of Women and the Reform Act of 1867', in Hall et al., *Defining*, p. 163.

81 E.g. Anna Clark, 'Manhood, Womanhood, and the Politics of Class in Britain, 1790–1845', in Laura L. Frader and Sonya O. Rose (eds.), *Gender and Class in Modern Europe* (Ithaca, NY: Cornell University Press, 1996); Michelle de Larrabeiti, 'Conspicuous before the World: The Political Rhetoric of the Chartist Women', in Eileen Janes Yeo (ed.), *Radical Femininity: Women's Self-Representation in the Public Sphere* (Manchester: Manchester University Press, 1998).

82 Anne Summers, 'Militarism in Britain before the Great War', *History Workshop Journal*, 2:1 (1976); cf. G.R. Searle, *A New England? Peace and War, 1886–1918* (Oxford: Clarendon Press, 2004), pp. 501–05, for a summary of some limits to this anti-militarism.

83 Duncan Bell and Casper Sylvest, 'International Society in Victorian Political Thought: T.H. Green, Herbert Spencer, and Henry Sidgwick', *Modern Intellectual History*, 3:2 (2006), pp. 211, 213.

84 P.J. Cain, *Hobson and Imperialism: Radicalism, New Liberalism, and Finance 1887–1938* (Oxford: Oxford University Press, 2002), pp. 148–49.

85 Howard Weinroth, 'Norman Angell and *The Great Illusion*: An Episode in Pre-1914 Pacifism', *Historical Journal*, 17:3 (1974).

reshape the existing garden into something satisfying to wartime senses. In the same way that individual gardeners tend their plants in their own ways, producing a massive variety of 'typical' gardens from similar materials, so too propagandists approached their tasks individually, producing a diverse range of patriotic depictions, from the same basic collection of premises.[86] The rest of Part 2 illustrates some of this range.

Before addressing the various sub-patriotisms in detail, however, the question remains as to whether the NWAC presented 'British' or 'English' identity. Clearly, the NWAC originally concerned itself with England and Wales. Though some meetings were held in Scotland and Ireland, the addition of £5000 for propaganda in Scotland as an afterthought in its estimates, prompting the eventual establishment of two central WACs for the whole country,[87] and the fact that an Irish WAC was not established until mid-1918 (and even then did not apparently operate normally, being under the control of Sir Horace Plunkett, chairman of the Irish Convention), leaves little doubt about the central focus. The Irish War Aims Committee appeared a much less elaborate organisation than that operating in England and Wales. Correspondence between two of its officers and Lloyd George's private secretary, W.G.S. Adams, suggests its primary function was to monitor Irish public opinion and, when necessary, provide a centralised statement on particular issues (most notably the extension of conscription to Ireland). As late as 31 October 1918, Adams received a complaint that if effective propaganda work were to be conducted, a larger professional staff was required.[88] Although two cinemotor tours were planned for October and November, apparently in conjunction with the Irish Recruiting Council,[89] the Irish War Aims Committee was clearly a very different type of organisation. Besides this organisational evidence, the NWAC's logo was seemingly England's patron saint (figure 18). Nevertheless, within the propaganda itself, there seems to have been no conscious attempt to privilege an English identity over a British one: the NWAC's handbook of over 90 pages, produced towards the end of the war, consistently discussed 'Britain' rather than 'England'.[90] Discussion and the use of symbols relating to

---

86 Cf. Jennifer Mori's description of the selective application of Enlightenment principles by 'loyalist' writers in the 1790s: 'Languages of Loyalism: Patriotism, Nationhood and the State in the 1790s', *English Historical Review*, 143:475 (2003), p. 45.

87 TNA:PRO T102/16, NWAC: Statement of Estimated Expenditure for 6 months ending March 31st, 1918, 16/10/17.

88 For the correspondence and details of the Irish War Aims Committee, see PA, Lloyd George Papers, LG/F/69/2.

89 See the list of tours contained in TNA:PRO T102/6, folder 'I'.

90 *Aims and Effort of the War: Britain's Case after Four Years* (London: NWAC, 1918). This is probably the closest evidence of a detailed NWAC 'guide' to propaganda content, but it was produced so late in the war that it cannot be treated as definitive for earlier months. Its 'limited' distribution only apparently commenced

Figure 18. The NWAC's logo, from its pamphlet, The Nation Made War and the Nation Must Make the Peace (n.d. [1917])

England seemingly rested on complacent assumptions of interchangeable English and British identities, rather than an intended denigration of the rest of Britain (and beyond), as with Lieutenant Aspinall's identification of Australia with 'England'. Later, however, he remarked that 'As Britishers they could not listen to any peace talk at the present time'.[91] Similarly, Smuts's Tonypandy speech discussed England and Wales, but the cherished ideals were those of the 'British Empire'. I will return to this issue as appropriate in subsequent chapters.

BY adapting traditional patriotic themes for a war-weary civilian population, NWAC propagandists produced a narrative of Britishness through various presentational sub-patriotisms which, though capable of independent application, were mutually dependent, interactive and reinforcing. The core appeal to duty which could be found in all pieces was essential, but meaningless without contextualisation by one or more of the other presentational patriotisms. The application of certain patriotic themes in this situation is itself interesting, in suggesting those considered sufficiently important or meaningful to be used in the urgent situation of 1917–18. However, the absence in many propaganda pieces of some sub-patriotisms arguably demonstrates an assumption of a general cognisance of the underlying narrative, aided by the use of existing patriotic stimuli in this form. By considering not only what was said, but also what was not, and how these thoroughly recognisable patriotic motifs were reconfigured into a narrative of total-war civilian experience, it may be

---

in October 1918 – see TNA:PRO T102/13, letter from W.H. Smith & Sons to unknown recipient, 13/10/18.

91 N. 15 above.

possible to develop a richer understanding of patriotic discourse, certainly in the period under examination, but perhaps also more generally. The significance of these presentational patriotisms for the broader study of British patriotism and national identity is that they offer a means of interpreting familiar themes of Britishness beyond simply recapitulating their presence. There is more to be said than that things which informed representations of Britain before 1914 continued to do so thereafter. By setting these common images within a framework of presentational patriotisms the broader purposes they served in a particular context are discerned. The extensive use of one or another idea or image does not automatically enshrine it as the most important 'source' of British identity. Rather, recognising the ways in which it interacted with other elements enables a more complete conceptualisation of Britishness. As in other settings, patriotism was not evoked for its own sake by the NWAC, but to motivate British civilians to continue playing their part in a total-war society. By arranging commonplace patriotic themes within a framework of presentational patriotisms, therefore, primacy is not necessarily assigned to those most apparent, but to the purposes for which they, in conjunction with other themes, were deployed. Although the manner of interaction and the centrality of certain elements may well vary in different historical settings, such an approach avoids an excessively focused alternative, whereby the most extensively discussed themes overshadow other, perhaps equally or more important, elements.

CHAPTER 5

Adversaries at Home and Abroad: The Context of Negative Difference

UNQUESTIONABLY, of all the presentational patriotisms employed, NWAC propaganda most extensively used adversarial patriotism. Harold Lasswell's claim that there 'must be no ambiguity about whom the public is to hate' is amply demonstrated in NWAC propaganda, though its adversarial patriotism was more refined than simply ensuring that that 'all the guilt [was] on the other side of the frontier'.[1] Britain's military enemies, especially Germany, received considerable opprobrium, but so did Bolshevik Russia, for betraying the allied cause, the so-called 'peace-at-any-price' movement at home and, less extensively, anyone at home who, by striking for work conditions to match the realities of wartime Britain, or simply through war-weariness, undermined the progress of Britain's war effort. By presenting the public with a range of adversaries varying both in their proximity and their degree of threat to Britain, the NWAC could produce a more complex adversarial patriotism than with a sole, over-arching adversary.

Adversarial patriotism is one of several interactive and mutually dependent presentational sub-patriotisms which *together* construct an image of patriotic identity. Marjorie Morgan is undoubtedly correct to suggest that middle-class Victorian travellers 'exhibited a flexible repertoire of national identities rather than a single one',[2] but her study nonetheless assumes, like Linda Colley, that this flexible identity depended upon the recognition of difference, 'the proximity, real or imagined, of the Other'. Unlike an 'otherness' approach, the concept of adversarial patriotism does not suggest that 'we usually decide who we ... are by reference to who and what we are not'.[3] While such an approach was certainly sometimes taken to demonstrate identity (both by NWAC propagandists and historically), the use of adversarial patriotism as an explanatory

---

1 Lasswell, *Propaganda Technique*, p. 47.
2 Morgan, *National Identities*, p. 217.
3 Colley, 'Britishness and Otherness', p. 311. See pp. 91–92 above.

category assumes that identity is substantially formed by an evocation of the values and virtues possessed by a community, and not by the 'mapping of difference'.[4] Edward Said argues that the 'construction of identity … involves establishing opposites and "others" whose actuality is *always* subject to the continuous interpretation and re-interpretation of their differences from "us"'.[5] A major purpose of the concept of adversarial patriotism is to avoid such presumptions of the universality of difference as the basis for identity. If such universality is not accepted, an alternative conceptualisation of the role of difference in identity construction is more appropriate than simply misapplying an existing paradigm. Further, whereas everything different supposedly becomes 'other', not all differences are threatening (as supranational patriotism shows), so not every 'different' group became an adversary. Adversarial patriotism is concerned only with difference which threatens the community and its identity, locating such difference to prevent complacency and ensure an active patriotism. These threats need not necessarily entail completely contrasted values, though they were often portrayed in this way; they could simply – especially in the wartime context – be rather crude threats of upheaval; violent, sexual or social. Thus, adversarial patriotism served as a negative motivator (whereas forms like supranational and aspirational patriotism acted as positive motivators), demonstrating threats to the community and its identity, and thereby reinforcing (rather than constructing) this identity by its defence.

NATURALLY, NWAC propaganda dealt extensively with Britain's most powerful adversary, Germany. Its newspaper, *Reality*, was tellingly subtitled 'The World's Searchlight on Germany', although it also contained plenty of material with other foci. Generally, propagandists employed a tripartite approach; highlighting atrocities, linking these to a broader critique of German society, culture and philosophy, and using the evidence of both, together with the examples of Belgium and (later) the peace treaties with Russia and Romania to demonstrate that a fair peace with Germany was impossible. The NWAC's role was not simply to bolster public morale in a vacuum, but to respond to criticisms by dissenters and their calls for negotiated peace.[6] Its critique of Germany thus met specific challenges rather than merely condemning Britain's principal opponent dogmatically.

The brutality of the events, the visceral language often employed and, perhaps, the post-war highlighting of atrocity stories to discredit

---

4   Hall, *Civilising Subjects*, p. 20.
5   Edward W. Said, 'Afterword (1995)', *Orientalism*, p. 332; emphasis added.
6   See above, p. 33 for the NWAC's 'Aims of Home Publicity'.

propaganda[7] have meant that the treatment of Germany in general studies of propaganda has tended to focus largely on this element.[8] NWAC propaganda went beyond this, but because of its sensationalism, and frequent employment to precede often divergent arguments, it is important that it be considered first. Though recognised by historians as a staple of propaganda throughout the war (for all sides),[9] at least one journalist praised the NWAC pamphlet, *Murder Most Foul!*, by the American clergyman Newell Dwight Hillis, because 'in these latter war days, we have not said much about them … though the crimes against humanity are not forgotten we do not bear them in mind perhaps so much as we should'.[10] Atrocity stories remained the simplest, quickest and most vivid means of appealing to the public, serving three major purposes. First, they sought to inspire civilians through both compassionate sympathy with the victims and plain fear. If British citizens did not play their part, the same things might (or, more forcefully, would) happen in Britain, as recruiters had similarly emphasised in 1914.[11] Second, concomitantly, atrocity stories played on issues of gender and identity, seeking to exploit ideas of chivalry.[12] Tammy Proctor has recently argued that 'home front' and 'civilian' became increasingly feminised categories, so that the idea of '"civilian man" [became] an oxymoron', and the battlefront was privileged at the expense of civilian service at home.[13] This interpretation bears considerable validity, but such categorisations concealed the reality of a significant remaining male population (including able-bodied adults, as well as youths and older men) within Britain. The NWAC's audience was seemingly predominantly male, as the decision, in October 1917, that 'special' women's meetings should be arranged, and the presence of propaganda specifically written for women suggests.[14] Proctor's perception of feminised categories should be treated with some caution, given the evidence of continuing propaganda seemingly aimed towards

---

7   E.g., Lasswell, *Propaganda Technique*, pp. 46–89; Ponsonby, *Falsehood*. On the weakness of some of Ponsonby's argument, see James Morgan Read, *Atrocity Propaganda, 1914–1919* (New Haven: Yale University Press, 1941), pp. 24–25.

8   E.g., Sanders and Taylor, *British Propaganda*, pp. 137–63; Haste, *Home Fires*.

9   Audoin-Rouzeau and Becker, *1914–1918*, pp. 45–69.

10 'Notes by the Chiel', *Evesham Standard and West Midland Observer*, 22/12/17, p. 2.

11 Good, 'England Goes to War', pp. 135–37.

12 On the gendered nature of atrocity stories, see Gullace, *Blood*, pp. 17–33; Grayzel, *Women's Identities*, pp. 50–85; Katie Pickles, *Transnational Outrage: The Death and Commemoration of Edith Cavell* (Basingstoke: Palgrave MacMillan, 2007), pp. 60–85. On chivalry, see Girouard, *Return to Camelot*; cf. Lucy Delap, '"Thus Does Man Prove His Fitness to Be the Master of Things": Shipwrecks, Chivalry and Masculinity in Nineteenth- and Twentieth-Century Britain', *Cultural and Social History*, 3:1 (2006).

13 Tammy M. Proctor, *Civilians in a World at War, 1914–1918* (New York: New York University Press, 2010), pp. 3–9 (4).

14 TNA:PRO T102/16, NWAC Minutes, 10/10/17.

male civilians' sensibilities. Alongside these concerns, Lasswell argues that atrocity stories served 'powerful, hidden impulses' with stories of rape providing 'secret satisfaction to a host of vicarious ravishers'.[15] Finally, atrocity stories sought to make Germany so abominable that it was impossible to consider 'premature' peace negotiations (facilitating further expositions on German *Kultur* and general untrustworthiness).

NWAC propaganda often presented atrocities en masse, trusting in both the shock caused by weight of numbers and public familiarity with the subject matter. A quick summary of various atrocities could provide a prelude for the rest of an argument. Basil Mathews, for instance, wrote that

> the rape of Belgium has bitten with acid into the minds of the world ... The cold catalogue is enough: a baby carried aloft, skewered on a bayonet in a regiment of singing soldiers; girls violated again and again until they died; matrons, old men and priests slaughtered; women and children thrust forward as a screen between 'the gallant troops of Germany' and their enemy; organised massacre; the abuse of the Red Cross and the White Flag.[16]

To this catalogue he added other familiar refrains – poison gas, the shelling of Scarborough, the execution of Edith Cavell, Zeppelins, attacks on hospital ships and many others – before spending the remaining eight pages of the pamphlet outlining the aims of Britain and its allies. In describing the 'rape of Belgium', Mathews succinctly presented a highly gendered image of an innocent female Belgium at the mercy of a powerful and brutal Germany. Moreover, such imagery was also intended to prompt British audiences to recognise their own good fortune thus far, and the continuing threat from Germany. This message was fortified by emphasising the chivalrous part played by Britain's armed services, and that which could be played at home. The Lord Lieutenant of Wales, Sir Powlett Milbank, told a Llandrindod Wells audience that 'their gallant soldiers were defending their hearths and homes, their women and children, as well as those of others, from these brutal Germans',[17] while in Woolfardisworthy, Devon, the Conservative speaker Bryan O'Donnell provided a similarly gendered image of Britain when he said that all Britons

> would rise with indignation at the thought that the hordes of Germany should ever ruin the fair lands of Devonshire or any other county ... [C]ome what might, the womanhood of our kind should be spared the sufferings of the women of Northern France, Belgium, Poland, Serbia and Montenegro.[18]

Such imagery was enhanced by examples such as the September entry of the NWAC's *German Crimes Calendar*, which showed a dead mother and

---

15 Lasswell, *Propaganda Technique*, p. 82.
16 Basil Mathews, *The Vista of Victory* (London, n.d. – probably 1917), p. 6.
17 'Allies' War Aims', *Radnor Express*, 27/9/17, p. 5.
18 'War Aims. Successful Meeting in the West Country', *North Devon Herald*, 8/11/17, p. 3.

GERMAN CRIMES CALENDAR

London Electrotype Agency

1918   SEPTEMBER   1918

Sunday	-	-	1	8	15	22	29
Monday	-	-	2	9	16	23	30

Figure 19. The NWAC's German Crimes Calendar, September

her children, recalling the anniversary of the first Zeppelin bombing of London (figure 19).[19] Significantly, seven of the twelve anniversaries on this calendar marked 'crimes' involving British victims, although Britain had avoided the worst excesses, suggesting that the NWAC used atrocities not simply to highlight abominable behaviour but to link it to British civilian experience, past, present and (potentially) future.

Listing atrocities en masse efficiently kept them in the public mind without extensively reiterating familiar stories. The cumulative effect of

---

19 The iconography echoes an earlier cartoon by Bernard Partridge of Germany's invasion of Belgium, depicting a German soldier standing proudly over the bodies of a mother and child amid smoking ruins: 'The Triumph of "Culture"', *Punch*, 23/8/14.

Reproduced by permission of "Life."

SOUL FLIGHTS.

" Have you bombed those Allied hospitals ? "
" Jah, Majesty."
" Spread the smallpox germs ? "
" Jah, Majesty."
" Mutilated all the Armenian women ?".
" Jah, Majesty."
" Poisoned the wells ? "
" Jah, Majesty."
" Well, you may go. I want a few silent moments with God."

Figure 20. 'Soul Flights' (reproduced from Life), Reality, *no. 105, 17/1/18, p. 1*

a number of atrocious acts, quickly listed, could lead to a specific point, delivered almost like a punchline. The cartoon 'Soul Flights', reprinted in *Reality* from *Life*, showed the Kaiser, sitting beneath the crucified Christ, asking a German soldier armed with diabolical weapons including a flamethrower, germs and poisons if he had completed a series of abominable tasks (figure 20). Having confirmed that he had, the soldier is dismissed so that Wilhelm can commune with God. The none-too-subtle spiritual patriotic message here was that a nation prepared to use such atrocious methods of war must surely be Godless. Atrocity stories, or generally terrible conduct, often led to religiously inflected condemnation. The Liberal MP, Charles McCurdy, insisted that 'German Christianity is a different Christianity from the rest of Europe',[20] and went further in *Reality*, arguing that Germany wanted 'to destroy the monuments of a Christian civilisation which the Germans have never themselves possessed, a civilisation which they hate ... [as] they have exhibited in the destruction of churches and cathedrals'.[21] The general 'inability to regard the enemy as Christian', noted by Stéphane Audoin-Rouzeau and Annette Becker,[22] was frequently apparent in discussions of atrocities, which confronted both propagandists and audiences with evident evil. The Bishop of Zanzibar, Frank Weston, demanded that Britain take responsibility for Germany's African colonies after the war since the 'German does not understand the elementary principles of humane Government'.[23] Such discussion complemented condemnation of German imperialism elsewhere, particular its vicious crushing of the Herero uprising of 1904, which *Reality* twice discussed, including graphic photographs of Africans in irons and hanged from trees.[24] Weston's clerical status perhaps provided a less controversial voice for imperial matters than was possible with a more political figure, who would enable dissenting claims that Britain fought for imperialistic aims, though Weston complained after the war that his letter was misleadingly reconfigured by propagandists, omitting additional criticism of British imperial policy.[25]

The NWAC also periodically gave longer expositions of particular atrocities, as in the *Reality* article featuring the testimony of a French nun, including a facsimile of her signed statement, that in Gerbéviller, in May 1916, German soldiers had committed various atrocities including covering a woman and an epileptic in petrol and burning them alive. To the suggestion that 'apes or gorillas' might operate a similar military organisation, Sister Julie reportedly replied, 'Don't let us insult

---

20 C.A. McCurdy, MP, *Freedom's Call and Duty: Addresses Given at Central Hall, Westminster, May and June, 1918* (London, 1918), p. 12.
21 C.A. McCurdy, MP, 'The Devil's Miscalculation', *Reality*, 144, 17/10/18, pp. 2–3. See Nicola Lambourne, 'First World War Propaganda and the Use and Abuse of Historic Monuments on the Western Front', *Imperial War Museum Review*, 12 (1999).
22 Audoin-Rouzeau and Becker, *1914–1918*, p. 120.
23 Frank Weston, DD, Bishop of Zanzibar, *The Black Slaves of Prussia: An Open Letter Addressed to General Smuts* (London, 1918), p. 12.
24 'The Kaiser as a Colonist. How "Kultur" was Practised in South-West Africa', *Reality*, 140, 19/9/18, p. 4; 'The Kaiser as a Colonist', *Reality*, 142, 8/10/18, pp. 2–3. For a fascinating account of German colonists' self-perceptions in Africa, which touches on the Herero War, see Daniel Rouven-Steinbach, 'Defending the *Heimat*: The Germans in South-West Africa and East Africa during the First World War', in Heather Jones, Jennifer O-Brien and Christoph Schmidt-Supprian (eds), *Untold War: New Perspectives in First World War Studies* (Leiden: Brill, 2008).
25 Ponsonby, *Falsehood*, pp. 114–15.

the gorilla.'[26] Nevertheless, Germans were occasionally simianised in NWAC propaganda (though generally through cartoons reprinted from elsewhere) as a means of making the German adversary as inhuman as possible. One such example was a cartoon reprinted in *Reality* from the *Bystander*, by Wilmot Lunt and the regular NWAC cartoonist W.F. Blood, 'The Go-Betweens', which showed three German soldiers surrendering, one a typical German stereotype – short, fat and wearing glasses – and another with distinctly simian facial features, continuing an established representation of adversaries threatening Britain, which originally exploited concerns that evolutionary theories undermined human identity.[27]

Despite the extensive evidence of atrocity material, one reason to reject atrocity stories as the quintessence of propaganda characterisations of Germany, and propaganda generally, is the frequent tendency, at least in NWAC propaganda, to lampoon and ridicule Britain's principal adversary. As Jay Winter and Jean-Louis Robert note, during the war 'the enemy was mocked as much as he was hated'.[28] In 'The Teutonic Thermometer' (figure 21), Blood played upon pre-war concerns about German competition by showing an unwell Kaiser Wilhelm looking anxiously at the mercury on his 'Victory' thermometer, conspicuously labelled 'Made in Germany'. Similarly, mocking a German speech proclaiming 'the constant activity' of Germany's navy, the Liberal MP T.J. Macnamara drew laughter from his audience at Ipswich by remarking that such activity was 'often veiled from view', a reminder of the High Seas Fleet's reluctance to put to sea.[29] Excessive concentration on atrocities as the source of British wartime views of Germany risks overlooking this more confident note and depicting wartime Britons as paralysed with either fear or rage.

Moreover, NWAC propaganda rarely used atrocities as ends in themselves. Pamphlets like *"Gentlemen" of Germany*, describing the torpedoing of the British steamer *Belgian Prince* and the subsequent deliberate drowning of sailors by a German U-boat submerging with the captured sailors still on deck, without relating the atrocity to a wider picture, were relatively rare.[30] Generally, as with the comment by McCurdy cited above, atrocities were part of a broader critique of

---

26 Wilson Crewtson, 'The Great German Crime at Gerbéviller. The Authorised Testimony of Sister Julie', *Reality*, 120, 2/5/18, pp. 2–3.

27 Wilmot Lunt and W.F. Blood, 'The "Go-Betweens"', *Reality*, 143, 10/10/18, p. 1; L.P. Curtis, *Apes and Angels: The Irishman in Victorian Caricature* (rev. edn, Washington and London: Smithsonian Institution Press, 1997), pp. 98–107.

28 Jay Winter and Jean-Louis Robert, 'Conclusion', in Winter and Robert, *Capital Cities at War*, II, pp. 472–73.

29 *East Anglian Daily Times*, 'War Aims of the Allies. Mr. T.J. Macnamara at Ipswich', 3/12/17, p. 6.

30 *"Gentlemen" of Germany* (London, n.d. [1917]). This was one of the original fifteen NWAC pamphlets, possibly requested by the War Cabinet, which discussed the event and asked the First Sea Lord to 'take steps to publish particulars of the outrage'; TNA:PRO CAB23/3/1365-204: War Cabinet 204, 3/8/17.

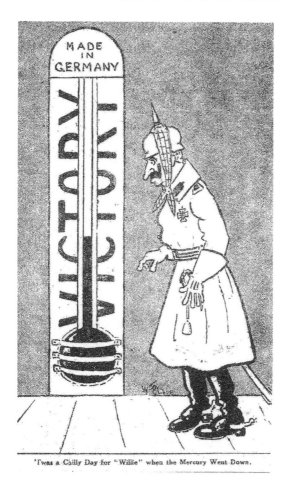

'Twas a Chilly Day for "Willie" when the Mercury Went Down.

Figure 21. W.F. Blood, 'The Teutonic Thermometer', Welcome, no. 20, 14/8/18, p. 235

German culture (*Kultur*) and society, designed to demonstrate that peace was impracticable until Germany changed its internal conditions. This meant reforming German political institutions to something genuinely democratic (an idea that Germans contested, claiming only Germany possessed 'true' democracy),[31] and the abolition of 'Prussian militarism' as a way of life. Despite its title, *Murder Most Foul!* was not simply a compendium of atrocities, but a larger critique of Germany. It was not the atrocities themselves which most horrified Hillis but that they were 'committed, not in a mood of drunkenness nor an hour of anger, but were

---

31 Stibbe, *German Anglophobia*, p. 171.

organised by a so-called German efficiency and perpetrated on a deliberate, cold, precise, scientific policy of German frightfulness'.[32] NWAC propaganda presented Germany as a nation saturated with militarist and expansionist ideology. This was usually blamed (not uniquely by the NWAC) on an intellectual triumvirate of the philosopher Friedrich Nietzsche, the historian Heinrich von Treitschke and the military theorist Friedrich von Bernhardi, who 'glorified war as a civilising agent, a beautiful and necessary method of national advance',[33] though Treitschke, at least, was largely neglected in Germany, except via Bernhardi's writings.[34] As Gregory Moore has discussed, these figures were held responsible for the establishment of *Kultur*, as distinct from Matthew Arnold's '"culture" … understood as "the pursuit of sweetness and light"'.[35]

More moderate writers and speakers confined criticisms to the military and the Prussian Junker class. Asquith asserted at Liverpool that 'it has never been part of our policy to annihilate or to mutilate Germany. Our warfare is waged … against Prussian militarism (cheers)'.[36] Asquith retained the pre-war Liberal 'two Germanies' distinction described by Paul Kennedy, between 'the ruling clique … who were reactionary and bad' and most German people 'who were peace-loving and good'.[37] However, as Stuart Wallace notes, 'this distinction tended to lose its force … as propaganda concentrated on the dangers of premature peace',[38] and others were less circumspect. Charles S. Parker, prospective Unionist candidate for Barnstaple, told an audience that he disagreed with President Wilson's claim not to be at war with the German people. He accepted that 'Prussia' and

> the Kaiser had been responsible very largely for the creation of that spirit of militarism, and for the creation of the desire and determination to beat England, which had dominated the German people … [But] the German people would have to bear the penalty of these misdeeds, and … it would be impossible to sit down after this War, except in enmity with the German people. (Hear, hear.)[39]

---

32 Dr Newell Dwight Hillis, *Murder Most Foul!* (London, n.d. [1917]), p. 4. On the military basis for German civilian repression, see Horne and Kramer, *German Atrocities*, pp. 169–70.

33 'Philosophy and War', *Reality*, 103, 3/1/18, p. 3. On the vilification of these figures, see Gregory Moore, 'The Super-Hun and the Super-State: Allied Propaganda and German Philosophy during the First World War', *German Life and Letters*, 54:4 (2001); Hoover, *God, Germany and Britain*, p. 131; Wallace, *War and Image*, pp. 31–33, 47–50, 67–69.

34 Wallace, *War and Image*, p. 68.

35 Moore, 'Super-Hun', p. 323.

36 'Mr Asquith's Speech', *Liverpool Daily Post and Mercury*, 12/10/17, pp. 5–6.

37 Kennedy, *Anglo-German Antagonism*, p. 398. See also Wallace, *War and Image*, p. 31; Ramsden, *Don't Mention*, p. 123.

38 Wallace, *War and Image*, p. 170.

39 'War Aims Campaign in North Devon', *North Devon Journal*, 1/11/17, p. 2.

Propagandists claimed that, from infancy, Germans became accustomed through education to hating Britain. The Labour MP Ben Tillett proclaimed that Germany 'had taught its young children to hate us and had convinced its young men that they could overcome us',[40] while at Malmesbury the barrister, Bromhead Mathews said,

> The Kaiser claimed to be possessed of the spirit of the Most High ... He wished to make himself world-master, to impose on us his "kultur," which meant devilish ingenuity in the art of mutilation; the murder of women and children ... To bring their people into line with this was effected by thorough education with the aid of the philospher [*sic*], the historian, the soldier Bernhardi, with the aid of clergymen who instead of the doctrine of peace and goodwill on earth, preached the gospel of English hate ...[41]

This was not a new approach. Napoleonic-era propaganda had asserted that Englishmen were 'hated and envied ... by the French above all others'.[42] Nor was it a First World War perspective unique to Britain. Matthew Stibbe suggests that Germans rapidly identified Britain as their key enemy through a combined fear of Britain's supposed strength through racial purity and disdain for the effects of 'Manchesterism', meaning laissez-faire economics.[43] NWAC propagandists were, likewise, as keen as their Napoleonic-era predecessors to utilise arguments about the unpleasant situation of their principal adversary's workers to maintain public order at home.[44] To make this more convincing, such arguments were often put either by Labour figures or by 'good Germans', who criticised or disavowed some or all of their native country's deeds.[45] William Stephen Sanders wrote several pamphlets for the NWAC. His credentials were impeccable, and most of his pamphlets contained an editorial note stressing his connection 'with the Labour and Socialist movement ... for over thirty years', holding positions on the Executive Committee of the Labour Party, and as Secretary to the British section of the International Socialist Bureau and the Fabian Society. Further, he had served two years as a captain in the army during the war, and was qualified to speak authoritatively on Germany, 'having studied in that country for a considerable period'.[46] Two pamphlets, *Germany's Two Voices* and

---

40 Ben Tillett, MP, *Who Was Responsible for the War – and Why?* (London, 1917), p. 9. On Tillett's attitude to the war, see Jonathan Schneer, *Ben Tillett: Portrait of a Labour Leader* (Urbana: University of Illinois Press, 1982), pp. 175–97.

41 'National War Aims Campaign. Meeting at Malmesbury', *Wilts and Gloucestershire Standard, and Cirencester and Swindon Express*, 3/11/17, p. 6.

42 Cottrell, 'Devil', p. 267.

43 Stibbe, *German Anglophobia*, pp. 78, 106.

44 Robert Hole, 'British Counter-revolutionary Popular Propaganda in the 1790's', in Colin Jones (ed.), *Britain and Revolutionary France: Conflict, Subversion and Propaganda* (Exeter: University of Exeter, 1983), p. 60.

45 Cf. Wallace, *War and Image*, p. 163.

46 William Stephen Sanders, *Is it a Capitalist War?*, NWAC pamphlet no. 19 (n.p.d.).

Figure 22. Cover of W.S. Sanders's pamphlet Germany's Two Voices

If the Kaiser Governed Britain: The Lesson of Germany, were particularly devoted to socialism and workers' concerns in Germany. In the former (figure 22), Sanders argued that, despite their peaceful rhetoric, most German Social Democrats were committed to military conquest. Those, like the minority Socialist Karl Liebknecht, who refused to be 'tools' of such an expansionist parliament, were imprisoned. Liebknecht was implicitly a 'good German', responsible for the oft-quoted 'We [Germans] are slaves in everything but thought, and even thinking is dangerous if you talk in your sleep!',[47] though Sylvia Pankhurst claimed that the

---

47 E.g., *Reality*, no. 102, 26/12/17, p. 4.

Figure 23. Strikes in Germany, satirised in the Evening News *(reprinted in* Reality, *no. 109, 16/2/18)*

publication of Liebknecht's speeches, rather than serving the purposes intended by 'our jingo Press', in fact encouraged British 'pacifists' to believe that a strong peace movement existed in Germany with which a negotiated peace might be arranged.[48] Sanders cited the Reichstag member Paul Lensch, whose 'hatred of Britain includes the British working classes' who would 'lose their present privileged position ... [and] be reduced to the same level as the workmen of other lands'.[49] The latter pamphlet provided a broader critique of German society, informing readers that the 'baby of the working class ... represents [for Germany's rulers] future "cannon fodder" or factory fodder ... The higher storeys of "Kultur" are not for the child of the proletariat.' Sanders explained that Germany was virtually a police state, where trade unions received no governmental recognition and where strikes were dealt with, not by negotiation (as, implicitly, in Britain), but by the district military commander threatening to send the workers to the trenches, or worse (figure 23). The Reichstag

---

48 Sylvia Pankhurst, *The Home Front: A Mirror to Life in England during the First World War* (London: The Cresset Library, 1987 [1932]), p. 328.
49 William Stephen Sanders, *Germany's Two Voices*, NWAC no. 30 (London, 1918), pp. 5, 9–10.

was 'not a Parliament in the sense in which we understand that word' since the Kaiser appointed the government and the Reichstag could not make laws, while the 'ruling classes in Germany openly avow ... that political questions are matters upon which working people have no right to express an opinion'.[50] The German expatriate banker Otto Kahn insisted that Germans had been 'misled, corrupted and systematically poisoned by the Prussian ruling caste' which had instilled a 'demoniacal obsession of power-worship and world-dominion'.[51]

Again, spiritual patriotism had a role to play in this cultural critique of Germany. Other critics scoffed (somewhat hypocritically) at perceived German feelings of religious superiority. At Glyncorrwg, Labour MP William Brace said Germany was 'a nation which believed it was the Chosen People, and its Emperor the chosen instrument of the Almighty God'. The Earl of Denbigh likewise said Germans 'suffered from a swelled head, regarding themselves as heaven-sent people destined to rule the world'. Interestingly, Germans made identical complaints about Britain, claiming that in fighting British imperialists Germany also fought for small nations. In criticising perceived German religious arrogance, propagandists ignored the similarly presumptuous sentiments expressed by their own countrymen. In the same Glyncorrwg speech, Brace attributed the steadfastness of the outnumbered British during the 1914 retreat from Mons to 'some Divine Force', while the vicar of All Saints Church in Evesham, Revd Dr Walker, reminded his congregation that 'it was God's grace that we existed today, and that England stood at the head of nations that would be free'.[52] In Lanreath, Cornwall, Revd L.A. Williams regarded Britain as 'especially blessed by God' and a divine instrument, whereas 'there was no liberty or justice in Germany today'. Britain thus would surely win the war, though Williams warned that the 'invasion of German theology and teaching' had significantly weakened British religion, so that, if an unthinkable German victory occurred 'religion ... would be no more'.[53] Clearly such use of spiritual patriotism was Janus-faced. Where Britons described their own nation as blessed, it was meant as a reassuring comfort, 'proved' by the Christian nature of the principles for which Britain fought. Similar claims by Germans, however, supposedly demonstrated German arrogance and (in Denbigh's view)

---

50 William Stephen Sanders, *If the Kaiser Governed Britain: The Lesson of Germany* (n.p.d [1918]), pp. 2, 13, 15.
51 Otto Kahn, *Right above Race* (pamphlet – *Searchlight* series, 28, [1918]), p. 1.
52 'Rt. Hon. Wm. Brace M.P. at Glyncorrwg', *Glamorgan Free Press*, 1/11/17, p. 1; Col. the Earl of Denbigh, *Why Germany Made War* (*German Aims* Series, 2, n.p.d. [1918]), p. 13. Brace perhaps alluded to the 'Angel of Mons', on which, see Wolffe, *God and Greater Britain*, p. 241; Winter, 'Spiritualism'. On German attitudes, see Hoover, *God, Germany, and Britain*, p. 53; Welch, *Germany, Propaganda*, pp. 62–63. 'Evesham. Remembrance Day at Evesham', *Evesham Journal*, 10/8/18, p. 6.
53 'British War Aims. Campaign in South-East Cornwall', *Cornish Times*, 8/2/18, p. 3.

blasphemy, throwing further doubts upon their claims to be a genuine Christian nation.

Atrocity stories vividly dehumanised the German adversary, while the critique of German society and culture sought to illustrate that Britons would be worse off under German rule. To complete the image of Germany as an intransigent adversary with which negotiated peace was impossible, propagandists capitalised on examples of German diplomacy. The German Chancellor Theobald von Bethmann-Hollweg's exasperated complaint in 1914 that Britain was going to war for a 'scrap of paper' (the 1839 treaty guaranteeing Belgian neutrality, signed by Britain and Prussia), and Germany's subsequent violation of it, provided ammunition for responses to calls for negotiated peace. The Labour MP Stephen Walsh assured a Wigan audience that 'Germany knew no international law, and her treaties were scraps of paper'.[54] The evidence of Prince Lichnowsky, Germany's ambassador to Britain in 1914, an accidental 'good German' whose private memoir was smuggled out of Germany and published worldwide, ostensibly proved German duplicity in July 1914 and was gleefully utilised.[55] Furthermore, after the Treaty of Brest–Litovsk in March 1918, speakers and writers could also stress the harsh terms Britain could expect in any negotiated peace. In Watlington, Norfolk, the Liberal speaker J.A. Oglesby 'warned pacifists of the dangers of a premature peace as obtained in Russia'.[56] 'Russia, who threw down her arms', wrote W.S. Sanders, 'received a scrap of paper', which 'handed over to Prussian domination territory larger than that of the whole German Empire.'[57] A real peace, however, required complete victory, and the removal of Germany's iniquitous rulers.

BRITAIN'S other external adversaries received relatively little attention, and most of that involved tangential further criticism of Germany. Austria-Hungary played little part in the propaganda, probably because British confrontations with Austrians were largely confined to the stagnant Salonika front and the brief period after Caporetto in which British troops reinforced the Italian front. Where Austria was discussed it usually became a German stooge. Even regarding Serbia, Austrian misdeeds

---

54 'War Aims Meeting at Wigan', *Wigan Examiner*, 17/11/17, p. 2; also 'War Campaign. Meeting at the Kursaal', *Harrogate and Claro Times, Knaresborough & Ridderdale Guardian*, 9/11/17, p. 5.

55 E.g. C.A. McCurdy, MP, *Guilty! Prince Lichnowsky's Disclosures* (n.p.d.,[1918]); *Germany Condemned by Her Own Ambassador* (*Searchlight* series, 18 [1918]); on Lichnowsky's memoir, see Harry F. Young, *Prince Lichnowsky and the Great War* (Athens, GA: University of Georgia Press, 1977), pp. 145–61.

56 'Watlington. National War Aims', *Thetford & Watton Times*, 23/3/18, p. 3.

57 William Stephen Sanders, *Those German Peace Offers* (*German Aims* series, 3, [1918]), p. 2; and *The Tragedy of Russia* (London, [1918]), p. 9.

were linked to Germany, the Liberal MP Charles McCurdy writing that while to Austria Serbia represented the apotheosis of Slav nationalism, to Germany it was the means of conquering the Near East and that 'the high mission of Germany as a Kultur-bearer' had led to expropriation followed by 'simple pillage and loot'.[58] The Ottoman Empire, perpetrator of the single largest atrocity of the First World War, the massacre of possibly more than a million Armenians,[59] received some opprobrium. At Brecon, Liberal MP Sidney Robinson 'hoped ... that the hand of the Turk would be removed from [Palestine and Armenia], and that the blight which the Turk succeeded in spreading over any land he had anything to do with would be removed ... once and for all'.[60]

However, criticism of Turks was often expanded to incorporate Germany, implying that such behaviour was to be expected from a 'barbarous' (and non-Christian) civilisation like Turkey's, but that the supposedly more 'civilised' Germans should have intervened.[61] Such a propaganda approach continued that taken to the genocide since 1915.[62] Conservative MP E.F.L. Wood told a Harrogate audience that the world 'had seen thousands of Armenians massacred because Germany would not lift a finger to stop it',[63] while McCurdy declaimed that 'the hills are white with the bones of slaughtered Christians', adding that nearly a million died 'with the connivance of the German government, without any protest from the German people'. Despite the Armenians being 'systematically exterminated', at Brest-Litovsk 'Germany secured from the Bolsheviks the return to Turkey of those Armenians ... saved from massacre by Russian armies, and the Turkish Government thereupon proceeded to complete their work of extermination'.[64] A US official claimed the massacres had been carried out 'under the domination and

---

58 C.A. McCurdy, MP, *The Case of Serbia* (*Freedom of Nations* series, 1, London, n.d.), pp. 2, 9–10.

59 Artin H. Arslanian, 'British Wartime Pledges, 1917–19: The Armenian Case', *Journal of Contemporary History*, 13 (1978), p. 517; Donald Bloxham, 'The Armenian Genocide of 1915–1916: Cumulative Radicalization and the Development of a Destruction Policy', *Past & Present*, 181 (2003), p. 141; and Niall Ferguson, *The War of the World: History's Age of Hatred* (London: Allen Lane, 2006), p. 179, all suggest this.

60 'War Aims. Mr. Sidney Robinson, M.P. at Brecon', *Radnor Express*, 11/10/17, p. 6. See also Basil Mathews, *The Freedom of the Holy Land* (*Searchlight* series, 30, [1918]).

61 Cf. the cartoon 'Two Revelations' reprinted from *Life*, in *Reality*, no. 123, 23/5/18, p. 4, which claimed that 'the leprous heart of the Turk dominates the Teuton'.

62 Donald Bloxham, *The Great Game of Genocide: Imperialism, Nationalism, and the Destruction of the Ottoman Armenians* (Oxford: Oxford University Press, 2005), p. 129 – for analysis of the mixed accuracy of such claims, see pp. 115–33.

63 'Major the Hon. E. Wood, M.P., and the War', *Ripon Gazette*, 8/11/17, p. 3.

64 C.A. McCurdy, MP, *The Truth about the "Secret Treaties"* (London, n.d. [1918]), pp. 12, 13, 26–27.

Figure 24. W.F. Blood, 'Four Forlorn Hopes', Welcome, no. 18, 31/7/18, p. 211

leadership of German officers'.[65] Such criticisms added further fuel to suggestions of Germany's deviant religiosity. A pamphlet version of a sermon preached at Oxford by Bishop Frodsham called for Africa to be 'Christianised', since 'Mohammedanism' stood there for 'slavery, the degradation of women, and the love of war for war's sake'. Interestingly, Frodsham criticised German rule in his speech, seemingly implying that Germany followed Islamic principles.[66] The Ottoman Empire's separation from Europe is implied in the cartoon 'Four Forlorn Hopes' (figure 24) by the contrasted colours of the clothing, scimitar, and anxious expression of the Turk, compared to his German, Austro-Hungarian and Bulgarian allies (he may also be backing away), while Germany's domination of its allies is illustrated by the Iron Crosses they all wear.

---

65 Frederick C. Walcott, 'The Prussian System as I Found it', *Reality*, 137, 29/8/18, p. 3.

66 Bishop Frodsham, *The British Empire after the War: Being the Ramsden Sermon Preached before the University of Oxford on Whit-Sunday (May 19th), 1918* (London, [1918]), pp. 13–14. For biographical details, see John Charles Vockler, 'Frodsham, George Horsfall (1863 - 1937)', *Australian Dictionary of Biography*, vol. 8 (Melbourne: Melbourne University Press, 1981), pp. 590–91.

Bolshevik Russia had to be engaged as an object of adversarial patriotism for two reasons. The violent revolution by which the Bolsheviks claimed power was an alarming warning of what might happen if domestic unrest became too extreme, and consequently it was necessary to delegitimise their form of government to the public. Furthermore, the Bolsheviks' publication of several secret treaties between the allies, including agreements about post-war territorial arrangements, undermined allied claims to be fighting a moral war for civilisation, and could strengthen prominent dissenting groups like the UDC, which had made the abolition of secret diplomacy a key goal.[67] Fortunately, in propaganda if not strategic terms, the Bolsheviks also withdrew Russia from the war, endangering Britain, and thus it was relatively simple to criticise Bolshevik 'betrayal' while sidestepping more awkward issues.

Before the Bolsheviks' emergence, propagandists interpreted the Tsar's overthrow as positive for both Russia and the alliance. In October 1917 the Liberal speaker Herbert Woodger said at South Littleton, Worcestershire, that the Tsar's overthrow would *prevent* a separate peace with Germany, and when 'they had got rid of their Anarchists in Russia as we meant to in this country, Russia would come again'.[68] However, once it became clear that the Bolsheviks would make peace, the tone changed. By March, criticism of Bolshevism was wide-ranging. The Irish MP D.D. Sheehan, in his weekly column, wrote that many MPs believed 'that the Bolsheviks betrayed their country to the Germans', a point echoed by Mrs Elsdon, a BWNL speaker, at a Keighley NWAC meeting, who said defeatists were 'responsible for the present state of affairs in Russia' and warned that defeatism would cause the same result in Britain.[69] The Liberal MP J.M. Robertson believed 'the horrors and the humiliation of the Bolshevik régime in Russia ha[d] gone far to ban revolution everywhere else'.[70] W.S. Sanders, in a heavily distributed pamphlet, lamented that what might have become a 'strong, independent, democratic country, has developed, under the guidance of folly and fanaticism into an orgie [*sic*] of anarchism'. There was 'little difference between the despotism of the Bolsheviks and the autocracy of the Kaiser', and Sanders inverted the public school language of manliness and patriotism in asserting that Lenin and Trotsky had 'played the German game' by making themselves 'dictators of Russia', 'destroy[ing] industry, trade and commerce, and [bringing] starvation to the masses'.[71]

---

67 Swartz, *Union of Democratic Control*, pp. 26, 192.
68 'District News. Evesham. National War Aims', *Evesham Journal and Four Shires Advertiser*, 20/10/17, p. 6.
69 'The War & Westminster. By a Soldier M.P.', *Seaham Weekly News*, 8/3/18, p. 2; 'England's War Policy', *Keighley News*, 30/3/18, p. 5.
70 John M. Robertson, MP, *The Pacifist Blind Spot* (*Searchlight* series, 23).
71 Sanders, *Tragedy of Russia*, pp. 2, 3, 8–9; the National Archives library copy is

NAMES OF LENINITE LEADERS.

Below are the real names of some of the Russian Bolshevik
leaders of the counter-revolution :

Name under which known.	Actual name.	Name under which known.	Actual name.
Trotsky	Bronstein	Sutkhanov	Gimmer
Zinoviev	Apfelbaum	Gorev	Goldman
Kamenev	Rosenfeldt	Mishkovsky	Goldenberg
Steklov	Nahamkhis	Ladin	Lure

Figure 25. 'Names of Leninite Leaders', Reality, no. 97, 17/11/17, p. 4

The most surprising and disturbing piece of NWAC propaganda is
found in *Reality*, where a very brief section informed readers of 'the real
names of some of the Russian Bolshevik leaders' (figure 25). What is most
interesting here is not simply that the NWAC asserted several Bolsheviks'
Jewish origins, but that it was assumed to be sufficient merely to print
the names without additional commentary, suggesting an assumption
that anti-Semitism was sufficiently deeply ingrained in Britain to make
further observations unnecessary. Exposing some Bolsheviks' Jewish roots
seemed enough to discredit them. This supposition is supported by other
wartime evidence. The socialist Leeds Conference in June 1917 prompted
an anti-Semitic riot,[72] while right-wing writers like Leo Maxse combined
anti-German and anti-Semitic sentiment throughout the war, further
suggesting the perseverance of anti-Semitism in wartime British consciousness.[73] Such views echoed the anti-Semitic scapegoating by commentators
like J.A. Hobson or Arnold White during the Boer War.[74] Interestingly,
it also reflected German critiques of Britain, which occasionally blamed
Jewish influence for the divergence of opinion between two nations 'from
similar Nordic or Teutonic stock'.[75] By casting Bolshevism as a treasonous,
anti-democratic force, responsible for 'ruining' and subjugating Russia,

---

labelled '2nd million'. On 'playing the game', see J.A. Mangan, *Athleticism in
the Victorian and Edwardian Public School: The Emergence and Consolidation
of an Educational Ideology* (Cambridge: Cambridge University Press, 1981). For
another instance of this kind of inversion, see David Monger, '"No Mere Silent
Commander"? Sir Henry Horne and the Mentality of Command during the First
World War', *Historical Research*, 82:216 (2009), p. 355.
72 Millman, *Managing*, p. 210.
73 Susanne Terwey, 'Stereotypical Bedfellows: The Combination of Anti-Semitism
with Germanophobia in Great Britain, 1914–1918', in Macleod and Purseigle
(eds), *Uncovered Fields*. See also Gregory, *Last Great War*, pp. 238–41.
74 E.g., J.A. Hobson, *The War in South Africa: Its Causes and Effects* (London: J.
Nisbet & Co., 1900), pp. 189–97; Arnold White, *Efficiency and Empire*, ed. G.R.
Searle (Brighton: Harvester Press, 1973 [1901]), pp. 79–80.
75 Stibbe, *German Anglophobia*, pp. 55, 59.

NWAC propaganda aimed to deflect criticism of the secret treaties while making this extreme socialism unthinkable to Britons. Whilst devoting considerable attention to external adversaries, however, NWAC propaganda also dealt with those within, who, it was often claimed, were the only adversaries truly capable of defeating Britain.

A S important as it was to emphasise the threat posed by outsiders, it was also essential to avoid implying that such adversaries were so powerfully malign as to render victory impossible. NWAC propagandists sought to stress that, militarily, only Britain and its allies could win the war, while preventing complacency with warnings of the dire consequences which would accompany the undermining of British servicemen by a disruptive homefront. 'No', wrote the socialist Robert Blatchford, 'we cannot be beaten. The only danger is that our victory may be thrown away, that class or party dissensions or mistaken ideas about the enemy and the war may drive our Government into a hasty and inconclusive peace.'[76] Therefore, adversarial patriotism required the presentation of tangible targets for hostility within Britain itself. Anti-Semitism provided a limited opportunity, as did Germans still 'at large' in Britain.[77] However, 'foreign' members of the community were less effective adversarial threats than 'native' Britons who, by dissent, left themselves open to imputations of disloyalty. 'Pacifists', 'defeatists' and conscientious objectors were particularly reviled, as sometimes were profiteers, while strikers and anyone demonstrating war-weariness or discontent were vulnerable to lesser accusations that they lacked patriotism. By creating a dichotomy which placed dissent and complaint 'beyond the pale' of patriotic society, the NWAC sought to stifle discontent and maintain an image of a united, determined and willing Britain. This was the message of the abortive 'British National Film', scripted by the novelist Hall Caine with contributions from Thomas Hardy and Rudyard Kipling, and music by Alexander Mackenzie and Edward Elgar, at a cost of over £23,500. The film depicted a German occupation of Chester and was intended to emphasise to the 'ordinary working man' the need for maximum civilian exertion to prevent German atrocities in Britain. This was not only to be achieved by the startlingly realistic portrayal by the women of Chester of

---

76 Robert Blatchford, *Can We Win?* (probably *Searchlight* series – same design-style but not designated as such, 1918).

77 E.g. Sascha Auerbach, 'Negotiating Nationalism: Jewish Conscription and Russian Repatriation in London's East End, 1916–1918', *Journal of British Studies*, 46:3 (2007). For earlier periods of the war, see Catriona Pennell, '"The Germans Have Landed!": Invasion Fears in the South-East of England, August to December 1914', in Jones et al. (eds), *Untold War*; Nicoletta F. Gullace, 'Friends, Aliens and Enemies: Fictive Communities and the Lusitania Riots of 1915', *Journal of Social History*, 39:2 (2005).

a 'terrorised population',[78] but seemingly by linking atrocities to industrial discontent. A post-war committee hoping to recoup the film's extravagant costs commercially was informed that 'having special regard for the atrocity and strike scenes which form a prominent feature of the film' such a course would be unwise and (argued the Ministry of Information-linked producer Sir William Jury) 'given the present Labour situation ... might indeed be dangerous'.[79] Although the film never reached the public, the linking of threatened German atrocities with misguided British civilian conduct in NWAC propaganda was clear here.

While dissent in Britain was certainly not always motivated by pacifism,[80] the NWAC consistently labelled nearly all criticism, particularly organised criticism, as 'pacifist', even privately.[81] This designation perhaps contained an emasculating motive. Democracy dictated that 'criticism' and 'dissent' were viable, indeed essential, ingredients, but by rendering dissenters as 'pacifist', propagandists could question their courage, resolve and moral code.[82] Without such 'masculine' attributes, 'pacifist' men had no right to participate in public life and discussion. This moral code could also be challenged by accusations that dissenters received German funding. At Barnstaple, Lord Fortescue declared that

> Pacifists ... might be divided into roughly three classes – some were simply fools, some were in German pay, and some were degenerates, who, he was afraid, were always to be found in this country, and who were the friends of every country except their own. (Applause).

Whether fools, stooges or degenerates, Fortescue emphasised that pacifists were somehow aberrant, a point endorsed by the town's prospective parliamentary candidates, C.S. Parker and the Liberal Lieutenant J.T. Tudor-Rees, who maintained that the pacifist 'hidden hand' was 'covered with blood' and that 'if any Britisher had anything to do with that blood-stained hand, he ought not to be allowed to enjoy British rule and privileges, but ... sent to Germany, to be treated ... as Germans had always been'.[83] Even the War Cabinet was 'persuaded that German money is supporting these societies', even though the man responsible for

---

78 Reeves, *Official British Film*, pp., 125–30.
79 TNA:PRO T1/12519, file 13904/1920; H.C. Brook Johnson to Sir John Bradbury,19/5/19; Jury to Guest, 3/1/19.
80 Ward, *Red Flag*, pp. 126–29, 138–40.
81 One of its aims was to overwhelm 'the insidious and specious propaganda of pacifist publications'. TNA:PRO T102/16 '(Confidential) Aims of Home Publicity', n.d.
82 This was certainly part of strategies to demonstrate female fitness for citizenship (Gullace, *Blood*, pp. 137–41). David Thackeray suggests that BWL efforts against 'pacifists' also, and more directly, questioned their manliness: 'Building a Peaceable Party: Masculine Identities in British Conservative Politics, c. 1903–1924', *Historical Research* (forthcoming).
83 'War Aims Campaign', *North Devon Herald*, 1/11/17, p. 2.

monitoring 'pacifist' activity, Basil Thomson (perhaps not quite so 'paranoid' as Gregory suggests), believed 'that there is no German money'.[84] Labour Minister G.H. Roberts reported in October 1917 that there was no 'evidence' that the UDC or No-Conscription Fellowship were 'financed from enemy sources', instead deriving their funds from 'wealthy Quaker families', while the ILP contained 'wealthy individual members' and was increasing funds from its generally expanding membership.[85]

Regardless of factual accuracy, however, associating 'pacifists' with 'German money' was a simple, if crude means of undermining their claims to patriotism. By linking two adversaries, the NWAC attempted to invalidate the idea of an 'oppositional' patriotism harking back to earlier, radical interpretations,[86] and to refuse the permissibility of dissent or individualism. Having implanted doubt with such accusations, propagandists could then argue that 'pacifists' weakened the fabric of British society and prolonged the war either by providing Germany with hope that the homefront might collapse or by destabilising the war effort. Thus, Tudor-Rees argued, they did not deserve the protection and privileges of British citizenship.

As with criticism of German society, so the adversarialising of dissenters was best expressed by figures linked to the groups. At Tooting, the MP Charles Duncan told a sparse audience that he was a member of the Labour party, supporting the government's prosecution of the war, unlike the ILP which was 'doing [its] best against this country during the war'.[87] Another Labour MP, William Brace, informed a Breconshire audience that 'the inconsistencies of the pacifists appalled him. They were not prepared to lift a finger to help the country in her hour of need; they were, indeed, trying to create an atmosphere of war weariness. There was something worse than war, and that was the enslavement of free people.'[88] At Pwllgwaun, East Glamorgan, the Unionist speaker John Farnsworth suggested 'to the pacifists, the British Socialist Party, and that section of the Labour Party to which [Philip] Snowden and Ramsay Macdonald gelonged [sic], that the people whom Ramsay Macdonald called "our German friends" had got to clean their character'.[89] Snowden and MacDonald, as the most influential 'pacifist' speakers, were the individuals most commonly selected for abuse, and MacDonald was

84 Basil Thomson, *The Scene Changes* (Garden City: Doubleday, Doran & Co., 1937), diary entry, 22/10/17, p. 392; on Thomson's 'paranoia', see Gregory, *Last Great War*, p. 202.
85 TNA:PRO CAB24/28/2274, GT2274, Ministry of Labour's reply to memo G.157, 10/10/17. Thomson later made a similar report: CAB24/35/2980, 'Pacifism', 13/12/17.
86 See Ward, *Red Flag*; Cunningham, 'Language of Patriotism'.
87 '"War Aims" Meeting at Tooting', *Battersea Boro' News*, 26/10/17, p. 2.
88 'War Aims. The Builth Meeting', *Brecon & Radnor Express*, 11/4/18, p. 5.
89 'What We Fight for, and Why', *Glamorgan Free Press*, 22/11/17, p. 1.

particularly irked by the constantly used 'German friends' refrain, claiming he had 'never said anything of the kind'.[90] However, the NWAC did not generally appear to encourage attacks on individual 'pacifists'. Perhaps because of their MP status, Snowden and MacDonald were very rarely mentioned in NWAC written propaganda – MacDonald was quoted positively, expressing dissatisfaction with 'any [peace] terms the Germans have yet offered' in an edition of *Reality*, and his endorsement was attached to the summary of Lloyd George's January 1918 War Aims speech,[91] but he was not directly criticised. Unlike prominent external adversaries like the Kaiser or Hindenburg, or German socialist figures, no caricatures of individual 'pacifists' appeared. At meetings, however, individuals like Snowden and MacDonald were sometimes singled out for adversarialisation. This represents a paradox in analysing NWAC propaganda. As previously discussed, the NWAC privileged meetings and public oratory as the primary methods of public communication. Speeches are thus essential in understanding the NWAC's propaganda message. However, central direction of content was much stronger with published propaganda, as editorial staff could decide what was published and where. Though the NWAC could provide guidelines, notes and copies of pamphlets, they had minimal control over speakers' comments on any occasion, beyond the power to withhold future engagements if unacceptable arguments were employed.

The most notable personalised condemnation of 'pacifism' discovered (in the local press of 30 constituencies) occurred at Leicester on 5 May 1918.[92] Here, the local WAC held a meeting in the marketplace at the same time as the local Labour Party's annual May Day celebration. On the NWAC platform were Lieutenant C.R. Pearse of the Royal Naval Volunteer Reserve (RNVR), a Canadian soldier (Lieutenant Towers) and Albert Howarth, a local BWNL secretary. The major speakers on the Labour platform were the constituency MP (an unwell MacDonald) and alderman George Banton, a veteran Leicester Labour campaigner. Shortly after MacDonald began speaking, his meeting was disrupted, first by the national anthem at the NWAC meeting, then by a group of 'discharged' soldiers singing Rule Britannia and marching through the crowd waving a flag. Finally several men, including discharged soldiers, attempted to rush the Labour platform and place a French flag on it in honour of Britain's ally, prompting police to intervene and arrest three people. MacDonald left the meeting early under police escort. Banton blamed the mayor,

---

90 F.P. Armitage, *Leicester 1914–1918: The War-Time Story of a Midland Town* (Leicester: Edgar Backus, 1933), p. 281.

91 'No Offer Yet!', *Reality*, no. 114, 21/3/18; *Our United War Aims* (no. 33).

92 Ben Beazley, *Four Years Remembered: Leicester during the Great War* (Derby: Breedon Books, 1999), pp. 159–60, gives a brief account. The following reflects local press reports.

Jonathan North, for inciting the disruption at a NWAC meeting in April, at which North regretted that

> in some quarters Leicester had a doubtful reputation. ("Shame.") Some had called it the "Pacifists' Paradise." ... Notwithstanding their small number, the Pacifists were able to be mischievous, and it behoved all true patriots to see that the young men of the country were not led astray by their wiles. Perhaps they had made a mistake in Leicester in not counteracting the insidious attacks of the Pacifists. (Applause, and "There are plenty of lamp-posts in the town.")[93]

The event's repercussions continued to be felt in Leicester for some considerable time. Articles and letters in the local press called for MacDonald's resignation, with some also debating the propriety of the NWAC's involvement.[94] On 15 May, those arrested during the disruption, including Howarth, who unrepentantly asserted in court that MacDonald and Banton had been 'preaching sedition',[95] had their cases dismissed, prompting the local ILP organ, the *Leicester Pioneer*, to argue that since DORA had not been invoked against such 'sedition' it had not occurred, and to protest that although 'outsiders cause a disturbance one week and threaten in a public Police Court to do the same another week ... nothing will be done in the matter'.[96]

The use of adversarial patriotism had a strong impact here, prompting violent disruption reminiscent of pre-war political meetings.[97] Such events, however, were seemingly quite rare, as were suggestions as violent as that of the Australian soldier who told his audience 'if any pacifists come to Ilfracombe ... just toss them over one of your huge cliffs'.[98] Generally NWAC propaganda against 'pacifists' was less personal and more concerned to demonstrate the need for continuing unity and fortitude. 'Don't let pacifism creep into your hearts, and disorganise the common union of the country', the Unionist speaker Edward Gieve implored his Barnstaple audience. 'Pacifism means prolonging the War, and prolonging the War means more loss of life.'[99] Lord Leverhulme summarised the problem with 'pacifism' in a *Daily Chronicle* interview (reprinted as a NWAC pamphlet):

---

93 'Our War Aims. Meeting at De Montfort Hall', 13/4/18, *Leicester Daily Mercury*, p. 7. Note again the implied feminisation of 'pacifists' in the reference to their 'wiles'.

94 See esp. *Leicester Daily Mercury*, 6-17/5/18. Reactions to the event are discussed in chapters 9–10.

95 'Labour Demonstration Disturbances. Anti-MacDonaldites at the Police Court', *Leicester Daily Mercury*, 15/5/18, p. 5.

96 'Sequel to the May Day Disturbance', *Leicester Pioneer*, 17/5/18, p. 4.

97 Lawrence, *Speaking*.

98 Lieutenant P.H. Aspinall, cited in 'War Aims Campaign', *Ilfracombe Chronicle*, 3/11/17, p. 3.

99 'France's Day at Barnstaple', *North Devon Journal*, 18/7/18, p. 2.

THE FOOD HOG.

JACK: "WOT'S HE BIN DOING, MATE?"
BILL, THE CHAUFFEUR: "LOOKS LIKE EXCEEDING HIS FEED-LIMIT."

Figure 26. Frank Styche, 'The Food Hog', Welcome, no. 16, 17/7/18, p. 189

the pacifist suggests to Germany that timorous souls over here are looking for any other way out of this war than the way of victory ... The only thing that can dismay the German Government is our resolute announcement that we'll ... go on fighting ... if it takes us twenty years more ... That's the true Englishness of this war ...[100]

In addressing profiteering, which the NWAC believed was partly responsible for 'a state of mind in which anti-war propaganda secures sympathetic attention',[101] propagandists were often scarcely less harsh. At Seeton, South Yorkshire, the veteran socialist chairman, George Pickthorne, blamed public discontent partly on profiteering. 'The "food hoggs" [*sic*] and profiteers were criminals, and should be dealt with as such, for to make money out of the blood of the lads who were defending our shores was dreadful.'[102] Condemnation of profiteering and hoarding was particularly important since the crime was generally regarded as one committed by the wealthiest members of society and therefore corrosive of community solidarity (see figure 26).[103]

100 Harold Begbie, *Negotiate Now? A Business Man's Answer: An Interview with Lord Leverhulme* (London, n.d. [1918]), p. 7.
101 TNA:PRO T102/16, NWAC 'Report Up to 8th December, 1917'.
102 'National War Aims. The Campaign in Keighley and District', *Keighley News*, 13/10/17, p. 5.
103 Waites, *Class Society*, esp. pp. 61–71, 222–26.

Strikers could also receive short shrift from propagandists (as the 'National Film' shows). One pamphlet suggested infantrymen would rather shoot strikers 'than kill Huns. At least the Hun is not a traitor!' Striking for extra pay was outrageous when 'the infantryman received a shilling a day for the work he did for you!'[104] Another pamphlet, by F.H. Rose of the ASE, was a 'call from the workbench'. Rose complained that in recent months (the pamphlet was probably produced early in 1918) 'the decadence of the skilled worker has been marked and manifest'. He said workers' grievances were national rather than sectional problems, and that

> Millions of our countrymen and women are making sacrifices which put the rest of us to shame. We have sacrificed a few workshop regulations of doubtful value ... [with] a promise to have them restored ... Those who cheerfully make the supreme sacrifice ask us only to work steadfastly to give them the means to make it not in vain.[105]

Women were similarly reminded of their larger responsibilities. Discussing the successful strike of female omnibus conductors, Miss E.M. Goodman warned that it constituted a dangerous example to women earning less than the conductors and that 'though strikes are sometimes necessary, they are very wasteful, not only for the employer, but for the country and the worker himself [*sic*] ... In war-time it is not everyone for herself, but all for England!'[106] In a wartime context of increased scrutiny on the everyday life of individuals, where perceived waste or frivolity could be considered outrageous moral transgressions, civilians of all sorts could be criticised and placed outside the bounds of acceptable conduct.[107] NWAC propagandists' task was to bring such people back to the fold. Adversarial patriotic condemnations performed part of this function, but simply hurling abuse at recalcitrant workers, greedy food-hoarders or the exhausted and war-weary would not achieve the desired results. Such criticism was thus only part of the broader narrative deployed by propagandists, linked to other, more celebratory or reasoned elements.

BY identifying numerous adversaries, external and internal, with varying degrees of threat to Britain, NWAC propagandists could make audiences aware of the need for continued dedication and the avoidance of complacency. Adversarial patriotism did not, and was not intended

---

104 Holmes, *An Infantryman on Strikes*, pp. 10, 18.

105 F.H. Rose, *A Call to War Workers of the Engineering and Shipbuilding Industries* (London, 1918), pp. 5, 8, 13–14. Some of these themes are developed in subsequent chapters.

106 Margaret Osborne (Goodman), 'The Woman's Part. Strikers and Women's Wages', *Droitwich Guardian War Supplement*, w.e. 12/10/18, p. 2.

107 On increasing moral disapproval, see Monger, 'Sporting Journalism', pp. 376–78; Jan Rüger, 'Entertainments', in Winter and Robert (eds), *Capital Cities at War*, II.

to, define British identity, but rather to illuminate possible threats to it. Identity was constructed primarily through the recognition of various cherished values and a desire to maintain and enhance them, as discussed in ensuing chapters. Adversaries tested British identity and patriotism. British failure to recognise and defeat these adversaries would be a renunciation of that identity (as 'pacifists' had supposedly renounced their Britishness). Adversarial patriotism was, therefore, an essential part of a broader patriotic model meant to ensure that British identity did not stagnate or become brittle but remained robust, vigorous and adaptable.

CHAPTER 6

Civilisational Principles: Britain and its Allies as the Guardians of Civilisation

> The war is no longer one between two groups of nations. It is the civilised world fighting to chastise rebels against its fundamental laws ...
> To make an end of war nothing less is requisite than a shifting of the centre of human allegiance from nationality to something wider. We need to feel a super-national patriotism.[1] – Lord Hugh Cecil, MP

A S CHAPTER 5 demonstrated, the NWAC's interpretation of British identity looked both inward and outward. However, whereas adversarial patriotism provided a predominantly negative motivation, the supranational and proprietorial sub-patriotisms presented positive explanations of what being British meant. Both transcended national boundaries. Supranational patriotism celebrated Britain's similarities with, and differences from, its allies, especially the USA, France and the empire (usually restricted to the 'white' Dominions). By dwelling on examples of behaviour or attitude where Britons were putatively surpassed by their allies, NWAC propaganda sought not to inspire through fear or outrage but to appeal to British pride in positive ways. In lauding French or American civilians, or Dominion soldiers, propagandists combined an explicit message of praise and friendship towards Britain's allies with an implicit encouragement of patriotic rivalry. Additionally, supranational patriotism illuminated similarities between Britain and its 'great' allies, thereby fusing supranational and proprietorial patriotism. Four values – honour, liberty, justice and democracy – were constantly invoked (sometimes with attendant emphasis on Christianity) to demonstrate that Britain and its allies fought for 'civilisation'. The NWAC's handbook listed 26 countries which had 'given their verdict' in favour of the war aims of 'the Allied Democracies', up to Costa Rica's declaration of war on 25 May 1918,[2] all of which were designated parts of the civilised world. However, a 'great power' mentality was evident in NWAC propaganda,

---

1   Lord Hugh Cecil, 'Can We Make Peace To-day?', *Reality*, 138, 5/9/18, p. 1.
2   *Aims and Effort*, p. 52.

THE NEW ALLY.

TOMMY *(to Poilu):* "THE NEW CHUM'S ALL RIGHT, AIN'T HE, MATE?"

Figure 27. Frank Styche, 'The New Ally', Welcome, no. 17, 24/7/18, p. 198

with Britain and its settler colonies, the USA and France (the major military contributors on the pre-eminent western front) generally the foci of supranational patriotic rhetoric. Belgium and Serbia served different roles as heroic victims (or martyrs) of enemy aggression, providing important examples of the 'little nations' or 'small states' for which the 'great civilised powers' fought, and were usefully employed to appeal to the sympathy of Britain's own 'small' sub-nations. Italy – perhaps because of the ideologically awkward 'squalid … bribery' necessary to secure its allegiance,[3] perhaps because the near collapse at Caporetto in October 1917 unhappily exemplified allied fragility – featured hardly at all, despite the presence of Italy's Foreign Secretary, Sonnino, at the NWAC's inaugural meeting.

By privileging Britain and its 'great' allies within supranational discourse, NWAC propaganda sought to foster patriotic pride in Britain's global position as a key representative of 'civilisation'. Furthermore, proprietorial patriotism, when slightly removed from supranational issues, also suggested that Britain might be superior even to its most prestigious allies. By emphasising Britain's heritage of liberty and democratic institutions, and its particularly strong identification with

---

3   Wilson, *Myriad Faces*, p. 27. On Italy's demands, see Stevenson, *First World War and International Politics*, pp. 47–58.

honourable conduct, NWAC propagandists could (gently) suggest British civilisational pre-eminence. Hence, while supranational patriotism placed Britain among several 'civilised' nations, proprietorial patriotism, emphasised in particular ways, allowed Britain to claim to be *primus inter pares*. This (unsurprisingly) differed from earlier Wellington House propaganda for US consumption which, while similarly stressing common Anglo-American values, had suggested that the civilisational principles in question were particularly American.[4] Persuasive patriotic appeals to British citizens required reasons for specifically British pride, even in a situation where affinities with other nations were being stressed.

OF Britain's allies, NWAC propaganda gave most attention to the USA. A new ally (technically an 'associate power'), having declared war in April 1917, the US represented enormous military and economic resources, making Allied defeat extremely unlikely. While this was recognised and celebrated (figure 28), most relevant NWAC propaganda was concerned with the ideological meaning of US involvement. Generally, propagandists approached the USA in two (sometimes interrelated) ways. First, it could be described as an impartial, democratic judge, which had stood aloof, calling for peace, until circumstances compelled it to abandon isolationism and join the war on Britain's side. Its delayed entry allowed propagandists to depict US intervention as a judgement on the justice of the allied cause and enemy iniquity. This judgement supposedly endorsed allied decisions and behaviour, prompting the second propaganda treatment of the USA, which extended this general approval to more specific claims about close Anglo–US ties. Thus, NWAC propagandists strove to use supranational patriotism relating to the US both to show how Britain could improve, and as a source of patriotic pride that Britain was not only supported by, but culturally, ideologically and linguistically bound to the war's supposed moral arbiter.

A regular speaker for the NWAC, the American judge Henry Neil informed his Leicester audience that 'America had been in no great rush' to declare war, but that Germany's behaviour had persuaded US citizens of their 'duty to the rest of the world ... to fight, not only for their own freedom, but for the freedom of others'. In Cheltenham, Revd P. Campbell Morgan claimed that the USA's 'sword' was 'unstained' having never been 'unsheathed ... save in the cause of liberty'.[5] NWAC propaganda

---

4   Jessica Bennett and Mark Hampton, 'World War I and the Anglo-American Imagined Community: Civilization vs. Barbarism in British Propaganda and American Newspapers', in Joel H. Wiener and Mark Hampton (eds), *Anglo-American Media Interactions, 1850–2000* (Basingstoke: Palgrave MacMillan, 2007), pp. 157–63.

5   'America's Part in the War', *Leicester Daily Mercury*, 11/10/18, p. 3; 'America's Part in the Great War', *The Looker-On. A Social, Political and Fashionable Review for Cheltenham and County*, 6/4/18, p. 4.

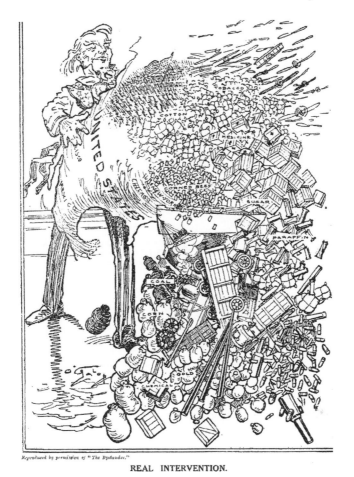

REAL INTERVENTION.

Figure 28. 'Real Intervention', Reality, no. 107, 31/1/18, p. 1 (reproduced from The Bystander)

emphasised the disinterested and unselfish motivations behind the US's entry into the war (though, given the immense financial links with the allies, particularly Britain, the USA eventually had little alternative but to protect its investment).[6] Nevertheless, the USA's moral authority was exploited by publishing American accounts of German misdeeds, including the former ambassador in Germany, James W. Gerard and a former consul in Ireland, Wesley Frost, who claimed to have 'collected ... much of the

---

6   Kathleen Burk, 'The Diplomacy of Finance: British Financial Missions to the United States 1914–1918', *Historical Journal*, 22:2 (1979); idem, *Britain, America and the Sinews of War, 1914–18* (London: Allen & Unwin, 1985); Strachan, *First World War*, pp. 815–992.

AMERICA'S VIEW OF UNITY.

"TOGETHER YOU WILL WIN."

Figure 29. 'America's View of Unity', Reality, no. 119, 25/4/18, p. 1

evidence on which America [had] entered the war',[7] citing 21 examples of German naval barbarity against civilian shipping.

Further, with its exalted status, the USA was an example ostensibly worthy of British emulation. British workers were regularly provided with evidence of the hard work of patriotic Americans. *Reality* quoted the US labour leader Samuel Gompers's appeal to 'fellow-workers' in Britain to acknowledge their duty to soldiers making 'the supreme sacrifice' by themselves making 'the greatest physical sacrifice possible' at work.[8] In Sheffield, local Trades and Labour Council 'Bolsheviks' were reportedly dismayed by the US labour delegate W.H. Shortt's strident patriotism. Shortt declared 'that if the criticisms he had just listened to were uttered in Germany the man who uttered them would promptly be in jail', adding that although US workers had taken years to be convinced of the war's

---

7   James W. Gerard, *When Germany Will Break* (*Searchlight* series, 9, n.p.d. [1918?]); Wesley Frost, *Devils of the Deep* (n.p.d., [1917?]), p. 3.

8   'Time to Do and Dare', *Reality*, 140, 19/9/18, p. 1.

necessity, they now fully supported their Government, having 'set aside for the time being trade union principles'.[9]

However, while the USA served as an object of emulation, NWAC propagandists also sought to stress the nations' very close bonds, converting effusive praise of US moral authority into patriotic self-congratulation. In a speech on 4 July 1918, Woodrow Wilson, a noted Anglophile,[10] compared the US revolutionary hero George Washington with the arbiters of Magna Carta, asserting that 'Washington ... like the Barons at Runnymede, spoke and acted, not for a class, but a people', a statement reprinted more than once by the NWAC.[11] The NWAC had already claimed Wilson's allegiance, quoting Sir Mark Sykes's assertion in December 1917 that Wilson 'had blood in his veins of English stock'.[12] Similarly, at Malmesbury, Bromhead Mathews had remarked that Americans were 'only a bit of Old Britain after all'.[13] The NWAC's Liberal assistant editor, E.W. Record, twice returned to turn-of-the-century language, asserting that with civilian steadfastness 'the united Anglo-Saxon race' would triumph. 'Britain's word is pledged. America's word is pledged ... It is not the Anglo-Saxon way to juggle with the obligations of honour ...[or] compromise with those ... without honour.' Record averted the paradox of the USA fighting for liberty alongside its erstwhile oppressor by arguing that Britons were glad the USA had won independence, since the 'American Colonists fought for English ideals while we fought against them.'[14] By contrast, a Texan clergyman, Dr Fort Newton, claimed the revolution was irrelevant since the 'American forefathers stirred themselves to war ... not in anger against Britons, but because a German sat upon the throne of England in 1776.'[15]

In discussing the USA, NWAC propaganda used supranational patriotism simultaneously to exhort, by suggesting that morally and effort-wise the USA surpassed Britain, and to exult by providing examples of the close ties between the nations, allowing citizens to comfort themselves by basking in reflected transatlantic moral sunlight. Proprietorial patriotism

---

9 'American's Plain Talk. No Sympathy with Sheffield Malcontents', *Sheffield Daily Telegraph*, 16/5/18, p. 2; 'A Straight Talk. U.S. Labour will Not Meet German Workers Till Liberty is Assured', *Sheffield Independent*, 16/5/18, p. 3.

10 Perkins, *Great Rapprochement*, pp. 289–91.

11 'What are the Conditions of Peace? President Wilson's Answer', *Reality*, 130, 11/7/18, p. 4; Woodrow Wilson, *Wilson's Message: The Conditions of Peace* (*Message* series, 3, n.p.d. [1918]).

12 'What Britain Has Done', *Reality*, 101, 18/12/17, p. 4.

13 'National War Aims Campaign', *Wilts and Gloucestershire Standard*, 3/11/17, p. 6.

14 (Record), 'Letter from London', *North Devon Herald*, 8/11/17; 12/9/18; 18/7/18, all p. 3. This was apparently not a permanent attitude: the 1924 film *America* was banned because its portrayal of the War of Independence 'was considered offensive to Britain': John M. Mackenzie, *Propaganda and Empire: The Manipulation of British Public Opinion, 1880–1960* (Manchester: Manchester University Press, 1984), p. 79.

15 Dr Fort Newton, 'Seen above the Smoke of Battle', *Reality*, 124, 30/5/18, p. 3.

THE BRITISH BULLDOG: "YOU KNOW, ALPHONSE, I'M SURE WE'RE OF THE SAME BREED. THE WAY YOU HAVE HUNG ON TO THE HUNS HAS QUITE PUT MY REPUTATION FOR "GRIP" INTO THE SHADE." THE FRENCH BULLDOG: "MONSIEUR, I AM PROUD TO COUNT MYSELF OF YOUR BRAVE FAMILY."

Figure 30. David Wilson and W.F. Blood, 'The Same Strain', Welcome, *no. 15, 10/7/18, p. 175*

attempted to provide even greater self-satisfaction, but this was also attainable by inverting supranational patriotism and awarding Britain's allies British attributes. Hence, in Harrogate a speaker referred to 'the bulldog tenacity of the British and French troops, and lately that of the Americans',[16] thus deeming Britain's allies honorary Britons by categorising them as one of Britain's national animal symbols (figure 30). Both of Britain's principal allies had only recently become 'friendly powers', the USA in the mid- to late 1890s[17] and France since the 1904 Entente Cordiale. While Anglo-Saxonism provided a pre-war point of Anglo-

---

16 'Remembrance Day', *Ripon Gazette*, 8/8/18, p. 3.
17 On earlier attitudes, see James Epstein, '"America" in the Victorian Cultural Imagination', in Fred M. Leventhal and Roland Quinault (eds), *Anglo-American Attitudes: From Revolution to Partnership* (Aldershot: Ashgate, 2000).

American unity, no such idea linked Britain and France, and culturally and socially Britain had less in common with France than with the USA or Germany. Therefore, France played a different supranational role to the USA in NWAC propaganda. As a 'front-line' nation, French civilian experience (unlike American) demonstrated how much harder life could be for Britons. Further, France had fought alongside Britain since 1914, and was thus more appropriately the subject of gratitude and admiration. Finally, exalting Britain's traditional enemy in comparison to its current adversaries served to highlight the issues at stake in the war.

The occasion for most NWAC propaganda treatments of France was 'France's Day', 12 July 1918 (the Friday before Bastille Day). Other nations' public holidays had been celebrated in Britain before. During the height of Anglo-Saxonism in 1898, 4 July 'was celebrated as a holiday throughout Britain',[18] and various national holidays were marked in Britain during the war. However, on France's Day, 117 constituency WACs planned some sort of event.[19] Unusually, this was a centrally promoted NWAC event organised to 'let our gallant Allies see that our people are not unmindful of the debt we owe to the French people' and to reciprocate France's celebration of St George's Day. The NWAC suggested that mayors should lead meetings and towns should send telegrams to the French president, fly the French flag on all public buildings, play the *Marseillaise* at places of public entertainment and address schoolchildren on the day's significance.[20] At Keighley, where the *Keighley News* stressed that few places had 'established closer relations with France than this district' (Keighley had had pre-war ties with the Parisian communes of Suresnes and Puteaux), the corporation declined to hold an official meeting though it enacted the other suggestions.[21]

Elsewhere, more marked enthusiasm was evident. In Evesham every schoolchild saluted the *tricolore* and sang the *Marseillaise*.[22] According to Avner Ben-Amos, in wartime France, communal singing of the *Marseillaise* was used to 'evoke the memory of the Revolutionary wars', becoming a 'myth' that reduced the complex meanings of the French national anthem to a morale-boosting public activity.[23] In Britain, it arguably symbolically

18 Anderson, *Race*, p. 119.
19 Statistics from Register Database. Average events per day was 13.54.
20 Letter from Boraston, Wallace Carter and Thompson to Keighley WAC, reprinted in 'War Aims Committee and Corporation. Correspondence About France's Day', *Keighley News*, 13/7/18, p. 4.
21 'Local Topics. Keighley Townspeople's Greeting to France', *Keighley News*, 13/7/18, p. 4.
22 'France's Day', *Evesham Journal*, 13/7/18, p. 8.
23 Avner Ben Amos, 'The *Marseillaise* as Myth and Metaphor: The Transfer of Rouget de Lisle to the Invalides during the Great War', in Valerie Holman and Debra Kelly (eds), *France at War in the Twentieth Century: Propaganda, Myth and Metaphor* (Oxford: Berghahn Books, 2000), pp. 29–30.

removed the historical distinction between the ordered progress of British constitutional development and the violent development of French democracy. Propagandists now stressed the common civilisational concerns motivating British and French involvement in the war. At Barnstaple, the Unionist speaker Edward Gieve remarked,

> France and England had often been at each other's throat during the olden days, but whether on land or sea there had always existed between the two countries a knightly chivalry, which had made us cherish a great respect for France ...[24]

In saying this, Gieve subtly emphasised civilised values, suggesting that though traditional enemies Britain and France had always fought according to certain principles, implicitly absent from the current war. Similarly, Record acclaimed 'France, clean of soul, the pattern of chivalry ... our once "sweet enemy", now our truest and noblest friend', arguing that Joan of Arc's defeat in fighting against a 'wrong done ... by England' was a higher victory, vindicated by its cause, in the same way that (an unthinkable) defeat would be against Germany.[25] In Liverpool, the lord mayor argued that the storming of the Bastille was 'the first great act of democracy asserting its right' and symbolised contemporary principles, ignoring traditional English uses of 'civilisation' as a counterweight to French 'democracy'.[26]

At Ipswich, the local MPs, Asquithian Liberal D.F. Goddard and Unionist Captain F.J.C. Ganzoni, both argued that France was at the pinnacle of civilised resistance. Goddard reminded his audience that France had 'suffered in a good many ways far more than we had in England' (a point already stressed by the mayor, H.D. Phillips) and that France fought for 'good feeling between peoples, for freedom, for justice, and England shared ... her ideals'. Ganzoni quoted France's revolutionary ideals of liberty, equality and fraternity and asked whether any other nation 'had given more evidence of its real love for liberty and the lengths for which it was prepared to go in order to defend it'.[27] Taken together, these arguments presented a cultivated example of supranational patriotism. While stressing France's strong heritage of liberty, and that it suffered more than Britain (or England), Goddard's linking of English and French ideals blurred this privileging of France. Furthermore, the phraseology

24 'France's Day at Barnstaple', *North Devon Journal*, 18/7/18, p. 2.
25 (Record), 'Letter from London', *North Devon Herald*, 18/7/18, p. 3.
26 'Homage to France. Her Suffering and Glory', *Liverpool Daily Post and Mercury*, 13/7/18, p. 3. On civilizational traditions, see Mandler, *National Character*.
27 'France's Day. Ipswich Celebrations', *East Anglian Daily Times*, 13/7/18, p. 5. On French propaganda uses of Revolutionary rhetoric, see Michael Moody, '"Vive la Nation!" French Revolutionary Themes in the Posters & Prints of the First World War', *Imperial War Museum Review*, 3 (1988); Horne, '"L'impôt du sang"'; Ben Amos, '*Marseillaise*'.

of Ganzoni's question enabled the consideration that Britain could actually claim to be more liberty-loving, since it had declared war without being directly threatened. Ganzoni also celebrated the 'knitting together' of Britain and France by the war, a point emphasised elsewhere. At Liverpool the French consul, Baron Barriere, referred to the 'communion of hearts' between the nations 'in defence of liberty', while in Wakefield the deputy mayor, C. Hardy-Richards, insisted that after the war 'we wanted ourselves and France to be more friendly, to be, as it were, as of one race and one nation (cheers)'.[28]

Like the pre-war social reformers discussed by E.P. Hennock, NWAC propagandists regarded France with a 'highly selective eye', seeking examples to influence 'the condition of England [Britain]'.[29] Admiration expressed for 'hardy, wholesome, untiring folk, who knew the value of work and who seemed to find in the performance of duty its own absolute and sufficient blessing' (which sounded rather more like a traditional description of Englishmen),[30] or claims that one 'does not hear of strikes in France',[31] suggested a wholly committed home front, whereas areas of France were actually rife with strikes and discontent, if not defeatism, throughout 1917 and 1918.[32] Nevertheless, France was an important example as it had both (unlike Britain or the USA) suffered the indignity of invasion, showing Britons that life could be worse, and (unlike Belgium or Serbia) continued to play a major role militarily, economically and industrially, thus providing a positive rather than negative motivation for British civilian exertion.

WITH the USA and France, supranational patriotic propaganda proclaimed ties of culture, language or ideals, and could use comparisons to reflect credit upon Britain. This was extended in discussing the empire, which was portrayed as the ultimate proof of Britain's civilisational credentials. The empire enabled patriotic self-congratulation because of the voluntary involvement of imperial nations in the war (ostensibly demonstrating both the liberty enjoyed by British possessions and their adoption of British values),[33] and because the empire arguably constituted a prototype League of Nations. Imperial figures, from the former anti-British Boer War hero and Imperial War Cabinet member

---

28 'France's Day', *Liverpool Courier*, 13/7/18, p. 3; 'France's Day', *Wakefield Express*, 13/7/18, p. 7.
29 Hennock, *Social Reform*, p. 206.
30 (Sheehan), 'The Homes of France. Their Glory and Their Grandeur', *Cornish Times War Supplement*, w.e. 24/8/18, p. 2; for an English comparison, see Parry, *Politics*, p. 62.
31 Holmes, *Infantryman on Strikes*, p. 12.
32 P.J. Flood, *France 1914–18: Public Opinion and the War Effort* (Basingstoke: MacMillan, 1990), pp. 145–81; Becker, *Great War*, pp. 238–66.
33 *Aims and Effort*, pp. 8, 54–55.

Figure 31. Wilmot Lunt and W.F. Blood, 'Four of the Finest', Welcome, *no. 16, 17/7/18, p. 181*

Smuts to ordinary soldiers, provided comforting illustrations of benevolent British rule and the desirability of Britain's way of life. NWAC propaganda usually focused on the 'white' Dominions (figure 31), probably reflecting an assumption that they were culturally closest to Britain, and the awkwardness of discussing self-determination or the 'rights of small nations' while maintaining control over colonial possessions with little or no self-government. Where non-white colonies were discussed, it was not in terms of equality but condescension. Bonar Law displayed a paternalist attitude towards India when discussing its part in Palestine, arguing that

> as an indication of the differences of spirit between the Alliance and our enemies, I think that we have as much reason to be proud of the fact that Indian troops, after our rule in India, have played that part as in the part which has been given to us.[34]

---

34 *Bonar Law's Message: The Way to Security* (*Message* series, 7, n.p.d. [1918]), p. 16. Germany had accused France and Britain of barbarity in using colonial troops in a 'white man's war'. Audoin-Rouzeau and Becker, *1914–1918*, pp. 150–52.

Bishop Frodsham, preaching at Oxford, celebrated that

> Not only in India, but also among the less developed races of Africa and the South Seas, there is apparently a genuine appreciation ... that the British Empire stands for the moral principles of justice, truth, and recognition of the rights of all humanity.

Nevertheless, he warned that involving 'tropical African races' in 'killing ... white men ... at the instigation of white men', together with German militarism made it essential to maintain peace and order by replacing native religions and customs with Christianity. Frodsham also added a further spiritual patriotic angle to his discussion. Regarding British imperial responsibilities, he wrote that Britons were 'in earnest in their desire to uphold the rights of the natives, and [thus] vindicate ... their Christian principles'. Frodsham's reference to vindication implied that Britain's failure to accept its responsibilities would forfeit its right to claim such Christian values for itself.[35]

By contrast, discussion of the white Dominions reflected considerably more identification between Britain and its colonies. In Wigan, the Conservative MP Rigby Swift asserted that 'so long as the blood of Englishmen flowed through English veins, so long as this people peopled the British Empire', Germany would be prevented from wreaking destruction.[36] At Barnstaple, Australian lieutenant P.H. Aspinall told his audience that in Britain's 'great colonies were people who were English as much as [the audience] were English, who had the same passionate love of being Britishers', while Smuts stressed he had 'fought ... for freedom in the Boer War', claiming (incredibly, given the guerrilla tactics, farm-burning and concentration camps) that it had been 'carried on by both sides in a sportsmanlike manner, and in a clean, chivalrous way'.[37] The involvement of Smuts, and South Africa, in the war was therefore claimed to demonstrate Britain's superior civilisation – even Britain's most recent enemy fought willingly alongside it. The theologian P.T. Forsyth wrote that Britons were recognised as 'trustees of justice over the world, and apostles of constitutional liberty', and boasted that Britain had 'given' its franchise and constitution to the Boers, because we 'could win the peoples we conquer, and neither carries malice'.[38]

In acknowledging ties between Britain and its dominions, some also advocated closer and more widespread post-war imperial unity. Former First Sea Lord, Admiral Sir Francis Bridgeman, referred at Ripon to the

---

35 Bishop Frodsham, *Empire after War*, pp. 4, 8–9, 12–14.
36 'To Combat Pacifism', *Wigan Examiner*, 10/11/17, p. 7.
37 'War Aims Campaign in North Devon', *North Devon Journal*, 1/11/17, p. 2; 'Prussianism Must Go', *Sheffield Daily Telegraph*, 25/10/17, pp. 5–6; General Smuts, *The British Commonwealth of Nations: A Speech Made by General Smuts On May 15th, 1917* (London, 1917), p. 2.
38 P.T. Forsyth, *The Root of a World-Commonwealth* (London, 1918), p. 8.

debt owed to 'those galant [*sic*] patriots from our great Colonial Empire', asking,

> Are our Crown Colonies after the war to remain in the same subordinate position ... or shall they be invited to ... take their place by the side of the legislators of the Old Country? We owe them this, and we ought to be proud of their co-operation.[39]

The empire's wartime service prompted a more general revival of ideas of imperial federation and imperial patriotism; a competition was even launched to add an imperial verse to the National Anthem.[40]

Other propagandists suggested the empire constituted a miniature League of Nations. Smuts said it was 'a community of states and nations far greater than any empire', like Germany's or Rome's, while both Curzon and Lloyd George less subtly insisted that both the empire and the allied nations were leagues of nations, Lloyd George adding bombastically that the empire's dissolution would be 'a crime against civilisation'.[41] In discussing empire, NWAC propaganda sought ideological legitimacy by glossing over the less creditable domination of Britain's non-white possessions and focusing on voluntary imperial support and the cultural sympathy between Britain and the white Dominions. The propaganda thus attempted to divert discussion from embarrassing considerations of imperial power towards expositions of international cooperation between amicable states which redounded to Britain's credit and enabled it to claim proprietorship of ideas of liberty and international democracy.

AS previously discussed, Belgium featured in NWAC propaganda largely as a victim (often heavily gendered) of German aggression. Rather than an active military ally, 'brave little Belgium' had been 'ruthlessly violated by a nation sworn to protect her'.[42] Belgians were sometimes imbued with similar values to their 'great' allies: Belgium was held to be particularly honourable in refusing to assist Germany by allowing free passage through its territory.[43] This conformed with commentary in earlier periods of the war, when Belgian resistance had been held up as a demonstration to the world of what was possible,

---

39 'Major the Hon. E. Wood, M.P., and the War', *Ripon Gazette*, 8/11/17, p. 3.
40 Percy A. Scholes, *God Save the Queen! The History and Romance of the World's First National Anthem* (London: Oxford University Press, 1954), pp. 141–43; Keith McClelland and Sonya Rose, 'Citizenship and Empire, 1867–1928', in Hall and Rose (eds), *At Home*, p. 290.
41 *Aims and Effort*, pp. 84–85, 89–90; Lloyd George's speech on this subject was also reprinted as *Lloyd George's Message: Looking Forward* (*Message* series, 6, n.p.d., [1918]).
42 F.J.C. Ganzoni cited in 'France's Day', *East Anglian Daily Times*, 13/7/18, p. 5.
43 E.g., Mathews, *Vista of Victory*, pp. 7–8.

which added 'heroism' to 'our comfortable liberal-minded western civilisation'.[44] However, in NWAC propaganda, Belgium was very rarely considered an object of supranational patriotism like France, which had similarly suffered invasion and was frequently offered sympathy for its sufferings. One limited example was the Labour MP William Brace's argument at Llandrindod Wells that 'Wales was a small nation, and it would be passing strange if Wales were to be indifferent to the claims of Belgium, Servia [sic], Montenegro, Roumania, and all the other small nations.'[45] The explanation, seemingly, was a 'great power' mentality amongst NWAC propagandists – it was appropriate to link Belgium and Wales via supranational patriotism because Wales, too, was a 'small nation', a sub-section of Britain; by contrast, supposedly, Britain and its 'great' allies protected small nations, defending the principles of a civilisation for which they were most responsible. Once again this was a case of enabling British pride in the war, and a pragmatic acknowledgement that if nations like Belgium and Serbia were considered 'equals' of Britain, protests against British involvement would be harder to refute. Rather than melodramatically emphasising principles and chivalry, arguments for continuing the war would have to rely on the much less appealing issues of British diplomatic interests which, although important, were unlikely to mollify disgruntled and war-weary civilians.

When mentioned, Italy was generally an adjunct to the 'great' allies. The NWAC's handbook noted that Italy was one of the 'four most important powers' which acted together in military, economic and supply matters.[46] Similarly, on France's Day at Keighley, the Liberal MP, W.H. Somervell, described Italy as one of the 'three great European States' which had 'long stood as a special representative of the cause of liberty', perhaps recalling British Liberals' fascination with Italian unification.[47] However, probably for the reasons suggested above, little was said about Italy. McCurdy defended Italy's territorial ambitions, claiming it had 'entered the war to free Italians ... suffering under an oppression which Englishmen have happily never known',[48] but this was unusual. It may simply be that Italy was too remote in the British imagination to be of much propaganda value. Shortly after Caporetto, Major General Sir George Aston reported that the setback had made Italy 'one in the determination to see the war through', before recalling that Napoleon

---

44 Contribution of Sir Gilbert Murray to Hall Caine (ed.), *King Albert's Book: A Tribute to the Belgian King and People from Representative Men and Women throughout the World* (London: Daily Telegraph, 1914), p. 83. Similar sentiments are expressed by many of the other contributors to this collection.
45 'Allies' War Aims', *Radnor Express*, 27/9/17, p. 5.
46 *Aims and Effort*, p. 85.
47 'France's Day at Keighley', *Keighley News*, 13/7/18, p. 5.
48 McCurdy, *Truth about "Secret Treaties"*, p. 17.

had been defeated by strategic withdrawals,[49] thus creating a meaningful message about remaining united in adversity. Generally, however, Italy was overlooked in NWAC propaganda, too powerful to be a victimised 'small nation', too ideologically and militarily weak to often rank alongside the 'great' allies fighting.

IN claiming that the war was fought on behalf of civilisation, NWAC propaganda sought to elevate it above matters of national interests and power politics, recognising that, important as these were, they were inappropriate for maintaining civilians' emotional investment in a physically and mentally draining total war. As is already evident, supranational and proprietorial patriotism were often closely interwoven. At Shrewsbury, the Earl of Powis said that although the war was arduous and painful, Britons could take comfort that

> we are steadily being drawn into closer relations with those of our own kin and race – (applause) – and … making what we hope and believe will be lasting friendship with the noble Allies with whom we are fighting for the cause of civilisation. (Loud applause.)[50]

Propagandists continually stressed that Britain and its allies fought for liberty, honour, democracy and justice. However, there were also persistent underlying attempts to stress Britain's special part in establishing these values. Despite representing Woodrow Wilson as the icon of democracy, and referring to France's association with liberty, NWAC propagandists frequently sought to establish Britain as the progenitor of modern civilisation, continuing long-held assumptions about Britishness. At Liverpool, in October 1917, the Conservative Attorney General, F.E. Smith, explained that British soldiers would have to bear the brunt of the fighting 'until the daughter nation, the United States, took her stand by [Britain's] side … in the last great struggle for civilisation'. Following Smith, Asquith developed the civilisational theme and, while using the USA as a moral example, again suggested British pre-eminence in establishing civilised principles. Arguing that Britain entered the war simply to defend Belgium and Serbia, Asquith claimed the question was now

> whether or not the world is to hold with the best ideals which civilised races have framed for themselves …
> Why has America come into the contest? Has she any selfish interest to serve, any territory to acquire[?] … We have seen the practical and universal aggregation of the free democracies of the world fighting side by side for the cause of triumph on which the whole prospects of future freedom

---

49 Major General Sir George Aston, 'The Situation in Italy', *Reality*, 96, 10/11/17, p. 4.
50 'Remembrance Day at Shrewsbury', *Shrewsbury Chronicle*, 9/8/18, p. 2.

depends ... When we ... feel depressed and despondent we can ... recall the great struggles our forefathers made, both at home and abroad, in the same sacred cause ...[51]

Hence, proprietorial patriotism served two purposes. Combined with supranational patriotism, it established Britain among a community of like-minded nations fighting for principles which should be universal, attempting to provide reassuring assumptions about strength, security and unanimity. However, by extending the argument to suggest Britain's primary responsibility for the development and distribution of these principles NWAC propaganda was intended both to allow pride and self-satisfaction in Britain's civilisational pre-eminence, and to illuminate more clearly what was at stake for Britons in the war. Making war on behalf of principles was one thing, but proprietorial patriotism was used to illustrate concrete reasons for continuing British commitment to the war. Not only was Britain fighting for principles, but for *British-made* principles integral to national life and threatened by adversaries adhering to different, un-British principles. At Golborne, Lancashire, Viscount Wolmer explained that

> They were defending their own birthright. (Loud cheers.) Did they realise what a great thing it was to be Englishmen? ... [I]t was our nation which had given to the world its conception of political liberty and civil justice and right. That achievement ... was the result of many centuries of struggle and development ... To-day we are a self-governing people ... because we, as a nation, had been able to establish certain vital principles. We had learned, and we had taught others – (hear, hear) – that ... a pledge once given must be adhered to – (hear, hear) – at all costs. (Applause.) They had learned as Englishmen – that a man's word was his bond ... They had also learned that those who governed had responsibilities to those whom they governed ... [T]he whole fundamental consideration upon which their civil rights were built, their political power, their national stability and safety depended upon those very principles ... challenged by the Central Powers ...[52]

A frequent stress of NWAC propaganda was on the principle of honour. This reflected long-standing preoccupations. The proverb 'an Englishman's word is his bond' (and its antecedents) had been part of the national lexicon since the early sixteenth century,[53] while concern with 'fair play' and chivalrous behaviour were key tenets of British conduct, inculcated especially at public schools, at least since the mid-Victorian

---

51 'Picton Hall. Mr. Asquith & Unruly Women', *Liverpool Daily Post and Mercury*, 12/10/17, p. 6.
52 'Lord Wolmer, M.P., at Golborne', *Wigan Examiner*, 4/12/17, p. 3.
53 'An Englishman's Word Is His Bond', in Jennifer Speake (ed.), *The Oxford Dictionary of Proverbs* (Oxford: Oxford University Press, 2003). Accessed online (10 May 2007) at www.oxfordreference.com.

period.[54] Basil Mathews argued that 'Europe [was] the first home of that great and ever-growing tradition of simple honour in the relations of human life ... that code of loyalties and faith which stands between us and barbarism'.[55] Frequently, however, 'honour' was claimed to be a particularly British virtue, providing an effective response to suggestions that Britain should have remained neutral. Britain's declaration of war in defence of Belgian neutrality, which it had guaranteed by treaty in 1839, provided considerable opportunity for self-congratulation. W.S. Sanders observed that 'Great Britain could have kept out of the war if she had chosen to place capitalistic interests ... above national honour',[56] while at Cheltenham the mayor argued that anyone who claimed Britain should have avoided war meant it should have 'denied our pledged and sworn word to Belgium', ignored France and 'made as much profit' as possible from 'nations to whom we had given our word of honour'.[57] The speaker thus accused dissenters of dishonourable greed, inverting a common dissenting critique of the war. By contrast, Sir Edward Grey's speech in the House of Commons on 3 August 1914 had stressed Britain's honourable obligations and the danger to its 'good name and reputation' alongside a pragmatic assertion that in the event of non-intervention Britain 'should not escape the most serious and grave economic consequences'.[58] This divergence can be explained by the differing purposes of the rhetoric. The purpose of Grey's speech was to appeal to both the honourable instincts and the businesslike sense of MPs in persuading them to endorse a war. NWAC propagandists, on the other hand, aimed to inspire continuing public commitment to the established reality of the war, and apparently judged that economic considerations could not be used in regard to this issue in a positive sense.

As noted in the previous chapter, honour could also be discussed adversarially against Germany by highlighting its disregard of international law and obligations. With this in mind, propagandists could develop expositions of honour containing threats to proprietorial patriotism, emphasising that if Britain did not accept its obligations it would cease to be the same nation. At Barnstaple the Liberal Tudor-Rees asserted that for 'a thousand years our ancestors had built up a record for rectitude, honour, and integrity'; and had Britain not aided Belgium, our 'honour, our credit, our traditions would have been gone', while the Unionist John Farnsworth

---

54   E.g., Mangan, *Athleticism*; Jonathan Rutherford, *Forever England: Reflections on Masculinity and Empire* (London: Lawrence and Wishart 1997), pp. 12–19; Girouard, *Return to Camelot*.

55   Mathews, *Vista of Victory*, p. 13.

56   William Stephen Sanders, *Is It a Capitalist War?* (NWAC pamphlet no. 19, n.p.d. [1917?]), p. 3.

57   'Remembrance Day', *Looker-On* (Cheltenham), 10/8/18, pp. 9–10.

58   PDC(5), 65 (3/8/14), col. 1825.

argued at Hirwain that such a 'stain' on Britain's honour would have 'handed down a heritage of littleness'.[59] Because of Germany's dishonourable conduct, demonstrated not only by atrocities but by the Treaty of Brest–Litovsk, Lord Leverhulme claimed that peace with an unreformed Germany would 'undermine our Anglo-Saxon mentality for centuries. We should never be the same race again.' 'Isn't there a time', he asked, 'when a nation must say, and mean it, Death rather than Dishonour?'[60]

B RITAIN'S reputation for honourable conduct was also held to place it at the forefront of the democratic world. *Reality* quoted the Greek prime minister Eleutherios Venizelos's assertion that after Germany's provocation of war, 'the democracy of the entire world turned enquiring eyes ... [towards] the attitude of England'.[61] NWAC propaganda extensively considered 'democracy'. This served, within adversarial patriotic discussion, to identify a significant difference between Britain's external adversaries, including Bolshevik Russia, and Britain and its allies, which was considered an effective way of addressing working-class grievances, as was a less oppositional approach of elucidating the benefits and virtues accompanying democratic behaviour.[62] Wilsonian democracy was highlighted as principled statesmanship which, by association and endorsement, NWAC propagandists could use to validate Britain's role in the war,[63] simultaneously undermining opponents by fervently embracing the figure and principles to which many dissenters had looked for assistance and inspiration.[64] Furthermore, by noting Wilson's connections with Britain, and demonstrating Britain's democratic heritage, attempts were made to claim British ownership of the principle.

Wilson's claim, that the USA intended to 'make the world safe for democracy', was a refrain taken up repetitively in NWAC propaganda, used almost as a simple catchphrase by speakers and writers as padding for their arguments.[65] Wilson himself was also effusively praised. The

---

59 'War Aims Campaign in North Devon', *North Devon Journal*, 1/11/17, p. 2; 'What We Fight for, and Why', *Glamorgan Free Press*, 22/11/17, p. 1.
60 Lord Leverhulme, *One or the Other* (*Searchlight* series, 14, n.p.d. [1918]).
61 'Greek Faith in Victory', *Reality*, 98, 24/11/17, p. 4.
62 E.g. 'The Meaning of Democracy', *Reality*, 135, 15/8/18, p. 4, quotes the Labour Minister J.R. Clynes advocating change by peaceful voting rather than revolution.
63 For links between Wilsonian and Lloyd Georgian democracy, see Roland Quinault, 'Anglo-American Attitudes to Democracy from Lincoln to Churchill', in Leventhal and Quinault (eds), *Anglo-American Attitudes*, pp. 129–32. An interesting corrective of views of Wilson as 'apostle of liberty' is provided by Erez Manela, 'Imagining Woodrow Wilson in Asia: Dreams of East–West Harmony and the Revolt against Empire in 1919', *American Historical Review*, 111:5 (2006).
64 Paul Mulvey, 'From Liberalism to Labour: Josiah C. Wedgwood and English Liberalism during the First World War', in Purseigle (ed.), *Warfare and Belligerence*.
65 E.g. *Aims and Effort*, pp. 77, 91; R. McNeill, MP, cited in 'Lest We Forget. What We Are Fighting For. National War Aims', *East Anglian Daily Times*, 27/11/17,

Irish nationalist, Sheehan, labelled Wilson 'our greatest "moral" leader' in his (anonymous) weekly column for the NWAC, while at least four pamphlets were produced in his name and he was quoted regularly in *Reality*.[66] However, while applauding Wilson's principles, propagandists were equally pleased to exploit his credentials to illuminate Britain's own democratic qualities. The Labour MP James Parker told a Leicester audience that 'Mr. Lloyd George, President Wilson and the Labour Party were in substantial agreement' over war aims, while at Swaffham, Norfolk, the Liberal MP Sir Richard Winfrey claimed that Wilson's peace terms were the same as those established by Asquith in 1914.[67]

In a speech in October 1918, reprinted as a pamphlet, Viscount Grey asserted that 'the people of this country are perfectly capable ... of knowing a democracy when they see it'.[68] Nevertheless, NWAC propaganda carefully explained the meaning of British democracy. Sheehan stressed the contemporary significance of parliament as 'the great centre of civic liberty'. He celebrated the fact that the vote, previously 'the privilege of property, is now proudly regarded as the badge of citizenship', adding that the proposed enfranchisement of some women was a 'mighty and tremendous' event.[69] This exemplifies the melodramatic democratic narrative which Patrick Joyce claims formed social identity through the inclusiveness that the presentation of democratic motifs inferred,[70] although by 1918 such inclusiveness was more directly provided by increased enfranchisement.

Elsewhere, propagandists dwelt on Britain's democratic heritage. At Llandrindod Wells, Brace reminded listeners that 'they stood on the same ground as Pitt, Palmerston and Gladstone ... and the ground was firm', adding that Britain

> was to all intents and purposes a republic ... as free in its constitution as any republican government ... was ever likely to be. (Cheers.) The people were supreme ... in the people's House of Parliament. The monarch was guided not by his own will, as in Germany, but by the opinion of his Parliament ... Their present constitution fitted in with the genius of their race.[71]

---

p. 5; C.A. McCurdy, *Freedom's Call and Duty: Addresses Given at Central Hall, Westminster, May and June, 1918* (London, n.d. [1918]), p. 20.

66 (Sheehan), 'The War & Westminster', *Seaham Weekly News*, 26/4/18, p. 2. The pamphlets were: *A World Peace. President Wilson's Programme* (NWAC pamphlet no. 34, n.p.d. [1918]); *Our Two Duties* (*Searchlight* series, 8, n.p.d.); *Why Are We Enlisted? President Wilson's Answer* (*Searchlight* series, 26, n.p.d. [1918]); *Wilson's Message*.

67 'Our War Aims', *Leicester Daily Mercury*, 13/4/18, p. 4; 'War Aims. Sir R. Winfrey, M.P., at Swaffham', *Thetford & Watton Times* 9/3/18, p. 1.

68 *Grey's Message: The League of Nations* (*Message* series, 8, [1918]), p. 10.

69 (Sheehan), 'The War and Westminster', *North Devon Herald*, 26/9/18, p. 6.

70 Patrick Joyce, 'The Constitution and the Narrative Structure of Victorian Politics', in James Vernon (ed.), *Re-reading the Constitution: New Narratives in the Political History of England's Long Nineteenth Century* (Cambridge: Cambridge University Press, 1996), esp. pp. 181–87.

71 'Allies' War Aims', *Radnor Express*, 27/9/17, p. 5.

Brace unambiguously linked democracy with British identity (continuing long-standing traditions),[72] and, in praising Britain's relative freedom compared to republics, also suggested British democratic pre-eminence. By attempting to establish incontrovertible links between Britain and democratic principles, NWAC propaganda also used democratic rhetoric to criticise internal adversaries who considered the increasingly pro-scriptive governance of Britain anti-democratic and Prussianised.[73] Brace argued that striking imperilled democracy: 'Down tools, and the divine right of kings will soon become an established fact; work, and Democracy will reign.'[74] At Wigan the Unionist MP R.J. Neville retorted to a heckler who shouted that 'Democracies' should try Germany for its wartime actions: '"Well go and do it ... you are a democrat["]', thus inverting dissenters' interpretations of democratic language. Neville's assumption (which received 'loud applause') was that Britain indisputably fought for democracy, therefore all 'democrats' should willingly fight in that cause.[75] In appropriating democracy as an ideological lodestar, NWAC propaganda again had a dual purpose; democracy provided an intellectually satisfying reason to make war while responding to dissenting challenges by trying to undermine their interpretation of democracy.

'JUSTICE' had three major meanings within NWAC propaganda. It could be discussed with regard to justice for small nations – that is, providing self-determination and national security; in reference to bringing Germany to justice for its crimes; or to emphasise that Britain fought a 'just war'. NWAC propagandists submerged these ideas into calls for a 'peace of justice', which again signified a rhetorical undermining of dissent (and German peace proposals) by providing an alternative to the 'peace with no annexations or indemnities' proposed by Kerensky in May 1917 and subsequently adopted by Bolsheviks, British dissenters and, when the war turned against the Central Powers, by Germany. In this case, dissenters were arguably misrepresented by NWAC propaganda. At Bath, for instance, the prominent dissenter Ethel Snowden (protected from prosecution under DORA by her husband's MP status),[76] argued that 'No peace would be democratic and worthy which did not include the complete destruction of German and all other kinds of militarism, and was not founded upon justice for all the peoples of the world.'[77] The

---

72 Robert Colls, 'The Constitution of the English', *History Workshop Journal*, 46 (1998).

73 Ward, *Red Flag*, pp. 133–37.

74 'Rt. Hon. Wm. Brace M.P. at Glyncorrwg', *Glamorgan Free Press*, 1/11/17, p. 1.

75 'War Aims Meeting at Wigan', *Wigan Examiner*, 17/11/17, p. 2.

76 Millman, *Managing*, pp. 185–86.

77 '"To a Democratic Peace." Mrs. Philip Snowden in Bath', *North Wilts Guardian*, 1/3/18, p. 5.

rhetoric deployed here was close to that used by NWAC propagandists, though Snowden's interpretations of militarism and justice may have been more expansive. Nevertheless, propagandists claimed that the disruptiveness of dissenters meant they constituted an adversarial threat to the war's prosecution.

As already discussed, references to the protection of the rights of small nations aimed to foster pride in British chivalry. Linking these rights to justice provided another reason for the necessity of continued effort. In Harrogate the Conservative MP, E. Wood, claimed that

> They maintained that the weaker individual should have the same consideration as the stronger ... applied that doctrine internationally and said that every State, be it as powerful as the German Empire or as weak as Belgium, had an equal right of just treatment before the great international bar of nations. (Applause.)[78]

The socialist A.S. Neill said 'vengeance' against Germany should be divine, but that 'foul outrages' like the *Lusitania*'s sinking had to be punished. 'Justice demands it in order that it may be shown that crime is still crime.'[79] In *Reality*, a cartoon portrayed a scene from *The Merchant of Venice*, with Wilson, as Portia, telling the Kaiser (Shylock), 'be assured thou shalt have justice, more than thou desir'st' (figure 32).[80]

NWAC propagandists combined discussion of the rights of small nations and the need for Germany to be brought to account for its actions into calls for a 'peace of justice'. For instance, Lloyd George asserted that there was 'no right you can establish, national or international, unless you establish ... that the man who breaks the law will meet inevitable punishment', further insisting that 'complete victory for the cause of justice and international freedom' was the only way to establish a viable League of Nations, which would otherwise be dominated by an abidingly militarist nation.[81]

Justice could also mean a 'just war'. Such discussion was usually linked to a spiritual approach to patriotism. Record insisted the war was 'a war of principles ... [involving] the first principles of our religion'. He noted that it had been called the 'Last Crusade' and reminded readers that a crusade was a religious war, adding that Germany had begun the war not 'for a religious end' but 'as a war of greed'.[82] Record's endorsement of the idea of a holy war was predicated upon both Britain's religious principles and what he considered German indifference to such ideals. Similarly, the Texan pastor Fort Newton insisted that the war was 'a holy

---

78 'Major the Hon. E. Wood, M.P., and the War', *Ripon Gazette*, 8/11/17, p. 3.
79 (A.S. Neill), *Our Real War Aim: By a Socialist* (*Searchlight* series, 15, n.p.d. [1918]).
80 Note again the possible anti-Semitism in this choice of characters.
81 *Lloyd George's Message*, pp. 5–7. Chapter 8 discusses the League of Nations further.
82 (Record), 'A Letter from London', *North Devon Herald*, 15/8/18, p. 3.

Figure 32. Detail from 'A Daniel Come to Judgment', Reality, no. 146, 31/10/18, pp. 2–3 (reproduced from The Bystander)

war ... for the preservation of those opportunities for which mankind has striven ... a war for the high privilege of spiritual growth'.[83] At Llandrindod Wells, Liberal MP Sir Francis Edwards agreed that Britain was fighting a 'righteous war' for the 'common good of humanity', asserting that the nation would otherwise be unable to bear the strain.[84] Edwards again linked Christianity closely with civilisational principles here, implying that it was the 'righteousness' of those ideals which moved Britons to accept the war's necessity. Here, spiritual patriotism arguably overrode a more constitutional or legalistic interpretation of British values. Alternatively it could be suggested that such constitutional values had permeated the national consciousness so considerably that they were almost sacred tenets, the breaching of which sanctified war in their defence.[85] In either case, spiritual patriotism enriched proprietorial

---

83 Newton, 'Seen above the Smoke of Battle', *Reality*, 124, 30/5/18, pp. 2–3; reprinted as *Fighting for the Faith* (*Searchlight* series, 10, n.p.d. [1918]).
84 'Allies' War Aims', *Radnor Express*, 27/9/17, p. 5.
85 See Wolffe, *God and Greater Britain*, p. 256.

patriotic arguments about liberty, justice, democracy and honour in a way which reiterates the vitality of religion in Britain during the war. Not only were these principles presented as rational requirements of civilised society, but also as articles of faith.

One interesting version of 'just war' rhetoric that did not involve a spiritual interpretation related to Ireland. In July 1918, Sheehan referred to Irish recruitment, lionising the nationalist MP Colonel Arthur Lynch who had fought against Britain in the Boer War and been sentenced to death for treason. Sheehan praised Lynch's 'strong sense of natural and political justice' in offering to assist in Irish recruiting, quoting Lynch's trust in Ireland's 'traditional regard' for 'right and justice'. In this instance, Sheehan sought both to re-justify the war and place Ireland alongside Britain and its 'great' allies as a principled nation, while also attempting to pique Irish patriotic pride by hoping Ireland would 'right herself before the world' by providing more soldiers.[86]

FREQUENTLY, 'justice' went hand-in-hand with 'liberty' in NWAC propagandists' arguments.[87] Justice for small nations invariably also meant liberty, and Grey spelt out liberty's importance to a League of Nations, avowing that 'you must have every Government in the League of Nations representing a free people' (though he did not define 'freedom', perhaps fearing awkward imperial questions).[88] However, the general NWAC argument was not merely that liberty was essential to peace, but that Britain was peculiarly endowed with it. Basil Mathews claimed that Britain's successful Middle Eastern campaign meant that 'from Gaza up to Damascus ... the chains of the ancient despotism of Turkey are broken and a new era of freedom, justice and security lies ahead'.[89] NWAC propaganda frequently referred to Britain's heritage of liberty. In so doing it created another key part of British civilisation that was threatened by adversaries, and another reason for continuing efforts to preserve Britain's identity. Additionally, propagandists acknowledged the necessary wartime restrictions on British liberty, stressing the importance of continuing the war to victory so that these liberties could be reinstated. Hence, the propaganda again sought to respond to criticism. By recognising complaints that British liberties were infringed by the war, the patriotic

---

86 (Sheehan), 'The War and Westminster', *Seaham Weekly News*, 12/7/18, p. 2. Note the similarity in discussion of Lynch's and Smuts's erstwhile opinions here. On Ireland, see also Sheehan's columns in the *Seaham Weekly News*, 26/4/18, 17/5/18, both p. 2.

87 E.g., 'War Aims Campaign. "Liberty, Justice, and Right"', *Ripon Gazette*, 25/10/17, p. 2; 'Downham Market. War Aims Meeting', *Dereham & Fakenham Times*, 2/3/18, p. 5.

88 *Grey's Message*, p. 10.

89 Basil Mathews, *The Freedom of the Holy Land* (*Searchlight* series, 30, n.p.d. [1918]). Note the inherent spiritual element here.

narrative again inverted criticism, arguing that the government intended to restore full freedom as soon as possible, and that by interfering with the war's progress dissenters served only to prolong such infringements. Furthermore, without total victory some restrictions (especially a permanently militarised state) might remain, since unreformed militaristic adversaries would necessitate continuing, semi-mobilised vigilance.

As already shown, NWAC propaganda presented the empire as proof of British liberties, since Britain's imperial possessions voluntarily involved themselves in the war. However, it was often stressed that Britain was peculiarly suffused with liberty and had introduced it to the world. Milner declaimed on St George's Day that 'Ordered liberty, the golden mean between anarchy and despotism, is our country's great gift to the world.'[90] As with democracy, Britain's long association with liberty was carefully demonstrated. Churchill described the US Declaration of Independence as 'the third of the title-deeds on which the liberties of the English-speaking race are founded', along with Magna Carta and the Bill of Rights, adding that the principles it embodied matched those of British contemporaries Lord Chatham and Edmund Burke, 'who in turn received them from John Hampden and Algernon Sidney'.[91] At Evesham, the vicar of All Saints' Church, Revd Dr Walker recalled the Battle of Evesham of 1265, at which Simon de Montfort was killed and his rebellion largely crushed. Walker said the battle had 'helped to make English liberty' labelling de Montfort 'the father of the English Parliament, the champion of liberty', and implying that this was responsible for the contemporary position of England 'at the head of nations that would be free'.[92] Here Walker linked local identity with national patriotic pride,[93] suggesting that Evesham's specific links to Britain's heritage of liberty made it partially responsible for Britain's position several hundred years later. Such a tendency also corroborates recent historiographical suggestions about the significance of anniversaries to British identity.[94] It is noteworthy that no references have been found to historical Welsh, Scottish or Irish attempts for liberty, despite the positive gloss put on US and French resistance to English authority, presumably to maintain the image of a totally and timelessly united nation and (certainly with Ireland) for fear of stirring up nationalist sentiments.

---

90 '"Beyond All Price." The Secretary of State for War', *Reality*, 120, 2/5/18, p. 4.

91 'Mr. Churchill on a "Union of Hearts"', *Reality*, 130, 18/7/18, p. 4. Note the irony that Magna Carta's arbiters neither spoke English nor considered themselves Englishmen, but nevertheless became national symbols. Anderson, *Imagined Communities*, p. 118.

92 'Evesham. Remembrance Day at Evesham', *Evesham Journal*, 10/8/18, p. 6.

93 On links between local and national identity, see the discussion in chapter 7.

94 Roland Quinault, 'The Cult of the Centenary, *c.*1784–1914', *Historical Research*, 71:176 (1998); Readman, 'Place of the Past'.

By tracing British associations with liberty through history, NWAC propagandists also retorted to Germany's attempt to subvert British naval supremacy by endorsing Wilson's demand for 'freedom of the seas'. At Keighley, H.F. Wyatt, the former Navy League figure who co-founded the Imperial Maritime League,[95] suggested that Britain's navy made Britain more suffused with liberty than was the case elsewhere: 'Military power had proved fatal to the liberties of the people, but sea power stopped at the shore and safeguarded popular liberty, and had ... allowed us to develop our own institutions of which we are now so proud.'[96] In *Reality*, an article lampooned Germany's demand for the reduction of British maritime influence, arguing that 'the German conception of "freedom" at sea means the removal of the policeman!', and citing Britain's naval heritage and 'pre-eminence' in exploring the oceans, establishing harbours, depots and coaling stations for international use and acting as global policeman (in suppressing the slave trade, for instance).[97]

By dwelling on Britain's heritage of liberty, NWAC propaganda also suggested what would be lost without complete victory. The *New Age*'s socialist editor, A.R. Orage, warned that if Germany were not fully defeated, Britain would be either conquered or would have to 'adopt the most rigorous militarism' to deal with the German threat.[98] Similarly, in Ripon the Liberal speaker James Dockett warned that a premature peace would mean that 'Instead of bring[ing] liberty and freedom to the world, we should have an armed truce' and compulsory national service.[99] NWAC propaganda again served a dual purpose here. Propagandists attempted to flatter audiences and dignify British identity by emphasising Britain's traditional (and pre-eminent) association with liberty. Simultaneously, repetitive dwelling on liberty's importance to Britons (for whom it was implicitly more important than for more recently 'free' peoples) meant that threats of its loss, either by conquest or an inconclusive peace necessitating continuing wartime restrictions, could be used both to persuade war-weary civilians to continue doing their utmost for the war effort and to present dissent as unpatriotic, interfering with the war effort, delaying success and forcing the government to limit civil liberties for longer than it wished.

---

95 Frans Coetzee, *For Party or Country: Nationalism and the Dilemmas of Popular Conservatism in Edwardian England* (Oxford: Oxford University Press, 1990), pp. 78–84.

96 'The Navy and Popular Liberty', *Keighley News*, 16/3/18, p. 5.

97 'The Freedom of the Seas', *Reality*, 103, 3/1/18, p. 2.

98 'Answers to a Few Questions', *Reality*, 114, 21/3/18, p. 1; reprinted as *A Socialist Talks It Over* (*Searchlight* series, 5, n.p.d. [1918]).

99 'War Aims Campaign', *Ripon Gazette*, 8/11/17, p. 4.

PROPRIETORIAL patriotism, then, identified a range of key values that combined to make up a set of key values which Britain's war effort protected. 'Civilisation' was often completed by the enlistment of Christianity, adding an otherworldly dimension to the tangible heritage of civilisational principles traced by propagandists. At Wakefield's War Anniversary (organised by Wakefield WAC's secretary), the mayor, G. Blakey, accompanied by at least five clergymen of different denominations on the platform, assured his audience that because Britain fought

> for such high ideals, the very fundamentals of religion ... we have no doubt in our minds and hearts. We have a special right, it seems to me, to approach God and ask him to bless our arms and give us victory.[100]

Here, Christianity became synonymous with civilisational values and thus victory was assured, provided Britons continued to work and fight for these principles. Indeed, the NWAC undoubtedly viewed the principles for which Britain supposedly fought as Christian. The resolution moved at its inaugural meeting contained the assertion that the war was a 'struggle in maintenance of those ideals of Liberty and Justice which are the common and sacred cause of the Allies'.[101] This terminology should not be brushed aside as a mere linguistic convenience. Had the Committee simply wished to emphasise the allies' deep commitment to the ideals, it could have expressed itself in plenty of secular terms instead of 'sacred': 'firm', 'indissoluble' or 'profound', for instance. Rather, it evokes an intense faith in civilisational principles. Even if this faith was, for some, one of rational enlightenment, the fact remains that a religious term was used to give it rhetorical force. 'Nationalism', Smith claims, was originally used in English 'to express the doctrine of the divine election of a nation'. Britain's assumed status as a chosen people, which Smith traces at least to Elizabethan England, meant that principles asserted as British effectively became 'sacred' by association.[102]

Such religious and quasi-religious rhetoric within NWAC propaganda unsurprisingly sometimes extended into millenarian attitudes. Millenarianism, whether distinctly religious or more general and secular, added a purposive edge to spiritual patriotism that fitted well with the high-minded discussion of civilisational principles. The eminent Scottish theologian P.T. Forsyth wrote that 'Even a war like this is but a province of a profounder strife which runs through history ... the standing world-war for the Kingdom of God and its righteousness; and [Christianity] regards it as the first charge on humanity.' Forsyth added that 'neither sacrifice,

---

100 'Entering the Fifth Year of War', *Wakefield Express*, 10/8/18, p. 5.
101 PA, Lloyd George Papers, LG/F/160/1/10, Primrose Stevenson, 'Report of Proceeding at the Inaugural Meeting of the National War Aims Committee', p. 22.
102 Smith, *Chosen Peoples*, pp. 46–48.

martyrdom nor obedience has in itself moral value'; Germans 'sacrifice[d] to a God without a conscience'. Sacrifice and society became moral when it 'establishe[d] the moral righteousness of the world, and recover[ed] the moral soul of universal things'. For the Congregationalist Forsyth, 'righteousness ... gives the law to patriotism and consecrates liberty'. Hence it was man's duty to act with a moral 'passion', without which 'religion is hollow and patriotism ignoble'. Thus the war became 'a war for the moral salvation of mankind'.[103] Forsyth's extensive calls for moral righteousness and the restoration of the Kingdom of God amounted to a millenarian rallying cry to Britain. It was imperative not only that Britain won the war, but won it in a manner that would ensure a better society emerged. At Bethany chapel in Pwllgwaun, East Glamorgan, Conservative speaker J. Farnsworth expressed similarly strong views. He believed Britain's declaration of war, based on principles of honour and justice, served 'to establish human brotherhood' far better than 'international Socialism' ever could. Britain 'had written out the articles of a new charter of international righteousness', and 'God's Kingdom was being brought a little nearer'.[104]

The professional religious thinker Forsyth's views, and those expressed at a chapel by Farnsworth, exceeded most propagandists' arguments. However, with less intensity propagandists frequently argued that Britain's involvement in the war had regenerated British society. Alan Wilkinson indicates the widespread 'conviction that pre-war England had been selfish, lazy, squabbling and morally enfeebled', but was reunited by the war which would 'purify' the nation.[105] Such a view was often expressed generally in NWAC propaganda, frequently as a counterpoint to celebrations of increased social closeness and cohesion developed through the emergent wartime concrescent community (discussed in the next chapter). Occasionally this went further in a millenarian direction. At Evesham's War Anniversary meeting (arranged by Evesham WAC), the Conservative speaker A.H. Coulter reflected that before the war 'the country was engaged in petty strife, class was set against class and the people were selfish-minded ... [whereas] today the people were full of selflessness, charity, brotherliness and self-sacrifice'. Coulter assured his audience that victory was near, and with it 'righteousness, the true righteousness which alone exalteth a nation, would reign supreme'.[106] Here again, the principles Britain ostensibly fought for – 'right' against 'might', 'truth' against 'falsehood' – were attached to a more religious and millenarian viewpoint which meant for Coulter that 'righteousness'

---

103 Forsyth, *Root of Commonwealth*, pp. 3, 15–16, 20.
104 'What We Fight for, and Why', *Glamorgan Free Press*, 22/11/17, p. 1.
105 Wilkinson, *Church of England*, p. 188.
106 'Evesham. Remembrance Day at Evesham', *Evesham Journal*, 10/8/18, p. 6.

would 'reign supreme' over a nation united and converted by the war into a cooperative, selfless and 'brotherly' community. Coulter suggested an impending golden age for Britain in which everyday principles of good conduct, bound to Christian 'righteousness', would create a peaceful and happy society. Such a viewpoint was also expressed by Lord Curzon, albeit in less religious language. Concluding a speech (reproduced in two NWAC pamphlets) on Britain's war effort in July 1918, Curzon argued that Britons felt they were

> fighting for something bigger than the War itself, bigger, even, than the peace [to follow] ... A new world is in process of being built up out of the smoking and battered ruins of the old; and it ... will be to us a great and crowning and sufficient reward.[107]

Curzon's claims about a new world emerging from the ruins of the old suggests a millenarian interpretation of the war as a purgative (divine or otherwise) of Britain's pre-war societal ills. Such less well-defined millenarian attitudes towards British society, together with broader demands for a more equitable society reflecting all citizens' efforts during the war, contributed to a sense of aspirational patriotism (discussed in chapter 8) – an idea that the patriotic efforts of the community were not only rewards in themselves, but would have material post-war benefits.

WHILE both supranational and proprietorial patriotism transcended national boundaries – one locating commonalities between Britain and its major associates, the other identifying key (shared) elements of civilised culture – they were both also intended to demonstrate British uniqueness and the nation's pre-eminently civilised society. Supranational patriotism provided comforting images of military, economic, industrial and cultural strength and security, alongside a chivalric purpose in uniting Britain with its 'great' allies to protect the rights of small nations. Additionally it aimed to motivate British competitive patriotism, suggesting that US or French civilians outdid Britons in their work ethic, enthusiasm or resolution. Combined with proprietorial patriotism, however, supranational patriotism simultaneously encouraged British assumptions of superiority. While, for example, the USA ostensibly demonstrated by its involvement the justice of Britain's cause, praise of US democratic instincts was tempered by asserting British biological and ideological ancestry.

Proprietorial patriotism provided the key ideological basis for British identity. In highlighting the major tenets of civilisation – honour, democracy, justice and liberty – it drew Britain and its allies closer together, acclaiming their common protection of these values against adversarial

---

107 Earl Curzon of Kedleston, *Great Britain's Share* ([London], 1918), p. 20.

threats. In recognising common values, it also partly enabled the endorsement of an international body, the League of Nations, which would inevitably impinge upon Britain's liberty.[108] In another way, however, it was meant to demonstrate that Britain was at the forefront of civilisation, thus boosting patriotic self-esteem. Care was taken to demonstrate the British heritage of each key civilisational value, suggesting that Paul Readman may be correct to argue that 'history formed a normative basis for ... conceptualizations of national belonging' and that 'historic continuity functioned as ... perhaps *the* essential repository ... of English (or British) conceptions of nationhood'.[109] Certainly, NWAC propagandists were not content to discuss contemporary issues solely with reference to the present. However, it is worth reiterating that NWAC propaganda was created for a purpose and was partly reactionary. By constructing evidence of 'historic continuity', propagandists could more successfully answer dissenting criticism. Further, as the next chapter shows, proprietorial patriotism, combined with the threats embodied in adversarial patriotism and the rivalry represented within supranational patriotism, was held to provide both the reasons why British citizens had done so well in the war and the motivation to strain every sinew to maintain the British way of life.

---

108 See chapter 8.
109 Readman, 'Place of the Past', pp. 150, 197–98.

CHAPTER 7

Patriotisms of Duty: Sacrifice, Obligation and Community – The Narrative Core of NWAC Propaganda

IN the NWAC's patriotic narrative, the values celebrated by propri- etorial patriotism supplied the foundations of British national identity. Supranational patriotism provided a validation of this value-based iden- tity and a means of demonstrating that more could be done. Adversarial patriotism reminded Britons of threats to their identity to revitalise their commitment to the war effort. Quantitatively, these sub-patriotisms represented a substantial proportion of NWAC propaganda, often the majority of a speech or article. However, purposively they merely con- textualised the NWAC's core message, that the British people not only had a particular national identity, but were duty-bound to maintain it. Sometimes this message amounted to a minuscule proportion of the overall piece – the 'moral of the story'. Over-explication of Britons' duties without such contextualisation might be counter-productive, potentially discouraging citizens by making stark demands for public exertion without a reasonable purpose.

Propagandists' recognition of the danger of antagonising war-weary civilians with unreasonable demands was manifested in their discussions of duty. Together with a rhetoric of sacrifice, NWAC propaganda espoused a complementary view of duty stressing obligations but emphasising the praiseworthy meeting of these by most individuals and communities, with 'consent and coercion [becoming] reciprocal functions of each other'.[1] In this dual approach, civic patriotism extended the contextual sub- patriotisms, especially proprietorial patriotism. Since, so NWAC rhetoric assumed, Britons lived in a privileged nation with institutions and laws to protect key civilisational values, citizens should work unstintingly to maintain the British way of life. Because they were Britons, however, they amply understood the relationship between responsibilities, rights and privileges, and had responded to the crisis in such a way that they grew

---

1   See Pierre Purseigle's discussion of civil society, 'Introduction', in Purseigle (ed.), *Warfare and Belligerence*, pp. 24–27.

closer together within several concrescent communities; occupational, local, regional and national (also imperial or international, when blended with supranational patriotism). By highlighting communal ties, NWAC propaganda sought to override sectional distinctions such as class or political affiliation.

In this (probably coincidentally) NWAC propagandists echoed the views of the Idealist sociologist R.M. MacIver, whose 1917 study, *Community*,[2] stressed that 'rank and wealth and religion are properly accidental in respect of the right of citizenship, and where they determine citizenship the community is incomplete'. Nationality, MacIver argued, was merely 'the colour of community ... a way of being human, a communal individuality'.[3] 'Our life' he maintained,

> is realised within not one but many communities, circling us round, grade beyond grade. The near community demands intimate loyalties and personal relationships, the concrete traditions and memories of everyday life. But where the near community is all community, its exclusiveness rests on ignorance and narrowness of thought ...

Instead, community expanded, but without obliterating smaller communities, which 'fulfil[led] a service which the greater cannot fulfil'.[4] NWAC propaganda adhered to similar principles, discussing the war in local as well as national contexts, seemingly hoping that appeals to the 'intimate loyalties and personal relationships' of the 'near community' would ensure dedication to the wider national community.

Ernest Renan defined a nation in 1882 as 'a large-scale solidarity, constituted by the feeling of the sacrifices one has made in the past and of those one is prepared to make in the future'.[5] Within NWAC propaganda, civic patriotism and the concrescent community idea were linked by consistent references to 'sacrifice' which completed the evocation of duty. As already discussed, NWAC propaganda demonstrated an interesting mix of religious and secular language, and this is clearly illustrated by its varied interpretations of 'sacrifice'. Servicemen exemplified sacrificial

---

2   José Harris warns that English 'ideas about community may have flourished, not when the social reality of community was strong, but when it was relatively week [*sic*]'. 'English Ideas', p. 157.

3   R.M. MacIver, *Community: A Sociological Study: Being an Attempt to Set Out the Nature and Fundamental Laws of Social Life* (4th edn, London: Frank Cass, 1970 [1917]), pp. 253, 280. On MacIver, see Sandra M. den Otter, *British Idealism*, pp. 200–02; Matthew Grimley, 'MacIver, Robert Morrison (1882–1970)', *Oxford Dictionary of National Biography* (Oxford: Oxford University Press, 2004), www.oxforddnb.com (accessed 26 June 2007).

4   MacIver, *Community*, pp. 260, 262. See also David Miller, *On Nationality* (2nd ed., Oxford: Clarendon Press, 1999), pp. 65–92.

5   Ernest Renan, *Qu'est-ce Qu'une Nation?* (1882), cited in Anthony D. Smith, *The Nation in History: Historiographical Debates about Ethnicity and Nationalism* (Cambridge: Polity Press, 2000), p. 12.

patriotism, willingly fighting (conscription notwithstanding) and, if necessary, dying for Britain. Allen J. Frantzen, linking sacrifice closely with chivalry, argues that such emphasis on sacrifice 'countered the impersonal scale of mechanized warfare':

> The belief that soldiers had freely sacrificed their lives to protect noncombatants was not merely a topos. Self-sacrifice was, rather, the foundational idea of the chivalric tradition, and it served to ennoble and particularize the good that each warrior had given to the cause.[6]

Consequently, propagandists insisted civilians were duty-bound to accept their own, smaller 'sacrifices'. However, servicemen's sacrifices were also presented as religiously charged events requiring commemoration. Religious rhetoric thus sanctified servicemen's actions and, by association, the war itself.

While 'sacrifice' is used extensively in this chapter, a more appropriate term might arguably be 'self-sacrificial patriotism', acknowledging the 'willing' nature of sacrifice. For Frantzen, in both the medieval period and the twentieth century, chivalry fused 'sacrificial' (vengeful) and 'antisacrificial' (forgiving) responses to the death of Christ into a third, 'self-sacrificial' conflation of 'powers and piety'. Chivalry 'enshrined the ideal of voluntary suffering and portrayed military exploits as a form of ascesis'.[7] René Girard, whose thought Frantzen adapts, argues that Christ's crucifixion 'is in no way presented as a sacrifice' in the Bible, misunderstanding of which leaves humans 'still clinging to the sacrificial vision that the Gospel rejects'.[8] For Girard, sacrifice represents a diversion of the community's inherent violence (caused by the 'mimetic rivalry' of members of the community desiring the same object) onto a single '"sacrificeable" victim' – a 'scapegoat' – so that 'sacrificial catharsis' prevents 'the unlimited propagation of violence' within the community.[9] Sacrifice is a 'collective murder or expulsion' carried out upon an arbitrarily chosen 'surrogate victim', whom the community can 'unite against' to maintain community stability by restricting violence to a single act rather than 'an onslaught of reciprocal violence'.[10]

Girard's definition of sacrifice seemingly invalidates the term here, having more of an adversarial patriotic implication. However, if 'violence' is considered a manifestation of 'imitation' (mimesis) whereby

---

6 Frantzen, *Bloody Good*, p. 198.
7 Frantzen, *Bloody Good*, pp. 3, 42.
8 René Girard, 'The Nonsacrificial Death of Christ' (1987), in idem, *The Girard Reader*, ed. James G. Williams (New York: The New York Publishing Company, 1996), pp. 178–79.
9 René Girard, 'Mimesis and Violence' (1979), in idem, *Girard Reader*, pp. 12–13; idem, *Violence and the Sacred*, trans. Patrick Gregory (Baltimore: Johns Hopkins University Press, 1979 [1972]), pp. 4, 30.
10 Girard, 'Mimesis and Violence', p. 11; *Violence*, pp. 257, 102, 94–95.

'two or more partners try to prevent one another from appropriating the object they all desire through physical *or other* means',[11] then, figuratively, violence may be deemed a fragmentary disturbance or disruption of the community (in other words, 'to do violence to' the community by disruption). Considered thus, Girard's arguments about sacrifice become more relevant to sacrificial patriotism. The

> common denominator [in all sacrifices] is internal violence – all the dissensions, rivalries, jealousies, and quarrels within the community that the sacrifices are designed to suppress. The purpose of the sacrifice is to restore harmony to the community, to reinforce the social fabric.[12]

Alexander Watson and Patrick Porter have recently made a similar argument in relation to servicemen's sacrifice, arguing that, beyond reducing the horror of death, 'Sacrificial ideology ... channelled men's grief and guilt in ways which raised armies' resilience.'[13] Sacrificial patriotism may thus arguably be reconciled with Girard's interpretation. Discussing the sacrifices of servicemen, together with those of civilians, aimed to prevent more widespread societal disruption. 'Self-sacrifice' will not be widely used because NWAC propagandists used an extensive 'language of sacrifice' similar to that identified by Max Jones for the pre-war period and Adrian Gregory for wartime.[14] Put simply, both propagandists and civilians considered rationing (for instance) a 'sacrifice'.

SACRIFICIAL patriotism in NWAC propaganda was most effective when stressing servicemen's roles. Girard argues that an appropriate sacrificial victim should be 'neither too familiar to the community nor too foreign to it' and 'should belong both to the inside and to the outside of the community'.[15] This encompasses servicemen's status admirably. By alluding generally to servicemen's sacrifices, propagandists could maintain some distance between servicemen and civilians, while concomitantly most civilians probably had personal ties to a serviceman.[16] Where appeals were more closely linked – references to particular regiments, for example – servicemen could remain both inside and outside the community insofar as they were known to it but separated by their

---

11 Girard, 'Mimesis and Violence', p. 9; emphasis added.
12 Girard, *Violence*, p. 8.
13 Alexander Watson and Patrick Porter, 'Bereaved and Aggrieved: Combat Motivation and the Ideology of Sacrifice in the First World War', *Historical Research*, 83:219 (2010), p. 162.
14 Jones, 'Our King upon His Knees', esp. pp. 115–19; Jones, *Last Great Quest*; Gregory, *Last Great War*, esp. chapters 4–6.
15 Girard, *Violence*, pp. 271–72.
16 Much recent scholarship has been concerned to demonstrate the continuing close links between soldiers and civilians. See e.g. Joanna Bourke, *Dismembering the Male: Men's Bodies, Britain and the Great War* (London: Reaktion Books, 1996), chapter 3; McCartney, *Citizen Soldiers*; Roper, *Secret Battle*; Proctor, *Civilians*.

service abroad. Servicemen were thus simultaneously close to civilians' hearts but often far from their embrace.

Sacrifice carried a heavy imperative, an expected reciprocation.[17] By emphasising servicemen's sacrifices, the message, usually explicit, was that civilians must match them. At Barnstaple, the Conservative speaker Edward Gieve insisted that

> we could not allow the work of the men who had made the great and supreme sacrifice, whether they were French or English, to go for nought ... These men from the factory, the farm, or the field, from the office or from the shop ... willingly came forward in the cause of liberty and freedom and for our protection ... and everyone must make sacrifices to help those men who were making so many sacrifices for us.[18]

Gieve's message created distance from the local community by referring generally to French and English servicemen, but simultaneously added a connection by referring to several civilian occupations from which they were drawn. His typical emphasis on willingness was somewhat disingenuous given that conscription had been in effect in France throughout the war, and in Britain since 1916, but such rhetoric aimed to enhance the self-sacrificial nature of death *pro patria*, the image of 'discipline, duty, and sacrifice willingly – but not easily – made',[19] and stressed that civilians were expected, accordingly, to play their part.

At Wigan, Liberal MP T.J. Macnamara struck a more personal note by relating that his father had served in a Lancashire regiment and that he had been brought up among the 'rough heroes of the Crimea':

> I have seen the red poppies waving over the heaped up clay of stalwart Lancashire heroes, and shall it be said that you for whom they made their last great sacrifice ... were so ... indifferent that you made terms with your enemy and left the work for which they gave their lives unaccomplished?

Here again heroism and sacrifice appeared synonymous, requiring similarly 'heroic' responses from civilians. Macnamara stressed that peace with an undefeated Germany was unacceptable – or, in the blunt words of Unionist speaker G.W. Worsey elsewhere, 'an everlasting insult to the brave fellows who had made the supreme sacrifice' – particularly, as Macnamara suggested at Wigan, to those most closely connected to the local community.[20]

There were plenty of propagandists prepared to make self-sacrificial duty even more explicit. In a pamphlet intended for women, Mary

---

17 On sacrifice's repetition and re-creation, see Girard, *Violence*, pp. 93–95.
18 'War Aims', *North Devon Herald*, 18/7/18, p. 7.
19 Frantzen, *Bloody Good*, p. 232.
20 'War Aims Meeting at Wigan', *Wigan Examiner*, 17/11/17, p. 2. On the changing status of soldiers after the Crimean War, see Anderson, 'Christian Militarism'; 'National War Aims', *Keighley News*, 13/10/17, p. 5.

Martindale wrote that we 'know that love is the greatest force in the world, and we know that love means self-sacrifice', associating women with what Frantzen sees as a particularly manly and chivalric sentiment by reminding them of their duty to stoically bear their burdens, and not 'to turn coward, to fail our men'.[21] Women's acceptance of sacrifice was essential, not only to maintaining domestic productivity, but to servicemen's morale. Interestingly, a religious interpretation of 1880 by Revd John Cooper had chosen a feminised analogy to describe self-sacrifice, describing its pain as a 'momentary and limited' one, 'like that of a woman in travail' (a comment unlikely to endear Cooper to female Christians), whereas the joy of self-sacrifice equated to that of a mother watching her child grow.[22] As Christabel Pankhurst's adoption of Scott and Oates as sacrificial comrades also shows, self-sacrifice could appeal beyond mere 'manly' chivalry.[23] At Chippenham, the barrister Bromhead Matthews reminded his audience that they 'had been making great sacrifices', especially acknowledging the suffering of parents who had 'given a son to the great cause':

> They [civilians] had greater sacrifices going on not far off … Blood had been poured out like water … they must make sacrifices in such things as Tea and Sugar [*sic*]. Let them remember what the Wiltshire Regiment had already done and they were going to do more …

Bromhead Matthews did not hide the war's horrors, instead using the bloody violence of the battlefield (linked to a local regiment) to persuade his audience that further domestic sacrifices were necessary to obtain 'the thing for which our boys had died'. In his interpretation this meant maintaining democracy (rather than autocracy), truth, justice, the rights of small nations and most importantly freedom.[24] Limited access to tea and sugar was negligible compared to the military sacrifices and the principles for which they were made.

Frequently, calls to recognise servicemen's sacrifice or demands for civilian self-sacrifice were couched in overtly Christianised terms (as in figure 33, which appeared above a poem entitled 'The Supreme Sacrifice'). Trevor Wilson argues that 'sacrifice' was 'the key word' that enabled clergymen to endorse the war (which contradicted many of their teachings) by erroneously conflating the sacrifice of Christ (who could have prevented his own death) and of soldiers.[25] In some examples, this

---

21 Mary Martindale, *One Englishwoman to Another* (Oxford, [1918]), pp. 7, 2.
22 Revd John Cooper, *Self-Sacrifice: The Grandest Manifestation of the Divine, and the True Principle of Christian Life; or, The Lost Power of Christian Zeal Restored to the Church* (London: Hodder & Stoughton, 1880), p. 131.
23 Jones, *Last Great Quest*, pp. 235–36.
24 'War Aims Meeting', *North Wilts Guardian*, 2/11/17, p. 2.
25 Wilson, *Myriad Faces*, p. 179.

Figure 33. L. Raven Hill, untitled, Welcome, *no. 18, 31/7/18, p. 207*

seems incidental – indicating the continuing power of Christian rhetoric over everyday language in wartime Britain. Alan Wilkinson argues that soldiers often used 'the language of Christian redemption ... because it was the only one available which seemed to give [events] some positive meaning',[26] and this was presumably equally true for civilians or propagandists, though the latter found ways to speak positively about the war. In his 'call from the workbench', the ASE member F.H. Rose liberally used religious language to bolster demands for greater industrial output and less union discord. The war was a 'life and death struggle' for civilisation, and its 'cause and conditions call for sacrifices by all orders of the community, demand faithful service, and exhort to every holy and righteous impulse'.[27] Rose's pamphlet rejected selfish over-protection of industrial privileges regardless of the wartime emergency, and was couched mostly in plain language. Michael Snape contends that 'the Christian culture of contemporary British society could serve to ameliorate the brutality

26 Wilkinson, *Church of England*, p. 192.
27 Rose, *Call to War Workers*, pp. 5–7.

and bitterness of war',[28] and Rose's resort to religious terminology like 'faithful service' and 'holy and righteous impulse', along with the call for sacrifice, suggests the underlying strength of this culture.

Other propagandists provided more overt references to the inter-connectedness of sacrifice and Christianity. The Texan pastor of the City Temple, Dr Fort Newton, described the allies as like 'knights of old, linked in a crusade', arguing that democracy required a complementary 'spiritual vision' to eradicate the world's evils. 'Spirituality', he concluded, 'includes the impulse of self-sacrifice'.[29] On 4 August 1918, the anniversary of Britain's declaration of war, commemorated throughout Britain with special interdenominational services and civic events (often organised with the encouragement or involvement of local WACs), the mayor of Croydon, Howard Houlder, celebrated

> that spirit of self-sacrifice which had animated all sections of the community, and more particularly ... the way in which the women of the land had come forward ...
>
> It was essential that the people ... recognise that Almighty God was above all things, and unless the nation ... showed a spirit of true religion and acted up to Christian principles then the war would be prolonged ... [H]e believed the country must ascertain the will of God and do its best to carry it out ...[30]

Such an argument might seem unremarkable from a clergymen, but from the secular head of the town it presents an interesting picture of the continuing vitality, at least among some, of strong Christian sentiments.[31] This did not merely reflect the religious nature of the commemoration, though such associations clearly prompted propagandist attention. E.W. Record assured readers in April 1918 'that the pain and suffering, not only of our men in the battle but also of our women in the home ... shall not have been endured in vain' since the 'freedom of mankind has been bought, like the Redemption of Mankind, only by the greatest of sacrifices'. Record congratulated industrial workers who had foregone Easter holidays after the German offensive of March 1918 for exhibiting 'the spirit, not only of true patriotism, but of true democracy working for the highest ends'.[32] Interestingly, in both examples, care was taken specifically to acknowledge women's suffering and sacrifices, with Record explicitly comparing their tribulations with those of Christ while also (like Rose) placing industrial issues within a Christian context.

---

28 Michael Snape, *God and the British Soldier: Religion and the British Army in the First and Second World Wars* (London: Routledge, 2005), p. 192.
29 Newton, 'Seen above the Smoke of Battle', *Reality*, 124, 30/5/18, pp. 2–3; reprinted as *Fighting for the Faith* (*Searchlight* series, 10, n.p.d. [1918]).
30 'Remembrance Day in Croydon', *Croydon Times*, 7/8/18, p. 1.
31 See also Wolffe, *God and Greater Britain*, pp. 92–93, 128–34.
32 (Record), 'Letter from London, *North Devon Herald*, 11/4/18, p. 3.

Naturally, clergymen also made such comparisons. At Wigan the rector, Canon R.G. Matthew, insisted that 'no life was wasted that was spent for righteousness and self-sacrifice, for it was by lives given for others that the whole nation was ennobled and lifted up to a higher standard of devotion'.[33] Although not referring directly to self-sacrifice by servicemen or civilians, he was addressing a congregation gathered to commemorate the war anniversary, meaning that he, implicitly at least, consecrated the actions of Britons involved in the war, who 'ennobled' the nation. By inference, such consecration also helped render the war 'holy'. It is unclear whether Wigan's War Anniversary events were influenced significantly by the NWAC. The local secretary merely advised the national organisation to write to the mayor, as he felt local clergyman would not respond to an initiative suggested by him.[34] Possibly, therefore, Matthew's sermon was composed without the NWAC's instigation (though he certainly attended NWAC events, including Macnamara's meeting).[35] If so, this suggests that NWAC propaganda corresponded significantly to the ways in which other public opinion-formers expressed themselves.[36]

The NWAC also appropriated sermons for its ends, twice reprinting one preached by the Congregationalist J.H. Jowett at Westminster chapel. The publication of material by prominent nonconformists like Jowett and P.T. Forsyth was presumably an attempt to entice British nonconformists to NWAC propaganda, alongside attempts to circulate propaganda through Methodist circuit plans.[37] Jowett cited Psalm 121 ('I will lift up mine eyes unto the hills') as part of a larger demand to 'keep in communion with the mountains of rectitude' (that is, to continue to fight for the right reasons). Continuing the metaphor with quotations from Lowell and Milton, Jowett celebrated that

> even now ... in our long strugglings we can cherish their mountain visions, and even breathe their mountain air, while we are toiling along the dull, low road that is getting filled up with graves and is heavy with the scent of death and sacrifice.[38]

Here, Jowett sought not to glorify sacrifice, which carried the 'scent of death', but to encourage his audience to take comfort in the higher ideals

---

33 'Wigan's "Remembrance" Day: Mayoral Visit to the Church', *Wigan Examiner*, 6/8/18, p. 2.
34 TNA:PRO T102/13, Southworth to NWAC, 6/7/18. Sometimes (e.g. Evesham, Keighley or Wakefield) press reports mentioned the involvement of local WAC figures at War Anniversaries, either explicitly as WAC representatives or by name, but often they did not, making debatable the extent of NWAC involvement.
35 'War Aims Meeting at Wigan', *Wigan Examiner*, 17/11/17, p. 2.
36 On clergymen's views and role in wartime 'propaganda', see especially Wilkinson, *Church of England*; Hoover, *God, Germany, and Britain*.
37 On the effectiveness of these attempts, see pp. 258–59 below.
38 Dr J.H. Jowett, '"We Can Endure, We Are Going to Endure"', *Reality*, 126, 13/6/18, pp. 2–3; Jowett, 'We Can Endure' (*Searchlight* series, 19, n.p.d. [1918]).

and 'lofty uplands of righteousness'. This demonstrates the diversity of the NWAC's 'language of sacrifice'. Jowett's interpretation equated sacrifice solely with death, whereas others adopted a much more comprehensive construction which compared less significant sacrifice – shortages and civilian hardships – with death, the 'supreme' sacrifice. Sacrificial patriotism thus contained its own dualism, comparable to that between civic patriotism and the concrescent community idea. While describing the tea shortage as a 'sacrifice' enabled civilians to feel a sense of commonality with servicemen, emphasis on the 'supreme' sacrifice reminded them that they had little right to complain but rather an obligation to match servicemen's examples.

Smith's interpretation of the 'sacred' elements of nationalism stresses the importance of 'national sacrifice', involving a recognition by 'each generation' of the need to 'fulfil our national destiny faithfully' and maintain the 'sacred communion of the dead, the living and yet unborn'.[39] The recourse to history that played so strong a part in NWAC propagandists evocation of Britain's civilisational principles reminded civilians of the great work done by their ancestors, and the sacrifice of servicemen showed that one portion of the present generation was meeting its obligations. The pressure that sacrificial patriotism exerted on civilians to conform to expectations was completed by warnings of the fate of the next generation if faint-hearted civilians did not see the war through. In September 1917, the joint chairman of the Battersea WAC, alderman W. Hunt, wrote to the *Battersea Boro' News* to explain the purposes of the NWAC. Hunt explained that

> One of the greatest dangers which the committee has to combat is ... the peace-at-any-price advocate, some of whom [sic] are regardless of the great sacrifice our men have paid and regardless of the unthinkable danger of leaving Germany in a position to renew the war at a future date ... Whatever repugnance we may have to war and the horrors it brings let us go through with it now, and so settle the question in one turn, rather than have the dread of anticipation of future trouble ... For the sake of our children and for the sake of humanity, we owe this thorough completion of the work to our men who have been in the dreadful operations at the front ...[40]

Hunt took the opportunity for a passing swipe at 'pacifists', but the thrust of his argument was that it was better to finish things once and for all than to have to fear for the future. However, in case this reasoning did not appeal to everybody, he also included an emotional appeal to protect the next generation while honouring British servicemen. In Leicester, towards the end of the war, a French soldier, Captain Georges Barbey,

---

39 Smith, 'Sacred Dimension', p. 809.
40 'The Objects of the War Aims Committee. Letter from Alderman W. Hunt, J.P., L.C.C.', *Battersea Boro' News*, 28/9/17, p. 2.

made a similar point to a meeting sufficiently crowded to merit attention in the history of the city's war.[41] Barbey said that he

> could quite understand the desire for peace at the earliest possible moment, but let us remember that if peace were established now the Hun would be the conqueror, and a few years hence our children would be embroiled in another bloody war, and the sacrifice we had made and the losses which we had sustained would all be in vain. There must be no compromise with those who make friends with the Hun. (Applause.)[42]

Again, Barbey could not resist a verbal assault on the 'pacifist' element of Leicester, with his final sentence almost certainly alluding to Ramsay MacDonald's reference to 'our German friends'. But again, the meat of the argument was the potential threat to children if the present generation did not fulfil its obligations.

A less aggressive approach was taken by the Liberal MP George Lambert at a meeting in Okehampton, Devon. Lambert sought to convince local residents of their obligation to sacrifice some of their food supplies to help industrial centres. He asserted that the war was 'a people's war', the purpose of which was 'to make sure that this England of ours and the world at large, should be a sweeter place for our children than it is to-day'.[43] This softer approach to the need for sacrifice for the sake of future generations fed into the forms of aspirational patriotism to be discussed in chapter 8, aiming at a general improvement of the condition of the world, but the underlying point was that children, as yet unable to fend for themselves, must have their futures safeguarded by the fulfilment of duty of the present generation.

That there was no definitive meaning of sacrifice within NWAC propaganda is demonstrated by the Liberal MP W.H. Somervell's address at Keighley's (NWAC-influenced) War Anniversary meeting. Somervell argued that all at the interdenominational service

> were trying to rise above the level of politics and above even patriotism, because religion, being greater than either, included the less and excelled it [*sic*]. No one could deny the patriotism of our enemies, who had endured far greater sacrifices than we had done.

Somervell suggested that 'the enemy's' patriotism (he was not specific) lacked 'the higher touch'. He asked his audience to exceed 'mere patriotism' and 'be an expression of the highest religious devotion'.[44] Somervell reversed the usual interaction of sacrifice and religion, making

---

41 See Armitage, *Leicester, 1914–1918*, pp. 281–82 for discussion of the meeting.
42 'Allies' War Aims. Great Meeting in the Corn Exchange', *Leicester Daily Mercury*, 9/9/18, p. 4. On the critique of MacDonald, see pp. 134–36 above.
43 'War Aims. Mr Lambert Addresses Okehampton Meeting', *North Devon Herald*, 10/1/18, p. 6.
44 'Fourth War Anniversary', *Keighley News*, 10/8/18, p. 5.

sacrifice something Britain's enemies made more extensively, attempting to encourage civilians that they were suffering less, rather than acknowledging Britons' difficulties. In stressing that Britain's superiority lay not with patriotism or sacrifice, but with its more devoted Christianity, he offered assurance that through Britons' affinity with God their position was unassailable. Nonetheless, though not using sacrificial language, Somervell asked his audience to tolerate 'the trifling inconveniences of our comfortable life here for the sake of our men'. Hence, though his terminology differed dramatically, Somervell still addressed the same key issues of sacrificial patriotism: the need to accept privations and match servicemen's examples. This is a salutary reminder that the patriotic categorisations employed in the analysis of the narrative framework of NWAC propaganda (as with all such) remain permeable and unable to perfectly fit every case, though Somervell's speech still fits well within the broader patriotic narrative.

CLEARLY, as chapter 4 demonstrated, NWAC discussion of citizenship and community was indebted to a lengthy discursive heritage.[45] Nevertheless, these broad principles required adaptation to the wartime situation.[46] The underlying principle for most expositions of civic patriotism was a reference to Britain's armed forces. Often explicitly linked to the rhetoric of sacrifice sketched above, elaborations on servicemen's continuing contributions negated claims of civilian hardship. Discussing soldiers in Wigan, the Labour MP Stephen Walsh asserted that through 'their wonderful courage … indomitable cheerfulness, [and] the majesty of their continued effort' Britain's civilian army had 'reached the high-water mark … [of] British valour'. Similarly, Britain's navy ensured that 'food was brought to our homes, that raw material came to our factories, that the … [people] of these islands were protected'. Civilians had 'a responsibility … only secondary to that of our soldiers and sailors' which, given such examples, they should willingly bear.[47]

Walsh's note about the navy's role in supplying food to Britain contextualises persistent demands for economy as a civic duty.[48] At Malmesbury, the barrister Bromhead Mathews told his audience to remember 'that every little bit of food saved meant probably the life of a soldier or sailor saved'. Economising on food meant fewer ships were needed for delivering and protecting food supplies, thus ending the war sooner

45 On the problematic relationship between citizenship and patriotism, however, cf. Stapleton, 'Citizenship versus Patriotism'.
46 Gullace, *Blood*, deals extensively with the 'renegotiation' of citizenship during the war, towards a recognition of service as its ultimate arbiter.
47 'War Aims Meeting at Wigan', *Wigan Examiner*, 17/11/17, p. 2.
48 For some examples of the wider context of this rhetoric, see Gregory, *Last Great War*, esp. pp. 131–51; Proctor, *Civilians*, pp. 84–97.

through their redeployment elsewhere.[49] Similarly, in June 1918, Record wrote in his regular column that the success of rationing and the extra US assistance 'does not absolve us from continued effort to economise food' or produce it at home, since any 'slackening of effort' would undermine the work already done.[50]

Alongside economising on provisions, civilians were told it was their civic duty to invest as much money as possible in war bonds and war savings certificates. In asking for £25 million per week from the public, the Chancellor of the Exchequer, Andrew Bonar Law, appealed 'to the patriotism of the people' who should realise that 'it is the clear duty of everyone to have the country's need first in his mind' and not invest anywhere else unless national coffers were full.[51] Speakers' reports confirm they sometimes stressed civilians' financial responsibilities (occasionally also sharing platforms with National War Savings Committee [NWSC] speakers). At Weymouth, the Liberal speaker R.J. Allen lectured on '"Our duties as citizens." Special stress was laid on our financial obligations, [because] of the asserted refusal of many to subscribe.'[52]

Civilian reluctance was evidently targeted here by Allen. In some cases, civic patriotism sought to convince civilians of their duties through shame. In October 1918, *Reality* quoted Ben Tillett's letter to Dock and General Workers' Union secretaries, which argued that since 19 out of 20 servicemen were working class, strikes were 'nothing better than assassination'.[53] In February Sheehan criticised 'young men [in industry] who have had three years' exemption from fighting' but wanted to 'evade their patriotic obligations' by opposing dilution through outdated industrial agreements. Sheehan, who had 'put in ... time at the Front' regarded such actions as 'undiluted selfishness and rank disloyalty'.[54] Such criticism was the strongest and most propagandistically hazardous element of civic patriotism. It needed to balance the intent to expose recalcitrant civilians to the community's obloquy with the risk of further antagonising essential workers. In such situations, concrescent community ideas were particularly important since discussing the majority of loyal and hard-working citizens assisted propagandists' attempts to prefabricate public opinion and place individuals or groups ('adversaries' in some cases) outside this 'consensual' patriotic community. Janet Watson's argument that some people regarded their wartime activities more as 'work' than as 'service' must be acknowledged here. While the notion of

---

49 'National War Aims Campaign. Meeting at Malmesbury', *Wilts and Gloucestershire Standard*, 3/11/17, p. 2.
50 (Record), 'A Letter from London', *North Devon Herald*, 20/6/18, p. 3.
51 *Bonar Law's Message*, pp. 7–9.
52 TNA:PRO T102/23, SDRs – R.J. Allen, South Dorset (Weymouth), 2/7/18.
53 'What Ben Tillett Says', *Reality*, 143, 10/10/18, p. 4.
54 (Sheehan), 'The War & Westminster', *Seaham Weekly News*, 1/2/18, p. 2.

service was pervasive, not every civilian necessarily thought about things in such terms.[55] Nonetheless, as Nicoletta Gullace stresses, in recognising the superior claims of 'service' to the right of citizenship, emphasis was also placed upon 'ideological conformity', and this is certainly borne out in NWAC propaganda.[56]

To stress the importance of civic patriotism and the local population's duties, most NWAC meetings were chaired by prominent local representatives. At large meetings local MPs or mayors might preside and make short introductory speeches. At smaller meetings local councillors or clergymen often filled the same role. Other representatives might also propose votes of thanks. This symbolically tied community figureheads to the NWAC's message while also indicating the likelihood of local censure for those who avoided their patriotic duties. In extreme examples, this could easily extend into adversarial patriotism, as in Leicester when the mayor was accused of inciting violence against Ramsay MacDonald.[57]

AS previously mentioned, the idea of a concrescent community functioned partly as an extension of civic patriotic pressure by placing dissent outside the community's embrace. However, such rhetoric should be considered more a means of acknowledging and congratulating the consenting majority. The coercive element is only apparent within broader contextual interactions with adversarial and civic patriotism. While the NWAC's remit was partly to isolate and invalidate dissent, it intended also to communicate with 'the great majority of the people', 'strengthen the national morals' and provide 'tangible proof of the Government's appreciation ... to brace and hearten them'.[58] By identifying sources of civilian pride, concrescent community rhetoric enabled NWAC propagandists to motivate by both heartening and hectoring, recognising civilians' agency, not their incapacity. The same sort of dualism can be seen earlier in the war in relation to recruiting propaganda. While post-war attention increasingly focused on Kitchener's famous pointing finger and other morally coercive approaches, Nicholas Hiley has suggested that the most successful recruiting posters were actually those that used messages about participation, enabling men to feel positively included by choice rather than negatively compelled by shame.[59] In the NWAC's written

---

55 Janet S.K. Watson, *Fighting Different Wars: Experience, Memory, and the First World War in Britain* (Cambridge: Cambridge University Press, 2004), chapter 1.

56 Gullace, *Blood*, p. 196. See also Howell's contention that '"the people" could always be a principle of social exclusion as well as of social inclusion'. 'Industry and Identity', p. 86.

57 See pp. 135–36 above.

58 TNA: PRO T102/16 'Aims of Home Publicity', n.d.

59 Nicholas Hiley '"Kitchener Wants You" and "Daddy, what did YOU do in the Great War?": The Myth of British Recruiting Posters', *Imperial War Museum Review*, no. 11 (1999).

propaganda this celebratory element generally focused upon the strength and contribution of the national community. Locally conducted spoken propaganda, however, placed considerably more emphasis on reasons for local pride, implicitly or explicitly linking the bonds and qualities of a local community to the larger national context. As Helen McCartney has noted, before 1914, 'Most people lived their lives at the local level. Their aspirations, expectations and connections were limited to the local and their loyalties were tied to village, town and county', and NWAC propaganda at constituency level amply demonstrated propagandists' awareness of this.[60]

Speakers often dwelt on the special qualities or achievements of a locality to stimulate communal pride. For instance, in Devon the Conservative speaker C.S. Parker recognised that 'Combe Martin had done well, both in recruiting and in war work',[61] while his Liberal colleague Tudor-Rees 'was impressed ... with the grandeur of the scenery'. He told an Australian co-speaker that 'if all the scenery of Australia could be rolled up and gathered into one it would not compare for a moment with the beauty of the scenery between Combe Martin and Ilfracombe. (Applause and laughter)'.[62] This friendly rivalry could also be used more aggressively to highlight one locality's virtues. At Ipswich, the local Conservative MP, F.J.C. Ganzoni, told his audience that 'in East Anglia, in Suffolk, and in Ipswich, they could look with gratitude on their record ... They had not been losing time in Ipswich as they had in Coventry'.[63] Ganzoni's comment also demonstrated expanding communal ties, comparing not only the town, but also the county and region favourably with Coventry, in an example which seems to conform to MacIver's view of multiple communities 'circling us round, grade beyond grade'.[64]

Another means of tying smaller communities to a regional one was to stress local associations with the county regiment. Ganzoni stressed that

> The 4th Suffolks were one of the few Territorial regiments honoured with the 1914 star ... That Battalion was composed of men who had not waited to be fetched – and was still in the trenches. They had been nobly supported by the people of Ipswich.[65]

Ganzoni's lionisation of Suffolk's volunteers overrode problematic questions about the contributions of conscripts, who faced equal military peril, but were sometimes marginalised by 'the rigid correlation between

60 McCartney, *Citizen Soldiers*, p. 57.
61 'War Aims Meeting', *North Devon Herald*, 8/11/17, p. 5.
62 'War Aims Campaign', *Ilfracombe Chronicle*, 3/11/17, p. 3.
63 'War Aims of the Allies', *East Anglian Daily Times*, 3/12/17, p. 6. Strikes in Coventry were reported at the end of November.
64 MacIver, *Community*, p. 260.
65 See n. 63 above. See also Asquith at Liverpool: 'Picton Hall. Mr. Asquith & Unruly Women', *Liverpool Daily Post and Mercury*, 12/10/17, p. 6.

patriotism and voluntarism'. While Ganzoni's praise of Suffolk voluntarism attempted to demonstrate exceptional local patriotism, it also risked
alienating relatives of conscripts.[66] Rather than associating locality with
a regiment, individual servicemen could alternatively become foci of
local patriotism.[67] On France's Day 1918 at Wakefield, the deputy mayor
presented a Distinguished Conduct Medal to Sergeant Major Jones of
the King's Own Yorkshire Light Infantry, remarking that 'Everyone was
proud that another Wakefield lad had won that distinction (applause).'[68]

The NWAC also produced propaganda for soldiers on leave, contributing articles and cartoons to *Welcome*. Most of this material was heavily
concerned with inculcating community ideals. A regular contribution
was Owen's quirky guide, 'Bits of Old London', which generally recommended less renowned or metropolitan attractions (including six public
houses in 31 editions). He described Shepherd Market near Piccadilly
as 'a modest little country town' where 'the simple life of the village'
continued to exist in the middle of London. His column's title evoked
a timeless sense of place, and an earlier column portrayed houses in
Holborn as representative 'of what London must have been in the merrie
days when much-married Henry ruled'.[69] Another regular NWAC article
was J.E. MacManus's weekly 'Sport and Play'. MacManus reported the
week's entertainments and sporting events – predominantly football or
cricket and boxing, as well as rugby, athletics and slightly bemused
descriptions of baseball matches between North American servicemen.[70]
Servicemen were encouraged to feel part of the multi-layered community,
with sport (as recently stressed in another context) providing 'a reminder
of civilian life and identity'.[71] NWAC-employed cartoonists provided
comforting images of home and community, along with implied sexual
reward for soldiers, as demonstrated in figures 34–35. In both examples,
soldiers are accompanied by women, in idealised pastoral scenes. Many
other drawings showed servicemen with women either in rustic settings

---

66 Ilana R. Bet-El, 'Men and Soldiers: British Conscripts, Concept of Masculinity,
    and the Great War', in Billie Melman (ed.), *Borderlines: Genders and Identities
    in War and Peace, 1870–1930* (New York: Routledge, 1998), p. 74; also, idem,
    Conscripts: Forgotten Men of the Great War (2nd edn, Stroud: Sutton Publishing,
    2003). On recruiting and local patriotism, see Nicholas Mansfield, *English
    Farmworkers and Local Patriotism, 1900–1930* (Aldershot: Ashgate, 2001).
67 For examples of very similar activity beyond NWAC propaganda, see Michael
    Finn, 'Local Heroes: War News and the Construction of "Community" in Britain,
    1914–18', *Historical Research*, 83:221 (2010).
68 'France's Day', *Wakefield Express*, 13/7/18, p. 7.
69 Will Owen, 'Bits of Old London', *Welcome*, 11, 12/6/18, p. 126; 7, 15/5/18, p. 78.
70 E.g. J.E.M. (MacManus), 'Sport and Play', *Welcome*, 8, 22/5/18, p. 93.
71 Eliza Riedi and Tony Mason, '"Leather" and the Fighting Spirit: Sport in the British
    Army in World War I', *Canadian Journal of History*, 41:3 (2006), p. 499; also
    Fuller, *Troop Morale*, pp. 86–94. For extended discussion of MacManus's articles
    and their meanings for patriotic propaganda, see Monger, 'Sporting Journalism'.

"BLIGHTY."

Figure 34. Wilmot Lunt and W.F. Blood, 'Blighty', Welcome, no. 8, 22/5/18, p. 8

or at home. In these media, propagandists provided a generic summary of 'Blighty', representing less a 'highly differentiated mosaic of regions',[72] than a similar pursuit of 'symbols of unity and coziness [*sic*] which were [universally] applicable' to that portrayed within German conceptions of *Heimat*. In this system, 'community was the core symbol; it led to the related symbols of home and family, both evoking togetherness'. Alon Confino notes that *Heimat* constituted a uniquely German conception of national identity,[73] but the NWAC's propagandising of servicemen suggests at least partly recognisable local-national archetypes in Britain, while Keith Grieves has emphasised that for some soldiers 'Scenes of play, nature and normality ... *became* the loved vistas and occurrences for which men died' – reminders of home enabled them to cope with the horrors they faced at the battlefront.[74]

---

72 Brace, 'Finding England Everywhere', p. 94.
73 Alon Confino, *The Nation as a Local Metaphor: Württemberg, Imperial Germany, and National Memory, 1871–1918* (Chapel Hill, NC: University of North Carolina Press, 1997), pp. 170, 212–13.
74 Keith Grieves, 'The Propinquity of Place: Home, Landscape and Soldier Poets of the First World War', in Jessica Meyer (ed.), *British Popular Culture and the First*

"DON'T YOU WISH YOURS WERE BOYS, MY DEAR, SO AS THEY COULD JOIN THE ARMY?"
"IT DON'T SEEM TO MAKE MUCH DIFFERENCE, MRS. JONES. IF THEY ARE BOYS THEY JOIN THE ARMY, AND IF THEY ARE GIRLS THE ARMY JOINS THEM."

Figure 35. Frank Styche, untitled ('Joining the Army', NA: PRO T102/19, Publicity Department ledger), Welcome, no. 21, 21/8/18, p. 248

The NWAC's commitment to linking local and national identity was demonstrated by the lengths to which speakers went to hold meetings. At Great Comberton, Herbert Woodger struggled 'to reach meetings owing to floods'. Nevertheless, he considered that a total attendance of 33 constituted 'two very good village meetings' since the population was only 167. Days earlier he had held a meeting attended by only 20 people, 'there being 12 inches of snow down'. The importance of meetings to convince isolated localities of their national role was confirmed by Woodger's report that another meeting of 55 people 'resulted in £1000 being invested in War Bonds'.[75] Stressing the community leitmotif and presenting an interactive local/regional/national identity as most relevant also helped avoid discussion of sectional differences of class or internal

---

World War (Leiden: Brill, 2008), p. 37. For extended discussion of the NWAC's efforts to provide reminders of home for soldiers, including Owen's articles and the types of images discussed here, see Monger, 'Soldiers, Home and Community'.

75 TNA:PRO T102/23, SDRs – Herbert Woodger, Evesham (Great Comberton), 19/1/18; (Bushley), 16/1/18; T102/24, SDRs – Herbert Woodger, South-West Norfolk (Stow Bridge), 11/3/18.

nationalism. This, perhaps, best explains the anonymisation of the Irish nationalist MP Sheehan's 'War and Westminster' columns. The assistance of an Irish nationalist ought to have had significant propaganda value for the NWAC. However, he had been 'dropped overboard from the [Nationalist] Party ship', in 1906 alongside his political mentor William O'Brien over their advocacy of a policy of conciliation of Ulster sentiments in the hope of maintaining a united independent Ireland. He retained his seat as an All-for-Ireland League MP in December 1910.[76] Dissident Irish nationalists could, therefore, have disavowed his arguments as unrepresentative, undermining his message and damagingly demonstrating sectional discord. In parliamentary debates about the NWAC, John Dillon persistently highlighted the absence of Irish nationalists from the 'all-party' Committee.[77] Consequently, Sheehan's talents as a writer and status as a 'Soldier M.P.' were more valuable than his Irish nationalism. As previously discussed, Sheehan's articles often stressed the importance of parliamentary democracy to British identity. However, they also significantly propagated concrescent community ideas by partially breaking down the distinction between governors and governed and emphasising MPs' equal efforts and privations. While reverential about parliament, he was considerably more irreverent about its occupants, remarking in one article, regarding rationing, that the 'shilling lunch has been done away with, and the cheap wine is no longer to be had cheaply, as in the old days that delighted us all', thus associating MPs with regretful sentiments at the loss of accessible alcohol through restrictions imposed by the Central Liquor (Control Board) since 1915.[78] The implication was that MPs shared the concerns of the 'man in the street' and thus worked in his interests.

The concrescent community idea proposed that the community was growing closer together at all levels through the need to work together for victory. The former Trades Union Congress (TUC) president, Harry Gosling, wrote that the war had

> broken down many of the barriers which formerly existed between different classes. Men of various sections of society who are working together have come to know one another's good qualities, and have learned to understand each other's point of view ...[79]

---

76 D.D. Sheehan, *Ireland Since Parnell* (London: Daniel O'Connor, 1921), pp. 198–99, 218–41; Sally Warwick-Haller, *William O'Brien and the Irish Land War* (Dublin: Irish Academic Press, 1990), pp. 252–64.

77 See PDC(5), 99, 13/11/17, col. 305 (see also the question of Joseph King at col. 288); PDC(5), 100, 14/12/17, col. 1557.

78 Searle, *New England?*, pp. 815–16.

79 Harry Gosling, JP, LCC (President, TUC, 1916), *Peace: How to Get and Keep It* (London, n.d. [1917?]), p. 13.

Barriers of sex were also supposedly being dismantled. At Liverpool, despite heckling from female audience members, Asquith celebrated 'the magnificent ... co-operation of every class of the community'. Describing a munitions factory with eight thousand women workers, Asquith expressed delight that

> out of such varying walks of life women who were fitted for other work have done their duty nobly ... [W]omen have given to the cause an adaptability and flexibility that have made them largely responsible for the success of the war (cheers). No more striking tribute to the justice of their worth has ever been known ...[80]

Sheehan asserted that 'the war services of the feminine sex' had 'secured them [*sic*] those great social and political privileges' embodied by the Representation of the People Act.[81] Finally, propagandists stressed political cooperation. Hence most NWAC meetings were addressed (at least) by both a Liberal and a Conservative speaker. At Tooting (where Liberal and Labour MPs spoke) Revd H.E.D. Keppel remarked, 'Before the war, they found their politicians engaged in the merry game of party politics ... But when the war started, our politicians put patriotism first, and party politics afterwards.'[82] This conception of the war effort as a unifying force in British society had taken root at the beginning of the war, as Kit Good notes,[83] but it also drew upon existent pre-war political rhetoric. As with Liberals after the 1880s, NWAC propagandists (including politicians of all three major parties) propounded a message of 'inclusive, participatory cross-class political ideals', hoping it would 'underpin continued social stability at home'.[84] Some even predicted, like Gosling, that the experiences of the war would lead to a new, less factionalised and more cooperative domestic and international society afterwards.[85]

BOTH civic patriotism and the concrescent community idea, then, contained multiple rhetorical strands providing a flexible approach, modifiable to the perceived tastes of particular audiences. However, while either could provide compelling individual representations of civilian experience, their potency lay in combining exultant praise with exhortative recapitulations of civic patriotic duties. Each sub-patriotism modified the other, tempering praise with reminders of continuing expectations; softening criticism of weary civilians by acknowledging their great efforts

---

80 'Picton Hall. Mr. Asquith & Unruly Women. Tribute to Navy and Munition Workers', *Liverpool Daily Post and Mercury*, 12/10/17, p. 6.
81 (Sheehan), 'The War and Westminster', *North Devon Herald*, 7/11/18, p. 6.
82 '"War Aims" Meeting at Tooting', *Battersea Boro' News*, 26/10/17, p. 2.
83 Good, 'England Goes to War', pp. 44–52.
84 Parry, *Politics*, p. 341; Paul Readman, 'The Liberal Party and Patriotism in Early Twentieth Century Britain', *Twentieth Century British History*, 12:3 (2001).
85 See chapter 8.

and 'sacrifices'. The only medium in which this dual discussion was not employed was in NWAC propaganda for servicemen in *Welcome*. Here concrescent community rhetoric was heavily apparent, but there was little or no civic patriotic discussion, the NWAC presumably deciding that servicemen need not be reminded of their obligations. The remainder of this chapter provides examples and analysis of the general interaction of these principles to demonstrate their interdependence.

In his article 'The Home Offensive', Percy James Brebner concocted a scene in which a soldier awarded the Victoria Cross (VC) returned to his home town. Responding to admiration by friends and neighbours, Brebner's soldier argued that any soldier would have done the same: 'What makes heroes, as we call 'em, is doing the job which happens to lie alongside.'[86] The soldier asks what the people at home have done, and proceeds,

> Here's old man Collins growing taters and things to help out the food, like a good 'un, in spite of his age; and there's Mrs Tibble, bringing up clean, straight young 'uns to be good Englishmen and look after the Country when we've gone; and here's Sally doing in Huns as cheerily as the gunners themselves [as a munitions worker] ... Why you're all heroes, that's what you are, and I feel a bit of a fraud ... because of this 'ere cross. Thank God for you all, say I. We are all doing our bit, and that's what the Country wants.[87]

Brebner uses concrescent community language extensively here, emphasising that civilians were already doing their part towards the war effort. John Price has recently discussed the importance of 'everyday heroism ... performed during the course of everyday life' without 'enforced responsibility or duty' in prompting assumptions of heroism as 'integral' to a 'morally-upright national character [which] transcended accepted social divisions'.[88] In demonstrating the equal 'heroism' of winning a VC and growing potatoes, the argument was advanced of communal affinity between soldiers and civilians, reinforced by the soldier's familiarity with his friends, while the 'naturalised' dialogue was presumably intended to appeal to 'ordinary' people rather than an elite readership. Nevertheless, in asserting that heroism was 'doing the job alongside', which was 'what the Country wants', Brebner's soldier very lightly introduces civic patriotism, noting the underlying expectations of the national community.

---

86 Note the correspondence of this statement with the discussion of service vs work in Watson, *Fighting Different Wars*.

87 Percy James Brebner, 'The Home Offensive', in (e.g.) *Ilfracombe Chronicle War Supplement*, w.e. 2/11/18, p. 2. Judging by other submissions to the NWAC, Brebner was probably a religious journalist; most of his articles were sent to Christian journals like the *Church Monthly* and *The Kingdom*. Information from Articles database.

88 John Price, 'Heroism in Everyday Life: The Watts Memorial for Heroic Self-Sacrifice', *History Workshop Journal*, 63 (2007), pp. 273–75.

While in this example civic patriotic exhortations are downplayed, servicemen's opinions were useful to the NWAC partly because their criticisms of civilian shortcomings were more likely to be palatable than those of people who had not 'done their part' militarily. In Leicester, a genuine VC-winner, Captain Robert Gee, returned home to give a very critical speech concerning civilian efforts. Gee announced that

> they heard too much about people being sick and tired of the war. Tommy Atkins was tired of the war, but he did not want to come back home with his tail between his legs like a beaten cur. (Cheers.) ...
>
> [He] reminded those present that while civilians ... were enjoying high wages, under conditions of safety and comfort, the men at the Front went out to fight for their protection for 'a bob a day' ... [W]hen he looked at the rate of wages paid at home he did not think they had done their duty to the country in the amount of money they had subscribed to the war loans ...[89]

Gee's critique of civilian contributions to the war effort contained no softening language. Instead, however, his harsh judgements were softened by his localness and heroic soldierly status. As the 'Cottage Houses V.C.',[90] he could take a more uncompromising stance than either non-soldiers or outsiders whose credentials to criticise would be less secure.

One reason for Smuts's popularity during the war was the breadth of his 'qualifications' to address the public. As an imperial figure and former enemy he was an ideal exponent of the British empire's virtues. As a War Cabinet member he conveyed credible knowledge of the situation. As a soldier who had served during the war, he could claim, to an extent (limited somewhat by his seniority of command), to represent servicemen's opinions. At Sheffield, Smuts said that he knew

> that in Sheffield – in this part of Yorkshire, anyhow – the best relations ... continued to exist between the various sections of the industrial community ... [G]ood will between the various classes, co-operation and mutual confidence between them, were necessary, not only to win the war, but for the great tasks that awaited us after the war. (Cheers.) ...
>
> The older men and women ... had worked as they had never worked before, and so every part of the nation had contributed their all to this great common cause ... It was true there had been cases – lamentable cases sometimes of greed and selfishness [like profiteering and shirkers] but ... the vast bulk of the nation had done its duty magnificently. (Hear, hear.) And they had worked not for themselves ... [but] for their common mother – the nation, the empire, and the world. (Cheers.) ...
>
> Our armies at the front were filled with a matchless spirit of fortitude ... courage and ... endurance. All that we could hope and try for was that the nation at the rear, that the women and men before him and of this nation and of the nations of the Empire, and of our Allies, will be just as strong ...[91]

89 'France's Day. Stirring Speech by Captain Gee, V.C.', *Leicester Daily Mercury*, 13/7/18, p. 1.
90 'V.C.'s Straight Talk' (Editorial), *Leicester Daily Post*, 13/7/18, p. 2.
91 'Prussianism Must Go', *Sheffield Daily Telegraph*, 25/10/17, pp. 5–6.

In these portions of a much larger speech, Smuts interwove many themes of civic patriotism and the concrescent community idea. The concluding paragraph was a straight civic patriotic demand for civilians to match soldiers' examples, while his reference to 'lamentable' examples of 'greed and selfishness' verged on adversarial patriotism. Emphasis on the necessity of class-transcendent goodwill was also couched in terms of obligation rather than celebration. However, all these demands and admonishments were modified by references to the 'magnificent' work already done by most civilians, while his depiction of community embraced 'Sheffield', 'Yorkshire', 'the nation, the empire and the world'. In this way, Smuts could insist upon continuing civilian effort without suggesting (except implicitly) that civilians had not done enough. Smuts could also conceivably claim to speak as a 'local' since he and Sir John Jellicoe were to receive the freedom of the city, or, as the *Sheffield Independent*'s editor wrote, 'to become citizens of the Empire's busiest and most indispensable centre'.[92]

As a 'Soldier M.P.' (as his articles were labelled), Sheehan also claimed to speak for servicemen. In March 1918, Sheehan said soldiers on leave had told him that, despite their own high morale,

> they were more concerned about … certain manifestations at home of a disquieting character. The reluctance of some of our young and well-paid workers to serve calls forth strong comments on the part of the men who have been through it and done their bit …

Later, Sheehan returned to the issue of rationing, asserting that MPs were 'submitting cheerfully, as in duty bound, to the new rationing regulations', adding that it could not be said 'that we are faring any better than the humblest citizen in the land'.[93] Here again is the duality of the sub-patriotisms. In discussing soldiers' concerns, Sheehan made it clear that those who refused to play an appropriate part in the war evaded their civic obligations, again noting the lucrative wages earned by civilians. That the criticism was by servicemen was, again, intended to render it more acceptable. Furthermore, by equating MPs' experiences of rationing with those of 'the humblest citizen', Sheehan suggested that it benefited the community by bringing governors and governed closer together. Within this cosy (if unconvincing) assumption of equality, the phrase 'as in duty bound' both clarified that this abstemiousness was an obligation 'cheerfully submitted' to and seemingly suggested that the acceptance of such obligations was inherently tied to communal happiness and harmony. This equated to T.H. Green's supposition (summarised by José Harris) that humans found freedom 'only in "society"', which brought

---

92 'The Outlook. Smuts and Jellicoe' (Editorial), *Sheffield Independent*, 25/10/17, p. 4; also 'Honouring Sheffield' (Editorial), *Sheffield Daily Telegraph*, 24/10/17, p. 4.
93 (Sheehan), 'The War and Westminster, *Seaham Daily News*, 8/3/18, p. 2.

'individual will into conformity with the rules and well-being of the wider organic whole'.[94]

Food loomed large in E.M. Goodman's weekly articles 'The Woman's Part', published in 'War Supplements' supplied to provincial newspapers like the *Nuneaton Observer* and *Droitwich Guardian*. Each week Goodman provided recipes which made the most of wartime ingredients, and regularly admonished her readers to avoid waste. In April 1918, Goodman counselled that since meat joints were so small, 'we shall learn, like Tommy in France, that a good stew is better than a second-rate joint', and might even 'prefer the roast beef of Old England in this disguise'.[95] In July, she argued (like Bromhead Mathews) that everything imported risked sailors' lives. 'To be wasteful now is to be foolish and possibly cruel.'[96] Generally, Goodman's articles informed women about their duties to the nation, both at home and at work. Her articles were often patronising and hectoring, redolent of the pre-war advice to working-class mothers discussed by Anna Davin.[97] However, there were also elements of concrescent community rhetoric in her articles. Discussing women's involvement in aeroplane construction, Goodman wrote that the general training received was essential to women's futures since 'the woman living at home or in service has to be jack of all trades'. She added that

> To be taught well, to be paid for learning, to be sure of good money after eight weeks sounds too good to be true. There must, girls think, be a 'catch' somewhere. Is it that this is war-work, and will when peace comes? ... [E]ven if it does, the good money will have been earned, and the learner will have had her education.

The emphasis was on the benefits to be gained through war-work. Though Goodman also stressed an obligation to undertake war-work, she encouraged readers that if air power was essential to victory, 'women will help to win it, even if they do not fly'.[98] Goodman asserted that women's duties, at home and in the workplace, served multiple purposes – personal, familial, local and national. While elaborating on the responsibilities of womanhood, they also celebrated women's enhanced roles and status as a result of the war, and, in providing recipes and housekeeping tips, imbued mundane household tasks with enhanced national significance. Spring

---

94 Harris, *Private Lives*, p. 228.

95 Margaret Osborne (Goodman), 'The Woman's Part. Stews, and the Way They Cook Them in France', *Nuneaton Observer War Supplement*, w.e. 6/4/18, p. 2.

96 (Goodman), 'The Woman's Part. Household Salvage: A Real Way to Help', *Droitwich Guardian War Supplement*, w.e. 27/7/18, p. 2.

97 Davin, 'Imperialism and Motherhood'.

98 (Goodman), 'The Woman's Part. Housemaids for Aeroplane Making', *Droitwich Guardian War Supplement*, w.e. 17/8/18, p. 2.

cleaning became a patriotic rather than personal duty,[99] and cooking a stew made a housewife 'like Tommy'. Domesticity, previously considered a feminine and private sphere, became in this rhetoric part of public life, further extending pre-war challenges to the idea of the public sphere as men's province (and adding another strand of 'women's work' to Gullace's 'renegotiation of citizenship'). Thus, the articles sought (however patronisingly) to acknowledge women's domestic contributions to the war effort, whether in the home or the factory.[100]

The Minister of Munitions, Winston Churchill, also celebrated women's contributions to war-work in munitions factories, in a parliamentary speech converted into a pamphlet, praising their 'diligence and ... devotion ... their skill, their strength ... [and] their loyal and unwearying spirit'. Churchill stressed the positive contributions of war-workers, ignoring the discontent manifested by strikes (which he said cost much less than one per cent of total work time) and war-weariness. 'Instead of quarrelling, giving way as we do from time to time to moods of pessimism and irritation, we ought to be thankful', Churchill argued, that no 'strain is too prolonged for the patience of the people.'[101] However, his assertion that people should 'be thankful' nonetheless contained a civic patriotic message. While claiming not to doubt civilian reliability, Churchill emphasised the people's responsibility to continue to be cheerful, diligent and 'loyal'.

A similar underlying civic patriotism was apparent at meetings in Brecon and Keighley. At Brecon, the deputy mayor, David Powell, asserted that the war had

> drawn all persons in these islands closer together than ever before. Differences of all kinds – social, political, religious and others were all forgotten. (Hear, hear.) Reports from the battle-field, where 'Colonel' and 'Tommy' lie together – and looking around that hall both on the platform and in the audience it could truly be said that now [sic] –
>> 'None are for a party,
>> But all are for the State;
>> The rich man helps the poor,
>> And the poor man loves the great.'

The main speaker, the Coalition Liberal MP Sidney Robinson, continued the inclusive rhetoric, suggesting the meeting was needless, since he was sure the people of Brecon took 'the highest patriotic view of the situation'. He praised 'the services that Brecon had specially rendered'

---

99 (Goodman), 'The Woman's Part. How to Tackle Spring Cleaning Difficulties in War Time', *Nuneaton Observer War Supplement*, w.e. 11/5/18, p. 2.

100 Gullace, *Blood*, pp. 145–66. Interestingly, Goodman made no mention of either nurses or Women's Auxiliary Army Corps members, who served in dangerous military settings throughout the war.

101 Winston S. Churchill, MP, *The Munitions Miracle* (British Effort Series, 1, n.d. [1918]), pp. 10, 8, 15.

before extensively describing German behaviour. In conclusion, however, Robinson 'appealed to one and all to work together ... even if we had to suffer inconveniences [since those of servicemen were much worse] ... to strive and help forward our Empire in this great crisis'.[102] This is a classic example of NWAC propaganda. The bulk of the meeting was devoted to adversarial patriotism, criticising Germany and its allies, and 'pacifists', but it was book-ended by celebrations of Brecon's contributions, civilian and military (in praising the South Wales Borderers), and a reminder of civic patriotic duties to work together despite difficulties. Without initially celebrating local achievements, the long diatribe against Britain's various adversaries might have provided a negative motivation through fear and outrage, but alternatively might have demoralised the audience by implying insurmountable suffering. Furthermore, without the civic patriotic conclusion there was a risk of civilian complacency. They were warned about German conduct and the dangers of 'pacifism', but after hearing that they had done and were doing wonderfully, assumptions might be made that little else was required. By supplementing this praise with calls for continuing exertions, however, the message was that adversaries still threatened Britain, and needed to be counteracted by intensive civilian effort, which the speakers were sure, given Brecon's previous conduct, would be forthcoming.

In December 1917, local Liberal MP Sir Swire Smith was joined by the Labour MP Will Thorne, and J.W. Morkill, a Conservative county councillor, in extolling the virtues and explaining the responsibilities of the people of Keighley. Smith said that

> there was not a town in the whole of the kingdom ... that had been [completely] converted like Keighley ... to the manufacture of works for war. When the time came for them all to put their shoulders to the wheel Keighley sent a larger quota of volunteers ... in proportion to the population. The town had also taken a leading part in the War Loan and the management of the food department ... [for the assistance of which] one of their officials had been taken to headquarters in London ...

Smith's praise was based upon Keighley having accepted its civic patriotic responsibilities. Because Keighley had done more than its fair share in several ways, he implied, including providing a local representative to a national organisation, they could feel especially proud. Morkill, moving the resolution, declaimed that

> he ... had proof that of those men ... called up compulsorily it was not that they 'funked' or were disloyal, but because nine out of ten thought they had domestic circumstances which prevented them from leaving home with a quiet mind ... One thing that had struck him in his work at Keighley was the magnificent fellow-feeling which filled all hearts. (Applause.)

---

102 'War Aims. Mr. Sidney Robinson, M.P. at Brecon', *Radnor Express*, 11/10/17, p. 6.

Unlike Ganzoni's ambivalence towards conscripts at Ipswich, Morkill exonerated Keighley's conscripts from accusations of patriotic misconduct, thus promoting a vision of the town as a wholly united and committed community. Following Smith's praise of Keighley's recruitment record, Morkill's defence of conscripts suggested concern that conscripted manpower should not discredit the town's patriotic credentials. There was no reference to well-paid workers being forcibly 'combed-out'; rather, conscripts had been concerned about familial responsibilities.

Continuing Morkill's assertions of 'magnificent fellow-feeling', Thorne added a wider perspective. He 'thought the organised workers of the country had done their duty from top to bottom'. Unusually, he cautioned that food shortages could 'mean the defeat of the Government', thus introducing an element of discord and class politics, but tempered this by arguing that 'if the workers and others knew they were getting their fair share he [doubted] serious trouble would break out'. Thorne employed a slightly inflected form of concrescent community imagery, arguing that workers had thus far done their duty and would continue to do so, providing they were fairly treated. Thorne added a more censorious civic patriotic message by saying he 'could not see the utility' of food strikes. However, he also concluded that 'he did not think the working-class families would waste anything, at all, for ... they had nothing to waste'; to understand 'the difficulties', Lloyd George and the Food Commissioner, Sir Arthur Yapp, should 'send their wives to purchase like others had to'. This is all quite surprising at a NWAC meeting, where Labour speakers often took more straightforwardly patriotic lines, arguing for uncomplaining cooperation to more swiftly end the war, after which social grievances could be addressed. However, Thorne's approach seems a clever amalgam of exhortation and conditional inclusivity. While his co-speakers used more conventional arguments about a fully united local community, Thorne 'was compelled to speak from the working-class standpoint'. He praised the cooperation of 'organised workers' and moderately criticised the government and food shortages. This all suggested that Thorne remained a true representative of the working class and not, as some 'old colleagues' would argue, 'a Jingo standing upon a capitalist platform'. By withholding unequivocal backing of government policy, Thorne could more convincingly espouse workers' obligations. 'So long' he said, 'as they meant to bring [the war] to a victorious conclusion that Government would get ardent support' from the Labour party.[103] Thorne argued that complaint and criticism were legitimate alongside continuing support for the prosecution of the war. Further, by standing

---

103 'Mr Will Thorne, M.P., on War Aims. Making Germany Pay. A Successful Keighley Meeting. Mr. J. W. Morkill's Fine Tribute to Keighley', *Keighley News*, 15/12/17, p. 5.

on the same platform as Smith and Morkill, he tacitly endorsed their sentiments. His speech specifically addressed workers, told them they had done their duty and empathised with their discontent, but disavowed striking and pledged unequivocal support to the war effort. This was a subtler and probably more effective argument than Labour-affiliated speakers or writers making identical arguments to Liberal or Conservative colleagues.

Concluding, J.E. Haggas, the Conservative vice president of Keighley WAC, said 'it was the duty of Keighley to set an example to the rest of the country'. This epitomises the combination of civic patriotism and the concrescent community idea. By conducting local campaigns, NWAC propagandists tailored arguments to local susceptibilities, hoping to exploit 'intimate loyalties and personal associations' for national purposes.[104] Appealing to local vanity through praise of a locality's 'special' contributions to the war effort prepared audiences for (or moderated) insistence upon civilians' duty to match servicemen's examples and work even harder, as uncomplainingly as possible, for victory. The supposed nobility of this effort was sometimes corroborated by propagandists' reference to a sense of the community growing together through war's adversities. This occasionally amounted to an immanent millenarianism, sometimes secular, sometimes spiritual, or at least to predictions that better conditions could be maintained after the war.

S ACRIFICIAL patriotism, together with civic patriotism and the con-crescent community idea, created a core message of duty. It was a flexible concept, capable of use both as an instrument of moral and emotional blackmail, by stressing the 'supreme' sacrifices being made by servicemen (adding depth to the compulsive tone of civic patriotism), and as an additional means of creating a community of sentiment between civilians and servicemen, by emphasising common 'willing self-sacrifice'. The predication of national identity upon an interactive concrescent community meant sectional divisions could generally be overridden by a string of experiential communities, from family to nation, empire or 'civilised world'. It was difficult to tie individuals solely to bonds of solidarity with every other individual in the nation. Therefore, by focusing partly upon the tangibility of everyday experience, NWAC propagandists hoped to link each small community progressively to several larger ones, until Keighley became (and was assumed to desire to become) an example to the nation. By linking local communal destinies to larger 'imagined communities', national demands could be made locally. Residents of Okehampton, who 'did not see that scarcity of food in many of the great centres of industry', could therefore be asked to help in feeding

---

104 See n. 4 above.

'millions of workers' of 'this England of ours', although 'greater food production [and] more economy' could perceptibly only lead to more local discomfort.[105] Such community ideas, based on an understanding of contemporary experience strongly rooted in ideas of sacrifice, thus tempered the necessary obligations civilians were obliged to confront, and were reminded of by civic patriotism. This three-pronged approach to duty enabled propagandists to make demands without excessively demoralising already tired and frequently overstretched civilians. And the celebratory acknowledgement of civilian duty was further contextualised by an aspirational patriotism (discussed in the next chapter) which held out the prospect of tangible post-war rewards for services rendered.

---

105 Speech of George Lambert, MP, 'War Aims. Mr Lambert Addresses Okehampton Meeting', *North Devon Herald*, 10/1/18, p. 6.

CHAPTER 8

Promises for the Future: The Encouragement of Aspirations for a Better Life, Nation and World

ASPIRATIONAL patriotism developed the arguments of the other sub-patriotisms to provide a vision of Britain's future. Adversarial, supranational and proprietorial patriotism provided broad contextual milieux within which civilians could derive understandings of the war's meaning at a relatively impersonal national level, while discussions of duty through civic patriotism, the idea of a concrescent community and sacrifice emphasised the patriotic role and significance of individuals and smaller groups and communities, seeking to make patriotism a personal commitment to a collective cause. These sub-patriotisms were partially refined by spiritual patriotism, which attempted to endow high-minded civilisational values, criticism of adversarial proclivities, and sacrificial rhetoric alike with a sacral sense, enabling arguments that Britain was engaged in a holy war together with concomitant consolation for loss and deprivation. While the first three contextual sub-patriotisms were (largely) outward looking and homogenising in intent, the three core patriotisms of duty presented a more inward-looking, individualised account of British identity. Combined, these concepts provided a dualistic and comprehensive explanatory framework within which divergent civilian interests and imperatives could be accommodated.

Aspirational patriotism drew together these varied strands into an evocation of the post-war world – a world usually presumed to centre upon Britain, with British aspirations becoming civilisational and civilisation requiring a harmonious Britain. Notwithstanding pre-war concerns with 'imperial overstretch' and 'relative decline',[1] national efficiency or racial degeneracy (briefly addressed below), British national self-regard was still largely a sentiment on which the sun never set, judging by the comments of NWAC propagandists and the reactions of some of their audiences. In combination with the other sub-patriotisms, and extending

---

1   Aaron L. Friedberg, *The Weary Titan: Britain and the Experience of Relative Decline* (Princeton: Princeton University Press, 1988).

the broader millenarian tone of parts of the propaganda (traced in chapter 6), aspirational patriotism confirmed that individual 'welfare [was] bound up with the community', service to that community thus constituting a form of personal 'goal-fulfilment', according to David Miller.[2] In providing epilogues to other sub-patriotisms, aspirational patriotism similarly operated dualistically, offering both civilisational/ideological aspirations for 'a world without war' – to be effected by eradicating militarism and establishing international cooperation via a League of Nations – and a more material, pragmatic and individualised set of aspirations. These latter are neatly (though anachronistically) encapsulated by Lloyd George's promise at the 1918 general election to make Britain 'a fit country for heroes to live in',[3] and these equate to a Durkheimian form of 'patriotism ... directed towards the interior affairs of the society, and not its exterior expansion'. Emile Durkheim argued that if each state's 'chief aim [was] ... to set its own house in order', all would be 'diverted' from international rivalry.[4] NWAC propagandists prophesied a more harmonious and equitable society in post-war Britain, extending rhetoric about the social ameliorations already stimulated by the war. Reconstruction, social and electoral reform, class and gender harmonisation were all presented as rewards for the patient wartime service and sacrifices of servicemen and civilians, with the implicit corollary that any calls for such improvements before peace were selfish and short-sighted.

This may appear more the politics of self-interest than patriotism. However, aspirations for rewards and societal improvement could readily be endorsed as patriotic by assuming that Britain's national and international strength and prestige depended on the vitality of the individuals within. This was emphasised by Lloyd George in September 1918, when he declared that

> if Britain has to be thoroughly equipped to meet any emergencies of either war or peace it must take a more constant and a more intelligent interest in the health and fitness of its people ... You cannot maintain an A1 Empire with a C3 population.[5]

---

2   Miller, *On Nationality*, pp. 66–67.
3   'Mr. Lloyd George On His Task', *Times*, 25/11/18, p. 13.
4   Excerpt from Emile Durkheim, *Professional Ethics and Civic Morals*, in Anthony Giddens (ed.), *Durkheim on Politics and the State* (Cambridge: Polity, 1986), pp. 203–04.
5   *Lloyd George's Message*, pp. 9–10. A1 and C3 referred to the highest and lowest military service grades used by the army up to mid-1917. A1 meant fully fit for general service. C3 meant fit only for limited home service. In mid-1917, following a reduction of the required fitness standards prompted by the need for more manpower, the shocked deputy director of medical services, Northern Command, claimed (apparently with some exaggeration) that men passed C3 in Northern Command included 'the lame, the halt, and the blind'. See J.M. Winter, *The Great War and the British People* (Basingstoke: MacMillan, 1986), pp. 50–55 (52).

By utilising the language of national efficiency, as Lloyd George explicitly did in his speech,[6] civilian demands for material rewards for war service became justifiable concerns for the nation's welfare (to Conservatives, as well as Liberals),[7] and aspiration a patriotic virtue rather than a self-interested vice.

NWAC propaganda's promotion of an aspiration to a world without war was based substantially on the appropriation of one of the UDC's key ideas. In publicising their organisation in September 1914, the UDC's five co-founders – Norman Angell, Ramsay MacDonald, E.D. Morel, Arthur Ponsonby and C.P. Trevelyan – made 'the establishment of a Concert of Europe, whose deliberations and decisions shall be published' one of their 'Cardinal Points'. In 1914 the UDC member and historian G. Lowes Dickinson called for a league of nations to be established, and by March 1915, several UDC members had involved themselves with the Bryce group (headed by the former Ambassador to the USA and the man responsible for the influential report into German atrocities, James Bryce) which proposed the establishment of such a league. The UDC also cooperated with the League of Nations Society (later Union – LNU), established in May 1915, and later UDC 'proposals for an international framework for world peace' showed strong affinities with these two groups.[8] By late 1915 the UDC claimed to have influenced Woodrow Wilson's call for a League of Nations, and subsequently made much of the similarity of their foreign-policy views.[9] In adopting the League as a key part of the 'world without war' element of aspirational patriotism, NWAC propagandists were probably influenced more by enthusiasm for Wilsonian principles than an intention to undermine dissenters by embracing their ideas – nevertheless, this was a beneficial propaganda effect. By advocating the League, NWAC propagandists reduced its power as a weapon of dissent.

Wilson's Independence Day 1918 speech on 'the conditions of peace' was reprinted by the NWAC. In it, Wilson called for the 'destruction of every arbitrary power anywhere that can ... disturb the peace of the world', and the 'establishment of an organisation of peace ... [enforced by] the combined powers of free nations'.[10] In September 1918, Lloyd George claimed that it already existed in the form of both the British

---

6 'Remember that the health of the nation is the secret of national efficiency and national recuperation', *Lloyd George's Message*, p. 10.

7 Keohane, *Party of Patriotism*, pp. 191–92.

8 Cited in Sally Harris, *Out of Control: British Foreign Policy and the Union of Democratic Control, 1914–1918* (Hull: University of Hull Press, 1996), pp. 55, 101–02.

9 Harris, *Out of Control*, pp. 124, 136–8; Swartz, *Union of Democratic Control*, pp. 25–26, 135–38.

10 *Wilson's Message*, pp. 5–7.

empire and allied cooperation, fighting in the cause of 'international right', adding that 'a Germany freed from military domination will be welcome' in the League.[11] In a well-distributed pamphlet (reaching a '2nd million'), the former Foreign Secretary Sir Edward Grey emphasised this. Germany would be welcome only if it abandoned militarism and recognised that 'the condition of true security for one nation is a sense of security on the part of all nations'. Grey felt the League was 'essential ... to secure each person in a quiet life'.[12] The muted emphasis here was on a new world order of peace and cooperation, a point made more explicitly by the Liberal MP McCurdy:

> it must be a League of Nations, not of dynasties – a League of Peoples, not of emperors or kings ... [and] as President Wilson has said, a League of Honour ... it must rest on a basis of moral law; it must be more than an agreement, it must be a creed – the articles of faith of a new brotherhood of peoples, pledged to observe peace and renounce war ...

Such rhetoric promised a better post-war world, rewarding the contributions of all to peace, and asserted that the war would not be repeated. These were all arguments calculated to promote endurance – if civilians would never have to tolerate such disruptions again, they might bear them longer to ensure that outcome. McCurdy acknowledged that 'We cannot abolish the possibility of war any more than ... any other crime', but argued that the League's establishment would enforce a common international treatment of war as 'discreditable, disreputable [and] criminal'.[13]

The League of Nations enabled the NWAC to align itself with mainstream Labour opinion. The joint war aims memorandum of the Labour Party and TUC (28 December 1917) called for the League's establishment, together with an 'International High Court' and 'Legislature' to ensure peaceful international resolution of disputes. In introducing the text in a pamphlet, the ubiquitous McCurdy wrote that 'British Labour has gone boldly to the root of the evil' by denouncing autocracy, adding that 'Europe must be drastically disarmed'.[14] As early as September 1917, at Llandrindod Wells, the Labour MP, Brace, endorsed the League of Nations at a NWAC meeting, expressing the hope that its creation 'would make it impossible for such a disaster as that which they were experiencing to ever recur'.[15] Given the NWAC's troublesome relationship with much of

11 *Lloyd George's Message*, p. 7.
12 Viscount Grey of Fallodon, *The League of Nations* (London, [1918]), pp. 8, 11.
13 McCurdy, *Freedom's Call*, pp. 25–27.
14 Charles A. McCurdy, MP, *The War Aims of the British People: An Historic Manifesto* (London, [1918]), pp. 5–6. The NWAC also published the memorandum of the Inter-Allied Labour and Socialist Conference (23 February 1918): Charles A. McCurdy, MP, *A Clean Peace. The War Aims of British Labour* (London, 1918).
15 'Allies' War Aims', *Radnor Express*, 27/9/1917, p. 5.

the Labour movement, the opportunity to identify common ground in an endorsement of the League was invaluable.

The League constituted in NWAC propaganda the international enshrinement of Britain's civilisational principles, and its advocacy represented, in a sense, a perceived triumph of 'British' values. In this way, the supranational and proprietorial elements of NWAC propaganda's patriotic narrative also seem to at least partially correlate with Helen McCarthy's evocation of the 'liberal-internationalist' 'enlightened patriotism' of the LNU, which 'yoked man's natural love of country to his wider loyalty to the international community'.[16] By supporting the League's establishment, NWAC propagandists offered a vision of a world without war in which Britain could continue to flourish. Its successful establishment depended, however, upon eradicating 'militarism'. Though Germany (or, more frequently, Prussia) was often blamed for the development of militarism, NWAC propagandists also went further, again inverting dissenting arguments by acknowledging Britain's militarisation. By accepting this, however, propagandists hijacked dissenting criticism and argued that only complete victory could remove militarism from society. An inconclusive peace would force Britain to retain a strong military deterrent, consequently reducing the government's ability to effect societal improvements. At Ripon, in November 1917, Liberal speaker James Dockett argued that an immediate peace would mean that

> instead of having a peace so that we might begin to improve the lot of the people, instead of having a peace of liberty and freedom, we should have an armed truce. Instead of destroying militarism ... [it] would compel every nation to adopt militarism as its national policy ...[17]

Likewise, at the Liverpool chamber of commerce, the Conservative Earl of Denbigh said (in a speech reiterated at a NWAC meeting) that 'a happier and more contented England was impossible as long as a powerful and aggressive Germany ... forced us to maintain a great army and to remain a great military nation'.[18]

In both these examples, the duality of aspirational patriotism is evident. While eradicating militarism became a high principle, essential to establishing a better and more peaceful world, it was also closely linked to the possibility of societal improvement at home. Thus, propagandists attempted to merge more intangible civilisational benefits, which flattered individuals' sense of intellectual and moral probity, with assertions that such ideals affected everyday life. This also highlighted the interrelationship between everyday life and international affairs. Basil

---

16 Helen McCarthy, 'The League of Nations, Public Ritual and National Identity in Britain, c. 1919–56', *History Workshop Journal*, 70 (2010), pp. 111–12.

17 'War Aims Campaign. Public Meeting at Ripon', *Ripon Observer*, 8/11/17, p. 4.

18 'The Empire's Peril', *Liverpool Daily Post and Mercury*, 7/5/18, p. 3.

Mathews underscored the importance of a total victory which destroyed militarism:

> The regulation of life under military and official control to-day in our own lands we accept because of the War. But the thought of that permanent detailed direction of our actions by officials backed by military power is simply unendurable to men who have centuries of liberty in their blood ...
> If we do not win the War we and our children for generations will live and die under the lash of militarism.[19]

These were clear references to the language of the 'Norman Yoke' and the 'freeborn Englishman' (presumably extended to all Britons).[20] Britons, Mathews suggested, would willingly subordinate their freedom in the national or civilisational interest for a certain period, but could not countenance permanent limitations. Therefore, playing their individual roles in an endeavour to modify international behaviour became of personal as well as national importance.

Within such arguments is a sense of ongoing tension between comforting illusions of Britain as an island 'physically as well as morally and metaphorically separate',[21] and the reality, demonstrated during the war by Britain's dependence on imported food (or simply by its entanglement in a total war), and acknowledged by expectations of post-war international cooperation, that British life was affected considerably by global events and decisions often beyond British control. Arjun Appadurai's comment that the 'locality (both in the sense of the local factory or site of production and in the extended sense of the nation-state) becomes a fetish which disguises ... globally dispersed [driving] forces' may perhaps be extended beyond economic production to incorporate socio-political issues as well.[22] The interaction of supranational and proprietorial patriotism, and the dualism inherent in aspirational patriotism, suggest that NWAC propagandists felt it necessary to remind civilians that Britain and British life was not, and could not be, isolated from international influence, while simultaneously continuing to suggest the overriding significance and superiority of Britain.

Propagandists frequently dwelt on hopes of a better world, and most references carried the message that international improvement intrinsically meant fulfilling national and individual aspirations as well. In an elegant example (unlike the brutal descriptiveness of most of his pamphlet), Mathews wrote that

---

19 Mathews, *Vista of Victory*, p. 14.
20 On English (and British) associations with liberty see, e.g., Hill, 'Norman Yoke'; Ward, *Red Flag*; Mandler, *National Character*, esp. pp. 87–91; Parry, *Politics*.
21 Behrman, *Victorian Myths*, p. 40.
22 Arjun Appadurai, 'Disjuncture and Difference in the Global Cultural Economy', *Public Culture*, 2:2 (1990), p. 16.

> We have to be the architects of a new world ... [in which] the differences
> of class, the problems of capital and labour, the injustices inflicted by social
> and economic oppressions, the international and interracial competition of
> interests, indeed, the whole world-complex of modern civilisation can be
> ... unravelled and set right.[23]

Although described as problems of international civilisation, such inequalities and rivalries were largely transferable to a narrower, British
focus. By phrasing his arguments in this way, however, Mathews executed
a rhetorical sleight of hand. While mollifying British civilian disgruntle-
ment, he portrayed such social inequalities (accurately) as worldwide
civilisational problems to be addressed post-war, rather than uniquely
British. The argument thus sought to defuse civilian discontent through
international comparisons and by suggesting that the world generally
would become a fairer place following the successful conclusion of the
war. Additionally, by not acknowledging specifically British problems,
such discussion allowed a certain deniability for those wishing to ignore
or downplay British social inequality. Similar sentiments were expressed
by Ripon's mayor, T.H. Fleming, who argued that the world was being
tested by 'a great travail of soul', after which Fleming 'hoped that the
next generation would be a better generation for [our] sufferings ... and
that the next world would be an infinitely better world than the one in
which we were living'.[24] Fleming here extended sacrificial and spiritual
patriotic language to reassure his audience that their current discomfort
and loss was serving a greater end than the resolution of international
power-politics, but while he referred specifically to local experience and
suffering earlier in his speech, his call was notably for a new *world*.

Other propagandists, however, demonstrated some recognition of the
national/international/civilisational tensions discussed above. At Keighley
the Liberal MP Somervell believed that

> A new world was in process of being built ... in which war would be
> unknown, in which class war at home, industrial injustice and acrimony
> must be ended, and a cleaner, healthier, happier Britain, safeguarded for
> the successors of those who had given their lives ...[25]

Seemingly, to Somervell the world still largely meant Britain and some
other landmasses. While alternating between discussing global peace and
national harmony, his rhetoric does not suggest significant engagement
with the notion that international and intranational harmony were
interrelated.[26] References to the outside world seem almost a wartime

---

23   Mathews, *Vista of Victory*, p. 15.
24   'War Aims Campaign', *Ripon Observer*, 8/11/17, p. 4.
25   'Fourth War Anniversary', *Keighley News*, 10/8/18, p. 5. On patriotism's percep-
     tion as a means to maintain class harmony, see Parry, *Politics*.
26   Although cf. Somervell's laudation of France, which problematises this assertion.
     'France's Day at Keighley', *Keighley News*, 13/7/18, p. 5.

exception to the norm, although it is also possible that Somervell's rhetoric sought to demonstrate immediacy and relevance to his audience rather than reflecting his own views.

The best evocation of the ties between civilisational-ideological and internal-pragmatic aspirations in NWAC propaganda is found in the arguments of J.C. Smuts. His speech at Sheffield, in October 1917, merits lengthy quotation as it synthesised virtually the entire meaning of aspirational patriotism. Britons, Smuts said,

> had seen their privileges curtailed, their holidays go ... and they had done it all for the common cause and for their common mother – the nation, the empire, and the world. (Cheers.) The reward would come in time ... and he was sure ... [the same civilian resolution] would make of this country a new world. (Cheers.) ...
>
> They would have fought this war to small purpose and victory would be of little value if, after the war, they were going to indulge in class war or economic chaos ... They wanted to see the State in this country fulfilling its proper function; they wanted to see greater happiness more widely diffused among the classes, and they wanted to see more justice in this country. They wanted to see less poverty and less luxury ...
>
> He wanted to see ... [m]ore economic freedom and more security for all workers in that world after the war, in which he hoped there would be no idlers, rich or poor. (Cheers.) ... If we were to reap those fruits and see the new and better England ... that new world towards which we hoped to move, ... Militarism must be swept away from the face of the earth. (Cheers.) ...
>
> The practical achievement of the war should be the establishment of machinery for securing peace ... We wanted to see a league or society of nations which would have force behind it, and which would see that there was no future danger, no future threat against the peace of the world ...[27]

Smuts captured the essence of aspirational patriotism here, melding grand predictions of national and global societal change with practical demands for its achievement: the eradication of militarism, a League of Nations, the fulfilment of the state's 'proper function' of social amelioration. Like Somervell, Smuts's 'new world' was largely located in the North Sea. Unlike Somervell, however, Smuts – an international statesman who later coined the term 'holism' – displayed awareness of the multiple layers of human interaction and identification, labelling nation, empire and world the 'common mother' and nodding to international socialism (even communism) by referring to 'all workers in the world'. Smuts emphasised that material reward and ideological aspiration went hand-in-hand, that it was patriotic to expect social change as it would benefit not only individuals but the nation and the whole international society.[28]

---

27 'Prussianism Must Go', *Sheffield Daily Telegraph*, 25/10/17, pp. 5–6.
28 On the significance of Smuts's holism to his rhetoric, see Saul Dubow, 'Smuts, the United Nations and the Rhetoric of Rights and Race', *Journal of Contemporary History*, 43:1 (2008), pp. 59–60.

Such rhetoric was intrinsic to the NWAC's message. The third of its 'Aims of Home Publicity' was 'to dwell on' wartime political and social improvements and 'to suggest the prospect of further improvement and greater freedom when the war is over; generally to envisage the rewards of success'.[29] If propagandists' discussions often privileged British examples for specific promises, this was not necessarily a parochial rejection of the outside world, but a pragmatic understanding of the propaganda's ultimate purpose – to persuade Britons to continue their participation in the war effort. High-minded aspirations for a better world had some value, but individuals' aspirations also required attention. Concrescent community rhetoric stressed the (supposed) existing communal harmony, and such discussion often extended into an aspirational patriotic suggestion that such harmony would become permanent in post-war Britain. At Pwllgwaun, for instance, the Conservative speaker John Farnsworth claimed that

> With every strain of circumstance and danger that surrounds us we believed that we were coming out of the struggle a better nation than when we went in, and that the world would be a cleaner place to live in than it was before.[30]

Here again, Farnsworth referred to the wider world, but emphasised national development. British exertions would improve Britain and help to cleanse the whole world by its defence of high ideals.

Propagandists recognised, however, that vague allusions to change were insufficient to satisfy public opinion and made stronger claims for specific improvements. At Tooting, local speaker H.R. Selley said that Britain's politicians 'wanted to make this old England of ours a better place to live in that it had been in the past'. Selley asserted (optimistically) that political factionalism would be set aside in favour of introducing 'legislation which would better the social conditions of the boys who had fought, and the women who had suffered'.[31] Selley clearly linked service to the nation with future rewards, implicitly replacing the idea that civic participation was its own, 'character'-building, reward with one that offered material recompense for material assistance.[32] Sheehan, with his insider's view of parliament, wrote that 'for the future the claims of human beings as such are to have a new recognition', the most vital of which were 'Health, housing, education, secure employment and a "living wage"', along with the seemingly autarchic and protectionist concern for the 'urgent anxieties of national safety in the field and on

---

29 TNA:PRO T102/16, '(Confidential) Aims of Home Publicity', n.d.
30 'What We Fight for, and Why', 22/11/17, *Glamorgan Free Press*, p. 1.
31 '"War Aims" Meeting at Tooting', *Battersea Boro' News*, 26/10/17, p. 2.
32 On service and character, see Harris, *Private Lives*, p. 249.

the farm'.[33] Again, the 'welfare' of Britain was stressed, in a patriotism of 'set[ting the nation's] own house in order'.[34]

Such acknowledgements of necessary reform responded to labour demands. Indeed, figures like Harry Gosling, the former TUC President, and the MP Will Thorne, exploited NWAC propaganda to make demands, building upon the increased wartime governmental recognition of unions.[35] Gosling asserted that education was 'essential, and on education must be built ... assurances of future world peace'. Furthermore, he stressed that 'labour' expected extended pensions and health insurance, 'a fuller share in the gains of industry' and influence over industrial direction. While celebrating the increased closeness and harmony engendered by the war, Gosling concluded his pamphlet by insisting that it was 'to the good of the country that labour should grow to the full ... use its strength, and use it wisely. It is essential that the old artificial barriers of class should disappear'.[36] At Keighley, Thorne argued that 'we were never going to get back to the old economic conditions, and if we wanted to prevent an industrial war after the military conflict, it would all depend upon the attitudes taken up by the employers of labour'.[37] While Thorne's public outburst was largely uncontrollable by the NWAC, by publishing Gosling's views it accepted their validity (or their propaganda value).[38] Gosling's conclusion emphasised the patriotism of workers' aspiration, echoing some of the arguments of nineteenth-century franchise campaigners and social reformers in asserting that labour advancement benefited the whole nation. In allowing labour figures to issue such challenges within its own propaganda, the NWAC attempted to demonstrate continuing British free expression by featuring varying opinions, as well as a tacit endorsement of that opinion. If such challenges were made, however, it was imperative that they be answered with evidence either of action already taken, or of good future intent. Thorne had himself acknowledged the possible ameliorations represented by the Whitley Committee (established by the Ministry of Reconstruction), the first of whose four reports on the improvement of employer–employee relations was published in July 1917.[39]

Other speakers and writers responded to this need. Lloyd George, in a September 1918 speech published by the NWAC, acknowledged that there had been a 'community of sacrifice' which meant that after the

---

33 (Sheehan), 'War and Westminster', *Seaham Weekly News*, 21/6/18, p. 2.
34 See n. 4 above.
35 Waites, *Class Society*, pp. 29–31, 205–06.
36 Gosling, *Peace*, pp. 9, 11, 13–14, 16.
37 'Mr Will Thorne, M.P., on War Aims', *Keighley News*, 15/12/17, p. 5.
38 On the pamphlet's publication, see Harry Gosling, *Up and Down Stream* (London: Methuen, 1927), pp. 219–20.
39 For the Whitley reports and their reception, see Horne, *Labour at War*, pp. 245–49, 271.

war 'the nation ... will expect put right the wrongs, inequalities, and stupidities from which millions have suffered and the community has suffered'.[40] Lloyd George's rhetoric again bore a patriotic tone: individual sufferings (albeit in their millions) were important because they affected the community as a whole. Such rhetoric also served an important party political purpose, as Nigel Keohane suggests that Conservatives 'were ready to contemplate measures that contributed to industrial capacity and national wealth, but they drew the line when it impinged on social questions'.[41] In an organisation that 'knew no party' and forbade speakers to discuss 'any questions of ordinary party controversy',[42] it was essential that material promises for the future improvement of individuals' lives could be tied to national benefit.

Given the purpose of his articles (and his Labour candidacy at Stepney-Limehouse at the 1918 election), it is perhaps unsurprising that the most extensive and frequent references to reform were by Sheehan. Discussing H.A.L. Fisher's education bill in June 1918,[43] Sheehan rejoiced that 'the public is at last beginning to take education seriously', which was necessary so that Britons could 'hold our own' against German technical education. His conclusion espoused

> the hope that it will bring us a long way towards the abolition of class and caste in this country. Social equality is not a dream of the workers alone ... All the best social feeling of to-day revolts against a state of things which should condemn any boy to a lower place in the world than his natural gifts of mind, disposition, and character would enable him to fill.[44]

Sheehan's rhetoric confirmed the association of idealistic aspirations for social reform with more pragmatic national concerns with 'service'. Educational reform was not only good for workers, but for the nation which they could thus better serve. Furthermore, it is interesting that Sheehan's concern only extends to male education, suggesting that, despite the ongoing renegotiation of service and citizenship to include women,[45] it still remained implicitly permissible, at least to Sheehan, to 'condemn' girls to 'a lower place' than they might deserve. Again in celebratory mood in August 1918, Sheehan (an Irish nationalist) praised the 'wonderful equanimity of the British character' which enabled Parliament, during total war, to enact 'the most comprehensive and remarkable set of laws ... [of] any era'. Sheehan cited franchise expansion and educational reforms, 'questions of maternity of child welfare [*sic*], and public health',

40 *Lloyd George's Message*, p. 11.
41 Keohane, *Party of Patriotism*, p. 206.
42 TNA:PRO T102/16, 'Report up to 8th December, 1917'.
43 See Wilson, *Myriad Faces*, pp. 816–17.
44 (Sheehan), 'War and Westminster', *Seaham Weekly News*, 7/6/18, p. 2.
45 Gullace, *Blood*.

and the curbing and limiting of enemy alien activity as evidence that the government had already taken steps to ensure victory and a better post-war Britain.[46]

While primarily addressing civilian concerns, the NWAC also assured Britain's future (returning) civilians that reforms were in hand. In September, Bombardier John S. Cairns used his regular, NWAC-paid column in *Welcome* to inform fellow servicemen of Lloyd George's remark about an 'A1 Empire'. Reviewing Lloyd George's speech, Cairns continued:

> So he promises better conditions for the workers after the war. Well, we'll see that we get 'em. In the past it was pretty difficult to get a million or two out of the public purse for this particular purpose. But this war has changed everyone's outlook, and – provided we make a clean job of it – for the better.[47]

Generally, however, the NWAC seemingly recognised that servicemen's immediate aspirations were rather more fundamental than social reform (as figure 36 shows), and aspirational patriotism in this context was firmly rooted in images of home and family from which servicemen were necessarily separated.[48]

NWAC discussion of aspirational patriotism involving women confirms that aspiration and reward was linked to 'national' service. The 1918 Representation of the People bill, while enfranchising married women over 30 and some women who had seen active service abroad as nurses or in the Women's Auxiliary Army Corps or merchant marine, failed to enfranchise those munition workers (and other domestic female 'war-workers') who were acknowledged by propagandists to have contributed so significantly to the war effort.[49] Nevertheless, propagandists explicitly linked the partial female enfranchisement to war service. Once again, Sheehan was prominent in elucidating the significance of franchise reform. In September 1918, he wrote that the 'vote at one time, the privilege of property [sic], is now proudly regarded as the badge of citizenship. And, to a limited degree, women have been associated with the duty of government.' Sheehan compared the admission of women with that of significant numbers of Labour MPs after 1906, arguing that rather

---

46 (Sheehan), 'War & Westminster', *Seaham Weekly News*, 23/8/18, p. 2.
47 Bombardier B III (Cairns), 'Just between Ourselves', *Welcome*, 26, 25/9/18, p. 305.
48 For servicemen's continuing ties with home and community, see esp. McCartney, *Citizen Soldiers*; Fuller, *Troop Morale*; David Englander, 'Soldiering and Identity: Reflections on the Great War', *War in History*, 1:3 (1994). For the NWAC's addressing of soldiers' aspirations, see Monger, 'Sporting Journalism' and 'Soldiers, Home and Community'.
49 E.g., 'Picton Hall. Mr. Asquith & Unruly Women', *Liverpool Daily Post and Mercury*, 12/10/17, p. 6; Churchill, *Munitions Miracle*. On this paradox, see Gullace, *Blood*, pp. 167–94, esp. pp. 169–78.

Figure 36. Wilmot Lunt and W.F. Blood, 'Waiting for Daddy', Welcome, no. 21, 21/8/18, p. 241

than diminishing its authority or prestige, parliament had 'unquestionably gained in respect, authority and influence' through their admission. After hearing a female BWNL speaker named Elsdon addressing a war aims meeting in Keighley, the secretary of Keighley WAC, C.H. Foulds, remarked that although previously opposed to female enfranchisement, Elsdon's performance convinced him that nobody 'could oppose the right and justice of them having' the vote.[50] Both these examples suggest that women's war service was interpreted as 'proving' 'political fitness', as men supposedly had done throughout the nineteenth century.[51] By taking so public a role (and by espousing arguments desired by those in power – in this case, a strong critique of 'pacifists' and 'defeatists'), Elsdon not only ostensibly demonstrated that women served the nation, but also exhibited female 'independence' through civil activity which women's

50 (Sheehan), 'The War and Westminster', *North Devon Herald*, 26/9/18, p. 6. After their inclusion in the *Herald* in mid-September 1918, Sheehan's articles ran a week earlier there than in the *Seaham Daily News*; 'England's War Policy' *Keighley News*, 30/3/18, p. 5.

51 Garrard, *Democratisation*.

primary, 'respectable' status as head of the household had supposedly made questionable.[52]

An alternative interpretation was given by E.M. Goodman. Her weekly articles on 'The Woman's Part' frequently discussed domestic issues, offering advice on cooking and housekeeping within wartime constraints, with a lesser emphasis on female work outside the home. Assessing a speech by Christopher Addison on reconstruction in November 1918, Goodman noted his reference to children as 'the country's most important crop', scoffing that women had always known this, but celebrating that he had not scolded women about child-rearing 'as we have come to expect', instead recognising that 'not parents alone, but the whole nation, is to blame' for the unnecessary death of infants through poverty and ignorance.[53] Continuing, Goodman claimed that the Ministry of Reconstruction was transforming the understanding of women's work – rather than forbidding women to work in unsuitable jobs, 'the work must be made suitable for women' through the improvement by employers of working conditions. Goodman concluded that the Ministry's policy recognised

> that women play a great part in the prosperity of the nation, and that their part is a double one. Women are now recognized as citizens, and they have a citizen's duty, which I take it, is to give his [*sic*] country a little more than he costs it ... A woman's chief duty as a citizen is often the care of future citizens, but there is no reason why she should spend long years of idleness before this special task is done, and after it is finished ...
>
> Now that the nation is ... altering its house to suit us, what are we going to do for the nation? We cannot be helped much unless we help ourselves and each other ... most of the work of bringing up the new citizens of the world is women's work. If we are to receive, it is that we may give again.[54]

Goodman's emphases here were threefold. She rejoiced that the Ministry's interpretation of citizenship included women. This was based not so much on 'separate' but dual spheres of domesticity and employment, with the concomitant assumption that female work was not a necessary evil but a civic virtue contributing as much to the 'prosperity of the nation' as motherhood. With this enhanced status, however, Goodman reminded readers of the associated extension of women's civic duties, an 'equality' of expectation as well as opportunity integral to legitimate citizenship. In Goodman's rhetoric, aspirational patriotism again represented the promised acknowledgement of service but also, partially, service on women's own terms. Essential war-work undermined chauvinistic claptrap about a woman's 'proper place', demonstrating instead that women, like men, served their country multifariously, whether by making babies or

---

52 See, e.g., Rendall, 'Citizenship of Women', pp. 122, 161–62.
53 Cf. the pre-war situation described by Davin, 'Imperialism and Motherhood'.
54 Margaret Osborne (Goodman), 'The Woman's Part. Beginning in Time', *Droitwich Guardian War Supplement*, w.e. 9/11/18, p. 2.

bombs, cleaning the house or conducting a bus. By linking reward with obligation, the acknowledged aspiration endorsed female agency. Women had accepted their duties during the war, and would similarly accept the duties associated with enhanced civic status.

Sheehan's claim that women's right to stand as parliamentary candidates amounted to 'full equality with men' is laughable given the franchise exclusions, but his assertion that 'those great social and political privileges' were the result of the 'war services of the feminine sex' once again highlights the service–reward nexus of individualised aspirational patriotism.[55] The examples of propagandists' discussion of the meeting of individual aspirations through reform are noticeably drawn from a narrower field than most elements of the NWAC's patriotic message. There are seemingly two main explanations for this. The first is that it was difficult to allude to specific future reforms unless some government announcement had been made; hence Sheehan dwelt on Fisher's Education Bill and franchise reform, and Goodman responded to a ministerial speech. Specific references tended to be made in written rather than spoken propaganda, over which the NWAC had editorial control. Furthermore, speakers' instructions stressed that they 'must not refer to any questions of ordinary party controversy'.[56] While allusions to a better world or nation or to general societal reform were acceptable, speakers (usually representing a particular party) could not discuss reform in detail, since much of it was susceptible to differing interpretations. Nevertheless, the combination of civilisational aspirations for a better world, acknowledgement of individual grievances and the need for reform at home, alongside limited discussion of specific reforms, was sufficient to provide an optimistic element within the NWAC's narrative, recognising that civilians needed not just reminders of what they were working to defend but also of the beneficial possibilities of development *beyond* wartime and pre-war conditions which victory promised.

ASPIRATIONAL patriotism was the final element of the NWAC's patriotic narrative. Discussion of civic patriotism, the concrescent community and sacrificial patriotism portrayed duty as the cornerstone of British patriotism. Proprietorial patriotism established several key civilisational values, shared with other nations but over which, supposedly, Britain could claim particular ownership and as such had a special duty to defend. Supranational patriotism contextualised both Britain's war efforts and its civilisational credentials, offering encouragement that British ideals were held also by numerous powerful allies, and providing a means

---

55 (Sheehan), 'War and Westminster', *North Devon Herald*, 7/11/18, p. 6.
56 TNA:PRO T102/16, 'National War Aims Committee. Report up to 8th December 1917'.

of demanding further efforts through evocations of civilian contributions elsewhere. Adversarial patriotism enabled the NWAC to identify several adversaries, external *and* internal, who threatened the continuing vitality of these ideals, whether through militaristic or revolutionary (external) or moral (internal) destructiveness, which could be flexibly tailored to inspire fear or disgust. Spiritual patriotism generally acted as a comforting rhetoric, feeding off and inflecting other sub-patriotisms. Aspirational patriotism completed the NWAC's evocation of civilian experience by providing several reasons for continuing civilian optimism. Discussion of a 'world without war', in which militarism was eradicated and a League of Nations established to ensure international harmony, offered assurances that all the wartime discomfort and loss would serve a wider purpose for humanity of which individuals could be proud, rather than being the potentially renewable consequence of international power-politics. Suffering for a wider humanity was all very well but, as the other element of aspirational patriotic rhetoric demonstrated, NWAC propagandists recognised the necessity to offer British civilians encouragement through tangible improvements to their own communities, which would not only preserve Britain's way of life but enhance it. Aspirational patriotism amounted to a mediated negotiation between the state and civilians, trading wartime service for post-war rewards. Although propagandists' promises were limited by the need to avoid party controversy, and by the caveats often inherent in effectively crafted oratory, the burden of expectation adversarial patriotic discussion encouraged was considerable. The ultimate purpose of NWAC propaganda was to maintain, and where necessary remobilise, civilian patriotism and morale sufficiently to enable Britain to see the war through to victory. To some extent, what happened next was not the problem of the NWAC or its propagandists. The next section considers the NWAC's wartime reception and influence, but it may be surmised here that the implementation of aspirational patriotic rhetoric, encouraging increased civilian expectations, placed considerable pressure on parliament to deliver the promised rewards.

PART 3

The Impact of the NWAC

'A Premium on Corruption'? Parliamentary, Pressure Group and National Press Responses

Hitherto it has been both the theory and the practice of our constitutional organisation that public opinion should form itself under the influences of the free agencies of the Press, the Platform, the Theatre and of Literature, and that the public opinion thus formed should shape both Government and its policy. It is a dangerous innovation that the process should be reversed and that Government should set itself to shape public opinion otherwise than by the public utterances and actions of the statesmen who compose it. It may be excusable in a time of crisis like the present, but its ulterior possibilities cannot be overlooked. – Staffs Committee: War Aims Committee and Information Ministry, Report of Sub-Committee[1]

NOTWITHSTANDING the generally agreed importance of maintaining civilian morale, the existence of a publicly funded body intended to persuade civilians to act and think in certain ways offered troubling possibilities of future exploitation. In debates on the NWAC in the House of Commons on 13 November and 14 December 1917, and in the House of Lords on 8 May 1918, serious criticisms were expressed of the NWAC's purposes or conduct. Further evidence of the views of MPs, the national press and pressure groups like the UDC and BWL extended such criticism. Although commentary was rarely flattering, the continuing involvement of many MPs as NWAC speakers, alongside its declining discussion in later months, suggest it became, to some extent, an accepted (or tolerated) part of the wartime scenery.

BROCK Millman suggests that, had the war extended beyond 1918, Lloyd George's government might have created a Britain where 'national life would move to a beat established by a universal and uniform propaganda system in which functional distinctions between the government, the NWAC and the private press would cease to have any meanings at all'.[2] However, there is little contemporary evidence that

---

1 TNA:PRO T1/12292, file 10179.
2 Millman, *Managing*, p. 253.

prominent parliamentarians or pressmen, even those – like Snowden, MacDonald or Ponsonby, or H.W. Massingham at *The Nation* – who conspicuously dissented from government policy, were very seriously beset by such fears. While concerns about civil liberties were expressed, much opposition to the NWAC related to more prosaic fears of future electoral advantage. Major General Sir George Aston, who had been involved with the NWAC's operations, noted that 'Party politicians are suspicious folk, unwilling to trust any Government with money to spend on propaganda, for fear that they will spend it in their own interests, rather than in the country's.'[3] The *Daily News & Leader*'s Liberal editor, A.G. Gardiner, assumed that the NWAC would be maintained by party funds. In September 1917, he suggested that

> No question is likely to be raised of the value of sound propaganda work to the Allied cause ... Of course, if it were the intention to throw the costs upon the public funds, the taxpayer would have had a just right to complain ... The political parties are doing nothing: their funds must have been steadily increasing in the last three or four years. Patriotism and common-sense alike dictate their employment on so natural and suitable an object as national propaganda.

Despite his intense distrust of Lloyd George's attempts to influence public opinion, Gardiner admitted no hostility to domestic propaganda or to the fact that Carson's appointment as Cabinet liaison 'stamps [it] as purely Government work'.[4] However, he felt the appropriate funders were the parties, seemingly drawing little distinction between this and standard electoral propaganda. The difficulty was that, while providing premises, manpower and expertise, neither of the two largest parties were prepared to finance NWAC activities.

Consequently, parliament was asked to approve Treasury funding. At the committee stage in November 1917, in a debate lasting more than three hours, the principal objection was the potential political advantage which could accrue to the government from controlling such a publicly funded organisation. This was bolstered by objections to the presentation of a token vote, rather than a full estimate, which limited parliament's ability to check expenditure. Several MPs criticised the quality or value of NWAC propaganda, while some also highlighted the threat the organisation posed to civil liberties.

Perhaps surprisingly, the first critic was not a 'pacifist' MP, but the City of London Conservative, Sir Frederick Banbury. Banbury doubted

---

3   Sir George Aston, 'Propaganda – and the Father of It', *Cornhill Magazine*, 48:284 (1920), p. 240.
4   'The New Propaganda', *Daily News & Leader* (henceforth *Daily News*), 19/9/17, p. 2. Stephen Koss, *Fleet Street Radical: A.G. Gardiner and the Daily News* (London: Allen Lane, 1973), pp. 168–242.

'anyone would cavil at the expenditure' but demanded a full estimate. Further, he strongly protested

> against this use of public money for political agents. To set up a Committee ... and then to take money which is not accounted for to Parliament and distribute it amongst the various political agents, under the auspices of the Whips, is a very dangerous precedent ...[5]

Banbury feared the subsidisation of party machinery by public funds. By accepting a token vote, he implied, parliament became liable for maintaining party staffs. This, said the 'pacifist' Liberal Joseph King, was 'a perfect scandal, a mass of jobbery'.[6] The proposals were also mildly rebuked by the former wartime Chancellor of the Exchequer, Reginald McKenna, who noted that the NWAC, while representing 'the views of the vast majority of the country does not represent the whole of the country'. McKenna thus reiterated that party funds were the best way 'to instruct public opinion upon party questions'. McKenna denied that the NWAC's cross-party composition elevated it above party politics, equating its work with 'a Budget campaign, a land campaign, and a House of Lords campaign', all of which the Liberal party had subsidised.[7] This was the root of parliamentary opposition to the funding. Despite Carson's rejoinder that the NWAC's work was 'not a party purpose [but] a national purpose',[8] most speakers judged that since its major intention – counteracting 'pacifist' propaganda – placed it in opposition to a section of MPs, public funding advantaged one section of the House against another.

Naturally, this point was made most stridently by those who felt themselves targeted by the NWAC. The UDC founder, Charles Trevelyan, asserted that the public money requested was 'directed against us'. He considered it 'a party political move', employing 'public money for a political purpose'. Trevelyan warned the House that

> you are setting a precedent of attacking, with public money, what you say is a comparatively insignificant movement ... which will allow [a future] Socialist Government – or any other Government of the sort you dislike – to use public money ... for its own party purposes ...
>
> I implore Members of this House, whether we here are right or wrong, to consider whether it ought to have a campaign waged against us ... paid out of the public purse?[9]

---

5 Speech of Sir Frederick Banbury, PDC(5), 99 (13/11/17), cols 292–96. Subsequent references to this debate are from this volume. Banbury was, according to Nigel Keohane, a 'diehard' and 'libertarian' Conservative committed to a bare minimum of state interference in private life. Keohane, *Party of Patriotism*, pp. 133, 175.
6 Col. 324.
7 Cols 308–11.
8 Col. 314.
9 Cols 302–05.

Trevelyan's colleague, the disillusioned Liberal, Robert Outhwaite, suggested that, despite Guest's assurance that the NWAC's purpose was not to 'support or defend the Government', the money would be used corruptly for 'keeping this Government in office' should public opinion turn against it.[10] Extending these arguments, the Liberal MP for Coventry, David Mason, said it was inappropriate for the majority to seek to stifle minority views, either inside or outside parliament. Mason, who though outside the 'pacifist' parliamentary group (see table 7) retained strong affinities with them, having become an 'independent, anti-war Liberal' in 1914,[11] suggested that the public included people sympathetic to the 'pacifist' parliamentary minority who would be obliged to subsidise the suppression of their own views:

> There are eight or ten hon. Members on the second bench opposite who represent a considerable section of opinion in the country, and though the House may not agree with their views, you have no right to use public funds to advance a propaganda which is not in accordance with the views which they are not allowed to express in this House. This seems to me to be a most vicious principle ... a premium on corruption.[12]

This was the major concern for MPs. While most speakers acknowledged the right and appropriateness – sometimes the necessity – of instructing public opinion, there was considerable resistance to using taxpayers' money to fund the suppression of minority opinion. Trevelyan's reference to a future socialist government (a point echoed by Mason) sought to demonstrate the proposal's illiberality. Despite a supporter's claim that the vote constituted no precedent since it was an emergency war measure, and McNeill's claim that if the Committee was 'doing party work out of public funds' then it was the work of a party 'composed of the nation itself' against one 'deliberately attempting to frustrate the will of the nation',[13] such an appearance of limiting free speech was somewhat troubling. 'Pacifist' MPs like Trevelyan utilised an 'oppositional' patriotism, recalling earlier radical interpretations which saw the active holding to account of governments as 'true patriotism'. During the war, according to Paul Ward, exponents of this oppositional patriotism held that 'the government at war was not the nation, and misrepresented its interests', especially by 'the suppression of English liberties through the restriction of anti-war activities'.[14] In February 1917, for instance, Lady Margaret Sackville had condemned press jingoism, which 'narrowed ...

---

10 Speeches of Capt. Guest, col. 287; Robert Outhwaite, col. 320.
11 Harris, *Out of Control*, p. 203; Edward David, 'The Liberal Party Divided 1916–1918', *Historical Journal*, 13:3 (1970), p. 513, n. 11; Stenton and Lees, *Who's Who*, p. 240.
12 Cols 324–26.
13 Speeches of Commander Carlyon Bellairs, cols 321–23; Ronald McNeill, col. 340.
14 Ward, *Red Flag*, pp. 132–33.

love of England to a barren nationalism, which bickers and quarrels and shouts and slanders like a drunken fish-wife'. The UDC, by contrast, cared for the '*true* England' – its 'wide tolerance', 'generosity', 'humour', 'humanity and *richness* of outlook'.[15]

Beyond this, several MPs criticised the quality of NWAC propaganda, suggesting it was unworthy of public support. The Liberal Alexander Whyte (Parliamentary Private Secretary to Churchill until 1915) said that the use of public money for distributing pamphlets which were virtually a 'gramophone for the "Daily Mail"' was a 'public scandal'.[16] Arthur Ponsonby complained that he had seen 16 NWAC leaflets which consisted of 'snippets' of speeches, 'two pictures from "Punch," and a number of leaflets describing German atrocities'. He criticised the 'reckless' wastefulness of the distribution, claiming that 250,000 pamphlets had been sent to a recent by-election, and adding that NWAC meetings had 'not been a very striking success'.[17] The most damning verdict was offered by the Liberal John Whitehouse (who became a member of the UDC's general council on 31 October 1918).[18] He argued that NWAC propaganda was 'unworthy of this country ... of any country. It makes an appeal to ... the fleeting passions that sometimes sweep over the world.' Whitehouse suggested it should instead emphasise the steps taken to preserve peace in the future, including the League of Nations. He urged Guest 'not to use this propaganda to increase the hatred of the world, but to make it constructive, and to show us how all may be led into the paths of peace'.[19] Despite McNeill's attempt to brush aside Whitehouse's criticism, such specific denunciation was probably useful to the NWAC. If propagandists did not cease to condemn German behaviour, they did present a much wider discussion than that criticised in parliament.

This extensive criticism of NWAC propaganda and its purposes notwithstanding, a vote on an amendment to limit funding to £900 was defeated by 132 votes to 22 (plus two tellers). While non-'pacifist' MPs like Banbury, McKenna and Timothy Davies made critical comments, the majority derived from that opposition bloc. An article in *The U.D.C.* numbered this group at eleven, with four additional 'semi-detached members' (King, Chancellor, Harvey and Arnold), but overlooked Richard Denman, a UDC general council member in 1917 as well as Richard Holt and Noel Buxton who had close ties to the group. Other MPs who

---

15 Lady Margaret Sackville, 'Patriotism', *U.D.C.*, 2:4, February 1917, p. 46.
16 Cols 296–97.
17 Cols 298–99. Similar criticisms were offered by Tyson Wilson, Noel Buxton and Philip Morrell. On NWAC involvement at by-elections, see TNA:PRO T102/14, letter (unsigned) to Edward Turton, MP, 25/4/18, regarding his promise to speak at South Hereford by-election.
18 'Fourth Annual General Meeting of the U.D.C.', *U.D.C.*, 4:2, December 1918, p. 287.
19 Cols 336–38.

Table 7 *The parliamentary 'pacifist' group*[1]

Name*	Party[2]	Constituency (since)	1918 election result[3]	Debate[4]	Voted[5]
William Anderson*	Labour	Sheffield (Attercliffe) (1914)	lost vs CL	no/no	abs
Sydney Arnold*	Liberal	Holmfirth (1912)	won vs CC and ILP (Penistone)	no/no	yes
Noel Buxton	Liberal/Lib–Lab[6]	North Norfolk (Jan. 1910)	lost vs CC	yes/no	yes
Henry Chancellor*	Liberal	Shoreditch (Haggerston) (Jan. 1910)	lost vs CL (4th of 5 behind Con, ILP, Shoreditch)	no/no	abs
Richard Denman	Liberal	Carlisle (Jan. 1910)	retired (temporarily)	yes/no	yes
Thomas Harvey*	Liberal	Leeds West (Jan. 1910)	retired (temporarily)	no/no	yes
Richard Holt	Liberal	Hexham (1907)	lost vs CC (Eccles)	no/yes	yes
Fred Jowett*	Labour	Bradford West (1906)	lost vs NDP (2nd of 3, East Bradford)	no/no	yes
Joseph King*	Liberal	North Somerset (Jan. 1910)	retired	yes/no	yes
Richard Lambert*	Liberal	Cricklade (Dec. 1910)	retired	no/yes	yes
Hastings Lees-Smith*	Liberal	Northampton (Jan. 1910)	lost vs NDP (2nd of 3, Don Valley)	no/no	yes
Ramsay MacDonald*	Labour	Leicester (1906)	lost vs NDP (Leicester West)	no/no	yes
Philip Morrell*	Liberal	Burnley (Dec. 1910)	retired	yes/no	yes
Robert Outhwaite*	Liberal/Ind. Liberal	Stoke – Hanley (1912)	lost vs NDP (3rd of 4 behind Lab.)	yes/yes	yes
Arthur Ponsonby*	Liberal/Ind. Democrat	Stirling Burghs (1908)	lost vs CL (3rd, Dunfermline Burghs, behind ILP)	yes/no	yes
Tom Richardson*	Labour	Whitehaven (Dec. 1910)	lost vs CL (Bosworth)	no/no	abs
Philip Snowden*	Labour	Blackburn (1906)	lost vs CL/CC (3rd, 2 seats)	no/no	abs
Charles Trevelyan*	Liberal/Independent	Elland (1899)	lost vs CC (4th behind AL, Lab.)	yes/no	yes
John Whitehouse	Liberal/Ind. Liberal	Mid Lanarkshire (Jan. 1910)	lost vs Lab. (4th behind CC, NPD, Hamilton)	yes/yes	yes

*Named in a *U.D.C.* article, 'Pacifists in Parliament'.

1 'Pacifists in Parliament', *U.D.C.*, 3:11, September 1918, p. 261. Also Swartz, *Union of Democratic Control*, pp. 95, n. 38, 225 (for Buxton, Denman); A.J.P. Taylor, *The Trouble Makers: Dissent over Foreign Policy, 1792–1939* (London: Hamish Hamilton, 1957), pp. 132–66, esp. pp. 148–9 (for Buxton); Trevor Wilson, *The Downfall of the Liberal Party, 1914–1935* (London: Collins, 1966), pp. 30–31, 99, 128, 175; David, 'Liberal Party Divided'; Sir Richard Denman. *Political Sketches* (Carlisle: Charles Thurnam & Sons, 1948), p. 24; David J. Dutton (ed.), *Odyssey of an Edwardian Liberal: The Political Diary of Richard Durning Holt* (Gloucester: Allan Sutton Publishing, 1989), p. xxvi.

2 Format for parties: previous election/1918 election, where these are different.

3 Position if more than two candidates in brackets. Party abbreviations: AL = Asquithian Liberal; CC = Conservative (coupon); CL = (usually Lloyd George) Liberal (coupon); Lab. = Labour; NDP = National Democratic Party. Details from Stenton and Lees, *Who's Who*, vols 1–2; *Craig, Parliamentary Election Results*.

4 Format for debates: yes/no regarding whether spoke at 13 November/14 December 1917 debate.

5 Format for votes: yes/no/abs regarding whether against NWAC in November division.

6 Clare Griffiths, 'Noel Buxton (Lord Noel-Buxton of Aylsham)', in Greg Rosen (ed.), *Dictionary of Labour Biography* (London: Politico's, 2001), pp. 94–96.

voted to limit NWAC funding also had links to the group, but were less prominent, like Mason, Percy Molteno, John Burns (a 'silent' supporter) and the Welsh Liberal nationalist (soon to convert to Labour) Edward John.[20] Of the 24 MPs who voted for the amendment, only two – the unopposed Conservative, Banbury, and the radical Sydney Arnold (later a 'Wee Free' Liberal)[21] who defeated a Coalition Conservative and an ILP candidate at Penistone – retained their parliamentary places. Eight retired (temporarily in the case of Denman and Harvey), and the other fourteen lost their seats (all except Whitehouse to Coalition candidates).

Of those who defended the Committee, four (Guest, Greenwood, Cowan and McNeill) were members, Carson was its cabinet liaison, and only three, the Conservative chairman Sir George Younger, Commander Carlyon Bellairs and Clement Edwards – who welcomed any stick with which to beat 'pacifists' – acted independently. Yet they obtained a comfortable majority. This suggests that, for many MPs, Treasury funding of domestic propaganda was uncontroversial. The apparent mood was one of tolerant indifference towards the Committee. Sanders noted that, despite Guest's weak advocacy, 'eventually only 22 voted against it',[22] perhaps indicating that he had expected more opposition.

Upon its second reading, on 14 December, the token vote received substantially similar criticism as previously over four hours. Critics like Whitehouse, Outhwaite and Mason again condemned the means by which the money was sought and spent. Beginning the debate, the anti-conscriptionist Leif Jones reiterated the view that it was 'essentially corrupt … for the Government of the day to use the funds at its disposal to push purposes which are not entirely national purposes'; that the propaganda was inappropriate, including the advocacy of tariff reform, and in some cases 'vulgar and inane'; and claimed that NWAC operations compromised press freedom. Jones said Treasury funds were being used to place advertisements in newspapers, but were withheld from those whose 'views are obnoxious' to the NWAC's executive. He condemned this as 'a very dangerous, corrupting power … liable to misuse at any moment', a point reiterated by Whitehouse.[23] Replying for the Committee, Sanders suggested that private subsidisation would have undermined its effectiveness through suggestions that it was beholden to the rich, and that the parties had refused to supply the money. Seeking

---

20 Swanwick, *Builders of Peace*, pp. 34–35; David, 'Liberal Party Divided', pp. 513–14, 523 (on Molteno); Harris, *Out of Control*, p. 203 (on Mason and Molteno); Taylor, *Troublemakers*, p. 133 (on Burns); Kenneth O. Morgan, 'Peace Movements in Wales, 1899–1945', *Welsh History Review*, 10 (1981), pp. 412–16 (on John).

21 Wilson, *Downfall*, pp. 177, 189.

22 Sanders diary, 17/11/17, in Ramsden, *Tory Politics*, p. 91.

23 Speech of Leif Jones, PDC(5), vol. (14/12/17), cols 1515–25; Whitehouse, cols 1539–43. Subsequent references to the debate are from this volume.

to reassure critics about the costs, Sanders revealed that the NWAC had spent considerably less than their estimates, and that local committees had to submit estimates ahead of meetings. Furthermore, though some of the propaganda might be considered of dubious quality, 'experienced political organisers' assured him 'that speeches and pamphlets, and what for some absurd reason we call literature', did influence public opinion, and that it was important to respond when criticism was expressed elsewhere.[24] Sanders' insouciance, intended to placate critics, instead encouraged Molteno to insist that Sanders had 'no belief in the propaganda' and could therefore make no justified demand for public funds.[25]

Later, the UDC member Richard Holt added his dissent. 'This', he said, was 'a proposal to propagate certain views held by a majority, but it is rather remarkable that, coincident with this propaganda, we have an attempt made to prevent the expression of the opposite view.[26] Holt's criticism related to the introduction of Defence of the Realm Regulation (DRR) 27c in mid-November, requiring that every pamphlet include the author's name and address and be presented to the Press Bureau for possible censorship, as should any newspaper or periodical established after 18 November. NWAC publications, however, were exempt from these requirements, demonstrating to critics that the measure simply attempted to reduce critical publications by intimidation.[27] This, together with the proposed disfranchisement of conscientious objectors, represented to Holt the 'growing spirit of oppression by the Tory-jingo knock out blow lot'.[28] Holt asked whether the Treasury bench believed NWAC propaganda

> should be carried into any constituency in which there is likely to be an election, or ... be carried on during the period of a General Election? ... I cannot help entertaining a suspicion that the reason why the estimate has not been produced ... is the fact that we might find ourselves carrying on an electioneering campaign on the strength of this Vote.

Further, he wanted to know whether the vote would be rescinded if the Committee ceased to represent all (non-Irish) parties.[29] Shortly before the token vote's successful passage, Guest assented to Herbert Samuel's demand for a 'definite assurance' of a 'policy of not conducting any propaganda of any sort in connection with either a by-election or a general election'. Samuel also expressed relief that Carson had denied

---

24 Cols 1525–31.
25 Cols 1531–32.
26 Col. 1578.
27 Questions by Ponsonby (19/11/17) and W.C. Anderson (23/11/17) in PDC(5), 99, cols 850, 1531. For a disinterested condemnation, see the *Manchester Guardian*'s editorials, 16, 21, 27 and 29 November.
28 Holt diary, 22/11/17, in Dutton (ed.), *Odyssey*, p. 51.
29 PDC(5), 101 (14/12/17), cols 1578–79.

that he controlled the NWAC, since 'some of his speeches have not commanded absolutely universal confidence', and the NWAC would be most successful if it represented 'the concensus [*sic*] of opinion of the various schools of thought'.[30]

Carson's involvement clearly harmed the NWAC's reputation amongst MPs (and much of the press). He was too divisive a figure and too strident an orator to act as an effective administrator for the NWAC, though critics amplified his role beyond its real function as a conduit to the War Cabinet. The Committee member Walter Rea was told by Wallace Carter as early as September 1917 that there was 'a growing tendency for Labour to stand aloof and when it is generally known that Sir Edward Carson is a member of the Committee our difficulties are likely to be increased'.[31] *The Nation* lamented that Carson, previously 'denounced' as a rebel 'conspiring to overthrow law', now 'dominate[d] the country' by directing the NWAC and suppressing the statement of war aims, while *Labour Leader* suggested that 'Pacifist England was to him but another Sinn Fein Ireland – needing a Dublin Castle to destroy it!'[32] Carson's part in the armed opposition to Irish home rule rendered him unfit, in many eyes, for a position of governmental responsibility. Those who celebrated his resignation from Cabinet and propaganda duties in January 1918 were hardly comforted, however, by the installation of Beaverbrook (an unprincipled 'intriguer first, last & always', as Gardiner remarked in 1942, retaining his earlier animosity) as Minister of Information.[33] While the NWAC remained outside his control, preserving a fig leaf of independence from the government, Beaverbrook made every effort to absorb it until finally instructed by the War Cabinet in March that it was to remain separate. The NWAC also rebuffed his attempt to have a sympathetic MP, the Conservative J.A. Grant, appointed to the Committee to oversee its operations.[34]

Nonetheless, domestic propaganda was commonly elided with Beaverbrook's actual function by parliamentarians, the press and the public.[35] In the House of Lords in May, the Earl of Denbigh, a prominent NWAC speaker, concluded a long exposition of the continuing menace of pacifism in Britain with a resolution regretting 'that stronger measures have not been taken to combat the various agencies in this country who

---

30 Cols 1592–93.

31 TNA:PRO T102/12, Wallace Carter to Rea, 15/9/17.

32 'The New Magnificat', *Nation*, 22/12/17, pp. 407–08; 'Suppressing the Pacifists – And Freedom!', *Labour Leader*, 22/11/17, p. 5.

33 Koss, *Gardiner*, p. 246.

34 PA, Beaverbrook papers, BBK/E/3/8, memoranda, February–October 1918; BBK/E/3/9, correspondence with Grant, c. 5–26/3/18; Sanders and Taylor, *British Propaganda*, pp. 79–80.

35 E.g., TNA:PRO T102/1, letters to Beaverbrook by Rose Belcher, 25/4/18; Dorothy Bates, 14/9/18.

are serving the cause of the enemy'.[36] Denbigh was seconded by Lord Beresford, who hoped Beaverbrook would 'use propaganda in every way he can to let the people of this country know the tremendous danger the pacifists are in our midst'.[37] Beaverbrook was obliged to explain that while his Ministry could 'assist and support propaganda at home', its direction was the NWAC's responsibility.[38] When Denbigh again complained in the *Times*, Beaverbrook provided the official response, outlining the NWAC's difficulties. Because of its all-party composition it had to avoid discussing issues of party controversy and had instead to 'be content to preach the general doctrines of patriotism'. Beaverbrook suggested that it was a 'lesser evil' to leave things as they were 'than to stir the embers of party dissension by making that committee a Government office directly responsible to Parliament in the usual way'.[39] Seizing the opportunity, the BWL executive wrote to the *Times* to boast that they were holding 'thousands' of meetings and to reassure Denbigh that 'there is at least one workers' organisation that is carrying on patriotic propaganda with energy and enthusiasm'. Such crowing from the BWL demonstrates once again that the BWL and NWAC were not nearly so close as Millman suggests.[40]

Occasional broadsides in the House of Commons in 1918 continued to decry the 'fiddling and idiotic waste of public money' by what Ponsonby described as 'an extravagant fiasco', but there was no further extended discussion of the NWAC.[41] Apart from some enquiries into the number of meetings held and pamphlets distributed, often from the stridently anti-'pacifist' Conservative, Charles Yate, which enabled Committee members to demonstrate their continuing strenuous activities,[42] MPs seemingly maintained their tolerant indifference to the NWAC and its propaganda. That well over one hundred MPs of varied political outlooks consented to speak or write for the NWAC over its 15-month existence suggests the silence of many during the debates was more one of endorsement than opposition (as does the heavy defeat of the November amendment).[43] Though some MPs, like Sir Archibald Stirling, may have

---

36 Speech of the Earl of Denbigh, Parliamentary Debates (Lords), 5th series, 29, cols 1009–18. All subsequent references to the debate are from this volume.
37 Col. 1023.
38 Cols 1023–28.
39 'National War Aims. Lord Beaverbrook on Home Propaganda', *Times*, 22/5/18, p. 7.
40 J.A. Seddon, J.F. Green and Victor Fisher, 'War Aims' (letter), *Times*, 23/5/18, p. 7; Millman, *Managing*, esp. pp. 232, 245–46.
41 Speech of John Henderson, PDC(5), 107 (19/6/18), col. 423; question by Ponsonby, PDC(5), 108 (9/7/18), col. 171.
42 E.g. questions by Yate, PDC(5), 107 (18/6/18), cols 180–81 – answered by Parker; 108 (9/7/18), cols 170–71, (16/7/18), cols 886–87 – answered by Guest. On Yate's anti-'pacifism', see his correspondence with the Home Secretary, December 1917–January 1918: TNA:PRO HO45/10743/263275/300, 307.
43 See pp. 51–53 above for party affiliation statistics. The number of MPs who spoke at meetings may considerably exceed those in the incomplete meetings register.

been 'not very keen on War Aims meetings' because they were 'wholly unnecessary' and because of perceived bad treatment during the National Service campaign of early 1917, others, like George Peel, were markedly enthusiastic. Indeed, MPs sometimes actively sought NWAC assistance. The Conservative MP for Denbigh, Captain William Ormsby-Gore, wrote to ask Cox what was being arranged there. Similarly, Churchill, as Minister of Munitions, asked Guest in May 1918 to provide speakers in Cumberland, not to 'deal with any controversial topic [like trade disputes] whatever ... [but] to explain the military situation and the need for effort'.[44] The Asquithian Liberal Aneurin Williams meanwhile sought to influence the content of NWAC propaganda. As chairman of the Armenian Refugees Lord Mayor's Fund, Williams told Greenwood that Armenia should receive discussion equal to Belgium or Serbia, and that arrangements could be made for Armenian speakers, subject to expense.[45] Even some moderate critics, like McKenna and Herbert Samuel, who expressed reservations about certain issues during the debates, spoke at NWAC events, strengthening the supposition that the Committee had the tacit endorsement of most MPs.[46] Similarly, the 'pacificist', anti-conscription, Asquithian Liberal W. Llewellyn Williams, despite an apparently 'almost pathological' dislike for Lloyd George, spoke at several NWAC events, suggesting that his supposed 'recruitment' to the 'critics of the war' was at most partial.[47] If some, like Asquith, 'spoke with more satisfaction than I generally feel' at these meetings,[48] the fact of their having done so demonstrates that many were either untroubled about the propriety of government-funded propaganda or else considered such scruples secondary to patriotic duty.

For instance, neither Francis Edwards (who spoke for the NWAC at Llandrindod Wells) nor W.H. Somervell (at Keighley) are listed on the surviving register pages.

44 TNA:PRO T102/13, Stirling to Vesey, 2/11/17; T102/11, Peel to Wallace Carter, 13/2/18; T102/5, Ormsby-Gore to Cox, 7/12/17; T102/2, Churchill to Guest, 24/5/18.

45 TNA:PRO T102/1, Williams to Greenwood, 22/11/17. See also the encouraging response to Williams's suggestion: T102/15, letter, unsigned (Wallace Carter) to Williams, 17/12/17.

46 McKenna was scheduled to speak in East Denbigh, while Samuel took meetings in Cleveland and Paddington. TNA:PRO T102/17, nos 143–44, 865, 921. Cf., however, the letter from Vesey to Donald McMaster, MP, 22/2/18, regarding the increasing difficulty of getting MPs to speak at meetings by February: T102/8.

47 Williams was scheduled for 21 separate campaigns. E.g. TNA:PRO T102/17, nos 738, 1675. On Williams's views, see Morgan, 'Peace Movements', pp. 409–12. A 'pacificist' differed from a 'pacifist' in believing that war was 'sometimes necessary' but should at all costs be avoided where possible. Martin Ceadel, *Pacifism in Britain 1914–1945: The Defining of a Faith* (Oxford: Clarendon Press, 1980), p. 3.

48 Desmond McCarthy (ed.), *H.H.A.: Letters to a Friend, First Series, 1915–1922* (London: Geoffrey Bles, 1933), letter, 28/9/17, p. 35.

POLITICIANS' general indifference towards the NWAC was mirrored in print. Those MPs who wrote about it in the press belonged to the noisy dissenting minority. Condemning the eventual acceptance of the NWAC's token vote, Philip Snowden labelled the Committee 'a grotesque and ludicrous absurdity' which had failed 'to arouse any public interest in their campaign [while] their meetings, as a rule, are miserable fiascos'. He alleged (seemingly falsely, given the diversity of addresses discussed in Part 2) that speakers used a scripted address and were 'expressly forbidden' to take questions in case their answers betrayed ignorance or offered inappropriate information, while NWAC pamphlets contained 'hackneyed and meaningless phrases about the destruction of Prussian militarism' intended 'to excite a hatred and a passion against the enemy' by recycling disproved atrocity stories (again, such criticism was reductive).[49] Ramsay MacDonald had made similar criticisms in the *Leicester Pioneer*. He argued that the Committee's purpose was to bolster the political position of jingoistic MPs, but insisted that 'Government-made opinions advocated by Government-controlled speakers and Government-paid propagandists will have no weight in the country.' He suggested that the government would not seek unlimited funding 'to combat ideas unless it [was] afraid of these ideas and [was] being beaten by them'.[50] Elsewhere he highlighted the ideological inconsistency of NWAC propaganda. Contradicting Snowden's claim that speakers followed a script, MacDonald noted that 'no two speakers say the same thing' and that the NWAC generally discussed peace rather than war aims. These 'desirable ends' constituted 'a programme of reforms which no war can ever carry out' and, in MacDonald's view, confirmed a 'tendency to keep the war going by classing as war aims every democratic reform we want to see … in Europe'.[51] The NWAC's purpose, in this interpretation, was less the maintenance of civilian morale to facilitate victory than of war as a permanent status quo.

'Pacifist' critics tended to exhibit a complacent contempt for the NWAC's efforts in their public utterances, suggesting a strategic attempt to undermine it by apparent insouciance. Thus MacDonald encouraged *Labour Leader* readers to buy McCurdy's NWAC pamphlet *The Truth about the Secret Treaties*, because its blend of misleading discussion and deliberate omissions of fact provided excellent material 'to expose the methods of the peace-at-no-price party'. McCurdy was 'so busy addressing War Aims meetings, that he has not had the leisure to understand any

---

49 Snowden, 'Review of the Week', *Labour Leader*, 20/12/17, p. 1. For the significance of his allegation of scripted speeches, see the discussion of political meetings in Lawrence, *Speaking*.
50 MacDonald, 'From Green Benches', *Leicester Pioneer*, 16/11/17, p. 4.
51 MacDonald, '"War Aims"', *The Free Man*, 7 (Nov. 1917), p. 1. A copy is at LSE, ILP papers, ILP/6/17/4.

of the questions upon which he speaks', therefore rendering him more useful as a credulous 'Government apologist and advocate'.[52] However, MacDonald's note in his diary of 'a vote passed to corrupt public opinion under the guise of War Aims propaganda' did not suggest such unconcern.[53] Nor, unsurprisingly, did his public reactions to the violent disruption of his May Day 1918 demonstration in Leicester.[54] In an angry speech the next day, MacDonald labelled the NWAC a 'fraudulent organisation' which tried to 'flout the claims of organised labour' because the local committee 'was composed almost entirely of men opposed to trades unionism', some of them 'sweaters'.[55] In the *Pioneer*, MacDonald attributed the 'ignorant, rowdy, loud-mouthed' counter-demonstration to central funding, and encouraged 'Mr. Guest to hire it for general exhibition in the country'. Shortly thereafter, he castigated the NWAC's 'paid touts and cheap-jack orators who will espouse any cause for a fee', adding that it was fraudulent because it deliberately withheld 'information which was essential if it did its work', particularly details of the secret treaties.[56] If 'pacifist' criticism in the press was generally muted and mocking, therefore, MacDonald's reaction to provocation in his own constituency suggests that 'pacifists' were not quite so relaxed about the NWAC as they claimed.

Nonetheless, mockery remained a potent technique for the NWAC's critics. MacDonald's UDC colleague, J.A. Hobson, provided the most bitingly satirical condemnation of the Committee. In 'War Aims: 1920', one of a series of unsigned articles produced for *The Nation* in 1917,[57] Hobson imagined a conversation between 'Charteris', a man keen to understand Britain's war aims, and 'Poynton', a NWAC member whose response to Charteris's complaint that he could not find an 'explicit, and intelligible' statement of war aims was as follows:

> I should hope not. Why, the whole effort of our Committee is devoted to baulking the curiosity of people who are not satisfied to see the show, but want to go behind and see how it is worked ...
> The people are quite satisfied with what you call our rhetorical stunts about the liberation of small peoples, the rescue of the world from German domination, making the world safe for democracy, and so forth ... It is just fellows like you who try to butt in and spoil the game.[58]

The NWAC's purposes, Poynton explains, are to maintain national unity by avoiding difficult or controversial questions like economic protection

---

52 MacDonald, 'Mr. McCurdy's "Secret Treaties"', *Labour Leader*, 18/7/18, p. 5.
53 TNA:PRO, MacDonald papers, PRO30/69/1753/1, diary, 13/11/17.
54 See pp. 134–36 above.
55 'Women's Labour League. Mr. MacDonald and Sunday's Meeting', *Leicester Daily Mercury*, 7/5/18, p. 2.
56 MacDonald, 'From Green Benches', *Leicester Pioneer*, 10/5/18; 24/5/18, both p. 4.
57 On Hobson's authorship, see Swanwick, *Builders of Peace*, p. 183.
58 'Lucian' (Hobson), 'War Aims: 1920', *Nation*, 24/11/17, pp. 266–67.

or a fully developed commitment to the League of Nations; to maintain Allied unity by avoiding awkward discussions of territorial claims; and to prevent the enemy from knowing Britain's aims since 'He might accept them, and then where would our war be?' Eventually, Charteris is warned that 'this talk about aims that are definite and intelligible is treasonable' as it would interfere with the unified prosecution of the war. For Hobson, the Committee's *raison d'être* was to prevent the war's resolution by obfuscating Britain's war aims so sufficiently that no chance of facilitating discussion remained. The NWAC's patriotic narrative, in this analysis, consisted of platitudes designed to confound critical enquiry. NWAC discussion of the League of Nations was conducted from a 'safe Utopian elevation' rather than 'the ground of real and immediate politics'. Hobson's view was that such propaganda contained no intellectual or ideological commitment, merely gestures toward liberal ideals. As another of his characters commented, 'truth is a raw material, infinitely malleable and adaptable to the uses of the State'.[59] Once again, Hobson's attack revealed an alternative interpretation of patriotism, which considered the close scrutiny of governmental action essential, even in wartime, to the maintenance of Britain's moral world leadership.

WHILE the UDC was understandably hostile to the NWAC, other pressure groups made different judgements. BWL involvement with the NWAC, while not as extensive and malevolent as Millman contends, partly counterbalanced the disapproval of pressure groups like the UDC, and its support was augmented by other somewhat right-wing 'patriotic' groups (or their members) like the British Empire Producers' Organisation and the Never Forget and Never Forgive League. A representative of Havelock Wilson's National Sailors' and Firemen's Union (NSFU, previously responsible for preventing MacDonald and F.W. Jowett from travelling to the Stockholm socialist conference), meanwhile, asked for 78 copies of a poster depicting 'British Sailors in Germany with their heads shaved' to hang in each of its branch offices. While such right-wing associations were problematic for the NWAC's picture of an united Britain, the NSFU in particular had considerable reach, its nationwide offices purportedly 'cover[ing] the seafaring population of Great Britain'.[60] They

---

59 'Lucian' (Hobson), 'The Laboratory of War-Truth: 1920', *Nation*, 27/10/17, pp. 118–19.

60 TNA:PRO T102/4, F.W.W. Fisher (British Empire Producers' Organisation) to Pembroke Wickes, 5/10/17; Robert Forsyth (Never Forget and Never Forgive League), 19/8/17; T102/7, John Kealey, National Sailors' and Firemen's Union to NWAC, 10/4/18. On the latter organisation's role in the Stockholm controversy, see Lloyd George, *Memoirs*, IV, pp. 1896–98. The poster referred to is probably 'How the Hun Hates!', produced by David Wilson and W.F. Blood (Wilson was a regular collaborator of Blood's, but is not listed as a NWAC-paid artist). See Imperial War Museum, London (IWM), IWM PST 13551 for the poster. This is

thus constituted an influential endorsement of the NWAC, albeit one which the Committee did not have to work very hard to receive.

The NWAC's establishment was also welcomed by some papers. The Conservative *Morning Post* asserted that the 'importance of [the Committee's] ... work cannot be over-estimated',[61] while in September its editor, H.A. Gwynne, urged the Committee and the government on to greater efforts, as did Robert Donald at the *Daily Chronicle*:

> We welcome its activities. A counter-propaganda was necessary to that of the pacifists, who are working with tireless assiduity. Judging by a dozen separate leaflets ... the committee is doing its work with energy and intelligence ... But it is not enough to circulate leaflets. There is need also for a vigorous propaganda on the platform ... Opinion at home must be sustained and enlightened.[62]

In commenting on the November debate, Donald, who at this time enjoyed close contact with Lloyd George and, as a member of the Press Advisory Committee, knew more than most about the NWAC's administration, continued to offer supportive commentary.[63] He argued that home propaganda was 'necessary'; that, since party funds were un-available, the government was obliged to supply the finance; and that this was better than suppressing 'mischievous criticism' in the press.[64] In the *British Citizen and Empire Worker* (the organ of the BWL), meanwhile, Victor Fisher defended the token vote, but demanded more strident action against 'pacifist' critics, claiming that total war legitimised restrictions of free speech.[65]

Generally, however, press commentary was antagonistic. With the notable exception of Asquith's speeches at NWAC meetings, which newspapers of nearly all attitudes praised (though a NWAC meeting in Leeds antagonised both Lloyd George, who believed Asquith had exploited it to 'make difficulties' for him, and the Women's Social and Political Union

---

not recorded in the NWAC ledgers as a poster for which Blood was paid, although several early payments are recorded simply for 'large poster': TNA:PRO T102/19.

61 'National War Aims', *Morning Post* (henceforth *Post*), 30/7/17, p. 6.

62 'The Nation and the War', *Daily Chronicle* (henceforth *Chronicle*), 20/9/17, p. 2; 'The Marplots', *Post*, 19/9/17. Note the continued fascination with public meet-ings, on which see pp. 41–42 above. This wartime understanding contradicted the post-war assessment by an unnamed committee that doubted the value of em-ploying 'indistinguised [*sic*] orators sent to address artificially convened meetings': TNA:PRO INF4/1B, 'Staff of the National War Aims Committee'. Conceivably, a distinction was being made between 'genuine' public meetings and those attended by individuals under instruction.

63 On Donald's role: TNA:PRO INF4/4B, 7, 9; Stephen Koss, *The Rise and Fall of the Political Press in Britain*, II, *The Twentieth Century* (London: Hamish Hamilton, 1984), pp. 315–16.

64 'Making War Aims Known', *Chronicle*, 15/11/17, p. 2.

65 Victor Fisher, 'Malignants and Malcontents', *British Citizen and Empire Worker*, 17/11/17, p. 305.

[WSPU] newspaper, *Britannia*, which boasted of having disrupted it and thus prevented him from reviving his popularity),[66] most of the commentary expressed disappointment, or worse, with the NWAC. Naturally, dissenting publications like *Labour Leader* and *Common Sense* were particularly strong critics, but so were other left-leaning papers, like the *Daily News* and *Manchester Guardian*. Perhaps most damagingly, Horatio Bottomley's *John Bull* offered sustained criticism of the NWAC. Some of this hostility may be attributed to the juxtaposition of the NWAC's government-sanctioned free expression with increasing restrictions elsewhere, following the introduction of DRR 27c. Such restrictions seemed like further evidence of a declining commitment to liberty.[67] This was put most caustically by *The Nation*:

> the Government dips one hand into the public purse for secret funds to subsidize its own War Aims campaign, while it chokes the throat of criticism with the other! ...
> The Government is to push its own propaganda of opinion by Press and public meetings and circulars, using public money for the purpose, but opposing opinions are to be crushed by fines and imprisonment. That is one way of getting national unity. But what is the worth of a unity based upon ignorance, silence, and repression[?][68]

Access to Treasury funds was indispensable to the NWAC's continued operation but had the problematic side-effect of tying it more firmly to the government. Thus, although responsible for neither the introduction nor administration of DRR 27c, it was guilty by association. However, journalistic disdain for restrictions on free speech cannot explain the volume of criticism the NWAC received. Individual papers and editors reacted according to their own expectations and imperatives. The *Daily Mail*, for instance, saw little value in the NWAC's stated purpose of counteracting 'pacifists', believing that the Government should instead spend its money on their arrest and prosecution. Furthermore, the Committee's creation also demonstrated that the propaganda efforts of newspapers like the *Mail* were insufficient.[69] It therefore said little about the Committee.[70]

---

66 C.P. Scott, diary, 28/9/17, in Trevor Wilson (ed.), *The Political Diaries of C.P. Scott, 1911–1928* (London: Collins, 1970), pp. 303–04; 'Asquith Challenged', *Britannia*, 5/10/17, p. 143.

67 Cf. Robert Colls, 'Englishness and the Political Culture', in Colls and Dodd (eds), *Englishness*.

68 'The Assassination of Opinion', *Nation*, 24/11/17, pp. 262–63.

69 I owe this additional point to Jon Lawrence. For aspects of the *Mail*'s propaganda efforts, see Adrian Gregory, "A Clash of Cultures: The British Press and the Opening of the Great War', in Troy R.E. Paddock (ed.), *A Call to Arms: Propaganda, Public Opinion, and Newspapers in the Great War* (London: Praeger, 2004), and idem, *Last Great War*, pp. 47–69.

70 'Pacifist Poisoners', *Daily Mail*, 15/11/17, p. 2; 'Pacifist Wreckers. Time to Stop Them', *Daily Mail*, 16/11/17, p. 2.

Some publications were implacably hostile from the outset whereas others became disappointed by the campaign's progress and effect. Even supporters like the *Post* and *Chronicle* soon expressed frustration with what they considered the NWAC's limited progress. In this was a certain elision between criticism of the Committee itself and the government. Gwynne blamed weak governmental leadership for the fact that 'Necessary measures have too often been belated or half-hearted', while Donald noted that many speeches by the most prominent politicians remained unpublished and therefore largely unknown, lamenting that the government had not realised much earlier the 'need for a proper national propaganda at home'.[71] Such limited criticisms were extended by Bottomley, self-appointed representative of the 'man-in-the-street' and a direct rival to the NWAC's patriotic activities. He described the NWAC in November 1917 as simply 'a dodge for doctoring public opinion', a 'pretext' for politicians to claim 'that they have won the war' and scoffed at the suggested involvement of clergymen in the campaign, since they took no fighting part.[72] Through the winter, Bottomley's opinion worsened. In December he twice called for the Committee to abandon 'politicians' rhetoric' and 'fine phrases' and provide a plain statement of terms.[73]

In January Bottomley reported that he had told Lloyd George and Carson that the NWAC had 'so far dismally failed in its purpose', and was surprised when Carson agreed with him. Bottomley 'ridiculed the idea of holding packed little meetings' with 'second-rate speakers'. Carson supposedly blamed the Committee's difficulties on its cross-party composition, which entailed 'various political rivals watching each other in every move', prompting Bottomley to suggest the appointment of a single 'Director of Propaganda' responsible to Lloyd George. However, Bottomley was 'indifferent to the outcome' since, officially or otherwise, he was 'proud to be the Tribune of the Man in the Street'.[74] This may substantially explain his antipathy to the NWAC. A national campaign to influence public opinion constituted a challenge to his self-proclaimed position as the voice of the people, or Caroline Playne's description of the 'divine omniscience'.[75] Bottomley toured the nation throughout the war giving patriotic speeches, sometimes without charge, but more often taking a substantial share of the meeting's proceeds, having realised, according to Theodore Felstead, that he could 'keep himself afloat

---

71 'The Constant Mind', *Post*, 8/11/17, p. 6; 'War Aims and War Propaganda', *Chronicle*, 20/12/17, p. 4.
72 'Still Taking Odds!', *John Bull*, 3/11/17, pp. 10–11.
73 'Hands Down, Lansdowne!'; 'Where <u>Do</u> We Stand?', *John Bull*, 8/12/17, 22/12/17, both pp. 8–9.
74 'My Visit to the Premier', *John Bull*, 19/1/18, pp. 8–9.
75 Playne, *Britain Holds On*, p. 230.

financially by ... patriotism'.[76] In early 1917, he embarked on a lecture tour for which he obtained 65–85 per cent of the gross admission fees. Moreover, he convinced himself that he deserved a role in government. Earlier in the war, Asquith had politely rejected Bottomley's offer to act as Chief Recruiting Officer, and on Asquith's fall he apparently expected an important governmental position. He also believed Northcliffe would recommend him for an official mission similar to Northcliffe's own to the USA. All these expectations were frustrated, however, and much of Bottomley's ire towards the NWAC may be assumed to relate to professional and commercial rivalry.[77] Its activities were not only an affront to his governmental pretensions, but also a potential threat to his lucrative lecture tours.[78] Bottomley does not seem to have been invited to assist the NWAC campaign, despite offering Carson his services 'in any capacity', presumably further fuelling his disdain for its operations. When Lord Rhondda failed to offer him a post at the Ministry of Food, Bottomley responded with an 'irritable diatribe' against the Ministry.[79]

Bottomley had no use for 'fine phrases' which did not conform to his own views, while suggestions of political intrigue were sufficient to dismiss the Committee as a 'collection of Party wirepullers', each striving only to 'secure votes for his own party at the next election'.[80] He argued that, because of the mistrust between the party officials, NWAC meetings were 'a laughing stock for the Pacifists and an insult to patriotic men', contrasting well-organised, thousand-strong 'peace meetings' with sparsely attended NWAC events conducted from a 'rickety little stand, from which someone is bawling at a bare patch of gravel'. For Bottomley, there was, by June 1918, 'no decent excuse for the continuance of this discreditable Committee'.[81] His castigation of NWAC meetings was, however, a partial interpretation. Between 20 and 22 June, for instance, successful meetings in Barnstaple were attended by audiences of 100–125, 250 and 300–500 people, according to speakers' reports.[82] Bottomley criticised the cost and political jockeying involved in running the Committee – the same issues which exercised many MPs in the funding debates, possibly because criticism of such issues was considered more acceptable than criticising

---

76 S. Theodore Felstead, *Horatio Bottomley: A Biography of an Outstanding Personality* (London: John Murray, 1936), p. 214.

77 Again, I owe this point to Jon Lawrence.

78 Julian Symons, *Horatio Bottomley* (London: House of Stratus, 2001 [1955]), pp. 148–75.

79 Henry J. Houston, *The Real Horatio Bottomley* (London: Hurst & Blackett, n.d. [1923]), p. 69.

80 '"War Aims Committee"', *John Bull*, 20/4/18, p. 1.

81 'The War Aims Farce. Wild Merriment for Pacifists – Pain for Patriots', *John Bull*, 22/6/18, p. 4.

82 TNA:PRO T102/23, SDRs – T. Enfield, Barnstaple, 20–22/6/18; G. Crabbe, Barnstaple, 21/6/18.

the general project of patriotic inspiration. Ultimately, however, his condemnation reflected his own self-interested and delusional motivations. If the government was not prepared to give him the role he felt he so clearly deserved, then no other organisation could expect his support.

Other papers also stressed these concerns, further rejecting the NWAC as an affront to liberal and democratic principles. At the *Daily News*, Gardiner said that a 'more insolent demand could scarcely be made' than that public funds should be supplied without detailed estimates, or else the Government might 'abandon the country to the horrors of pacifist intrigue'. When the proposal was upheld in December, Gardiner, having discussed Carson's Janus-faced view of the League of Nations, called for Britain's war aims to be 'explicitly declared' by the government, if the NWAC was to 'have the smallest effect'.[83] In the same paper, the novelist Arnold Bennett (later involved in propaganda himself), infuriated by DRR 27c, said that the government was 'anti-democratic in desire, in tendency, in act'. It was

> encountering a great deal of opposition up and down the country. The opposition, however, is not to the war, but to the Government ... And the great Government publicity campaign is not really a pro-war campaign but a pro-Government campaign; that is to say, an anti-democratic campaign.[84]

THE timing of these criticisms was not coincidental. Discussion of the NWAC in the national press frequently followed the pattern of parliamentary discussion – debates on the token vote provoked similar discussion on Fleet Street. Likewise the coincidence that DRR 27c was introduced shortly after the first debate prompted the same comparisons as in parliament. DRR 27c was a government measure; the NWAC drew upon public funds and was, therefore, all-party status notwithstanding, a government organisation. DRR 27c thus made the NWAC appear a more sinister example of government assaulting civil liberties than was probably the case.

At the *Manchester Guardian*, C.P. Scott carefully avoided so crass an elision. Nonetheless, he was hardly complimentary about the NWAC's first 15 pamphlets. He suggested the Committee was 'preaching to the converted':

> For those ... heartened by denunciations of the KAISER and grim lists of German atrocities they provide generous fare, but one had expected from a War Aims Committee so weightily constituted something a little more intelligent and effective than this clumsy kind of bludgeon-work ... [M]uch of the dissension which impedes national effort is due to a widespread

---

83 'The Latest Economy', *Daily News*, 14/11/17, p. 2; 'The War-Aims Propaganda', *Daily News*, 15/12/17, p. 2.
84 Arnold Bennett, 'More Dangerous Than Bolo', *Daily News*, 29/11/17, p. 2.

feeling that civil liberties have been undermined to a degree that even war does not make necessary, and that there are in this country the makings of a militarism not less definite and dangerous than that which is condemned in Germany.[85]

This was a potent criticism, and Scott appealed to the NWAC executive's vanity to set its propaganda on a more sophisticated level, attuned to public concerns. Moreover, while Lloyd George claimed that 'Nobody cared what the *Daily News* & the *Nation* said because they made it their business to find fault', the *Guardian* was supposedly much more influential.[86] Previous chapters have shown that the NWAC acknowledged such criticism, and while condemnation of Germany and its allies continued, it was accompanied by much wider discussion. Propagandists, for instance, regularly embraced the UDC-originated calls for a League of Nations, although one critic suggested that the term had become simply 'a prophylactic against all the ills of mankind, the most diverse and most incompatible ... a shibboleth and a formula'.[87] W.S. Sanders's pamphlets on German society drew praise from H.W. Lee, editor of the SDF newspaper, *Justice*. Lee asserted that they were 'necessary for the people of this country' as much as for foreigners, and insisted that Sanders

> cannot be regarded as an anti-German, even by the most truculent of pacifists. If anything, he has a strong bias in Germany's favour. What he says ... is said from the point of view of one who has found the facts against what he had hoped to see, and regretfully recognises that it is so.[88]

Reviewing Sanders's pamphlets, Lee (a fierce critic of Labour 'pacifism') endorsed the majority of their contents and recommended them to those who suffered from a delusion that 'capitalism is the sole cause of this war' and those who were 'Bolshevik and Sinn Fein at the same time'. *Justice*'s endorsement extended to stocking copies of the pamphlets at its office and offering to send them to readers for the cost of postage, alongside reporting their availability at Smith's' bookstalls, while a reply to the review, in which Sanders elaborated upon his ideas (thus extending his propaganda), was also published.[89] By contrast, a *Labour Leader* article criticised Sanders's contribution to an issue of *Reality* ('the organ of the War Aims Committee for the propagation of war passion'). J. Jacks quoted Sanders's description of Germany providing workers with just enough education to be an 'obedient implement of a ruling class he can never enter', and questioned his interpretation, arguing that to 'make a man intelligent for one purpose is to make him intelligent for all purposes'.

---

85 'War Aims Propaganda', *Manchester Guardian* (henceforth *Guardian*), 20/9/17, p. 4.
86 Memorandum by C.P. Scott, 30 April–4 May 1917, cited in Koss, *Rise*, II, p. 312.
87 'Notes of the Week', *New Age*, 3/1/18, p. 183.
88 Lee, 'The Bookshop. "War Aims" Propaganda', *Justice*, 20/6/18, p. 7.
89 'A Personal Explanation' (letter by W.S. Sanders), *Justice*, 4/7/18, p. 8.

Jacks asked, 'is this the same Mr. Sanders who used to write Fabian tracts to show what a lot our Government could learn from Germany'?[90]

The *Guardian* seemingly remained unimpressed. Even in October 1918, welcoming Arnold Bennett's appointment as a director at the Ministry of Information, Scott complained that domestic propaganda had 'consisted too much in the dissemination of the literature of hate',[91] while in February the paper had anxiously reported the invitation of London publicans to a meeting addressed by the Master of Balliol, A.L. Smith, and Colonel Henry Gibbon (both of whom spoke for the NWAC).[92] Fear was expressed that the 'conversational autocrats of the bar' would become 'licensed propagandist[s]'.[93] Despite Scott's discomfort with NWAC propaganda, however, he arguably accepted the organisation's necessity. The *Guardian* ignored criticism of the NWAC's high salaries and expenses in the report of the Select Committee on National Expenditure in May 1918. Unlike the *Chronicle*, *Post*, *Daily News* and *Telegraph* (which all printed critical excerpts), and *Common Sense* and *John Bull*, which (later) both produced long condemnations, the *Guardian* omitted any reference to NWAC finances in its editorial and two-page discussion of the report.[94] While doubting the quality of its propaganda, therefore, it may have accepted its importance.

Besides *John Bull*, it was, unsurprisingly, the papers sympathetic to the UDC, *Labour Leader* and *Common Sense*, which provided the most sustained criticism. Together with the direct publication of parliamentary and UDC criticisms, Katherine Glasier's *Labour Leader* poured scorn on the NWAC in February 1918 with the reproduction of what it claimed was a 'model' war aims speech, issued by the Committee, which was 'too precious to be allowed to rest in the pockets of speakers or to echo in the empty halls they address'. The report ridiculed the speech, noting factual inaccuracies and contradictory elements, and encouraged readers attending a meeting to listen for various key phrases. 'Mr. Guest', it concluded, 'is a great asset in these mournful times'.[95] F.W. Hirst's *Common Sense*,

---

90 Jacks, 'The Madding Crowd', *Labour Leader*, 11/7/18, p. 4.
91 'Propaganda', *Guardian*, 2/10/18, p. 4.
92 PA, Lloyd George papers, LG/F/79/32–33.
93 'Propaganda and the Publican', *Guardian*, 21/2/18, p. 4.
94 '£10,000,000 a Year Lost', *Chronicle*, 20/5/18, p. 3; 'The Way the Money Goes', *Post*, 20/5/18, p. 5; 'War Propaganda. Method of Financing Criticised by Select Committee', *Daily News*, 20/5/18, p. 3; 'Waste of Public Money', *Daily Telegraph*, 20/5/18, p. 2; 'The War Aims Farce', *John Bull*, 22/6/18, p. 4; 'Public Expenditure on War Aims, Newspapers, &c.', *Common Sense*, 29/6/18, p. 295.
95 'Junius', 'A War Aims "Model Speech"', *Labour Leader*, 21/2/18, p. 4. NWAC correspondence confirms that skeleton lectures were prepared: TNA:PRO T102/7, NWAC to Ald. W.E. Lovsey, 4/12/17. However, the model speech does not substantially replicate anything discovered in over 100 local newspapers. The reference to a 'war map' may mean that the 'model' is based on the Earl of Denbigh's lectures.

meanwhile, maintained consistent criticism of the NWAC. A generally approving review of Asquith's NWAC speech at Birmingham nonetheless stressed that 'we must remember that Sir Edward Carson is Chief War Aims Propagandist to the British Government, with Mr. Asquith's parliamentary support', thus undermining its value and sincerity.[96] In April 1918, *Common Sense*'s fire turned upon Denbigh, who was labelled, after Lord Leverhulme, the NWAC's 'principal star'. Scoffing at his concerns about dissent, the article retorted that 'If peace meetings could win the war for the other side we should have won it long ago' since the press was full of stories of immense German and Austrian gatherings, and argued that Denbigh's discussion at meetings of Germany's *Mitteleuropa* scheme veiled more sinister preoccupations. 'One of the main obstacles to a good peace settlement, as well as to success in the war', the paper argued, 'is the lust for Asiatic conquests exhibited by Lord Denbigh and his school.' For Hirst and his writers, as for Massingham at *The Nation* and some MPs, the NWAC's involvement with figures like Carson and Denbigh reduced its campaign to imperialist and jingoistic posturing, no matter how many mild and encouraging speeches figures like Asquith made. In a poem accompanying the article, Denbigh's notorious 'war map' was lampooned as demonstrating 'why we must not cease to fight / Until all Asia's conquered quite'.[97] Denbigh's Habsburg heritage was also noted in *Common Sense*, though it was left to the *Leicester Catholic News*, outraged by what it considered Denbigh's near-apostasy, to castigate his 'shouting ... to assure all and sundry that the Count of Hapsburg is a loyal and furious and patriotic Jingo'.[98] Nonetheless, *Common Sense* condemned McCurdy, in discussing his pamphlet on the secret treaties, as 'a good jingo democrat'.[99]

National press attitudes towards the NWAC were thus rarely complimentary. Like MPs, editors and writers in several national papers questioned the value for money, the implications for civil liberties and the quality of NWAC propaganda. Whether such criticism demonstrates its failure, however, is less clear. Although the debates on the NWAC's token vote demonstrated marked hostility by some MPs, 'the Government got their blank cheque with only 22 dissentients'.[100] Coupled with the extensive involvement of MPs as NWAC propagandists, this suggests that such qualms as existed among the majority were either insufficiently troubling to prompt serious opposition or were overridden by a desire to publicly demonstrate patriotic commitment to the war effort through propaganda work.

96 'Mr. Asquith's Birmingham Speech', *Common Sense*, 15/12/17, p. 372.
97 'Lord Denbigh's Views'; 'A Soliloquy', *Common Sense*, 27/4/18, p. 211.
98 'Notes and Comments. The Reason Why!', *Leicester Catholic News*, 18/5/18, p. 2.
99 'War Aims Expenditure', *Common Sense*, 6/7/18, p. 3.
100 'Suppressing the Pacifists – And Freedom!', *Labour Leader*, 22/11/17, p. 3.

As for the press, though much commentary ranged between un-complimentary and hostile, the impression is less (excepting three or four publications) of sustained opposition to the organisation as of general indifference, interrupted by occasional criticism of particularly poor work. Journals linked to organisations like the UDC, such as *Common Sense, Labour Leader* and *The Nation*, predictably offered many trenchant criticisms. Nor is it surprising that the *Guardian*, edited by what Mark Hampton describes as 'an almost anachronistic character' of the 'old journalistic tradition', made some uncomplimentary assessments, though it is interesting that while it complained that 'some among our governors ... think that every time they trample upon a British liberty they are defeating the enemy', it did not draw the contrast that other papers did between NWAC funding and DRR 27c.[101] Apparently the *Guardian*, like most of the 'mainstream' national press, accepted the NWAC as an inevitable (if unfortunate) necessity, consequently confining itself to occasional critiques of propagandistic excesses. The absence of regular or substantial comment from papers like the *Mail, Express, Times* or *Telegraph* may be considered craven obedience or collusion with the government, but may equally suggest that they simply saw nothing par-ticularly significant about the Committee's activities, or embarrassment that their own propaganda efforts had been so ineffective that a formal organisation was required. Bottomley's disdain for the Committee's party political organisation, which he blamed for the supposed weakness of its propaganda campaigns, together with his demagogic determination to be 'Tribune of the people', accounts for his implacable hostility and this last issue perhaps undermines its significance as a 'genuine' expression of the NWAC's reception. Nevertheless, given its popularity, *John Bull* was certainly an enemy the NWAC could have done without.

The NWAC's opponents delighted in mocking criticism. It is paradox-ical, however, that such critics – apparently so certain the Committee was a shambolic failure – nevertheless demonstrated concern about its influence. Noel Buxton complained that the Asquithian Liberal W.H. Somervell had been assisted in his by-election victory at Keighley by free NWAC literature, disseminated by Smith's' bookstalls.[102] Alongside this seeming admission of NWAC propaganda's effectiveness may be placed the parliamentary demands by King and MacDonald that NWAC activities would be curtailed during the general election campaign.[103] It is curious that an organisation so readily derided by 'pacifist' critics

---

101 Mark Hampton, *Visions of the Press in Britain, 1850–1950* (Urbana: University of Illinois Press, 2004), p. 135; 'The Censorship of Opinion', *Guardian*, 16/11/17, p. 4.
102 Buxton, 'Liberalism and Keighley', *Nation*, 4/5/18, p. 108.
103 Questions of King and MacDonald PDC(5), 110 (14/11/18), col. 2869 – answered by Sanders.

as absurdly unsuccessful should need to be wound up to ensure a fair election. Once again, this suggests the NWAC was slightly more potent an organisation than its critics acknowledged.

In a memorandum on 'Industrial Unrest' suggesting alternative propaganda arrangements, Patrick Hannon, secretary of the right-wing pressure group the British Commonwealth Union, averred that the NWAC was

> grievously handicapped by the political factors involved in its constitution and [its] work is largely stultified from the fact that it is maintained by a parliamentary vote. Although the War Aims Committee has laboured energetically, and although much sound work must be placed to its credit, it is regarded by the people generally as the official protagonist of the interests of the Coalition Government.[104]

Hannon's interpretation certainly represented the expressed reception of the Committee by MPs and the national press. The extent to which the public reaction corresponded to his negative assessment is discussed in chapter 10.

---

104 PA, Hannon papers, HNN/13/4, memorandum, 'Industrial Unrest', n.d. (1918). Thanks to David Thackeray for this reference.

Individual and Local Reactions to the NWAC

THE NWAC did not enjoy the complete confidence of parliament or the national press, but it was geared towards convincing neither parliamentarians nor journalists but the general public. This chapter, therefore, discusses the Committee's public reception. It is difficult to assess individual civilians' reactions to the NWAC. Diaries and auto-biographies rarely mention the organisation specifically, and general allusions to propaganda must be treated cautiously, particularly since such discussion often focuses on the recruitment propaganda of the early years. Nonetheless, it is possible to make some assessment of the NWAC's reception, through official judgements of its effectiveness, including speakers' reports of individual meetings, through local press reports of events and through public correspondence with the Committee or local newspapers. This chapter examines these various indications of the NWAC's public reception. Each type, in isolation, is limited by possibilities of private, political or official agendas or self-justification. Neither individually nor in combination do they provide anything like a complete image of public reception. However, some suspicions of bias or atypicality can be allayed by comparison of the different forms of evidence. In combination, they suggest the Committee succeeded in gaining receptive and, significantly, often *attentive* audiences, even in some troublesome areas. While it did not attain universal success, it apparently played an important part in maintaining civilian resolution and effort.

BY July 1917, the War Cabinet had two consistent sources of in-formation on public opinion: the MoL's weekly reports on the 'Labour Situation' and fortnightly reports on 'Pacifist and Revolutionary Organisations' by Basil Thomson at CID. Neither organisation was en-tirely disinterested, but equally neither had any incentive to praise or criticise the NWAC. As such, their reports are valuable guides to official assessments of NWAC achievements, and much more impartial than equivalent judgements by the Committee itself or its denigrators. This evidence suggests that, at least until May 1918, the NWAC remained an effective tool of industrial pacification. Thereafter, its efforts are rarely mentioned, although other sources indicate that it continued to pursue active and reasonably effective campaigns.

Despite holding nearly 850 days of events in August and September 1917,[1] it was not until October that the NWAC's effects began to be noted. Before this, David Shackleton (permanent secretary at the MoL), who had earlier recommended the NWAC's establishment, lamented the limited effect of opposition to 'pacifist' propaganda by groups like the BWL, British Empire Union and WSPU, and that there had been 'little or no attempt to counteract [the ILP's] dangerous propaganda' on the Clyde.[2] Thereafter, however, both Shackleton and Thomson acknowledged the NWAC's contribution. On 11 October, Shackleton noted mixed results. While in Yorkshire NWAC activities were 'meeting with success', attempts to counteract 'pacifist agitation' in Finsbury Park attained 'scant success', owing to the long period of unchecked dissent there. A week later, the NWAC had reportedly 'quite definitely ... got the upper hand over the pacifist bodies in Yorkshire' and held 'a number of successful meetings' in the north-east, where the BWL had also established several new branches. Shackleton further recommended an NWAC campaign in South Wales to influence the outcome of a ballot of the South Wales Miners' Federation on a proposed 'down tools policy' against government attempts to 'comb-out' mines.[3]

The resulting campaign, addressed by high-profile speakers like Smuts, the Labour cabinet-member and trade unionist William Brace, and the Admiralty financial secretary T.J. Macnamara, was credited with turning local opinion against the resolution. Reports proclaimed 'outstanding results' and that 'serious efforts to organise opposition [to Smuts's speech] at Tonypandy ... failed entirely'. The 31 October report called Tonypandy 'the hotbed of pacifism', where trouble was most likely; the failure of the 'pacifists' thus suggested its 'vociferousness is out of all proportion to its influence'. The following week, the report announced that the ballot would be 'rejected by an overwhelming majority' and argued that the *South Wales Pioneer*'s depiction of Smuts's massively overcrowded visit as a 'negligible incident' demonstrated ILP concern at its effectiveness. Shackleton concluded that

---

1   Register database. Chapter 2 provides detailed discussion.
2   TNA:PRO CAB24/27, GT2199, 'The Labour Situation. Report from the Ministry of Labour' (henceforth MoL report), 3/10/17; CAB24/26, GT2087, MoL report, 19/9/17.
3   TNA:PRO CAB24/28, GT2266, MoL report, 11/10/17; CAB24/29, GT2331, MoL report, 18/10/17. On the contest for space in London parks, see Lawrence, 'Public Space', pp. 296–99.

the success of the War Aims meetings and of the miners' vote on the comb-out is a very serious defeat [for the 'pacifists'], and the loyal portion of the South Wales population is doubtless proportionately encouraged ... [However,] 15,000 men practically voted against the war with the eyes of the whole country on them ... and the number would doubtless have been larger but for the activities of the War Aims Committee. It is essential that these activities should continue in order to counteract the vigorous and well-organised pacifist propaganda, which unless regularly countered may yet produce deplorable results.[4]

Notwithstanding Adrian Gregory's assertion that fewer days were lost to striking throughout the war than had been lost in 1912 alone, Shackleton left no doubt of his belief that serious 'pacifist' dissent existed in the nation, and required continuing counteraction.[5]

Shortly thereafter, the Home Secretary, Sir George Cave, suggested that since the South Wales campaign had been so successful, 'every pacifist gathering should be brought to the attention of the War Aims Committee or the British Workers' League, in order that they may (if thought desirable) organize a loyal meeting to follow it'.[6] In late November, Basil Thomson reported that the 'set-back to Pacifism in the Provinces and in London [was] largely due to the efforts of the War Aims Committee'. Consequently arrangements were made to keep it abreast of developments, as Cave proposed.[7] Nonetheless, despite Cave's recommendation, this arrangement was apparently not extended to the BWL, which Lawrence contends was considered 'part of the problem, rather than ... of its solution'. While Cave's note and the apparent elision in the MoL's October report of NWAC and BWL actions in the north-east lends partial credence to Millman's 'home front conspiracy theory',[8] Shackleton's earlier report of the BWL's limited effectiveness, and Thomson's restriction of praise solely to the NWAC, suggest again that there is insufficient evidence for claiming that the organisations were brought closer together 'to streamline the process of suppression'. BWL involvement with the NWAC, while undeniable on occasion, was not a systematic partnership, and Millman's reconstruction of Cave's suggestion to imply the existence of a 'BWNL WAC – the chosen instrument of suppression' is inexcusably misleading.[9] Not only were many in Whitehall

---

4   TNA:PRO CAB24/30, GT2457, MoL report, 31/10/17; CAB24/31, GT2542, MoL report, 7/11/17. See also the report by R. Wherry Anderson, 29/10/17, in Hancock and Van der Poel, *Smuts Papers*, pp. 566–67.

5   Gregory, *Last Great War*, pp. 202–03.

6   TNA:PRO CAB24/4, G173, 'Pacifist Propaganda. Note by Sir George Cave and Draft Regulations', 13/11/17.

7   TNA:PRO CAB24/34, GT2809, 'Pacifism. (Report by Mr. Basil Thomson)', 24/11/17.

8   Lawrence, 'Public Space', p. 298; idem, 'Review, *Managing*', p. 86.

9   Millman, *Managing*, pp. 245, 251, n. 81; Millman cites Swartz's paraphrase of Cave's suggestion but apparently overlooks Swartz's use of the somewhat important word 'or'. See Swartz, *Union of Democratic Control*, p. 189.

uncomfortable with the BWL, but also many provincial Conservatives, as Sanders's diary shows.[10]

Having seemingly acknowledged the NWAC's value, MoL reports offered praise alongside suggestions for further progress through the winter. In Yorkshire and the East Midlands, NWAC efforts attained 'uniform success'. In December, it was credited with preventing the progress of 'pacifism' in Newcastle, while the 'quieter element' within Barrow-in-Furness was keen to host another large meeting after the success of one addressed by George Barnes.[11] Repeated assertions of NWAC success in Yorkshire offer an interesting contrast to Cyril Pearce's evocation of wartime Huddersfield. If that town was 'dominated' by unspectacular anti-war sentiment 'readily and regularly exemplified in the day-to-day conduct of affairs', it was seemingly the exception rather than the regional rule.[12]

As 1918 began, Shackleton warned that 'class-war propaganda' was sapping public morale. Alongside recommending 'even more drastic application of the Excess Profits Tax' to demonstrate government opposition to profiteering, and the imposition of compulsory rationing to 'destroy the charge of inequality of sacrifice in regard to food', he argued it was essential to 'dispose of the fable that the propertied classes ... have not made the same sacrifices on the battlefield as the working classes'. Shackleton recommended 'widespread and continuous' demonstration by the NWAC via casualty lists that officers suffered heavier casualties than 'the rank and file'. Shackleton unwittingly echoed suggestions made by Macnamara, based on his experiences at NWAC meetings. Macnamara recommended rationing, clamping down on profiteering and hoarding, prompt settlement of public grievances, immediate refutation of specious 'pacifist' criticism and the clear statement of war aims.[13] Shackleton also recapitulated (more than once) that the NWAC had not commenced serious operations on the Clyde.[14]

This criticism of NWAC inaction was augmented by a memorandum by the Labour Minister, G.H. Roberts, who doubted that the government had retained public sympathy:

---

10 Sanders diary, 3/3/18, 24/3/18, 9/6/18, 14/7/18, in Ramsden, *Tory Politics*, pp. 101–07.
11 TNA:PRO CAB24/33, GT2716, MoL report, 21/11/17; CAB24/34, GT2886, MoL report, 5/12/17; CAB24/35, GT2952, MoL report, 12/12/17.
12 Cyril Pearce, *Comrades in Conscience: The Story of an English Community's Opposition to the Great War* (London: Francis Boutle, 2001), pp. 216, 222.
13 TNA:PRO CAB24/37, GT3196, MoL report, 2/1/18; PA, Lloyd George Papers, LG/F/6/2/49, Memorandum by T.J. Macnamara, 'The Civil Population and the War', 27/11/17.
14 TNA:PRO CAB24/38, GT3293, MoL report, 9/1/18; CAB24/39, GT3369, MoL report, 16/1/18.

Speakers sent down by the War Aims Committee, pamphlets, and similar
means of propaganda are all valuable in their way and much good has
undoubtedly been done ... but the effects which they produce soon pass
away, whereas the whole essence of successful propaganda is constant
reiteration of a few fundamental truths through the newspapers which are
read every day ... To neglect the Press, therefore, and to rely principally on
public speakers, &c. is a suicidal policy ...[15]

Roberts recommended more systematically organised local officials informing provincial newspapers about war aims and the war situation, and
monitoring pacifist propaganda, so that 'an effective answer was always
forthcoming to local pacifist propaganda'. Roberts's memorandum fundamentally questioned the NWAC's operational basis which (as previously
discussed) followed pre-war political traditions by privileging public
meetings and open engagement with civilians as the most important form
of propaganda. Instead of sporadic meetings, Roberts believed continuous
written affirmation of important messages would best maintain civilian
assent. His arguments perhaps presage the declining faith of politicians
in the efficacy of claiming civic space through public meetings, which
Lawrence traces in the post-war period, though for Roberts it was not
so much any 'fear of brutalisation' or distrust of rowdiness or disorder
which invalidated public meetings, but their transitory nature.[16] As previously shown, however, the NWAC actively placed propaganda in the
provincial press while also, with MI7b and CID assistance, monitoring
'pacifist' attitudes in the press and in localities. Further, the NWAC's
establishment was originally necessitated because press propaganda was
considered insufficient, while one correspondent warned that published
propaganda was insufficient because 'the people rarely read anything
but that awful paper "The News of the World"'.[17] As such, Roberts's
critique may represent anxiety over a perceived increase in 'pacifist'
activity rather than a sudden decision that NWAC propaganda no longer
worked. Shortly afterwards, Thomson reported 'a rather sudden growth
of Pacifism among the actual workers ... [apparently] due entirely to their
desire to save their own skins' in response to the comb-out.[18] Gregory
interprets this assessment as 'the paranoia of a secret policeman' but,
alongside the worries expressed by Shackleton and Roberts, it is arguable
either that such views contained some validity, or that the paranoia
was sufficiently strong to capture the imaginations of officials closely

15 TNA:PRO CAB24/39, GT3360, memorandum by G.H. Roberts regarding the use
    of the press for propaganda purposes, 16/1/18.
16 Jon Lawrence, 'Forging a Peaceable Kingdom: War, Violence, and Fear of
    Brutalization in Post-First World War Britain', *Journal of Modern History*, 75:3
    (2003); idem, 'The Transformation of British Public Politics after the First World
    War', *Past and Present*, 190 (2006).
17 TNA:PRO T102/12, H.F. Russell to Cox, 1/5/18.
18 TNA:PRO CAB24/40 GT3424, Memorandum by Thomson, 'Pacifism', 22/1/18.

associated with the labour movement.[19] Moreover, dissenters also sensed a changed mood. UDC secretary E.D. Morel was assured in February by his colleagues MacDonald and Seymour Cocks, as well as the Liverpool UDC branch, that he would find himself 'in a very different world' to the one he had known before his six-month imprisonment in the autumn of 1917 (on dubious grounds relating to a pamphlet he sent to the French novelist Romain Rolland in neutral Switzerland). Cocks believed there had 'been a very great change in public feeling … and a distinct alteration in the popular temper' in the UDC's favour.[20]

This change in temperament, however, was seemingly only temporary. In mid-February, Shackleton reported a marked improvement on the Clyde owing most significantly to the 'national loyalty of the majority of the workers', secondly to a Scottish press campaign and finally to the NWAC's 'exceedingly satisfactory and effective action'. Shackleton emphasised the Committee's important intervention in 'the two most critical' recent disturbances in South Wales and the Clyde.[21] He extended his praise subsequently, arguing that its campaign 'had an effect out of all proportion to the area in which it was conducted' by inducing a marked 'diminution' of the Clyde Workers' Committee, the nation's most influential shop stewards' movement. Generally, Shackleton emphasised that industrial conditions were 'quieter than during any week since this Report was first instituted' in May 1917. Thomson agreed that the 'Pacifists have not had a good fortnight' attributing this partly to the NWAC's efforts.[22] Such evidence is significant. It is commonly asserted that industrial workers rallied to the nation and rejected industrial action after the German offensive on 21 March,[23] yet, demonstrably, 'industrial unrest was on the decline even before' then.[24] While (as Trevor Wilson notes) reports dwelt on the general loyalty of most workers, it is noteworthy that the NWAC was also credited with turning opinion against labour extremism. There may have been a 'loyal majority' in most places, but in areas like South Wales, Barrow or the Clyde, it required a mouthpiece. The NWAC's Clyde campaign, according to Shackleton, gave the 'revolutionary element' a 'decided check, and the loyal portion of the community [was] correspondingly encouraged'.[25] Historians including Wilson and Gregory have questioned Thomson's reliability, with Gregory describing

19 Gregory, *Last Great War*, p. 202.
20 LSE, Morel Papers, MOREL F1/5, Cocks to Morel, 3/2/18; also MacDonald to Mrs. Morel, 12/2/18; David Paterson (Liverpool UDC) to Morel, 17/2/18.
21 TNA:PRO CAB24/42, GT3606, MoL report, 13/2/18.
22 TNA:PRO CAB24/42, GT3677, MoL report, 20/2/18; GT3674, Thomson, 'Pacifist Revolutionary Propaganda', 20/2/18.
23 E.g. Horne, 'Remobilizing', p. 210; Turner, *British Politics*, pp. 382–83; Gregory, *Last Great War*, p. 205.
24 Wilson, *Myriad Faces*, pp. 654–56.
25 TNA:PRO CAB24/42, GT3606, MoL report, 13/2/18.

him as prone to 'alarmist rhetoric' and conspiracy theories. As noted earlier, there is also some evidence to suggest Thomson sought to restrain the wilder assumptions of Cabinet members. However, whether or not Thomson should be considered unreliably paranoid, his testimony on the apparent efficacy of NWAC propaganda remains revealing, particularly when placed alongside the views of labour and dissenting figures like Shackleton and the UDC members. Either Thomson's claims reflect the considered judgement of a senior policeman or, even more remarkably, they credit the NWAC with reducing 'pacifist' sentiments despite such achievements hindering Thomson's own supposed 'hidden agenda'.[26]

The German offensive enhanced the industrial quietism. The NWAC continued its work, successfully attending to pockets of 'pacifist spirit' in Coventry, Newcastle and Glasgow.[27] However, when unrest recurred after June, calls were no longer specifically made for NWAC rebuttals. Shackleton warned in late July that 'Organised labour is now very suspicious of any measure adopted by the Government to interfere with the normal industrial position', but again made no recommendation for NWAC involvement.[28] One possible explanation for this is Peters's withdrawal as the NWAC's Labour secretary. Despite the continued adherence of the 'patriotic Labour' MPs Parker and Tootill, critics broadcast Peters's withdrawal widely, and the MoL may have judged that this discredited NWAC propaganda with industrial audiences.[29] Similar criticism attended the report detailing its officials' salaries in May, which may also have undermined its credibility. Another limitation was highlighted in the *Conservative Agents' Journal*. In Western England, the NWAC's campaign was reportedly 'extremely successful in some constituencies, while in others the movement has not been so apparent ... [because] War Savings and Food Control organizations have somewhat absorbed the opportunity for War Aims propaganda'.[30] The NWAC was one section of what Bernard Waites calls the Government's 'formidable armoury of public persuasion' and, recognising that civilians might become 'not war-weary [but] meeting weary' through the efforts of various government

---

26 Descriptions of Thomson's rhetoric and views from Gregory, *Last Great War*, p. 202; see also Wilson, *Myriad Faces*, pp. 658–59, 823–24. For evidence of Thomson's restraining influence, see p. 134, n. 84 above.

27 TNA:PRO CAB24/49, GT4329, MoL report, 24/4/18; CAB24/50, GT4407, MoL report, 1/5/18; CAB24/52, GT4624, 'Pacifism and Revolutionary Organisations in the United Kingdom', 23/5/18. Thomson's report also praised the BWL and Navy League's work in Glasgow and Newcastle.

28 TNA:PRO CAB24/55, GT4984, MoL report, 26/6/18; CAB24/59, MoL report, 24/7/18.

29 PDC(5), 101 (6/2/18), col. 2241; 106 (6/6/18), cols 1741–42; Ramsay MacDonald, 'From Green Benches', *Leicester Pioneer*, 14/6/18, p. 4. Press coverage of Peters's withdrawal was noted in TNA:PRO CAB24/43, GT3769, MoL report, 27/2/18.

30 *Conservative Agents' Journal*, no. 47 (January 1918), p. 19.

agencies, tailored its plans around those of other organisations.[31] This, however, does not explain the MoL's reluctance to recommend its involvement. The loss of Peters and exposure of its officials' salaries probably damaged the NWAC's reputation, though its omission in MoL reports may alternatively suggest that it was working efficiently and need not be hectored to involve itself. The situation was also considered less serious when industrial unrest recurred in late June. Government action on food shortages, for instance, such as active prosecution of hoarding, exemplified by the fining of the novelist Marie Corelli (who, perhaps fortunately for the NWAC's reputation, apparently did not produce the pamphlet requested by Fiennes), meant, to one diarist, that though 'all were not fined who deserved to be', by May the 'rage' over food shortages had 'died down'.[32] Gregory contends that, while the NWAC's activities 'helped' to reduce labour unrest in early 1918, government action over food, war bonuses and manpower was most important, and concessions continued to be made when necessary for the rest of the year.[33] Equally, familiarity may have bred contempt – as the NWAC became part of the social scenery, its work may have gone unremarked. In any event, its activities continued to the armistice, as the evidence of its own files and of localities demonstrates.

ONCE the NWAC had established its organisational structure, it began to assess the effect of its propaganda. By December its campaign had reportedly 'covered' 186 constituencies, plus YMCA huts and canteens (for servicemen in Britain). According to NWAC speakers, there was 'no weakening of public opinion on the war', except that people wanted Britain's war aims clearly defined. Assumptions about the strength of public opinion may have been partially wishful thinking. MacDonald noted his belief in November 1917 that in Leicester 'the tide [had] definitely turned' in his favour, owing to public concerns over food, 'Labour muddles', casualties and the government's performance. The NWAC's report also warned that government interference with daily life might assist 'anti-war propaganda'. The Committee resolved that speakers should note specific grievances and report them for resolution in the hope of mollifying public opinion.[34] Additionally, Fiennes warned

---

31 Waites, *Class Society*, p. 232; TNA:PRO T102/16, NWAC Meetings Department Report, 10/10/17. For an example of this selective activity, see T102/3, NWAC to Clement Dennis, 2/4/18; T102/12, Vesey to Capt. H.K. Ryan, 2/4/18 (both explaining a cancelled meeting in Chester-le-Street).

32 IWM, 06/28/1, W.E. Pead, 'War Diary, Aug 5 1914 to Nov 20, 1918', 26/5/18; on the NWAC and Corelli, see p. 56 above.

33 Gregory, *Last Great War*, pp. 204–05.

34 TNA:PRO T102/16, NWAC 'Report up to 8th December, 1917'; for Ramsay MacDonald's view of the improving situation for dissent, see PRO30/69/1753, MacDonald Papers, Diary, 21/11/17.

cabinet members that – based on attitudes in Sheffield, Barrow and Derby – problems with housing, food queues and beer shortages caused discontent. The latter was important because

> men, in a discontented frame of mind, are left in the streets – where they easily become listeners to Pacifist oratory – While [sic] in the public houses they are safe ... as the Pacifists are generally teetotallers who will not show themselves in these bodes of iniquity.[35]

Evidently, Fiennes disputed Lloyd George's claim that drink was a deadlier foe than Germany.[36] Drunken workers were less worrisome than sober malcontents. Fiennes recommended reiterating Asquith's pledge to restore pre-war trade union conditions after the war, a promise of social legislation, and the introduction of covered markets to mitigate food queues, and said the NWAC required 'a lead from the Government'. As with the definition of war aims, therefore, NWAC activity was limited by governmental behaviour, and it is perhaps likewise noteworthy that elements of the advice offered by the Committee were subsequently pursued. NWAC surveillance work not only enabled the counteraction of 'pacifist' meetings but also supplied a further source of advice for policy-makers. Nonetheless, while some government actions helped the NWAC's efforts, others did not. An example was provided by a speaker in Southport. When Private Wilfred Rhodes's mother died, her separation allowance was cancelled. The Derby Scheme volunteer asked for its transferral to his sister, who had left service to look after her blind brother. However, this was refused by the War Office, 'and the neighbours discount War Aims meetings in the light of what locally is described [as] "heartless treatment".'[37] A local War Pensions Committee investigation had demonstrated that the sister was not entitled to assistance, but this hardly helped speakers obtain sympathetic audiences.

In September 1918, the Committee received detailed analysis of its efforts in the south-west. R. Wherry Anderson affirmed that the area was provided with 'only a small amount of propaganda' because 'people in Cornwall and North Devon are comparatively free from war troubles ... [and it] cannot be truthfully said that these remote districts are infected with the war-weariness that beats up for seditious outbursts'. Anderson insisted that discussions with 'representative people' revealed no anxiety for extended propaganda efforts. Anderson's report indicates that,

---

35 TNA:PRO CAB24/33, GT2798, Memorandum, Fiennes, 'Causes of Discontent and Labour Unrest', 29/11/17. For some context surrounding this report, see Carsten, *War against War*, p. 174.
36 Lloyd George himself was not wholly committed to this rhetoric. Wilson, *Myriad Faces*, p. 163; Alan Turberfield, *John Scott Lidgett: Archbishop of British Methodism?* (Peterborough: Epworth Press, 2003), pp. 160–61.
37 TNA:PRO T102/12, G.H. Bibbings to Wallace Carter, 10/7/18.

though extensive propaganda was unnecessary in the south-west, the NWAC remained active. He visited Smith's' shops and bookstalls in various towns and reported that their distribution of NWAC literature was 'thoroughly well done', although the Plymouth WAC secretary had never seen *Reality*, prompting Anderson's recommendation that all secretaries should receive weekly copies and information about its availability.[38] Such literature distribution was not confined to known supporters of NWAC propaganda. Dr Macleod Yearsley recorded finding 'two excellent pamphlets' in his letterbox in early February 1918, 'evidently counterblasts to the pernicious, lying stuff which the Pacifists were spreading'.[39] One pamphlet was Sanders's *Germany's Two Voices*, the other (for which Yearsley affirmed NWAC responsibility) was probably *Our United War Aims*, a précis of Lloyd George's January war aims speech. While Yearsley (an apparently unpleasant and paranoid figure) clearly sympathised with NWAC propaganda, the pamphlets were anonymously provided, demonstrating that distribution of NWAC pamphlets was not limited to those directly requesting them.[40] *Reality*'s distribution, however, was restricted. Although by October 1918 *Reality* boasted that weekly requests for it 'now exceed One Million', Fiennes had earlier explained to the Press Advisory Committee, after the *Newsagents' Review* criticised the probable waste of paper, that its distribution was 'by no means wholesale ... [and] we have always concentrated on particular districts [with] labour troubles or other agitation at the time of publication'.[41]

THE closest analysis of the NWAC's public reception was provided by the speakers themselves, who sent daily reports of meetings, stating times, specifying locations within towns, estimating attendance and summarising the event. A breakdown of 1521 reports of 833 meetings across 30 constituencies enables some statistical analysis.[42] Figures 37–38 show speakers' judgements of their receptions following (where possible) their own terminology.[43] They suggest that a majority of speakers considered their meetings to have been 'excellent', 'very good' or 'good'. These

---

38 TNA:PRO T102/1, R. Wherry Anderson, 'Report on Propaganda in Cornwall and Devon', 4/9/18. For some discussion of the impact of the war in Cornwall, see A.L. Rowse, *A Cornish Childhood* (London: Jonathan Cape, 1942), pp. 187–206. Note Anderson's previous link in reporting on Smuts's South Wales campaign (n. 4 above).

39 IWM, DS/Misc/17, 'The Home Front Diary of Macleod Yearsley, 1914–1918', pp. 253–54.

40 For Yearsley's suspicious nature, see Gregory, *Last Great War*, p. 239.

41 *Reality*, 143, 10/10/18, p. 1; PA, Beaverbrook papers, BBK/E/3/5, Press Advisory Committee minutes, 31/12/17, appended letter by Fiennes, 3/1/18.

42 Appendix 2 gives details of selected constituencies.

43 Statistics for this and following discussion based upon the Reports database. Where no explicit judgement was made, reception was recorded according to a report's tone – where this was ambiguous, it was recorded as 'unknown/unclear'.

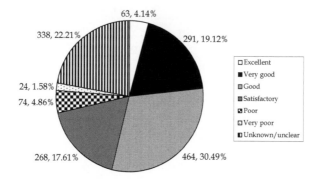

Figure 37. Speakers' reports, judgements of reception

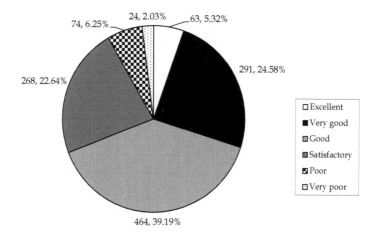

Figure 38. Speakers' reports, judgements of reception (excluding unknown/ unclear)

statistics must be treated cautiously. The speakers who completed these forms were lower-level, paid party speakers whose livelihoods sometimes depended upon such meetings. Speakers consistently reporting unsuccessful meetings might fear for future employment. Reports, therefore, tended to be positive. Furthermore, while some negative reports echoed the Conservative speaker T.H. Batty's lamentation of a 'ding dong' meeting in Wigan with 'plenty of interruption and organised I.L.P. opposition' in a town abounding in 'pacifists of an evil revolutionary type: regular Bolshevics [*sic*]', many more labelled meetings 'poor' or 'very poor' because of inclement weather or a poor pitch.[44] Nonetheless, speakers' judgements cannot be dismissed as self-serving vindications. Their descriptions often suggested significant audience interest (as discussed below).

A further means of gauging reception is to assess estimated audience size. Across the 30 constituencies examined, the average attendance recorded in 1521 reports was 348.8 people varying from zero to 12,000 at a May 1918 cinemotor event in Oldham.[45] In Weymouth, a town with a significant ILP presence for which exactly 100 days' meetings were recorded, the average attendance was 376.0, ranging from 30 (excluding 23 reports with no recorded figure) to 1800.[46] A comparison of events in Weymouth in each September, moreover, reveals a compelling further statistic. Over 19 days throughout September 1917, the average reported attendance was 191.2, ranging from 50 to 1500. By contrast, a year later, 24 days' events yielded an average attendance of 526.0, ranging from 60 to 1800. That is, average attendances in Weymouth were 2.75 times larger in September 1918 than a year earlier. This may partly be explained by the fact that the 1918 speakers held their second meeting at 6.30 in the evening, whereas the 1917 speakers held theirs at 3.00 in the afternoon – evening meetings, after the working day, usually attracted larger audiences. If, therefore, consideration is restricted to meetings held at 11.00 or 11.30 in the morning, an even closer comparison is possible. With these criteria, in 31 reports of 18 days' meetings in September 1917, the average attendance was 133.1 (ranging from 50 to 200). By contrast, in 36 reports of 22 days' meetings in September 1918, the average attendance was 280.7 (ranging from 60 to 800), more than twice as large as 1917. The NWAC enjoyed larger audiences in Weymouth in September 1918 than in earlier days. It may certainly be argued that the Committee's organisational foundations were much stronger than in September 1917; however, this reinforces a conclusion that, despite reduced official recognition, the NWAC was not defunct by the summer of 1918. At least in Weymouth, more people heard NWAC propaganda thirteen months after its inception than after six weeks.

Weymouth does not represent the whole nation. In Finsbury, for instance, 46 reports of 17 days' events in 1917 recorded an average

---

44 TNA:PRO T102/22, SDRs – T.H. Batty, Wigan, 1/9/18. Re. bad weather and poor pitch, see, e.g., SDRs – Ivan Davies, Leicester, 30/8/18; B. Bilcliffe, Leicester, 10/7/18.

45 TNA:PRO T102/26, SDRs – Tom Barnshaw, Oldham, 8/5/18. Many reports were duplicated by submissions by both speakers (although attendance estimates did not always agree).

46 The relatively consistent nature of Weymouth's meetings, mainly held in August and September 1917, and July, August and September 1918 – often near the seafront clock tower – enables reasonably equitable comparisons. Other constituencies showed greater variation of dates, times and locations, thus offering less equitable comparisons.

attendance of 289.3, declining in 1918 to 180.0 in 54 reports over 29 days (20 per cent of Finsbury reports were also 'poor' or 'very poor', compared to around 6 per cent generally).[47] Nonetheless, that attendances increased in some places seems clear, and even where they declined NWAC speakers still obtained audiences. The clearest evidence of public rejection of NWAC propaganda would be continual failure to obtain listeners, but this did not apparently happen. There were few reports like A.J. Fearnley's, whose meeting was cancelled because 'people wouldn't respond at all' to his efforts.[48] In most recorded cases, barring poor weather, speakers gathered sufficient audiences to make meetings worthwhile. John Williams's explanation that people attended public meetings to counteract the 'disappearance of so much of normal life',[49] seems an inadequate explanation for people's willingness to listen to what must have become familiar speeches. Kit Good suggests that 'the need to be *seen* to be committed and contributing was almost as important as the contribution itself',[50] and it is possible that civilians felt impelled to demonstrate their patriotism by attending such meetings. Whether this was so – whether they simply paused through curiosity or whether they were actuated by genuine affinity with the messages espoused – continuing audiences for NWAC speakers constituted some endorsement of its purpose and rhetoric.

A noticeable feature of many speakers' comments on successful meetings related to their audience's attentiveness. In several reports during a week in Leicester, J.A. Corner emphasised his 'very attentive' audience on each occasion (except one failed meeting).[51] At Normanton, another speaker, addressing 'mostly miners and Railway men', 'got a good and attentive audience' including 'Pacifist[s] of the I.L.P. order ...[who] took their "medicine" cheerfully', while at Bideford, the Liberal George Crabbe asserted that despite 'some slight interruption ... everything went smoothly and the audiences were very attentive'.[52] In all, 154 separate reports (over 10 per cent of the sample) used the terms 'attentive' or 'attentively' when describing an audience. Jonathan Crary has emphasised the increasing concern with attentiveness by the late nineteenth

---

47 For comparative purposes, Finsbury is less satisfactory than Weymouth as meetings were more scattered, both temporally and geographically, so that the comparison is more generalised – comparable months in each year cannot be isolated.

48 TNA:PRO T102/25, SDRs – A.J. Fearnley, Houghton-le-Spring (Fence Houses), 24/8/18. Fearnley blamed the large meeting addressed the previous night by Tom Wing, MP, for this outcome.

49 John Williams, *The Home Fronts: Britain, France and Germany, 1914–1918* (London: Constable, 1972), p. 185.

50 Good, 'England Goes to War', p. 72.

51 TNA:PRO T102/22, SDRs – J.A. Corner, Leicester, 23–28/6/18.

52 TNA:PRO T102/24, SDRs – A.M. Stones, Wakefield (Normanton), 14/7/18; T102/23, SDRs – G.F. Crabbe, Barnstaple (Bideford), 25/6/18.

century. By 1900, he argues, 'attention' became 'key to the operation of noncoercive forms of power', whereby the 'attentive subject [was] part of an *internalization* of disciplinary imperatives in which individuals [were] made more directly responsible for their own efficient or profitable utilization within various social arrangements'. That is, 'through the new imperatives of attentiveness ... the perceiving body was deployed and made productive and orderly'.[53] Civilians who listened attentively to NWAC speakers could also be relied upon to fulfil civil functions; attentiveness appears almost an index of civilian reliability in the reports.[54] The association of attentiveness and orderliness, explicitly linked in reports by the Conservative Robert Orrell,[55] further suggests that the post-war concern with orderly public meetings depicted by Lawrence was already becoming an issue. By contrast, speakers sometimes despaired of inattentive audiences. In Finsbury, one speaker complained that adults were 'passing + repassing' while two 'aeroplanes overhead [were] of more interest than war aims', and another pair blamed their failure on 'the large number of noisy children present', whose 'restlessness' made it difficult for adults to pay attention.[56] Elsewhere, J. Farnsworth complained that he had only found a small audience since it was 'pay night' and the '"pub" was doing a "roaring trade"', particularly among young men, prompting his churlish suggestion that 'it would be a good place for a "comb out"'.[57]

It is also clear that attentiveness cannot alone demonstrate the value of NWAC meetings. In Weymouth, Revd T.E. Jackson reported gathering 'a number of regular attenders [*sic*] who are present at every Meeting' and were 'attentive + enthusiastic'.[58] It did not apparently strike Jackson that in seeing the same faces each day he was preaching to the converted rather than convincing new civilians. For Jackson it was doubtless pleasant to see his efforts appreciated, but for his masters in the central Committee it may be surmised that more productive work among the uncommitted was desired. Audience attentiveness also took other forms. In the same Weymouth campaign, G.L. Paton reported that

---

53 Jonathan Crary, *Suspensions of Perception: Attention, Spectacle, and Modern Culture* (Cambridge, MA: MIT Press, 1999), pp. 73–74, 22–23. Emphasis in original.
54 This is bolstered by the emphasis in a report of a war aims meeting at Downham Market in the *Dereham & Fakenham Times*, 2/3/18, p. 5; and by the first MoL report to mention NWAC work, which recorded that audiences were 'large, attentive and sympathetic': TNA:PRO CAB24/28, GT2266, MoL report, 11/10/17.
55 E.g. TNA:PRO T102/22, SDRs – R. Orrell, Holderness (Withernsea [twice], Pateington, Hornsea, Beverley), 26–31/8/18.
56 TNA:PRO T102/22, SDRs – H. Morgan, Finsbury, 20/8/18; T102/16 and 26, SDRs – J.P. Whitestone/T.G. Harper (2 reports), Finsbury (Clerkenwell), 29/8/18.
57 TNA:PRO T102/23, SDRs – John Farnsworth, Evesham (Crabs Cross), 25/1/18.
58 TNA:PRO T102/23, SDRs – Revd T.E. Jackson, South Dorset (Weymouth), 10/8/18.

We had considerable attention from the Socialists + 'Peace by negotiation' pacifists, + outclassed them at answering questions.

It does seem as if the So' Dorset Labour Secty [*sic*] supported by his Party ... made organised efforts to molest us + obstruct our War Aims Meetings.

The great majority on our side.[59]

While Gregory may be correct to dismiss a depiction of Weymouth as a 'hotbed of revolutionary agitation', this does not mean that no organised dissent existed there. Speakers' reports throughout the summer of 1918 alluded to sometimes considerable opposition – in mid-August, Paton and Jackson reported that their meeting had been broken up by 'young socialist men and dilutees' supporting the local Labour secretary, necessitating police protection.[60] Speakers often seemingly relished a 'pacifist' presence, which added a controversial air to proceedings. At Wigan the local secretary described a meeting of 1200 people as 'excellent', despite several interruptions and the voting of 40–50 men for peace by negotiation, while at Ripon the public turned against 'pacifists' who called the speaker a 'coward' for refusing to answer a question, and 'rushed 3 of them off the Market + out of the town'.[61]

However, some speakers apparently enjoyed the combative element too much. Two separate Southport incidents provoked complaints about the conduct of NWAC speakers. In April 1918, Aeneas Henderson demanded Paton's address in order 'to have a writ served upon him for a slanderous statement made ... in public, to my serious hurt and detriment'.[62] Six weeks later, another Southport resident complained strenuously about his treatment by the speakers B. Billcliffe and G.H. Bibbings. James Jackson claimed he had sought to correct Bilcliffe's denunciation of 'pacifists' reluctant to ask questions as '"Cowards" and "Traitors" who dare not assert themselves'. Following Jackson's 'friendly overture' that such silence was caused by DORA's strictures, which 'menaced the liberties of Pacifists', Bilcliffe retorted, 'If you are not a pacifist you are damned near one.' On following days, Jackson was targeted for abuse. Jackson, who said he had chaired or spoken at 30 NWAC meetings without charge, was

not conscious of being less loyal to my sovereign or my services being of less value than those of the mob orators ... I shall not quietly submit to be held up by contumely, scurrility and abuse to the derision of the mob and have my life menaced by War Aims hooligans ...

59 TNA:PRO T102/23, SDRs – G.L. Paton, South Dorset (Weymouth), 7/8/18.
60 Gregory, *Last Great War*, pp. 207–08; TNA:PRO T102/22, SDRs – G.L. Paton/ Revd T.E. Jackson (2 reports), South Dorset (Weymouth), 16/8/18. Quotation from Paton's report.
61 TNA:PRO T102/25, SDRs – Thomas Southworth (organiser's report), Wigan, 25/8/18; A.M. Stones, Ripon, 5/9/18.
62 TNA:PRO T102/5, Aeneas Henderson to Cox, 16/4/18.

Cox replied that he believed that Jackson 'provoked any little difficulty there may have been' and lectured him on his duty to Britain, prompting Jackson's scornful reply that he had voluntarily assisted his country and 'it ill becomes a paid servant to lecture a free citizen and voluntary worker'. Concluding, Jackson emphasised the competing interpretations of patriotism at stake, asserting that 'For a speaker to first invite questions … [then] carry on a campaign of abuse against his victim is certainly not playing the game of a Britisher.'[63]

NWAC correspondence suggests it handled complaints in a high-handed manner, unlikely to remedy the situation or regain the complainant's sympathy. In October 1918, the Committee corresponded with a Lincolnshire chief constable over a dispute between a constable and a cinemotor crew. Captain Mitchell-Innes wrote in defence of Constable Ancliffe who had removed the cinemotor screen from the side of his house because his wife (who had allowed the speaker to use the wall) had not realised the prolonged disturbance the event would cause. Mitchell-Innes objected to the speaker's rude conduct and demanded advanced warning of future events. The NWAC criticised Mitchell-Innes's 'tone', reminding him that 'this is a Government Committee charged with carrying out propaganda in all parts of the country' and that cinemotor shows were very successful, 'the police generally heartily co-operating with us'.[64] Such arrogant dismissal of legitimate complaints again suggests the NWAC may have struggled in convincing those not already supportive to accept its propaganda.[65] In January, R.H. Glover, a speaker who 'specialised in attacks on the peace party', claimed from personal experience in attending NWAC meetings that Horatio Bottomley's characterisation of the Committee as a 'dismal failure' was 'only too true'. Consequently, he demanded an opportunity to demonstrate his own abilities. Cox's reply that the Committee had sufficient speakers for its purposes suggests that it was not unduly concerned with the problems Bottomley and Glover proclaimed, perhaps preferring the opinions of their own (often party-based) speakers to such self-serving estimations.[66]

The Committee seemed more conciliatory to political complaints. Like MPs, civilians also sometimes complained about apparent political advantages. A Surrey Conservative complained that allowing prospective

63 TNA:PRO T102/6, James Jackson to Cox, 31/5/18; Cox to Jackson, 11/6/18; Jackson to Cox, 13/6/18.
64 TNA:PRO T102/8, correspondence, Capt. C. Mitchell-Innes and NWAC, 10–19/10/18.
65 However, cf. E.W. Toye's letter praising the Committee's 'continued thoughtfulness [which] contrasts so favourably with some unappreciative officials of other Depts'. TNA:PRO T102/14, Toye to Cox, 28/2/18.
66 TNA:PRO T102/5, R.H. Glover to Cox, 17/11/17, 23/1/18; Cox to Glover, 24/1/18.

parliamentary candidates to address NWAC meetings 'may most dis-
advantageously affect the Conservative cause', while in South London
another correspondent objected to 'the advertisement of the Conservative
Party by a Coalition Government Department' at a meeting in Wallington,
complaining that both the speaker and chairman were Conservatives,
while the Conservative secretary was credited with the arrangements. The
first complainant was telephoned, while the second received a detailed
account of local cross-party arrangements to demonstrate that the NWAC
had 'done everything to ensure that no one side has an advantage'.[67]
The Committee was apparently more sensitive to accusations of political
exploitation than of ineffective propaganda, suggesting its members
recognised the precariousness of its role caused by political mistrust.

THE NWAC clearly had a mixed reception from two groups – clergymen and organised labour. The request that senior Methodists
provide the Committee with their circuit plans so that propaganda could
be circulated to local clergymen met with a lukewarm response. In
Birmingham, Revd W.R. Maltby refused to provide his circuit plan,
fearing that the NWAC wished to propagate to 'preachers ... certain
views ... which I think are not Christian ... I think we have had from the
[NWAC] some communications which were a gross insult to the Christian
ministry'. Others, while 'in complete sympathy with [the NWAC's] aims'
refused to provide their plan as they did 'not wish [their] pulpits to be
used for any War propaganda'. In Manchester, Revd A.E. Hutchinson
reported that though five of thirty local clergymen had 'pacifist views'
he believed the majority were doing patriotic work and needed no
central stimulation. Maltby's condemnation of un-Christian propaganda,
together with Revd F.W. Harrison's 'disquiet at the revelation of secret
treaties',[68] suggest NWAC efforts to incorporate spiritual patriotism
as part of its larger message were hampered by some other elements
and governmental actions. Nonetheless, clergymen were not invariably
hostile to NWAC propaganda. Both the Anglican *Church Times* and
the leading nonconformist newspaper *British Weekly* commended some
NWAC propaganda. The *Church Times* recommended the NWAC's initial run of pamphlets in September 1917, insisting that '[e]very household
should possess' the NWAC's *Kalendar of Kultur*. In February 1918, it
publicised the Bishop of Zanzibar's pamphlet on German imperialism,
claiming that it should be 'scattered broadcast over the country'. In

---

67 TNA:PRO T102/1, J. Allen to Cox, 14/3/18; T102/11, F.J. Palin to the Secretary,
    Ministry of Information (forwarded to NWAC), 22/5/18.
68 TNA:PRO T102/8, Revd W.R. Maltby to Wallace Carter, 20/3/19 [*sic*, but 1918];
    T102/5, Revd A.E. Hutchinson to NWAC, 20/3/18; Revd F.W. Harrison (Bath) to
    NWAC, 18/3/18. However, cf. the positive response to the NWAC's request by
    Revd R.M. Pope: T102/11, letter (unsigned) to Pope, 8/2/18.

the following edition it announced that demand for the pamphlet had been 'so great that the supply is exhausted', while Sanders's pamphlet *The Tragedy of Russia* was recommended as part of 'that fine collection of war literature which [W.H. Smith] is distributing with patriotic generosity'.[69] The Presbyterian W.R. Nicoll's Free Church *British Weekly*, perhaps the most stridently patriotic representative of a generally pro-war nonconformity, also endorsed NWAC propaganda, celebrating the Congregationalist theologian P.T. Forsyth's 'strong and noble' pamphlet on Britons' moral duties (the newspaper regularly published Forsyth's sermons).[70] Eminent Congregationalists were particularly prominent in NWAC propaganda. Alongside Forsyth, J.H. Jowett's views were given prominence in NWAC publications, while Revd P. Campbell Morgan spoke at several NWAC meetings.[71] Nor were Methodists apparently particularly susceptible to anti-war sentiment. The leading Wesleyan Dr Scott Lidgett had expressed wholehearted support for Methodist enlistments in 1914, also renouncing his previous opposition to conscription when it was introduced in 1916. Even Primitive Methodists, who before 1914 considered themselves (after Quakers) 'the most pacifist or peace-loving of all denominations', enlisted in large numbers, with only a small minority of Primitive Methodists expressing dissent in the *Primitive Methodist Leader*, the content of which was more usually characterised by 'patriotic fervour'. In 1916, the Quaker MP Arnold Rowntree was informed that 'pacifist' Methodist minsters 'had been placed on a black list'. Although the passage of conscription apparently turned some (most prominently Samuel Keeble) towards an opposition based on 'the traditional language of 19th-century Nonconformist liberalism', Michael Hughes contends that 'Most Methodists supported the war because they shared the instinctive patriotism exhibited by their fellow Britons.'[72]

Alongside the clerical cooperation discussed previously, correspondence reveals further instances of supportive clergy. In North Walsham, Norfolk, Revd Francis Knowles described the pamphlet *The Truth about the War* as 'just what is wanted' to counteract the 'wild talk going on among the working-classes in this parish and neighbourhood', while in

---

69 'Summary', *Church Times*, 21/9/17, p. 223; 'A Voice from Africa', *Church Times*, 22/2/18, p. 235; ibid., 28/2/18, p. 249; 'Summary', *Church Times*, 21/6/18, p. 435. For the significance of the newspaper's publicity, see, e.g., TNA:PRO T102/6, Revd H.E. Jones to NWAC, 24/9/17, requesting the pamphlets discussed on the 21st.

70 'War Pamphlet by Dr. Forsyth', *British Weekly*, 14/3/18, p. 431.

71 On Jowett, see pp. 177–78 above; on Morgan, see TNA:PRO T102/17, Meetings register, nos 1072, 1324, 1372, 1374, 1380–85.

72 Alan Wilkinson, *Dissent or Conform?*, esp. pp. 26, 29–38; Turberfield, *Lidgett*, pp. 151–62; Stephen Koss, *Nonconformity in Modern British Politics* (London: B.T. Batsford, 1975), p. 134; Michael Hughes, 'British Methodists and the First World War', *Methodist History*, 41:2 (2002), p. 328.

Leeds, Revd Frank Lord wanted a copy of the *Kalendar of Kultur* 'to hang in the church porch' and 'hearten my people whose boys are in the line of battle'.[73] At East Ham, a Wesleyan minister thanked the Committee for sending the American, Judge Henry Neil, to his mission, where two thousand men thoroughly enjoyed his speech. Neil, who also wrote a pamphlet for the NWAC, was a valuable propagandist, having previously been praised in the 'pacifist' press for championing a 'Mother's Pension scheme'.[74] Thus, if Maltby's criticism was particularly strong, it must be set alongside the endorsement of, and participation in, NWAC propaganda by other clergymen, suggesting that, while not universally approved by clerics, the Committee nonetheless received considerable support.

MoL reports suggest the NWAC successfully convinced workers to reject strikes in turbulent places like South Wales, Coventry and the Clyde. Further, general indications of the public mood in working-class autobiographies suggest attitudes which, notwithstanding UDC judgements of changing public opinion, provided an environment receptive to some NWAC arguments. An anonymous autobiographer, probably in his early forties by 1918, insisted that, despite prevailing 1930s assumptions that the war had been 'one gigantic blunder', 'there really was a great conflict of ideals involved'. The historian A.L. Rowse, son of a Cornish china-clay worker, recalled that in mid-1918, aged fourteen, he was 'very anti-German [and] drew up peace terms of a Draconian severity', while Arthur Newton, a teenage Hackney shoemaker, suggested that in 1917 there was

> a rather false sense of security ... people rather thought that they would never again see the dire poverty that they once knew ... Had this not been a war to end all wars? So things were going to be very different when it was all over.[75]

The NWAC's proprietorial and aspirational patriotic messages would have resonated with such attitudes, while Rowse's anti-Germanism offers an indication of adversarial patriotism's continuing vitality. However, it should not be assumed that NWAC activities were unremittingly successful. Obviously attitudes varied widely. If some 'romantic' feminists

---

73 TNA:PRO T102/7, Revd Francis Knowles to NWAC, 18/9/17; Revd Frank Lord to NWAC, 25/9/18.
74 TNA:PRO T102/1, Revd W.H. Armstrong to Wallace Carter, 9/4/18; George Bernard Shaw, 'Judge Neil's Business in Britain', *Labour Leader*, 19/7/17, p. 5; James Leakey, 'Judge Neil at Poplar', *Workers' Dreadnought*, 24/11/17, p. 889. On the value and success of American speakers in NWAC propaganda, see the letter by 'Trade Unionist 12 Years' regarding American Labour delegates in Sheffield, *Sheffield Daily Telegraph*, 17/5/18, p. 4; Brittain, *Pilgrims and Pioneers*, pp. 164–66.
75 'Authorship unacknowledged', *Narrow Waters: The First Volume of the Life and Thoughts of a Common Man* (London: William Hodge, 1935), pp. 205–06; Rowse, *Cornish Childhood*, p. 205; Arthur Newton, *Years of Change: Autobiography of a Hackney Shoemaker* (London: Centerprise Publications, 1974), pp. 50–51.

celebrated women's war work and, 'influenced by current propaganda wondered what kind of new society lay ahead', Gail Braybon suggested others were more interested in returning to the status quo antebellum.[76] Similarly Robert Roberts, discussing the war generally, doubted that

> any man joined the forces through the politicians' lures of a 'better world' to come ... [H]ow many expected social miracles or in fact even wished for basic change? ... [Most] were products of a class structure which conditioned them to defend, with all its faults and virtues, the country *they knew*, not to fight for some idealised land of the future.[77]

Roberts's argument, unlike those above, suggests aspirational patriotism was meaningless, unless it promised a return to comfortable familiarity. If NWAC messages seemed to match the attitude of some, then, they were apparently inappropriate to others, although the flexibility and variety of its patriotic messages might have assisted in appealing to those unimpressed by certain aspects.

The NWAC's difficulty in appealing to organised labour has been discussed.[78] Many local labour organisations rejected Peters's request to assist the Committee, though few went so far as the Brighton Trades' and Labour Council which resolved that his letter 'be burnt and ashes returned'.[79] Furthermore, correspondence indicates that the NWAC's presence was not always beneficial. From the colliery town, Ashington, the Committee was asked to clarify the role of Alfred Baker, who had been accused at a miners' meeting of being 'a paid agent of the National War Aims Committee, to go up and down the country to gull the Workers'. Their correspondent believed this accusation was damaging Baker's credibility, adding that Baker was the only person in the area attempting to 'further the War Aims Committee's view', and was undermined by 'a good many pacifists' holding leading positions. Baker himself complained that his accuser was

> a pasifist [sic] or as I call them enemies of our own country and I do not think it is right that they should be allowed to make these statements that are not true. I ... have never been engadeg [sic] by the War Aims Committee I only wish I had but ever since I was discharged from the army in 1916 I have felt it my duty to ... do what I can for my country ...[80]

A reply confirmed that Baker was not a paid speaker. Association with the NWAC was clearly considered counterproductive to successful 'patriotic'

---

76 Braybon, *Women Workers*, pp. 165–66.
77 Robert Roberts, *The Classic Slum: Salford Life in the First Quarter of the Century* (Manchester: Manchester University Press, 1971), p. 192. Emphasis in original.
78 See pp. 40–41 above.
79 TNA:PRO T102/12, G. Rayner to Secretary of NWAC, 18/8/17.
80 TNA:PRO T102/1, Joseph Armstrong to Cox, 21/8/18; Alfred Baker to Cox, 13/8/18.

propaganda here. While evidence of voluntary working-class action was doubtless heartening, the fact that association with the Committee rendered propaganda amongst workers less rather than more successful was alarming. Similarly, despite optimistic reports of NWAC success in Coventry, the businessman R.S. Morrish advised that the city was 'probably past praying for' but that good work might still be possible in Leamington.[81]

However, there was also considerable testimony to the NWAC's success among workers. Near Ashington, in West Stanley, a mine surveyor with 'good opportunities going amongst the miners underground' judged that a NWAC speaker had noticeably improved local attitudes:

> if you could have heard them yourself, you would have been surprised at the amount of good you did ...
> Every person I spoke to after your lecture both patriots, Socialist, Independent Labour men, + many Irishmen all exposed [sic] a genuine wish to hear you again ...[82]

Likewise, James Wright, formerly an ASE branch president and district councillor in Weymouth, informed George Barnes that 'the speakers now at Weymouth ... are doing a great, + grand work'. Arguably, participation is the best index of NWAC reception. As with clergymen, so too the involvement of working-class figures with NWAC propaganda demonstrated commitment beyond mere nodding acceptance. Wright's offer to 'do anything to help your representative at Weymouth' was a more impressive demonstration of the NWAC's reception than simple applause, though this was also very welcome.[83] Generally, correspondents were more positive than negative, though this is unsurprising – firm opponents did not generally waste time corresponding, but continued their own agitations regardless. However, the very fact that so many people contacted the Committee demonstrates some level of committed support of the NWAC's cause, and certainly engagement with its message (positive or negative) rather than apathy. Furthermore, voluntary activism continued beyond the armistice. In January 1919, a discharged officer asked for one of Lord Denbigh's maps showing Germany's *Mitteleuropa* ambitions to assist his teaching at a school. As with all post-armistice requests, he was informed that the Committee was no longer operating and so was unable to help. That people continued to approach the NWAC after its operations had ceased, however, suggests that it maintained some prestige throughout the final months of the war (and beyond).[84] At least among civilians enthusiastic enough to correspond, the NWAC seemingly remained in public consciousness throughout 1918.

81 TNA:PRO T102/8, R.S. Morrish to Cox, 10/9/18.
82 TNA:PRO T102/14, Harold Tarbuck to 'Stone Esq.', 21/1/18.
83 TNA:PRO T102/15, James Wright to Barnes, n.d.
84 TNA:PRO T102/6, Major J.S. Iredell to NWAC, 26/1/19.

NONETHELESS, most local press discussion of the NWAC, like official assessments, occurred before the summer of 1918. Later commentary usually focused on major events like France's Day and the War Anniversary, though this was not universal – in October 1918 newspapers in Evesham recorded a successful NWAC campaign, where 87 meetings had been held since July, attracting around 50 per cent of the adult populations of the villages visited.[85] The NWAC believed local newspapers were 'more consistent, less materialistic and more representative of solid English opinion' than their national equivalents.[86] As such it monitored their content, and presumably valued their comments as guides to the Committee's reception. Further, from an analytical perspective, the local press 'contributed to ... building and maintaining communities of locality and belief', 'proclaiming an image of the town itself', both for the town's inhabitants and for outside observers.[87] Commentary on NWAC activities may, therefore, be considered an indication both that the local press wished to demonstrate (or inculcate) a locality's patriotism, and that covering NWAC events was considered useful to this. As previous chapters demonstrate, local press coverage of NWAC events, often including verbatim reports of speeches, was extensive, despite the shrinking numbers of newspaper pages caused by paper shortages.

Local newspapers also sometimes commented separately on the importance of the NWAC's work. The Liberal *Montgomeryshire Express* 'rejoice[d] to note the energetic campaign' commenced by the NWAC in South Wales since 'all thoughtful persons recognise the potential dangers of permitting the pacifist an unchallenged innings'.[88] Most editorials were prompted by ongoing campaigns. Hence the Liberal *Radnor Express* devoted two editorials to the need for continuing civilian effort following meetings addressed by the MPs Sir Francis Edwards and Sidney Robinson. Their campaign was 'meeting with all the success their promoters desired', and the *Express*' editor was 'glad' that Robinson confronted

> one of those small groups of people ... whose views, as he said, did not savour of the most enthusiastic patriotism. They call themselves pacifists or reconciliators ... [but it] is extremely difficult ... to understand ... [their] attitude ... in certain parts of the country ...[89]

---

85 'County News. Evesham', *Evesham Standard*, 5/10/18, p. 3; 'Winchcombe. War Pictures', *Evesham Journal*, 5/10/18, p. 3.

86 See p. 68, n. 34 above.

87 Aled Gruffydd Jones, *Press, Politics and Society: A History of Journalism in Wales* (Cardiff: University of Wales Press, 1993), p. 199; Good, 'England Goes to War', p. 12.

88 'The Perilous Stage', *Montgomeryshire Express and Radnor Times*, 25/9/17, p. 5.

89 'The Testing Time', *Radnor Express*, 4/10/17, p. 5; 'The Real Need', *Radnor Express*, 11/10/17, p. 5.

Similarly, Smuts's Rhondda visit was heralded by the 'Liberal and Labour' *Rhondda Leader* as having 'once for all, dissipated the notion that the Rhondda was other than most loyal' and shown that 'pacifism', though noisy, was 'more or less a mirage' as 'the mass are made of the right patriotic mettle', noticeably echoing (or prompting) the MoL's assessment. The subsequent defeat of the 'down-tools' resolution redounded to the 'eternal credit ... of the working collier' who refused to 'kow-tow ... to the active anti-war section of the I.L.P. led by the academic Ramsay MacDonald and Snowden crowd of agitators'.[90] These editorial viewpoints demonstrate an important element in the NWAC's reception. Successful meetings like Smuts's at Tonypandy generated multiple responses. While the crowd's initial enthusiasm demonstrated endorsement of the Committee's general principles, it also prompted local press coverage. Speakers' messages were thus brought to larger audiences than could be reached at the meeting itself, spreading its effects more widely.[91] Furthermore, editorial commentary often extended the speaker's arguments, extrapolating from these and adding more pointed comments. Hence the *Rhondda Leader*'s editor specifically blamed discontent on MacDonald and Snowden, whereas NWAC speakers generally avoided direct criticism of MPs.[92] Speakers could therefore sometimes be allusive, expecting either that the audience would understand the implication or that a local newspaper would elucidate it; that is, that both journalists and audiences could draw 'inferences about inferences', as Hans Ruthrof puts it, which might not all be 'derived directly from the signals of the text'.[93] Local newspapers thus generated their own propaganda, extending the official line with their own less regulated interpretation. While this created potential for inappropriate messages, it also meant NWAC propaganda was publicised to civilians who might eschew meetings. In local papers, sometimes reduced to as little as four pages (including retained advertising space), discussion of a meeting via reports of the speeches and, sometimes, an additional editorial, could mean a substantial proportion of a day's or week's local news being devoted to NWAC messages.

NWAC propaganda began in Leicester in April 1918 with a meeting addressed by the Labour NWAC member James Parker, much to the

---

90 'From the Editor's Chair', *Rhondda Leader*, 3/11/17, p. 2; 17/11/17, p. 2.
91 On this publicity process, see Matthew, 'Rhetoric and Politics'.
92 This was also sometimes the case with national newspapers, such as Christabel Pankhurst's *Britannia*, which urged the NWAC to maintain an 'irreducible minimum' of war aims against calls for negotiation: 'Review of the Week', *Britannia*, 27/7/17, p. 58.
93 Hans Ruthrof, *The Reader's Construction of Narrative* (London: Routledge & Kegan Paul, 1981), p. 43. For an example of this sort of oratorical approach in practice in another context, see L.P. Curtis, 'Moral and Physical Force: The Language of Violence in Irish Nationalism', *Journal of British Studies*, 27:2 (1988).

relief of the *Leicester Daily Mercury*'s editor, who thought it a 'pity it was not called long ago and followed by others in the meantime'. The ILP's *Leicester Pioneer*, meanwhile, happily reported that an early NWAC meeting was closed prematurely because two audience members had settled an argument over conscription 'in the old-fashioned style (with their fists)'.[94] Following the May Day disruptions, however, the local press (except the *Pioneer*, which was rather less satisfied when violence affected MacDonald's meeting) took the NWAC's side against MacDonald and his supporters. Shortly after May Day, the *Mercury* printed a digest of public responses, concluding that 'a force has arisen in the town which will be directed to the rout of MacDonaldism' and the removal of the 'stain' of 'pacifism' from Leicester.[95] Leicester journalists, forthrightly critical of MacDonald since 1914, renewed their calls for his resignation. They also published numerous letters, mostly criticising MacDonald. One woman enquired whether 'the War Aims Committee agree with the suppression of Free Speech as a War Aim', and complained that while she could hear the 'patriotic' line anywhere it was much harder to get the other side of the story. However, most opprobrium not directed at MacDonald and his supporters was taken by Albert Howarth, a local BWL organiser arrested for his part in the incident, and who had been warned by the mayor – chairman of Leicester WAC – not to violently disrupt MacDonald's meeting.[96] Simply by staging a rival meeting, the NWAC stimulated local opinion to a largely self-sustained local campaign against a principal adversary, which did not abate until his electoral defeat in December. The NWAC challenged the legitimacy of MacDonald's gathering by occupying the same 'civic space'. 'An Old Trade Unionist' asked whether MacDonald 'seriously ... [claimed] a monopoly of the Market-place', adding that ILP trade unionists were merely a noisy minority.[97] Speakers subsequently reported 'quite a wave of patriotism' and that 'Leicester as a whole may be acquitted of any charge in favour of Pacifism'.[98] NWAC propaganda, a compliant local press and public antipathy towards critics like MacDonald formed a potent combination seemingly capable of transforming a town from a notorious 'Pacifists' paradise' to one where 'patriotic loyalty is as good as any ... I have been

---

94 'The War Aims Meeting', *Leicester Daily Mercury*, 13/4/18, p. 4; 'Are You Surprised to Hear?', *Leicester Pioneer*, 19/4/18, p. 4.

95 For May Day in Leicester, see pp. 135–36 above; 'Sunday's Meeting. What People Are Thinking', *Leicester Daily Mercury*, 8/5/18.

96 Letter by 'A Woman with a Vote', *Leicester Daily Mercury*, 10/5/18, p. 2; 'Ald. Banton's Allegation' (letter by Albert Howarth), *Leicester Daily Post*, 7/5/18, p. 3.

97 Lawrence, *Speaking*, p. 181; letter, 'An Old Trade Unionist', *Leicester Daily Mercury*, 8/5/18, p. 6.

98 TNA:PRO T102/24, SDRs – Abraham Williamson, Leicester, 12/5/18; T102/16, SDRs – T. Hemsley, Leicester, 23/8/18.

in'.[99] In reality, it may be assumed that Leicester's reputation had been undeserved all along, based solely on MacDonald's continuing role as MP, but the NWAC's campaign encouraged a noisy public restatement of local loyalty.

MOST local editorials discussing the NWAC were similarly positive to those discussed above. In Ipswich, the independent *East Anglian Daily Times*, while supportive, was more sceptical about the value of NWAC campaigns. Discussing Macnamara's efforts, the paper noted the quality of his argument, but asked 'was he not preaching to the converted? How are the careless, thoughtless, indifferent people to be reached?' It recommended short speeches in places of entertainment where more of the audience would benefit from '"a good talking to" than would be found at any "war aims" meeting'.[100] This was a pertinent observation, supported by the comment noted above about gathering a regular audience throughout a week in Weymouth and by a correspondent's observation that 'the working classes do not patronise Smith's bookstalls and shops' and so did not see the NWAC's publications.[101] If the same people heard the NWAC's speakers each time a campaign was held, there was a risk that the message reached only those who did not need to hear it. This difficulty was partly addressed by events like France's Day, which combined a public fête with speeches, exploiting entertainment in a way similar to that suggested by the *East Anglian Daily Times*. Further, the NWAC attempted to implement the suggestion more fully. In April, the entertainment agency Keith, Prowse & Co. was approached to assist in arrangements for short speeches to be made at theatres and music halls, preferably delivered by 'prominent actors and music hall "stars"'.[102] While this plan was abandoned due to running-time restrictions, the Committee maintained the general idea.[103] Besides the very successful cinemotor campaigns, a special War Anniversary message by Lloyd George was sent to over 4000 places of entertainment, to be simultaneously opened at nine o'clock to an audience expected to number 2,500,000 people, with others able to read it later in the local press.[104] Cox also explained to the Australian Directorate of War Propaganda that besides 'ordinary meetings exhibitions of war pictures and films take place in cinema

---

99 For the phrase 'Pacifists' paradise', see 'Our War Aims', *Leicester Daily Mercury*, 13/4/18, p. 4; TNA:PRO T102/25, SDRs – E. Rhodes, Leicester, 23/8/18.
100 'War Aims and War Means', *East Anglian Daily Times*, 3/12/17, p. 4.
101 TNA:PRO T102/1, extract of letter from Dr H.L.P. Baker, 9/7/18.
102 TNA:PRO T102/7, Vesey to E.M. Briggs, 11/4/18.
103 E.g. TNA:PRO T102/7, Wallace Carter(?) to Keith Kenneth (actor), 5/9/18.
104 TNA:PRO T102/1, Capt. Barber to J. Cabourn, 29/7/18. For the message, see, e.g., *Evesham Standard*, 10/8/18, p. 2.

house [sic], music-halls, theatres and other places of entertainment'.[105] The extravagant 'British national film', finally produced too late for wartime release, would have extended this activity still further, though officials' post-war reaction to it suggests this might have been a mixed blessing.[106] Evidently, the Committee attempted to extend its propaganda to those uninterested in public meetings, but these remained the principal means of communication. Nonetheless, this should not be dismissed as an outmoded medium. As some of the evidence above shows, these meetings were credited with much success.

IN November 1918, Charles B. Little, in Ryhill, near Wakefield, wrote to praise the Committee, particularly for 'the campaign that you are carrying on in the small towns and the villages ... the speeches given ... did good in enlightening the people ... and in stiffening the community in their determination to endure and have patience'.[107] While also praising the cinemotors, Little's acknowledgement is fitting testimony to the significance of the NWAC's work. While the major events addressed by Smuts or Asquith garnered most national attention, it was the smaller meetings in villages, small towns or city districts which typified the NWAC's output. At these local gatherings, talented speakers like Sergeant A.K. Hamilton 'held the people spell bound', producing an 'abiding' effect which was 'just what [was] wanted to rouse up more interest in national work'.[108] Though not all speakers were as skilled as Hamilton, nor all audiences so rapt as the 30 Wiltshire citizens he addressed, it was at this level, ultimately, that the NWAC was most important. Through its presence in small communities, the NWAC (and organisations like War Savings and Food Control Committees) became, in most (English and Welsh) constituencies, a small part of British wartime society, linking those 'shut away in sheltered nooks of the country' with the rest of the nation by reminding preoccupied minds of things outside their immediate horizon.[109] Whether individuals fully endorsed NWAC propagandists' arguments was arguably less important than that its presence refocused public *attention* on the nation's requirements 'in the interests of maintaining an orderly and productive world' capable of seeing the war through to a close.[110]

---

105 TNA:PRO T102/3, Cox to D.K. Picken, 28/10/18.
106 See pp. 132–33 above.
107 TNA:PRO T102/7, Charles B. Little to Barber, 7/11/18.
108 TNA:PRO T102/25, SDRs – A.K. Hamilton, Chippenham (Rodbourne), 10/9/18.
      Hamilton was (perhaps immodestly) quoting the local WAC secretary, A. George.
109 TNA:PRO T102/3, S.A. Earnshaw to NWAC, 5/10/17.
110 Crary, *Suspensions of Perception*, p. 17.

Conclusion

THE NWAC's activities ceased shortly after the armistice. Sanders told MPs on 14 November that the Committee had warned all WACs ten days earlier that activities would be suspended during a general election. Sanders reported that it 'has also been decided to suspend all meetings and publications during the period of the Armistice', barring a couple of final newspaper supplements, an edition of *Reality* and a pre-arranged tour of the western front for trade unionists. Sanders also confirmed that parliamentary candidates would not be permitted to use NWAC pamphlets in their campaigns.[1] Having been suspended, the Committee effectively ceased to exist. Its MPs, secretaries and the party staff speakers addressed themselves to the election, while salaried staff sought other appointments.[2] It was seemingly the first propaganda organisation to shut down fully, with responsibility for its cinemotors transferred to the National War Savings Committee on 14 December. The Ministry of Information, Lord Northcliffe's enemy propaganda organisation at Crewe House and the Press Bureau followed shortly thereafter. As Sanders and Taylor note, 'the reputation which the British government earned for the successful employment of propaganda was not one of which many contemporaries felt proud. It was ... a somehow "un-English" activity' only acceptable in retaliation to enemy efforts.[3]

Notwithstanding the unease at the use of domestic propaganda, however, Gerard Fiennes was appointed Commander of the Order of the British Empire in 1920 specifically for his wartime role in the NWAC's Publicity Department, suggesting governmental appreciation of domestic propaganda's worth.[4] Two other key Committee members were less well

---

1 PDC(5), 110, 14/11/18, col. 2869.
2 E.g. letter by Maynard Saunders (Publicity Department) in TNA:PRO HO139/35/146.
3 TNA:PRO T102/9, NWAC to Proprietor, North Eastern Railway Hotel Garage, York, 2/1/19. Sanders and Taylor, *British Propaganda*, p. 248.
4 'Civilian War Honours', *Times*, 31/3/20, p. 18.

rewarded. Its two Asquithian Liberal MPs, A.H. Marshall and Walter Rea, were not given the Coalition 'coupon' at the 1918 election. Marshall subsequently received only 14 per cent of the vote at Wakefield behind a Coalition Conservative and a Labour candidate, while Rea managed just 12.1 per cent, finishing fourth and failing to win either of Oldham's two seats (behind 'couponed' Conservative and Liberal candidates and Labour).[5] While Marshall and Rea benefited little politically from their involvement with the Committee, however, Guest and Sanders's collaboration as chairman and vice chairman probably helped facilitate arrangements for the post-war coalition.[6]

In February 1920, Major General Sir George Aston, who had written for the NWAC and been involved in coordinating Britain's various propaganda organisations, grandly claimed that British propaganda, unlike that of Britain's enemies, was based solely on truth: 'We never lied in our propaganda ... great care was taken not to use a word or a story that was not strictly true.'[7] However, the general post-war attitude towards propaganda overlooked the truthful elements within propaganda and focused upon the excesses of atrocity stories, resulting in the permanent assumption that propaganda was an activity based upon lies and deception. Although the NWAC was indeed largely geared towards 'truthful' propaganda, post-war criticism touched upon some NWAC propaganda. Referring to a nastily anti-Semitic allegation – which appeared in *Reality* in November 1917 – a 1920 discussion of 'The "Propaganda" Morass' recalled, 'At one time we were told that Bolshevism was run by a little gang of Jews. That was found to be untrue.'[8] Arthur Ponsonby's 1928 condemnation of British propaganda included a section discussing the Bishop of Zanzibar's disavowal of the pamphlet *The Black Slaves of Prussia*, based on his letter to Smuts, which he said had been doctored, omitting inconvenient discussion of the British Empire's flaws. Ponsonby also strongly criticised propaganda relating to war aims, ridiculing many key arguments (used by NWAC propagandists) as 'general high-sounding ideals which might give the war the character of an almost religious crusade'. He insisted that militarism, far from being crushed, was stronger than ever, citing Britain's higher post-war military expenditure, and complained that despite talk of fighting for small nations, 'Montenegro was wiped off the map by the Peace Treaties, although the restoration of Montenegro was specially mentioned by the Prime Minister on January

---

5 Craig, *Parliamentary Election Results*, pp. 261, 211.
6 See, e.g., Sanders diary, 24/3/18, 14/7/18, in Ramsden, *Tory Politics*, pp. 101, 106–07.
7 Aston, 'Propaganda', pp. 239–40.
8 'The "Propaganda" Morass', *Guardian*, 15/1/20 – cutting in University of London, Special Collections, GB 0096 MS 1112, Caroline Playne papers, folder 135. See p. 131 above.

5, 1918 (National War Aims pamphlet No. 33)'. Moreover, the empire had expanded, despite assertions that Britain had no territorial goals. The ambition to 'make the world safe for democracy' had been vitiated by several dictatorships in Europe and elsewhere, while the 'war to end war' had resulted in wars all over the world.[9] Harold Lasswell, with trademark ironic cynicism, suggested that the 'truth about the relation of truth to propaganda seems to be that it is never wise to use material which is likely to be contradicted by certain unconcealable events before the political objective of propaganda is attained'. To this extent, the NWAC largely succeeded – no question was raised about the Bishop of Zanzibar's letter in 1918; rather, following advertisement by the *Church Times*, demand for it exceeded supply.[10] Its patriotic narrative served its wartime purpose. Short-term success, however, may have been traded for contributing to the longer-term suspicion of propaganda, and the consequent striking of the NWAC activities from memoirs and much of the general historical record.

THIS book has explored the complexity of patriotic language in war-time Britain through close analysis of propaganda addressed towards civilians in 1917 and 1918. NWAC propaganda offered Britons a complex and flexible narrative of patriotic identity. Building upon familiar pre-war patriotic themes, its core message of duty was contextualised by several sub-patriotisms, which explained what being British meant through the explication of key civilisational values; claimed that these were British creations but were shared by their 'civilised' allies; and warned that they were threatened by adversaries, external and internal, whose conduct showed that Britain must maintain its effort to victory. Building on the celebratory elements of its evocation of duty, moreover, the 'concrescent community' was encouraged to believe that the post-war society would be a vast improvement on the struggle and division of pre-war Britain. The nation's 'holy war' had brought people together through shared sacrifice and, provided civilians maintained their effort and resolution long enough to win the war, the British way of life would be preserved, and the life of the individual and community improved. Despite the cynicism of some parliamentary and journalistic critics and concerns about the continued (though by no means omnipresent) use of atrocity stories and anti-German rhetoric, this message apparently captured the public's attention and imagination.

Despite such apparent success, the Committee's work soon faded from public and official memory. After 20 years of obscurity, the Second World War restored domestic propaganda to public attention. In response to

---

9 Ponsonby, *Falsehood*, pp. 114–15, 162–66.
10 Lasswell, *Propaganda Technique*, p. 208. See pp. 258–59 above.

the 1938 Munich crisis, a Ministry of Information was re-established, following plans begun in 1935. Despite the transferral of the NWAC's records to the Public Record Office in 1931, planners complained in 1938 that they knew nothing about its activities, and it was not until 1941 that a report examined the NWAC's papers and summarised its activities for the Ministry of Information.[11] A Home Publicity sub-committee was established in 1938 to assess the need for domestic propaganda in the event of war. Its former members reacted poorly to a Ministry of Information memorandum on 13 September 1939 which expressed strong distrust for the reliability of the public. According to Ian McLaine, morale 'was to be sustained by the propagation of three basic themes: the justice of the British cause, Britain's strength, and the commitment of the whole community to the war effort'; principles reminiscent of much NWAC propaganda. The Ministry of Information not having investigated its predecessors' methods, however, the first period of the war was characterised by 'unnecessary and inept' propaganda based on 'misunderstanding and distrust of the British public'. Familiar problems recurred. As in 1917, for instance, Second World War propagandists were hamstrung by the prime minister's refusal to make a statement of war aims.[12]

In September 1940, *The Times* published a letter by the historian Albert M. Hyamson, arguing that the Ministry of Information was attempting to fill too many functions and concentrating excessively on domestic propaganda: 'Public opinion in this country during the last war was in the hands of quite a small organization, the War Aims Committee, of which little was heard.'[13] In calling for the reinstitution of this supposedly unobtrusive body, Hyamson was presumably unaware that a War Aims Committee had been established in July, comprising Duff Cooper (Minister of Information since May), Neville Chamberlain, Lord Halifax, Clement Attlee, Ernest Bevin and Sir Archibald Sinclair. This committee of luminaries, unlike its namesake, did not administer propaganda, however, but advocated the discussion of (in Correlli Barnett's terms) a 'New Jerusalem' following the war, celebrating – in strikingly similar terms to NWAC evocations of a concrescent community and aspirational patriotism – that 'the war has broken down many old barriers and prejudices' and 'aroused the public's social conscience'. Commitments should therefore be made to make 'Britain in every way worthy of her heroic citizens'.[14]

11 Ian McLaine, *Ministry of Morale: Home Front Morale and the Ministry of Information in World War II* (London: George Allen & Unwin, 1979), pp. 13–14; TNA:PRO INF4/4A, 'Home Publicity during the Great War'.
12 McLaine, *Ministry*, pp. 27–30, 10, 173.
13 Albert M. Hyamson, 'Work of the M.O.I. A Diversity of Functions' (letter), *Times*, 11/9/40, p. 9.
14 Correlli Barnett, *The Audit of War: The Illusion & Reality of Britain as a Great Nation* (London: Macmillan, 1986), pp. 20–22; McLaine, *Ministry*, pp. 105, 172–73.

Echoes of the NWAC's approach also resonated in the BBC's recognition that 'loosely-defined nostalgia for home provided a far more potent and popular morale-booster both home and overseas than thumping jingoism'. The examples supplied had evolved – landscape and the countryside, for instance, though somewhat prominent in 1917–18, had become a much more important part of national identity during the 1920s – but the portrayal of Britain as 'essentially one vast and picturesque village' clearly shared similar ideological territory as the NWAC's concrescent community rhetoric. However, Siân Nicholas suggests that civilians felt considerable 'ambivalence about some of the implications of wartime community feeling', while assertions of 'national unity' often seemed 'an aspiration rather than a statement of fact'.[15] This of course was also true between 1917 and 1918, but while NWAC propaganda identified internal adversaries like 'pacifists', strikers or profiteers with which to contextualise its exhortation and celebration of duty, this seemed much less a part of Second World War propaganda strategies – those in Britain targeted for criticism were more likely to be foreign 'fifth columnists', or Jews accused of running the black market and avoiding war work, among other things. 'Pacifism', the great concern of NWAC propaganda, did not apparently much trouble Second World War propagandists.[16] Clearly, propaganda and the patriotism it propounded had changed since 1918. The idea of the public meeting as the crucial venue for propaganda had not endured – film and radio were much more important. Nonetheless, traces of the NWAC's patriotic narrative are still discernible after 1939, further supporting the suggestion that the First World War, although a time of great upheaval, remains also a place of continuity in British history.

T HIS book has explored the NWAC's wartime activities. Far from the canting menace to civil liberties portrayed by Millman, NWAC representatives were encouraged to report public grievances in the hope of finding solutions, or to try to set wartime discomforts in context. Propagandists developed a diverse patriotic narrative, alterable to the tastes of particular localities or types of audience. It was the speeches made to local audiences, often of only a few dozen, which constituted (in its own estimation) the NWAC's most important means of propaganda, and speeches were not simply verbalised pamphlets. The limited attention

15 Siân Nicholas, *The Echo of War: Home Front Propaganda and the Wartime BBC, 1939–45* (Manchester: Manchester University Press, 1996), pp. 239, 233; idem, 'From John Bull to John Citizen: Images of National Identity and Citizenship on the Wartime BBC', in Richard Weight and Abigail Beach (eds), *The Right to Belong: Citizenship and National Identity in Britain, 1930–1960* (London: I.B. Tauris, 1998), pp. 53–54.
16 McLaine, *Ministry*, pp. 55–58, 74–75, 116–17, 166–68. On the targeting of aliens, see also Sonya O. Rose, *Which People's War? National Identity and Citizenship in Britain, 1939–1945* (Oxford: Oxford University Press, 2003), esp. chapter 3.

to speeches in earlier studies has produced a thin understanding of the NWAC's messages. Published propaganda was important, but was necessarily standardised to reach as wide a national audience as possible, and was subject to close editorial control that ensured inappropriate (particularly party political) messages were restrained. By contrast, the central Committee could do much less to inhibit what speakers said spontaneously at a Wednesday afternoon meeting in a village square, while effective propagandists also particularised their messages to the localities in which they were delivered. The NWAC's evocation of patriotism was clearly tailored to a particular situation, but it is possible that the patriotic categories identified as elements of a wider narrative may also resonate in other areas of modern British history.

Far from pre-war patriotic conceptions losing their validity in the face of mass casualties taken by deluded and idealistic volunteers, it was the longevity of such ideas that gave them much of their strength. When woven into a narrative appropriate to the situation in which anxious, overworked civilians found themselves by 1917, the familiarity of the ideas presented assisted propagandists in constructing resonant messages that were easily absorbed. The busy and fraught final years of the war were no time to create a wholly new conception of what it meant to be British. They were a time to re-present the most potent ways in which people already understood such issues. Once it is recognised that propagandists drew from well-established language and imagery, it is possible to pay greater attention to the ways in which they were deployed, and the purposes served by particular references within a broader underlying narrative.

Much previous work on patriotism and propaganda has been too characterised by distrust. Perceptions that First World War propaganda was essentially about the cynical manipulation of the public by the state have encouraged equally cynical interpretations of propaganda content that often seem to start from condescending assumptions that, somehow, Britons were bamboozled by bayoneted babies into endorsing the war between 1914 and 1918. For generations that increasingly saw the war as immense folly it was necessary to explain how people could have been so stupid. As Gregory points out, 'No one stormed Buckingham Palace in 1917, but it was frequently used for garden parties for wounded soldiers.'[17] The British public remained substantially supportive of the war to the armistice, and part of the reason for this was that propagandists working for organisations like the NWAC did not actually spend their whole time bawling about bestial brutality, but provided discussion which directed familiar concepts to wartime purposes. Atrocities remained prominent in NWAC propaganda, but they were far from its be-all and end-all. By focusing on them without understanding the purpose they

---

17 Gregory, *Last Great War*, p. 136.

served within wider narratives, comprehension of their meaning is diluted rather than strengthened.

Considerable work remains to be done on the ways in which patriotic ideas and language shifted or remained constant across the war years – this study has only substantially addressed the work of one organisation, operating in the last months of the war. What this book has hopefully shown is the value of taking such patriotic language seriously as an expression of sentiments considered valid and meaningful by their proponents and at least some portions of the population at large. Rather than an 'obsolete' language, explorers of First World War patriotism may find a set of ideas that remained vibrant, relevant and resonant to those who lived through the period.

Local Case Studies

IN order to survey an adequate sample of propaganda in local areas, together with the related Speakers' Daily Reports, 30 local case studies were selected, using statistics from the card-index database.[1] A representative survey required that these constituencies should cover

1. varied regions (ten from each);
2. different types of social composition (and their numerical significance within each region);
3. different secretarial affiliations;
4. WACs established at varying times throughout their period of operations.

These four issues were all judged using the non-card-index data table (see appendix table 2.4). It also required examination of WACs of varying levels of activity. This was judged by the number of successful grant applications recorded in the Constituency economic activities table (see appendix table 2.3). An analysis of this data provided the following conclusions.

Regions and Constituency Classifications

The 'non-card-index data' table in the card-index database (see appendix table 2.4 for sample) shows that the three regions (as defined in that table) contained broadly similar numbers of constituencies, and much more similar numbers of constituencies with WACs:

1. North: 146 (108 with WACs; 107 excluding 1 unclassified constituency)
2. Midlands/Wales: 186 (120 with WACs; 113 excluding 7 unclassified constituencies)
3. London/South: 196 (116 with WACs)

---

1   A complete and accessible version of the database, together with further appendices and samples, is available in Monger, 'National War Aims Committee'.

Each region was, therefore, broken down to ten case studies each. The percentages of classification of constituencies with WACs were then taken into account in each region (ignoring unclassified constituencies). Smallest classifications potentially had to be ignored altogether in one region (for example, urban, mainly middle-class constituencies in the North). Percentages in parentheses are the percentage of each constituency with a WAC classification in a region, excluding unclassified constituencies.

North[2]
Urban working class: 3 (30.84%)
Urban mixed: 3 (25.23%)
Mining: 2 (19.63%)
Urban/rural: 1 (14.95%)
Rural: 1 (6.5%)
Urban middle class: 0 (2.8%) – since so small a percentage.

Midlands/Wales[3]
Rural: 3 (33.63%)
Urban mixed: 2 (18.58%)
Urban/rural: 2 (15.93%)
Mining: 1 (15.04%)
Urban working class: 1 (9.73%)
Urban middle class: 1 (7.08%)

London/South
Urban working class: 2 (21.55%)
Urban/Rural: 2 (20.69%)
Rural: 2 (19.83%)
Urban mixed: 2 (19.83%)
Urban middle class: 2 (18.10%)
Mining: 0 (0%)

Totals (percentage of constituencies with WACs, excluding unclassified)
Urban mixed: 7 (21.13%)
Urban working class: 6 (20.54%)
Rural: 6 (20.24%)
Urban/rural: 5 (17.26%)
Mining: 3 (11.31%)

---

2   Discrepancy with rural and middle-class constituencies was resolved by fitting to national totals.
3   Discrepancy for urban/rural and mining constituencies was resolved by comparing prospective numbers of classifications examined to national percentages.

Urban middle class: 3 (9.52%)
Total: 30 (100%)

These are, therefore, reasonable allocations of classification in each region. Rural constituencies are technically over-represented in the North but balanced by being under-represented in the Midlands.

Party Representation
Of 344 WACs, in 31 cases the party affiliations of the secretaries are unknown. Of the remaining 313: 295 (94.25%) had a Conservative representative; 281 (89.78%) had a Liberal representative; 27 (8.63%) had a Labour representative. Therefore: no more than 3 of the 30 case studies should have a Labour representative; no more than 1 or 2 of the 30 should not have a Conservative representative; no more than 3 of the 30 should not have a Liberal representative.

Further, of the 313 WACs with known affiliations: 238 (76.04%) comprised Conservative and Liberal reps; 32 (10.22%) were Conservative only; 22 (7.03%) were Conservative, Liberal and Labour; 16 (5.11%) were Liberal only; 3 (0.96%) were Unionist and Labour; 2 (0.64%) were Liberal and Labour. Therefore: at least 22 of the 30 case studies should be WACs with Conservative and Liberal secretaries; of the remaining 8, 3 should be Conservative only; the 3 WACs with Labour reps should have Conservative Liberal and Labour secretaries; 2 should be Liberal only.

Establishment Date Group
Of the 344 WACs the date of origin of 4 cannot be established. If the remaining 340 are divided into 3 groups of 4 months and 1 group of 5. These are: (1) July–October 1917; (2) November 1917–February 1918; (3) March–June 1918; and (4) July–November 1918. Of these, 230 (67.65%) were established in (1); 42 (12.35%) in (2); 27 (7.94%) in (3); 41 (12.06%) in (4). Therefore: at least 20 of the 30 case studies should have been established before 1 November 1917; 3 or 4 should have been established between 1 November 1 1917 and 28 February 1918; 2 should have been established between 1 March and 30 June 1918; 3 or 4 should have been established between 1 July and 11 November 1918.

Grants
About a third (10) of the case studies should only have received one grant from the NWAC, about a fifth (6) should have received two, and the others should be reasonably evenly spread between three and eight grants. Since the highest number of grants (12 to Forest of Dean) is so anomalous, it should be omitted.

With these requirements in mind, therefore, the following constituencies were selected for examination.

Appendix table 1.1 Northern case studies

Case study	Classification	Constituency	Party affiliations	Establishment group	Grants
1	Urban, w-c	Keighley	UL	Jul–Oct 17	2
2	Urban, w-c	St Helens	ULLA	Jul–Oct 17	2
3	Urban, w-c	Oldham	UL	Nov 17–Feb 18	1
4	Urban, mixed	Liverpool City	UL	Jul–Oct 17	1
5	Urban, mixed	Sheffield City	UL	Jul–Oct 17	1
6	Urban, mixed	Wakefield	UL	Jul–Oct 17	4
7	Mining	Wigan	U	Jul–Oct 17	3
8	Mining	Houghton-le-Spring	UL	Jul–Oct 17	4
9	Urban/Rural	Ripon	UL	Jul–Oct17	5
10	Rural	Holderness	UL	Jul–Nov18	3

Appendix table 1.2 Midlands/Wales case studies

Case study	Classification	Constituency	Party affiliations	Establishment group	Grants
1	Rural	Evesham	ULLA	Jul–Oct 17	7
2	Rural	Radnorshire	UNK	Jul–Oct 18	2
3	Rural	South West Norfolk	UL	Nov 17–Feb 18	1
4	Urban mixed	Lichfield	UL	Jul–Oct 17	3
5	Urban mixed	Ipswich	L	Nov 17–Feb 18	3
6	Urban/rural	Nuneaton	U	Mar–Jun 18	1
7	Urban/rural	Shrewsbury	UL	Jul–Nov 18	1
8	Mining	Rhondda	UL	Jul–Oct 17	2
9	Urban, w-c	Leicester	UL	Jul–Oct 17	8
10	Urban, m-c	Cheltenham	UL	Jul–Oct 17	4

Appendix table 1.3 London/South case studies

Case study	Classification	Constituency	Party affiliations	Establishment group	Grants
1	Urban, w-c	Battersea	U	Jul–Oct 17	3
2	Urban, w-c	Finsbury	UL	Jul–Oct 17	2
3	Urban/rural	St Albans	UL	Jul–Nov 18	1
4	Urban/rural	Barnstaple	UL	Jul–Oct 17	3
5	Rural	Bodmin South East Cornwall	UL	Nov 17–Feb 18	1
6	Rural	Chippenham	UL	Jul–Oct 17	5
7	Urban mixed	Croydon	ULLA	Mar–Jun 18	1
8	Urban mixed	South Dorset	UL	Jul–Oct 17	3
9	Urban, m-c	Dulwich	UL	Jul–Nov 18	1
10	Urban, m-c	Eastbourne	UL	Jul–Oct 17	2

APPENDIX 2

Card-Index Database

This database is constructed from the card-index contained in TNA:PRO T102/26.

Appendix table 2.1* 'Constituencies' card

Constituency	County/Borough	Con. before 1918?	Con. after 1918?	Evidence of Committee	Secretaries/contacts	Date began	Notes	Other evidence of Committee
Aberavon	Glamorganshire	no	yes	yes	T. Thomas (U); Edward Hopkin (L)	7/8/17	'Part of Rural Dist. of Neath, Penybont –P– Municipal Borough of Aberavon –P– Urban Dists. of Briton Ferry, Glencorwg, Margam, Porthcawl'; see also Mid Glamorgan entry (from which date began is taken)	no
Abertillery	Monmouthshire	no	yes	no			'Urban Dists. of Abercarn, Abertillery, Nantyglo, Blaina' No record of committee	no
Abingdon North Berks	Berkshire	yes	yes	yes	W. Bernthal; G. Hemming	5/10/17	'Rural Dists. of Abingdon, Wallingford, Wantage, part of Bradfield, Farindon –P– Municipal Boroughs of Abingdon, Wallingford –P– Urban Dist. of Wantage'	no
Accrington	Borough	yes	yes	yes	Mrs L. Hudson (U); F. Baker (L)	4/9/17	'Municipal Borough of Accrington –P– Urban Dists. of Church, Clayton-le-Moors, Oswaldtwistle, Rishton'	no
Acton	Middlesex	no	yes	no			'Urban Dist. of Acton' no record of committee (though might come up in London Boroughs section)	no
Aldershot	Hampshire	no	yes	yes	W.T. Mignot Tucker (U)	7/10/18	'Rural Dist. of Hartley Wintney –P– Urban Dists. of Aldershot, Farnborough, Fleet' WAC formed but may never have done anything owing to late date	no

Constituency	County					Date began	Constituency notes	
Altrincham	Cheshire	yes	yes	yes	F. Milne (U; later replaced); T. Bradbury (U); H. Hetherington (L).	17/4/18	'Part of Rural District: of Bucklow –P– Urban Dists. of Altrincham, Ashton-upon-Mersey, Bowdon, Cheadle and Gatley, Hale, Handforth, Lymm, Sale' May only have been an ad hoc committee	no
Andover	Hampshire West Hants	yes	no	no	F.C. Grant (L)		'Now merged in Basingstoke' See also Basingstoke entry	no
Anglesey	Anglesey	yes	yes	yes	O. Caewyn Roberts	2/9/18	'Administrative County of Anglesey'	no
Appleby	Westmorland	yes	no	no			'Now merged in Westmorland Division' See also Westmorland entry	no

*This sample contains the first ten entries in this table, from a total of 528. County/Borough: contains information relative to original card index. Records either in the counties section, in which case they have a county name, or in the Boroughs section (usually large towns), in which case they are to be labelled 'Borough' (although London Boroughs, Welsh counties and Scotland are also in this section, they have their own designations). Constituency before/after 1918: all information for this is based upon Kinnear, *The British Voter*. Evidence of committee: Evidence of Committee means there was some evidence that a Committee was formed and active. This does not include examples where constituency political party representatives met and decided a campaign was unnecessary (however, it does include examples such as St Austell, which explicitly state that a WAC has been set up, but does not think campaign is necessary). Date began: contains the date on which the committee was apparently formed, rather than necessarily the first entry on the activities/economic activities cards. In some cases may simply refer to the first (or only) date on the activities card, if no explicit reference can be found. No record/s of committee/constituency: in Constituency notes column. Refers only to constituencies with no activity/economic activity card records at all. Does not refer to those constituencies where NWAC was told they weren't interested in forming a committee, which instead may begin 'Now merged with'. These quotations are typed on the index card for the constituency. –P– represents a paragraph break on the original card. Constituencies notes: *see also*: where constituencies merge into others in 1918, 'see also' refers to a relevant corresponding constituency, usually relating to issues of constituency boundary redistribution, regardless of whether link leads to any interesting information. Other evidence of Committee: this field exists to reflect the discrepancy between the card-index data and evidence from a list of WACs in T102/18. Those constituencies that appear on this list are recorded as other evidence. When citing statistics from the database, it should be noted that these possible WACs existed, but have not been included in the statistics as evidence not from the card index, except those for which there was already evidence of a WAC (where the letter prompted an altered establishment date, for instance).

Appendix table 2.2 * 'Constituency activities' card

actID	Constituency	Date	Activity/correspondence	Notes
1	Bedford	01/10/1917	formation of Committee	
2	Bedford	17/10/1917	report of plans	'M.P. Bowles - decided to hold Mass meeting in the Corn Exchange – to hold dinner hour meetings in all the works – house to house distribution of literature also in Cinemas.'
3	Bedford	23/10/1917	estimate enclosure	re meetings
4	Bedford	07/12/1917	details of Committee	2 enclosures of list of members (by Bowles and G. Lee Roberts)
5	Bedford	18/01/1918	estimate enclosure	re distribution of literature
6	Bedford	19/01/1918	progress report	re campaign (unspecified)
7	Biggleswade North Beds	01/10/1917	formation of Committee	should be 1st in the list
8	Biggleswade North Beds	06/10/1917	report of plans	meetings to begin on 19/10. Entry for 1/10/1917 should be 1st on list (actID 7)
9	Biggleswade North Beds	12/10/1917	report of plans	meetings to begin on 22/10
10	Biggleswade North Beds	15/01/1918	estimate enclosure	re distribution of literature

*This sample contains the first ten entries in this table, from a total of 2382. **actID**: these are code numbers attached to the database to assist calculations in queries (primary keys). They do not appear on the card itself. **Activity classifications**: these are standardised to a degree; i.e. 'letter', 'formation of Committee', 'WAC not required', 'estimate enclosure' etc. The difference between 'letter' and 'correspondence with NWAC': 'letter' = fairly banal correspondence, mostly before formation of Committee, can also be used to represent phone call, telegram etc. (recorded in notes); 'correspondence' = ongoing discussion with NWAC, often haggling over estimates etc. The various standardised terms used in this column are: correspondence with NWAC; details of Committee; estimate enclosure; formation of Committee; letter; literature request; open-air form returned; progress report; report of plans; report of situation; WAC not required; other (left blank). **Activity notes**: where notes mention a list enclosed (e.g. list of members/list of meetings planned etc.), unless the list is given in the notes field, means that the existence of the list was mentioned in the card entry.

Appendix table 2.3* 'Constituency economic activities' card

econID	Constituency	Period start	Period end	Estimate	Reason	Grant	Notes
1	Bedford			£46	meetings	none	estimate for '2 or 3 meetings daily[,] 1 Mass meeting Oct: 24' no dates for this record
2	Bedford			£10	distribution of literature	£10	
3	Biggleswade North Beds	19/10/17	7/11/17	£60	meetings	£35	
4	Biggleswade North Beds			£15	distribution of literature	£15	no dates
5	Luton South Beds						no card attached to this file
6	Mid Bedford	15/7/18	31/7/18	£32–35	none given	none	
7	Mid Bedford	1/9/18		£26	none given	£26	unspecified fortnight in September, not necessarily 1st
8	Abingdon North Berks	1/11/17	5/12/17	£56	meetings	£45	20 meetings planned
9	Abingdon North Berks			£12–100	distribution of literature	£12–100	no dates
10	Abingdon North Berks			£20	other special day (specify in notes)	£20	France's Day

*This sample contains the first ten entries in this table, from a total of 1012. **econID:** database code numbers (primary keys). **Economic activities:** there are 16 types of economic activity used in the database: Meetings (explicitly named as meetings on card); Special meeting (speaker named); Mass meeting; Distribution of literature; Lantern lectures; Cinemotor; Conference; Special Campaign; War Anniversary (this refers to arrangements made for events on 4 August 1918, in response to suggestion by the NWAC central organisation); Other special day (specify in notes) (this usually refers to France's Day – 12 July 1918 – and is recorded in notes column); Postage; Printing; amended estimate; none given; other (specify in notes); Meetings (likely) (inferred from Activities card). **Economic activities notes:** when no dates are attached to an estimate on the Constituency economic activities card, there is often an estimated date attached, which will relate to an entry in the Constituency activities card. Usually the date (c. ?/?/?) will refer to the date of the activity on the Activities card, unless there is any more explicit evidence of planned dates of activity.

Appendix table 2.4* Non-card-index data

CID	Constituency	Establishment group	Classification	Blewett?	Turner?	Region	Secretaries/contacts
1	Abingdon North Berks	Jul–Oct 17	R	yes	yes	London/South	UNK
2	Newbury	Jul–Oct 17	R	yes	yes	London/South	UNK
3	Windsor	Nov 17–Feb 18	UMC	yes	yes	London/South	UL
4	Wokingham	Jul–Oct 17	R	yes	no	London/South	UL
5	Aylesbury Mid Bucks	no WAC	R	yes	yes	Midlands/Wales	UL
6	Buckingham	Nov 17–Feb 18	R	yes	yes	Midlands/Wales	UL
7	Wycombe	no WAC	UR	yes	no	Midlands/Wales	L
8	Cambridge-shire	unknown	R	no	yes	Midlands/Wales	L
9	Chesterton West Cambs	Nov 17–Feb 18	R	yes	no	Midlands/Wales	L
10	Newmarket East Cambs	no WAC	R	yes	no	Midlands/Wales	U

* This sample contains the first ten entries in this table, from a total of 528. This data was compiled to assist in the selection of local case studies (see appendix 1) after the construction of the main data tables. **CID**: database code numbers (primary keys). **Establishment group**: constituencies were assigned one of six 'establishment groups', depending upon the date on which they formed a WAC, where known. **Classification**: contains details of each constituency's classification, based on those supplied by either Neal Blewett, *The Peers, the Parties and the People: The General Elections of 1910* (London: MacMillan, 1972), pp. 488–94; or John Turner, *British Politics and the Great War: Coalition and Conflict, 1915–1918* (New Haven: Yale University Press, 1992); or both, where they agree. Where there is disagreement, classification will depend either on their establishment date or whether they are a new constituency etc. As a general rule, WACs formed up to the end of February 1918 will follow Blewett. Those thereafter will follow Turner, in case of disagreement with note of disagreement (but not lack of information). The 'Blewett' and 'Turner' columns indicate where the attribution has been taken from. Discrepancies are recorded in the notes column. **Region**: each constituency/regional WAC was assigned to a region, based upon map 4 in Kinnear, *British Voter*. All constituencies/WACs north of the southern boundary of Cheshire or Yorkshire are categorised 'North'; all south of Cheshire and Yorkshire and north of the northern boundary of Somerset, Wiltshire, Berkshire, Hertfordshire and Essex are categorised 'Midlands/Wales'; all others are categorised 'London/South'. **Secretaries/contacts**: each constituency/WAC was categorised according to the affiliations of its secretaries. The eight alternatives are: U (Unionist only); L (Liberal only); LA (Labour only); UL (Unionist and Liberal); ULA (Unionist and Labour); LLA (Liberal and Labour); ULLA (Unionist, Liberal and Labour); UNK (Unknown).

Bibliography

Unpublished Primary Material

National Archives
T102/1–26: Papers of the National War Aims Committee.
CAB 23 and 24: War Cabinet Minutes and Papers.
HO45/10741/263275: Files relating to 'Anti-Recruiting and Peace Propaganda'.
HO139/35/146–47: Press Bureau files relating to NWAC.
INF4: Papers relating to the Ministry of Information and First World War Propaganda.
PRO30/69: J. Ramsay MacDonald Papers.
T1/12519: Files related to 'British National Film'.
T1/12292: Post-War Report on Ministry of Information and NWAC.
WO106/367: Papers of the Parliamentary Recruiting Committee.

Parliamentary Archives
Beaverbrook Papers.
Hannon Papers.
Lloyd George Papers.

London School of Economics Library
Harry Brittain Papers.
Labour Party Conference Reports.
Leicester ILP Journals.
E.D. Morel Papers.

Senate House Library, University of London
GB 0096 MS 1112 – Playne collection.

Keighley Public Library
BK424: H.A. France, Notebooks and scrapbooks concerning Keighley and the First
    World War.

Published Primary Material

Parliamentary Debates

National Archives Library
Reality (NWAC Weekly Newspaper).
NWAC Pamphlets (5 vols).

Bodleian Library
Welcome.

British Library
NWAC Pamphlets, calendars.
Archives of British Liberal Party: National Liberal Federation Reports.
Archives of British Conservative and Unionist Party: Minutes of National Union
   Executive Committee.
Archives of British Conservative and Unionist Party: *Conservative Agents' Journal.*

British Library Newspaper Archive (Colindale)

National publications
Britannia.
British Citizen and Empire Worker.
The British Weekly.
The Church Times.
The Clarion.
Common Sense.
The Daily Chronicle.
The Daily Express.
The Daily Mail.
The Daily News & Leader.
The Daily Telegraph.
John Bull.
Justice.
Labour Leader.
The Manchester Guardian.
The Morning Post.
The Nation.
The New Age.
The Times.
Workers' Dreadnought.

Local publications
The Battersea Boro' News.
Brecon & Radnor Express, Carmarthen and Swansea Valley Gazette and Brynmawr
   District Advertiser.
The Bromsgrove, Droitwich & Redditch Weekly Messenger, County Journal and General
   Advertiser.
The Central Wales News, Radnorshire Standard and Llandrindod Wells Gazette.
The Cheltenham Chronicle and Gloucestershire Graphic.
The Cornish Times and General Advertiser.
Coulsdon & Purley Weekly Record.
The Croydon Advertiser and Surrey County Reporter.
The Croydon Times.
Dereham & Fakenham Times.
Downham Market Gazette.
The Droitwich Guardian, and Brine Bath Visitors' Record.
East Anglian Daily Times.
Eastbourne Chronicle.
The Eastbourne Gazette.
Evening Star and Daily Herald.
The Evesham Journal and Four Shires Advertiser.
Evesham Standard & West Midland Observer.
The Finsbury Weekly News, Clerkenwell Chronicle & St. Luke's Examiner.
The Harrogate Advertiser.
Harrogate and Claro Times, Knaresborough and Ridderdale Guardian.

The Harrogate Herald.
The Holborn and Finsbury Guardian.
The Ilfracombe Chronicle.
The Ilfracombe Gazette and Observer.
The Illustrated Leicester Chronicle.
Glamorgan Free Press, Pontypridd, Rhondda and Caerphilly Chronicles.
The Gloucestershire Echo.
The Keighley News.
Leicester Advertiser for the Midland and Adjoining Counties.
The Leicester Catholic News.
The Leicester Daily Mercury.
The Leicester Daily Post.
The Leicester Pioneer.
The Liverpool Catholic Herald.
The Liverpool Courier.
The Liverpool Daily Post & Mercury.
The Liverpool Echo.
The Looker-on. A Social, Political and Fashionable Review for Cheltenham and County.
Mid-Rhondda Gazette.
North Devon Herald.
North Devon Journal.
North Wilts. Guardian.
The Norwood Press and Dulwich Advertiser.
The Nuneaton Chronicle.
Nuneaton Observer.
The Radnor Express.
The Rhondda Leader, Maesteg, Garw & Ogmore Telegraph.
The Ripon Gazette; Thirsk, Bedale, and Northallerton Times, West and North Yorkshire Advertiser.
The Ripon Observer.
The Saltash Gazette.
The Seaham Weekly News, and Seaton, Murton, Hetton, Rainton and Houghton-le-Spring Advertiser.
The Sheffield Catholic Herald.
The Sheffield Daily Telegraph.
Sheffield Independent.
The Shrewsbury Chronicle.
The Southern Times and Dorset County Herald.
The Swanage and Wareham Guardian, Visitors' Directory, and Dorset and Hampshire Advertiser.
Thetford & Watton Times.
The Wakefield Advertiser & Gazette.
The Wakefield Express.
The Weymouth & Portland Standard.
Weymouth Telegram, Abbotsbury, Broadwey, Upwey and Wyke Regis Express.
The Wigan Examiner.
The Wigan Observer and District Advertiser.
Wilts. and Gloucestershire Standard, and Cirencester and Swindon Express.
Yorkshire Telegraph and Star.

Leicestershire, Leicester and Rutland Record Office
The Leicester Mail.

Other Published Primary Material

Addison, Christopher, *Four And a Half Years: A Personal Diary from June 1914 to January 1919*, 2 vols, London: Hutchinson & Co., 1934.
Aston, Sir George, 'Propaganda – and the Father of It', *Cornhill Magazine*, vol. 48, no. 284, 1920, 233–41.
'Authorship unacknowledged', *Narrow Waters: The First Volume of the Life and Thoughts of a Common Man*, London: William Hodge, 1935.
Bradley, F.H., *The Limits of Individual and National Self-Sacrifice,* pamphlet reprinted from the *International Journal of Ethics*, n.p.d., 1894.
Brittain, Sir Harry, *Pilgrims and Pioneers*, London: Hutchinson, 1945.
Cooper, Rev. John, *Self-Sacrifice: The Grandest Manifestation of the Divine, and the True Principle of Christian Life; or, The Lost Power of Christian Zeal Restored to the Church*, London: Hodder & Stoughton, 1880.
Denman, Sir Richard, *Political Sketches*, Carlisle: Charles Thurnam & Sons, 1948.
Dutton, David J. (ed.), *Odyssey of an Edwardian Liberal: The Political Diary of Richard Durning Holt*, Gloucester: Allan Sutton Publishing, 1989.
Gosling, Harry, *Up and Down Stream*, London: Methuen, 1927.
Hancock, W.K. and Van der Poel, Jean (eds), *Selections from the Smuts Papers*, vol. 3, *June 1910–November 1918,* 7 vols, Cambridge: Cambridge University Press, 1966.
Hobson, J.A., *The War in South Africa: Its Causes and Effects*, London: J. Nisbet & Co., 1900.
Houston, Henry J., *The Real Horatio Bottomley*, London: Hurst & Blackett, n.d. (1923).
Jones, David, *In Parenthesis*, London: Faber & Faber, 1937.
Lloyd George, David, *War Memoirs of David Lloyd George*, 6 vols, London: Ivor Nicholson & Watson, 1933–36.
McCarthy, Desmond (ed.), *H.H.A.: Letters to a Friend, First Series, 1915–1922*, London: Geoffrey Bles, 1933.
MacIver, R.M., *Community: A Sociological Study: Being an Attempt to Set Out the Nature and Fundamental Laws of Social Life*, 4th edn, London: Frank Cass, 1970 (1917).
Milner, Lord, G.C.B., *The Nation and the Empire, Being a Collection of Speeches and Addresses: with an Introduction by Lord Milner, G.C.B.*, London: Constable and Company, 1913.
Newton, Arthur, *Years of Change: Autobiography of a Hackney Shoemaker*, London: Centerprise Publications, 1974.
Playne, Caroline E., *Britain Holds On: 1917, 1918*, London: George Allen & Unwin, 1933.
Ramsden, John (ed.), *Real Old Tory Politics: The Political Diaries of Sir Robert Sanders, Lord Bayford, 1910–35*, London: The Historians' Press, 1984.
Roberts, Robert, *The Classic Slum: Salford Life in the First Quarter of the Century*, Manchester: Manchester University Press, 1971.
Rowse, A.L., *A Cornish Childhood*, London: Jonathan Cape, 1942.
Sheehan, D.D., *Ireland Since Parnell*, London: Daniel O'Connor, 1921.
Society for Promoting Christian Knowledge, *Self-Sacrifice*, tract no. 1653, London: SPCK, (1872).
Thomas, Edward, *The South Country*, London: Everyman and J.M. Dent, 1993 (1909).
Thompson, Basil, *The Scene Changes*, Garden City, NY: Doubleday, Doran & Co., 1937.
White, Arnold, *Efficiency and Empire*, ed. G.R. Searle, Brighton: Harvester Press, 1973 (1901).
Wilson, Trevor, *The Political Diaries of C.P. Scott, 1911–1928*, London: Collins, 1970.

Secondary Material

Anderson, Benedict, *Imagined Communities: Reflections on the Origin and Spread of Nationalism*, rev. edn, London: Verso, 1991.

Anderson, Olive, 'The Growth of Christian Militarism in Mid-Victorian Britain', *English Historical Review*, vol. 86, no. 338, 1971, 46–72.

Anderson, Stuart, *Race and Rapprochement: Anglo-Saxonism and Anglo–American Relations, 1895–1904*, London: Associated University Presses, 1981.

Andrews, Katherine, 'The Necessity to Conform: British Jingoism in the First World War', *The Dalhousie Review*, vol. 53, no. 2, 1973, pp. 227–245.

Appadurai, Arjun, 'Disjuncture and Difference in the Global Cultural Economy', *Public Culture*, vol. 2, no. 2, 1990, 1–24.

Armitage, F.P., *Leicester 1914–1918: The War-Time Story of a Midland Town*, Leicester: Edgar Backus, 1933.

Arslanian, Artin H, 'British Wartime Pledges, 1917–19: The Armenian Case', *Journal of Contemporary History*, vol. 13, 1978, 517–29.

Audoin-Rouzeau, Stéphane and Becker, Annette, *1914–1918: Understanding the Great War*, trans. Catherine Temerson, London: Profile Books, 2002.

Auerbach, Sascha, 'Negotiating Nationalism: Jewish Conscription and Russian Repatriation in London's East End, 1916–1918', *Journal of British Studies*, vol. 46, no. 3, 2007, 596–620.

Badsey, Stephen, 'Press, Propaganda and Public Perceptions', in Michael Howard (ed.), *A Part of History: Aspects of the British Experience of the First World War*, London: Continuum, 2008, 27–35.

Barnett, Correlli, *The Audit of War: The Illusion & Reality of Britain as a Great Nation*, London: Macmillan, 1986.

Beazley, Ben, *Four Years Remembered: Leicester during the Great War*, Derby: Breedon Books, 1999.

Becker, Annette, *War and Faith: The Religious Imagination in France, 1914–1930*, trans. Helen McPhail, Oxford: Berg, 1998.

Becker, Jean-Jacques, *The Great War and the French People*, trans. Arnold Pomerans, Oxford: Berg, 1993.

Behlmer, George K. and Leventhal, Fred M., *Singular Continuities: Tradition, Nostalgia, and Identity in Modern British Culture*, Stanford, CA: Stanford University Press, 2000.

Behrman, Cynthia Fansler, *Victorian Myths of the Sea*, Athens, OH: University of Ohio Press, 1977.

Bell, Duncan and Sylvest, Casper, 'International Society in Victorian Political Thought: T.H. Green, Herbert Spencer, and Henry Sidgwick', *Modern Intellectual History*, vol. 3, no. 2, 2006, 207–38.

Ben Amos, Avner, 'The *Marseillaise* as Myth and Metaphor: The Transfer of Rouget de Lisle to the Invalides during the Great War', in Valerie Holman and Debra Kelly (eds), *France at War in the Twentieth Century: Propaganda, Myth and Metaphor*, Oxford: Berghahn Books, 2000, 27–48.

Bennett, Jessica and Hampton, Mark, 'World War I and the Anglo-American Imagined Community: Civilization vs. Barbarism in British Propaganda and American Newspapers', in Joel H. Wiener and Mark Hampton (eds), *Anglo-American Media Interactions, 1850–2000*, Basingstoke: Palgrave MacMillan, 2007, 155–75.

Bentley, Michael, *The Liberal Mind, 1914–1929*, Cambridge: Cambridge University Press, 1977.

Bet-El, Ilana R., 'Men and Soldiers: British Conscripts, Concept of Masculinity, and the Great War', in Billie Melman (ed.), *Borderlines: Genders and Identities in War and Peace, 1870–1930*, New York: Routledge, 1998, 73–94.

Bet-El, Ilana R., *Conscripts: Forgotten Men of the Great War*, 2nd edn, Stroud: Sutton Publishing, 2003.

Betts, Robin, *Dr Macnamara, 1861–1931*, Liverpool: Liverpool University Press, 1999.

Billig, Michael, *Banal Nationalism*, London: Sage, 1995.

Blewett, Neal, *The Peers, the Parties and the People: The General Elections of 1910*, London: MacMillan, 1972.

Bloxham, Donald, 'The Armenian Genocide of 1915–1916: Cumulative Radicalization and the Development of a Destruction Policy', *Past & Present*, vol. 181, 2003, 141–91.

Bloxham, Donald, *The Great Game of Genocide: Imperialism, Nationalism, and the Destruction of the Ottoman Armenians*, Oxford: Oxford University Press, 2005.

Bourke, Joanna, *Dismembering the Male: Men's Bodies, Britain and the Great War*, London: Reaktion Books, 1996.

Brace, Catherine, 'Finding England Everywhere: Regional Identity and the Construction of National Identity, 1890–1940', *Ecumene*, vol. 6, no. 1, Jan. 1999, 90–109.

Braybon, Gail, *Women Workers in the First World War*, London: Routledge, 1989 (1981).

Burk, Kathleen, 'The Diplomacy of Finance: British Financial Missions to the United States 1914–1918', *The Historical Journal*, vol. 22, no. 2, 1979, 351–72.

Burk, Kathleen, *Britain, America and the Sinews of War, 1914–18*, London: Allen & Unwin, 1985.

Burton, Antoinette, 'New Narratives of Imperial Politics in the Nineteenth Century', in Catherine Hall and Sonya O. Rose (eds), *At Home with the Empire: Metropolitan Culture and the Imperial World*, Cambridge: Cambridge University Press, 2006, 212–29.

Buitenhuis, Peter, *The Great War of Words: Literature as Propaganda, 1914–18 and after*, London: B.T. Batsford, 1989.

Cain, P.J., *Hobson and Imperialism: Radicalism, New Liberalism, and Finance 1887–1938*, Oxford: Oxford University Press, 2002.

Carsten, F.L., *War against War: British and German Radical Movements in the First World War*, London: Batsford Academic and Educational, 1982.

Ceadel, Martin, *Pacifism in Britain, 1914–1945: The Defining of a Faith*, Oxford: Clarendon Press, 1980.

Cecil, Hugh and Liddle, Peter (eds), *Facing Armageddon: The First World War Experienced*, London: Leo Cooper, 1996.

Chambers, Frank P., *The War behind the War, 1914–1918: A History of the Political and Civilian Fronts*, New York: Arno Press, 1972 (1939).

Chickering, Roger, *The Great War and Urban Life in Germany: Freiburg, 1914–1918*, Cambridge: Cambridge University Press, 2007.

Chickering, Roger and Förster, Stig (eds), *Great War, Total War: Combat and Mobilization on the Western Front, 1914–1918*, Cambridge: Cambridge University Press, 2000.

Clark, Anna, 'Manhood, Womanhood, and the Politics of Class in Britain, 1790–1845', in Laura L. Frader and Sonya O. Rose (eds), *Gender and Class in Modern Europe*, Ithaca, NY: Cornell University Press, 1996, 263–79.

Clark, J.C.D., 'Protestantism, Nationalism, and National Identity, 1660–1832', *The Historical Journal*, vol. 43, no. 1, 2000, 249–76.

Coetzee, Frans, *For Party or Country: Nationalism and the Dilemmas of Popular Conservatism in Edwardian England*, Oxford: Oxford University Press, 1990.

Coetzee, Frans and Shevin-Coetzee, Marilyn (eds), *Authority, Identity and the Social History of the Great War*, Providence: Berghahn Books, 1995.

Colclough, Stephen, '"No such bookselling has ever before taken place in this country." Propaganda and the Wartime Distribution Practices of W.H. Smith & Son', in Mary Hammond and Shafquat Towheed (eds), *Publishing in the First World War: Essays in Book History*, Basingstoke: Palgrave MacMillan, 2007, 27–45.

Colley, Linda, 'Britishness and Otherness: An Argument', *Journal of British Studies*, vol. 31, no. 4, October 1992, 309–29.

Colley, Linda, *Britons: Forging the Nation, 1707–1837*, London: Pimlico, 2003 (1992).

Colls, Robert, 'Englishness and the Political Culture', in Robert Colls and Philip Dodd (eds), *Englishness: Politics and Culture, 1880–1920*, London: Croom Helm, 1986, 29–61.

Colls, Robert, 'The Constitution of the English', *History Workshop Journal*, vol. 46, 1998, 97–127.

Colls, Robert, *Identity of England*, Oxford: Oxford University Press, 2002.

Colls, Robert and Dodd, Philip (eds), *Englishness: Politics and Culture, 1880–1920*, London: Croom Helm, 1986.

Confino, Alon, *The Nation as a Local Metaphor: Württemberg, Imperial Germany, and National Memory, 1871–1918*, Chapel Hill, NC: University of North Carolina Press, 1997.

Cottrell, Stella, 'The Devil on Two Sticks: Franco-phobia in 1803', in Raphael Samuel (ed.), *Patriotism: The Making and Unmaking of British National Identity*, vol. 1, *History and Politics*, London: Routledge, 1989, 259–74.

Cragoe, Matthew, '"We Like Local Patriotism": The Conservative Party and the Discourse of Decentralisation, 1947–51', *English Historical Review*, vol. 122, no. 498, 965–85.

Craig, F.W.S., *British Parliamentary Election Results, 1918–1949*, rev. edn, Basingstoke: Macmillan Press, 1977.

Crary, Jonathan, *Suspensions of Perception: Attention, Spectacle, and Modern Culture*, Cambridge, MA: MIT Press, 1999.

Cubitt, Geoffrey (ed.), *Imagining Nations*, Manchester: Manchester University Press, 1998.

Cubitt, Geoffrey and Warren, Allen (eds), *Heroic Reputations and Exemplary Lives*, Manchester: Manchester University Press, 2000.

Cunningham, Hugh, 'The Language of Patriotism, 1750–1914', *History Workshop Journal*, vol. 12, 1981, 8–33; repr. as 'The Language of Patriotism', in Raphael Samuel (ed.), *Patriotism, The Making and Unmaking of British National Identity*, vol. 1, *History and Politics*, London: Routledge, 1989, 57–89.

Curtis, L.P., 'Moral and Physical Force: The Language of Violence in Irish Nationalism', *Journal of British Studies*, vol. 27, no. 2, 1988, 150–89.

Curtis, L.P., *Apes and Angels: The Irishman in Victorian Caricature*, rev. edn, Washington and London: Smithsonian Institution Press, 1997.

Daniel, Ute, *The War from Within: German Working-class Women in the First World War*, Oxford: Berg, 1997.

David, Edward, 'The Liberal Party Divided, 1916–1918', *The Historical Journal*, vol. 13, no. 3, 1970, 509–33.

Davidoff, Leonore, *Worlds Apart: Historical Perspectives on Gender & Class*, Cambridge: Polity Press, 1995.

Davidoff, Leonore, L'Esperance, Jeanne and Newby, Howard, 'Landscape with Figures: Home and Community in English Society' (1976), in Leonore Davidoff, *Worlds Between: Historical Perspectives on Class and Gender*, Cambridge: Polity Press, 1995, 41–72.

Davin, Anna, 'Imperialism and Motherhood', *History Workshop Journal*, vol. 5, 1978, 9–65.

Dawson, Graham, *Soldier Heroes: British Adventure, Empire and the Imagining of Masculinities*, London: Routledge, 1994.

DeGroot, Gerard J., *Blighty: British Society in the Era of the Great War*, London: Longman, 1996.

Delap, Lucy, '"Thus Does Man Prove His Fitness to Be the Master of Things": Shipwrecks, Chivalry and Masculinity in Nineteenth- and Twentieth-Century Britain', *Cultural and Social History*, vol. 3, no. 1, 2006, 45–74.

Douglas, Roy, 'Voluntary Enlistment in the First World War and the Work of the Parliamentary Recruiting Committee', *Journal of Modern History*, vol. 42, no. 4, 1970, 564–85.

Douglas, Roy, 'The National Democratic Party and the British Workers' League', *The Historical Journal*, vol. 15, no. 3, 1972, 533–552.

Douglas, Roy, 'Britain and the Armenian Question, 1894–7', *Historical Journal*, vol. 19, no. 1, 1976, 113–33.

Dubow, Saul, 'Smuts, the United Nations and the Rhetoric of Race and Rights', *Journal of Contemporary History*, vol. 43, no. 1, 2008, 45–74.

Dyck, Ian, 'Local Attachments, National Identities and World Citizenship in the Thought of Thomas Paine', *History Workshop Journal*, vol. 35, 1993, 117–35.

Eastwood, David, *Government and Community in the English Provinces, 1700–1870*, Basingstoke: MacMillan, 1997.

Englander, David, 'Soldiering and Identity: Reflections on the Great War', *War in History*, vol. 1, no. 3, 1994, 300–18.

Epstein, James, '"America" in the Victorian Cultural Imagination', in Fred M. Leventhal and Roland Quinault (eds), *Anglo-American Attitudes: From Revolution to Partnership*, Aldershot: Ashgate, 2000, 106–23.

Farrar Jr, L.L., 'Nationalism in Wartime: Critiquing the Conventional Wisdom', in Frans Coetzee and Marilyn Shevin-Coetzee (eds), *Authority, Identity and the Social History of the Great War*, Providence: Berghahn Books, 1995, 133–51.

Feldman, David, *Englishmen and Jews: Social Relations and Political Culture, 1840–1914*, New Haven: Yale University Press, 1994.

Felstead, S. Theodore, *Horatio Bottomley: A Biography of an Outstanding Personality*, London: John Murray, 1936.

Ferguson, Niall, *The Pity of War*, London: Allen Lane, 1998.

Ferguson, Niall, *The War of the World: History's Age of Hatred*, London: Allen Lane, 2006.

Finn, Michael, 'Local Heroes: War News and the Construction of "Community" in Britain, 1914–18', *Historical Research*, vol. 83, no. 221, 2010, 379–408.

Flood, P.J., *France 1914–18: Public Opinion and the War Effort*, Basingstoke: MacMillan, 1990.

Förster, Stig, 'Introduction', in Roger Chickering and Stig Förster (eds), *Great War, Total War: Combat and Mobilization on the Western Front, 1914–1918*, Cambridge: Cambridge University Press, 2000, 1–15.

Frantzen, Allen J., *Bloody Good: Chivalry, Sacrifice and the Great War*, Chicago and London: University of Chicago Press, 2004.

Freeden, Michael, *The New Liberalism: An Ideology of Social Reform*, Oxford: Clarendon Press, 1978.

French, David, 'Who Knew What and When? The French Army Mutinies and the British Decision to Launch the Third Battle of Ypres', in Lawrence Freedman, Paul Hayes and Robert O'Neill (eds), *War, Strategy and International Politics: Essays in Honour of Michael Howard*, Oxford: Clarendon Press, 1992, 133–53.

French, David, *The Strategy of the Lloyd George Coalition, 1916–1918*, Oxford: Clarendon Press, 1995.

Friedberg, Aaron L., *The Weary Titan: Britain and the Experience of Relative Decline*, Princeton: Princeton University Press, 1988.

Fuller, J.G., *Troop Morale and Popular Culture in the British and Dominion Armies, 1914–1918*, Oxford: Clarendon Press, 1991.

Fussell, Paul, *The Great War and Modern Memory*, London: Oxford University Press, 1975.

Garrard, John, *Democratisation in Britain: Elites, Civil Society and Reform since 1800*, Basingstoke: Palgrave, 2002.

Giddens, Anthony (ed.), *Durkheim on Politics and the State*, Cambridge: Polity, 1986.

Girard, René, *Violence and the Sacred*, trans. Patrick Gregory, Baltimore and London: Johns Hopkins University Press, 1979 (1972).

Girard, René, *The Girard Reader*, ed. James G. Williams, New York: The New York Publishing Company, 1996.

Girouard, Mark, *The Return to Camelot: Chivalry and the English Gentleman*, London: Yale University Press, 1981.

Goldfarb Marquis, Alice, 'Words as Weapons: Propaganda in Britain and Germany during the First World War', *Journal of Contemporary History*, vol. 13, 1978, 467–98.

Good, Kit, 'England Goes to War, 1914–15', PhD dissertation, University of Liverpool, 2002.

Gough, Paul, *A Terrible Beauty: British Artists in the First World War*, Bristol: Sansom & Company, 2010.

Grainger, J.H., *Patriotisms: Britain, 1900–1939*, London: Routledge & Kegan Paul, 1986.

Grayzel, Susan R., *Women's Identities at War: Gender, Motherhood, and Politics in Britain and France during the First World War*, Chapel Hill, NC: University of North Carolina Press, 1999.

Gregory, Adrian, 'British "War Enthusiasm" in 1914: A Reassessment', in Gail Braybon (ed.), *Evidence, History and the Great War*, Oxford: Berghahn Books, 2003, 67–85.

Gregory, Adrian, 'A Clash of Cultures: The British Press and the Opening of the Great War', in Troy R.E. Paddock (ed.), *A Call to Arms: Propaganda, Public Opinion, and Newspapers in the Great War*, London: Praeger, 2004, 15–49.

Gregory, Adrian, *The Last Great War: British Society and the First World War*, Cambridge: Cambridge University Press, 2008.

Green, E.H.H., *An Age of Transition: British Politics 1880–1914*, Edinburgh: Edinburgh University Press for the Parliamentary History Yearbook Trust, 1997.

Grieves, Keith, *The Politics of Manpower, 1914–18*, Manchester: Manchester University Press, 1988.

Grieves, Keith, 'The Propinquity of Place: Home, Landscape and Soldier Poets of the First World War', in Jessica Meyer (ed.), *British Popular Culture and the First World War*, Leiden: Brill, 2008, 21–46.

Grieves, Keith, 'War Comes to the Fields: Sacrifice, Localism and Ploughing Up the English Countryside in 1917', in Ian F.W. Beckett (ed.), *1917: Beyond the Western Front*, Leiden: Brill, 2009, 159–76.

Griffiths, Clare, 'Noel Buxton (Lord Noel-Buxton of Aylsham)', in Greg Rosen (ed.), *Dictionary of Labour Biography*, London: Politico's, 2001, 94–96.

Grimley, Matthew, 'MacIver, Robert Morrison (1882–1970)', in *Oxford Dictionary of National Biography*, Oxford: Oxford University Press, 2004, www.oxforddnb.com (accessed 26 June 2007).

Gullace, Nicoletta F, 'White Feathers and Wounded Men: Female Patriotism and the Memory of the Great War', *Journal of British Studies*, vol. 36, 1997, 178–206.

Gullace, Nicoletta F., *'The Blood of Our Sons': Men, Women, and the Renegotiation of British Citizenship during the Great War*, Basingstoke: Macmillan, 2002.

Gullace, Nicoletta F., 'Friends, Aliens and Enemies: Fictive Communities and the Lusitania Riots of 1915', *Journal of Social History*, vol. 39, no. 2, 2005, 345–67.

Hallifax, Stuart, '"Over by Christmas": British Popular Opinion and the Short War in 1914', *First World War Studies*, vol. 1, no. 2, 2010, 103–21.

Hall, Catherine, *Civilising Subjects: Metropole and Colony in the English Imagination, 1830–1867*, Cambridge: Polity, 2002.

Hall, Catherine, McClelland, Keith and Rendall, Jane, *Defining the Victorian Nation: Class, Race, Gender and the British Reform Act of 1867*, Cambridge: Cambridge University Press, 2000.

Hall, Catherine and Rose, Sonya O., *At Home with the Empire: Metropolitan Culture and the Imperial World*, Cambridge: Cambridge University Press, 2006.

Hall, Stuart and Schwarz, Bill, 'State and Society, 1880–1930', in Mary Langan and Bill Schwarz (eds), *Crises in the British State, 1880–1930*, London: Hutchinson, 1985, 7–32.

Hamilton, Malcolm B., 'Sociological Dimensions in Christian Millenarianism', in Stephen Hunt (ed.), *Christian Millenarianism: From the Early Church to Waco*, London: Hurst & Company, 2001, 12–25.

Hampton, Mark, *Visions of the Press in Britain, 1850–1950*, Urbana: University of Illinois Press, 2004.

Hanna, Martha, *The Mobilization of Intellect: French Scholars and Writers during the Great War*, Cambridge: MA: Harvard University Press, 1996.

Harling, Philip, 'The Centrality of Locality: The Local State, Local Democracy, and Local Consciousness in Late-Victorian and Edwardian Britain', *Journal of Victorian Culture*, vol. 9, no. 2, 2004, 216–34.

Harling, Philip, 'The Powers of the Victorian State', in Peter Mandler (ed.), *Liberty and Authority in Victorian Britain*, Oxford: Oxford University Press, 2006, 25–49.

Harris, José, *Private Lives, Public Spirit: A Social History of Britain, 1870–1914*, Oxford: Oxford University Press, 1993.

Harris, José, 'English Ideas about Community: Another Case of "Made in Germany"?', in Rudolf Muhs, Johannes Paulman and Willibald Steinmetz (eds), *Aneignung und Abwehr: Interkultureller Transfer zwischen Deutschland und Großbritannien im 19. Jahrhundert*, Bodenheim: Philo, 1998, 143–58.

Harris, José (ed.), *Civil Society in British History: Ideas, Identities, Institutions*, Oxford: Oxford University Press, 2003.

Harris, Sally, *Out of Control: British Foreign Policy and the Union of Democratic Control, 1914–1918*, Hull: University of Hull Press, 1996.

Harrison, Brian, 'Civil Society by Accident? Paradoxes of Voluntarism and Pluralism in the Nineteenth and Twentieth Centuries', in José Harris (ed.), *Civil Society in British History: Ideas, Identities, Institutions*, Oxford: Oxford University Press, 2003, 79–96.

Haste, Cate, *Keep the Home Fires Burning: Propaganda in the First World War*, London: Allen Lane, 1977.

Hendley, Matthew, '"Help us to secure a strong, healthy and peaceful Britain": The Social Arguments of the Campaign for Compulsory Military Service in Britain, 1899–1914', *Canadian Journal of History*, vol. 30, no. 2, 1995, 261–88.

Hennock, E.P., *British Social Reform and German Precedents: The Case of Social Insurance, 1880–1914*, Oxford: Clarendon Press, 1987.

Hiley, Nicholas, '"Kitchener Wants You" and "Daddy, what did YOU do in the Great War?": The Myth of British Recruiting Posters', *Imperial War Museum Review*, vol. 11, 1999, 40–58.

Hill, Christopher, *Puritanism and Revolution: Studies in Interpretation of the English Revolution of the 17th Century*, London: Mercury Books, 1962.

Hinks, John, *Ramsay MacDonald: The Leicester years (1906–1918)*, Leicester: private publication, 1996.

Hinton, James, *Labour and Socialism: A History of the British Labour Movement, 1867–1974*, Brighton: Wheatsheaf Books, 1983.

Hole, Robert, 'British Counter-Revolutionary Popular Propaganda in the 1790's', in Colin Jones (ed.), *Britain and Revolutionary France: Conflict, Subversion and Propaganda*, Exeter: University of Exeter, 1983, 53–69.

Hollis, Patricia, *Ladies Elect: Women in English Local Government, 1865–1914*, Oxford: Clarendon Press, 1987.

Hoover, A.J., *God, Germany, and Britain in the Great War: A Study in Clerical Nationalism*, New York: Praeger, 1989.

Horne, John, '"L'impôt du sang": Republican Rhetoric and Industrial Warfare in France, 1914–18', *Social History*, vol. 14, no. 2, 1989, 201–23.

Horne, John, 'Remobilizing for "Total War": France and Britain, 1917–1918', in John Horne (ed.), *State, Society and Mobilization in Europe during the First World War*, Cambridge: Cambridge University Press, 1997, 195–211.

Horne, John (ed.), *A Companion to World War I*, Oxford: Wiley-Blackwell, 2010.

Horne, John N., *Labour at War: France and Britain, 1914–1918*, Oxford: Clarendon Press, 1991.

Horne, John and Kramer, Alan, 'War between Soldiers and Enemy Civilians, 1914–1915', in Roger Chickering and Stig Förster (eds), *Great War, Total War: Combat and Mobilization on the Western Front, 1914–1918*, Cambridge: Cambridge University Press, 2000, 153–68.

Horne, John and Kramer, Alan, *German Atrocities, 1914: A History of Denial*, New Haven: Yale University Press, 2001.

Howell, Philip, 'Industry and Identity: The North–South Divide and the Geography of Belonging, 1830–1918', in Alan R.H. Baker and Mark Billinge (eds), *Geographies of England: The North–South Divide, Material and Imagined*, Cambridge: Cambridge University Press, 2004, 64–87.

Hughes, Michael, 'British Methodists and the First World War', *Methodist History*, vol. 41, no. 2, 2002, 316–28.

Hunt, Stephen, *Christian Millenarianism: From the Early Church to Waco*, London: Hurst & Company, 2001.

Hyam, Ronald, *Britain's Imperial Century, 1815–1914: A Study of Empire and Expansion*, 3rd edn, Basingstoke: Palgrave MacMillan, 2002.

Hynes, Samuel, *A War Imagined: The First World War and English Culture*, London: Bodley Head, 1990.

Johnson, Graham, '"Making Reform the Instrument of Revolution": British Social Democracy, 1881–1911', *The Historical Journal*, vol. 43, no. 4, 2000, 977–1002.

Jones, Aled Gruffydd, *Press, Politics and Society: A History of Journalism in Wales*, Cardiff: University of Wales Press, 1993.

Jones, Heather, O'Brien, Jennifer and Schmidt-Supprian, Christoph (eds), *Untold War: New Perspectives on First World War Studies*, Leiden: Brill, 2008.

Jones, Max, '"Our King upon His Knees": The Public Commemoration of Captain Scott's Last Antarctic Expedition', in Geoffrey Cubitt and Allen Warren (eds), *Heroic Reputations and Exemplary Lives*, Manchester: Manchester University Press, 2000, 105–22.

Jones, Max, *The Last Great Quest: Captain Scott's Antarctic Sacrifice*, Oxford: Oxford University Press, 2003.

Jowett, Garth S. and O'Donnell, Victoria, *Propaganda and Persuasion*, 4th edn, London: Sage Publications, 2006 (1986).

Joyce, Patrick, *Visions of the People: Industrial England and the Question of Class, 1848–1914*, Cambridge: Cambridge University Press, 1993.

Joyce, Patrick, 'The Constitution and the Narrative Structure of Victorian Politics', in James Vernon (ed.), *Re-reading the Constitution: New Narratives in the Political History of England's Long Nineteenth Century*, Cambridge: Cambridge University Press, 1996, 179–203.

Kearney, Hugh, *The British Isles: A History of Four Nations*, 2nd edn, Cambridge: Cambridge University Press, 2006 (1989).

Keatley Moore, H. (ed.), *Croydon and the Great War: The Official History of the War Work of the Borough and Its Citizens from 1914 to 1919, Together with the Croydon Roll of Honour*, Croydon: Corporation of Croydon, 1920.

Kennedy, Paul M., *The Rise of the Anglo–German Antagonism, 1860–1914*, London: George Allen & Unwin, 1980.

Keohane, Nigel, *The Party of Patriotism: The Conservative Party and the First World War*, Farnham: Ashgate, 2010.

Kinnear, Michael, *The British Voter: An Atlas and Survey since 1885*, Ithaca, NY: Cornell University Press, 1968.

Kitchen, James E., '"Khaki Crusaders": Crusading Rhetoric and the British Imperial Soldier during the Egypt and Palestine Campaigns, 1916–1918', *First World War Studies*, vol. 1, no. 2, 2010, 141–60.

Koss, Stephen, *Fleet Street Radical: A.G. Gardiner and the* Daily News, London: Allen Lane, 1973.

Koss, Stephen, *Nonconformity in Modern British Politics*, London: B.T. Batsford, 1975.

Koss, Stephen, *The Rise and Fall of the Political Press in Britain*, 2 vols, London: Hamish Hamilton, 1981/1984.

Kramer, Alan, *Dynamic of Destruction: Culture and Mass Killing in the First World War*, Oxford: Oxford University Press, 2007.

Krebs, Paula M., *Gender, Race, and the Writing of Empire: Public Discourse and the Boer War*, Cambridge: Cambridge University Press, 1999.

Kumar, Krishan, *The Making of English National Identity*, Cambridge: Cambridge University Press, 2003.

Lambourne, Nicola, 'First World War Propaganda and the Use and Abuse of Historic Monuments on the Western Front', *Imperial War Museum Review*, vol. 12, 1999, 96–108.

Langan, Mary and Schwarz, Bill (eds), *Crises in the British State, 1880–1930*, London: Hutchinson, 1985.

Larrabeiti, Michelle de, 'Conspicuous before the World: The Political Rhetoric of the Chartist Women', in Eileen Janes Yeo (ed.), *Radical Femininity: Women's Self-Representation in the Public Sphere*, Manchester: Manchester University Press, 1998, 106–26.

Lasswell, Harold D., *Propaganda Technique in the World War*, 2nd edn, London: Kegan Paul, 1938.

Lawrence, Jon, 'Class and Gender in the Making of Urban Toryism, 1880–1914', *English Historical Review*, vol. 108, 1993, 629–52.

Lawrence, Jon, 'The First World War and its Aftermath', in Paul Johnson (ed.), *Twentieth-Century Britain: Economic, Social and Cultural Change*, London: Longman, 1994, 151–68.

Lawrence, Jon, 'The Dynamics of Urban Politics, 1867–1914', in Jon Lawrence and Miles Taylor (eds), *Party, State and Society: Electoral Behaviour in Britain since 1820*, Aldershot, Scolar Press, 1997, 79–105.

Lawrence, Jon, *Speaking for the People: Party, Language and Popular Politics in England, 1867–1914*, Cambridge: Cambridge University Press, 1998.

Lawrence, Jon, 'Review: Brock Millman, *Managing Domestic Dissent in First World War Britain*', *Twentieth Century British History*, vol. 14, no. 1, 2003, 86–88.

Lawrence, Jon, 'Forging a Peaceable Kingdom: War, Violence, and Fear of Brutalization in Post-First World War Britain', *Journal of Modern History*, vol. 75, no. 3, 2003, 557–89.

Lawrence, Jon, 'The Transformation of British Public Politics after the First World War', *Past and Present*, vol. 190, February 2006, 185–216.

Lawrence, Jon, 'Public Space, Political Space', in Jay Winter and Jean-Louis Robert (eds), *Capital Cities at War: Paris, London, Berlin, 1914–1919*, vol. 2, *A Cultural History*, Cambridge: Cambridge University Press, 2007, 280–312.

Leventhal, Fred M. and Quinault, Roland (eds), *Anglo-American Attitudes: From Revolution to Partnership*, Aldershot: Ashgate, 2000.

Liddle, Peter H. (ed.), *Home Fires and Foreign Fields: British Social and Military Experience in the First World War*, London: Brassey's Defence Publishers, 1985.

McCarthy, Helen, 'The League of Nations, Public Ritual and National Identity in Britain, c. 1919–56', *History Workshop Journal*, vol. 70, 2010, 108–32.

McCartney, Helen B., *Citizen Soldiers: The Liverpool Territorials in the First World War*, Cambridge: Cambridge University Press, 2005.

McClelland, Keith, '"England's Greatness, the Working Man"', in Catherine Hall, Keith McClelland and Jane Rendall, *Defining the Victorian Nation: Class, Race, Gender and the British Reform Act of 1867*, Cambridge: Cambridge University Press, 2000, 71–118.

McClelland, Keith and Rose, Sonya, 'Citizenship and Empire, 1867–1928', in Catherine Hall and Sonya O. Rose (eds), *At Home with the Empire: Metropolitan Culture and the Imperial World*, Cambridge: Cambridge University Press, 2006, 275–97.

Mackenzie, John M., *Propaganda and Empire: The Manipulation of British Public Opinion, 1880–1960*, Manchester: Manchester University Press, 1984.

Mackenzie, John M., 'Heroic Myths of Empire', in idem (ed.), *Popular Imperialism and the Military, 1850–1950*, Manchester: Manchester University Press, 1992, 109–38.

Mackenzie, John M. (ed.), *Popular Imperialism and the Military, 1850–1950*, Manchester: Manchester University Press, 1992.

McKibbin, Ross, *The Evolution of the Labour Party, 1910–1924*, 3rd edn, Oxford: Clarendon Press, 1986 (1974).

McLaine, Ian, *Ministry of Morale: Home Front Morale and the Ministry of Information in World War II*, London: George Allen & Unwin, 1979.

Macleod, Jenny and Purseigle, Pierre (eds), *Uncovered Fields: Perspectives in First World War Studies*, Leiden: Brill, 2004.

Malvern, Sue, *Modern Art, Britain and the Great War: Witnessing, Testimony and Remembrance*, New Haven: Yale University Press, 2004.

Mandler, Peter, *History and National Life*, London: Profile Books, 2002.

Mandler, Peter, *The English National Character: The History of an Idea from Edmund Burke to Tony Blair*, New Haven: Yale University Press, 2006.

Mandler, Peter (ed.), *Liberty and Authority in Victorian Britain*, Oxford: Oxford University Press, 2006.

Manela, Erez, 'Imagining Woodrow Wilson in Asia: Dreams of East–West Harmony and the Revolt against Empire in 1919', *The American Historical Review*, vol. 111, no. 5, December 2006, 1327–51.

Mangan, J.A., *Athleticism in the Victorian and Edwardian Public School: The Emergence and Consolidation of an Educational Ideology*, Cambridge: Cambridge University Press, 1981.

Mansfield, Nicholas, *English Farmworkers and Local Patriotism, 1900–1930*, Aldershot: Ashgate, 2001.

Marsh, Peter, 'Lord Salisbury and the Ottoman Massacres', *Journal of British Studies*, vol. 11, no. 2, 1972, 62–83.

Marwick, Arthur, *The Deluge: British Society and the First World War*, Boston: Little Brown, 1965.

Matthew, H.C.G., *The Liberal Imperialists: The Ideas and Politics of a Post-Gladstonian Élite*, Oxford: Oxford University Press, 1973.

Matthew, H.C.G., 'Rhetoric and Politics in Great Britain, 1860–1950', in P.J. Waller (ed.), *Politics and Social Change in Modern Britain: Essays Presented to A.F. Thompson*, Hassocks: Harvester Press, 1987.

Messinger, Gary, *British Propaganda and the State in the First World War*, Manchester: Manchester University Press, 1992.

Meyer, Henry Cord, *Mitteleuropa in German Thought and Action, 1815–1945*, The Hague: Martinus Nijhoff, 1955.

Miller, David, *On Nationality*, 2nd edn, Oxford: Clarendon Press, 1999.

Millman, Brock, *Managing Domestic Dissent in First World War Britain*, London: Frank Cass, 2000.

Millman, Brock, *Pessimism and British War Policy, 1916–1918*, London: Frank Cass, 2001.

Millman, Brock, 'HMG and the War against Dissent, 1914–1918', *Journal of Contemporary History*, vol. 40, no. 3, 2005, 413–40.

Monger, David, 'The National War Aims Committee and British Patriotism during the First World War', PhD dissertation, King's College London, 2009.

Monger, David, '"No Mere Silent Commander"? Sir Henry Horne and the Mentality of Command during the First World War', *Historical Research*, vol. 82, no. 216, 2009, 340–59.

Monger, David, 'Sporting Journalism and the Maintenance of Servicemen's Ties to Civilian Life in First World War Propaganda', *Sport in History*, vol. 30, no. 3, 2010, 374–401.

Monger, David, 'Soldiers, Propaganda and Ideas of Home and Community in First World War Britain', *Cultural and Social History*, vol. 8, no. 3, 2011, 331–54.

Moody, Michael, '"*Vive La Nation!*" French Revolutionary Themes in the Posters & Prints of the First World War', *Imperial War Museum Review*, vol. 3, 1988, 34–43.

Moore, Gregory, 'The Super-Hun and the Super-State: Allied Propaganda and German Philosophy during the First World War', *German Life and Letters*, vol. 54, no. 4, October 2001, 310–30.

Morgan, Kenneth O., 'Peace Movements in Wales, 1899–1945', *Welsh History Review*, vol. 10, 1981, 398–430.

Morgan, Marjorie, *National Identities and Travel in Victorian Britain*, Basingstoke: Palgrave, 2001.

Mori, Jennifer, 'Languages of Loyalism: Patriotism, Nationhood and the State in the 1790s', *English Historical Review*, vol. 143, no. 475, 2003, 33–58.

Mulvey, Paul, 'From Liberalism to Labour: Josiah C. Wedgwood and English Liberalism during the First World War', in Pierre Purseigle (ed.), *Warfare and Belligerence: Perspectives in First World War Studies*, Leiden: Brill, 2005, 189–214.

Nicholas, Siân, *The Echo of War: Home Front Propaganda and the Wartime BBC, 1939–45*, Manchester: Manchester University Press, 1996.

Nicholas, Siân, 'From John Bull to John Citizen: Images of National Identity and Citizenship on the Wartime BBC', in Richard Weight and Abigail Beach (eds), *The Right to Belong: Citizenship and National Identity in Britain, 1930–1960*, London: I.B. Tauris, 1998, 36–58.

Otter, Sandra den, *British Idealism and Social Explanation: A Study in Late Victorian Thought*, Oxford: Clarendon, 1996.

Otter, Sandra den, '"Thinking in Communities": Late Nineteenth-Century Liberals,

Idealists and the Retrieval of Community', in E.H.H. Green (ed.), *An Age of Transition: British Politics 1880–1914*, Edinburgh: Edinburgh University Press, 1997, 67–84.

Packer, Ian, *Lloyd George, Liberalism and the Land: The Land Issue and Party Politics in England, 1906–1914*, London: Boydell Press, 2001.

Pankhurst, Sylvia, *The Home Front: A Mirror to Life in England during the First World War*, London: The Cresset Library, 1987 (1932).

Parry, J.P., 'The Impact of Napoleon III on British Politics, 1851–1880', *Transactions of the Royal Historical Society*, 6th series, vol. 11, 2001, 147–75.

Parry, J.P., 'Liberalism and Liberty', in Peter Mandler (ed.), *Liberty and Authority in Victorian Britain*, Oxford: Oxford University Press, 2006, 71–100.

Parry, Jonathan, *The Politics of Patriotism: English Liberalism, National Identity and Europe, 1830–1886*, Cambridge: Cambridge University Press, 2006.

Pearce, Cyril, *Comrades in Conscience: The Story of an English Community's Opposition to the Great War*, London: Francis Boutle, 2001.

Pennell, Catriona, '"The Germans Have Landed!": Invasion Fears in the South-East of England, August to December 1914', in Heather Jones, Jennifer O'Brien and Christoph Schmidt-Supprian (eds), *Untold War: New Perspectives on First World War Studies*, Leiden: Brill, 2008, 95–116.

Perkins, Bradford, *The Great Rapprochement: England and the United States, 1895–1914*, London: Victor Gollancz, 1969.

Petersoo, Pille, 'Reconsidering Otherness: Constructing Estonian Identity', *Nations and Nationalism*, vol. 13, no. 1, 2007, 117–33.

Pickles, Katie, *Transnational Outrage: The Death and Commemoration of Edith Cavell*, Basingstoke: Palgrave MacMillan, 2007.

Pocock, J.G.A., 'The Limits and Divisions of British History: In Search of the Unknown Subject', *American Historical Review*, vol. 87, no. 2, 1982, 311–36.

Ponsonby, Arthur, *Falsehood in War-time: Containing an Assortment of Lies Circulated throughout the Nations during the Great War*, London: Allen & Unwin, 1928.

Porter, Bernard, *The Absent-Minded Imperialists: Empire, Society, and Culture in Britain*, Oxford: Oxford University Press, 2004.

Price, John, 'Heroism in Everyday Life: The Watts Memorial for Heroic Self Sacrifice', *History Workshop Journal*, vol. 63, 2007, 255–78.

Prior, Robin and Wilson, Trevor, *The Somme*, New Haven: Yale University Press, 2005.

Proctor, Tammy M., *Civilians in a World at War, 1914–1918*, New York: New York University Press, 2010.

Pugh, Martin, *The Tories and the People, 1880–1935*, Oxford: Basil Blackwell, 1985.

Pugh, Martin, 'The Rise of Labour and the Political Culture of Conservatism, 1890–1945', *History*, vol. 87, no. 288, October 2002, 514–37.

Purseigle, Pierre, 'Beyond and below the Nations: Towards a Comparative History of Local Communities at War', in Jenny Macleod and Purseigle (eds), *Uncovered Fields: Perspectives in First World War Studies*, Leiden: Brill, 2004, 95–123.

Purseigle, Pierre, 'Introduction: Warfare and Belligerence: Approaches to the First World War', in idem (ed.), *Warfare and Belligerence: Perspectives in First World War Studies*, Leiden: Brill, 2005, 1–37.

Purseigle, Pierre (ed.), *Warfare and Belligerence: Perspectives in First World War Studies*, Leiden: Brill, 2005.

Quinault, Roland, 'The Cult of the Centenary, *c.*1784–1914', *Historical Research*, vol. 71, no. 176, 1998, 303–23.

Quinault, Roland, 'Anglo-American Atttitudes to Democracy from Lincoln to Churchill', in Fred M. Leventhal and Roland Quinault (eds), *Anglo-American Attitudes: From Revolution to Partnership*, Aldershot: Ashgate, 2000, 124–41.

Rae, J., *Conscience and Politics: The British Government and the Conscientious Objector to Military Service 1916–1919*, London: Oxford University Press, 1970.

Ramsden, John, *A History of the Conservative Party*, vol. 3, *The Age of Balfour and Baldwin, 1902–1940*, London: Longman, 1978.

Ramsden, John, *Don't Mention the War: The British and the Germans since 1890*, London: Little Brown, 2006.

Read, J.M., *Atrocity Propaganda, 1914–1919*, New Haven: Yale University Press, 1941.

Reader, W.J., *'At Duty's call': A Study in Obsolete Patriotism*, Manchester: Manchester University Press, 1988.

Readman, Paul, 'The Liberal Party and Patriotism in Early Twentieth Century Britain', *Twentieth Century British History*, vol. 12, no. 3, 2001, 269–302.

Readman, Paul, 'The Place of the Past in English Culture c.1890–1914', *Past and Present*, vol. 186, February 2005, 147–99.

Reeves, Nicholas, *Official British Film Propaganda during the First World War*, London: Croom Helm, 1986.

Reeves, Nicholas, *The Power of Film Propaganda: Myth or Reality?*, London: Cassell, 1999.

Reid, Alastair, 'Dilution, Trade Unionism and the State in Britain during the First World War', in Stephen Tolliday and Jonathan Zeitlin (eds), *Shop Floor Bargaining and the State: Historical and Comparative Perspectives*, Cambridge: Cambridge University Press, 1975, 46–74.

Rendall, Jane, 'The Citizenship of Women and the Reform Act of 1867', in Catherine Hall, Keith McClelland and Jane Rendall, *Defining the Victorian Nation: Class, Race, Gender and the British Reform Act of 1867*, Cambridge: Cambridge University Press, 2000, 119–75.

Renton, James, 'Changing Languages of Empire and the Orient: Britain and the Invention of the Middle East, 1917–1918', *Historical Journal*, vol. 50, no. 3, 2007, 645–67.

Richards, Jeffrey, 'Popular Imperialism and the Image of the Army in Juvenile Literature', in John M. Mackenzie (ed.), *Popular Imperialism and the Military, 1850–1950*, Manchester: Manchester University Press, 1992, 80–108.

Riedi, Eliza and Mason, Tony, '"Leather" and the Fighting Spirit: Sport in the British Army in World War I', *Canadian Journal of History*, vol. 41, no. 3, 2006, 486–515.

Rix, Kathryn, 'The Party Agent and English Electoral Culture, 1880–1906', PhD dissertation, University of Cambridge, 2001.

Rix, Kathryn, '"Go Out into the Highways and the Hedges": The Diary of Michael Sykes, Conservative Political Lecturer, 1895 and 1907–8', *Parliamentary History*, vol. 20, no. 2, 2001, 209–31.

Roper, Michael, *The Secret Battle: Emotional Survival in the Great War*, Manchester: Manchester University Press, 2009.

Rose, Sonya O., *Which People's War? National Identity and Citizenship in Britain, 1939–1945*, Oxford: Oxford University Press, 2003.

Rosen, Greg, *Dictionary of Labour Biography*, London: Politico's, 2001.

Rothwell, V.H., *British War Aims and Peace Diplomacy, 1914–1918*, Oxford: Clarendon Press, 1971.

Rouven-Steinbach, Daniel, 'Defending the *Heimat*: The Germans in South-West Africa and East Africa during the First World War', in Heather Jones, Jennifer O-Brien and Christoph Schmidt-Supprian (eds), *Untold War: New Perspectives in First World War Studies*, Leiden: Brill, 2008, 179–208.

Rüger, Jan, 'Entertainments', in Jay Winter and Jean-Louis Robert (eds), *Capital Cities at War: Paris, London, Berlin 1914–1919*, vol. 2, *A Cultural History*, Cambridge: Cambridge University Press, 2007, 105–40.

Ruston, Alan, 'Protestant Nonconformist Attitudes to the First World War', in Alan F.P. Sell and Anthony R. Cross (eds), *Protestant Nonconformity in the Twentieth Century*, Carlisle: Paternoster Press, 2003, 240–63.

Rutherford, Jonathan, *Forever England: Reflections on Masculinity and Empire*, London: Lawrence and Wishart, 1997.

Ruthrof, Hans, *The Reader's Construction of Narrative*, London: Routledge & Kegan Paul, 1981.

Said, Edward W., *Orientalism*, 5th edn, London: Penguin Books, 2003.

Salvidge, Stanley, *Salvidge of Liverpool: Behind the Political Scene, 1890–1928*, London: Hodder & Stoughton, 1934.

Samuel, Raphael (ed.), *Patriotism: The Making and Unmaking of British National Identity*, 3 vols, London: Routledge, 1989.

Samuel, Raphael, *Island Stories: Unravelling Britain. Theatres of Memory*, vol. II, ed. Alison Light, Sally Alexander and Gareth Stedman Jones, London: Verso, 1998.

Sanders, M.L. and Taylor, Philip M., *British Propaganda during the First World War, 1914–18*, London: MacMillan, 1982.

Schneer, Jonathan, *Ben Tillett: Portrait of a Labour Leader*, Urbana: University of Illinois Press, 1982.

Scholes, Percy A., *God Save the Queen! The History and Romance of the World's First National Anthem*, London: Oxford University Press, 1954.

Searle, G.R., *The Quest for National Efficiency: A Study in British Politics and Political Thought, 1899–1914*, London: Ashfield Press, 1990.

Searle, G.R., *A New England? Peace and War, 1886–1918*, Oxford: Clarendon Press, 2004.

Sheffield, Gary, *Forgotten Victory: The First World War: Myths and Realities*, London: Review, 2001.

Silbey, David, *The British Working Class and Enthusiasm for War, 1914–1916*, London: Frank Cass, 2005.

Simkins, Peter, *Kitchener's Army: The Raising of the New Armies, 1914–1916*, Manchester: Manchester University Press, 1988.

Smith, Anthony D., *National Identity*, London: Penguin, 1991.

Smith, Anthony D., 'The "Sacred" Dimension of Nationalism', *Millennium – Journal of International Studies*, vol. 29, 2000, 791–814.

Smith, Anthony D., *The Nation in History: Historiographical Debates about Ethnicity and Nationalism*, Cambridge: Polity Press, 2000.

Smith, Anthony D., *Chosen Peoples*, Oxford: Oxford University Press, 2003.

Smith, Anthony D., *The Cultural Foundations of Nations: Hierarchy, Covenant, and Republic*, Oxford: Blackwell, 2008.

Snape, Michael, *God and the British Soldier: Religion and the British Army in the First and Second World Wars*, London: Routledge, 2005.

Snell, K.D.M., *Parish and Belonging: Community, Identity and Welfare in England and Wales, 1700–1950*, Cambridge: Cambridge University Press, 2006.

Sondhaus, Lawrence, *World War I: The Global Revolution*, Cambridge: Cambridge University Press, 2011.

Sorlin, Pierre, 'Film and the War', in John Horne (ed.), *A Companion to World War I*, Oxford: Wiley-Blackwell, 2010, 353–67.

Squires, James Duane, *British Propaganda at Home and in the United States from 1914 to 1917*, Cambridge, MA: Harvard University Press, 1935.

Stanley, Brian, 'Church, State, and the Hierarchy of "Civilization": The Making of the "Missions and Governments" Report at the World Missionary Conference, Edinburgh 1910', in Andrew Porter (ed.), *The Imperial Horizons of British Protestant Missions, 1880–1914*, Grand Rapids: William B. Eerdmans, 2003, 58–84.

Stapleton, Julia, 'Citizenship versus Patriotism in Twentieth-Century England', *The Historical Journal*, vol. 48, no. 1, 2005, 151–78.

Stapleton, Julia, *Christianity, Patriotism and Nationhood: The England of G.K. Chesterton*, Lanham: Lexington Books, 2009.

Stenton, Michael and Lees, Stephen, *Who's Who of British Members of Parliament, A Biographical Dictionary of the House of Commons: Based on Annual Volumes of 'Dods' Parliamentary Companion' and Other Sources*, vols II (1885–1918) and III (1919–1945), Hassocks: Harvester Press, 1978, 1979.

Stevenson, David, *The First World War and International Politics*, Oxford: Oxford University Press, 1988.

Stevenson, David, *1914–1918: The History of the First World War*, London: Penguin, 2004.

Stibbe, Matthew, *German Anglophobia and the Great War, 1914–1918*, Cambridge: Cambridge University Press, 2001.

Strachan, Hew, *The First World War*, vol. 1, *To Arms*, Oxford: Oxford University Press, 2003.

Stubbs, J.O., 'Lord Milner and Patriotic Labour, 1914–1918', *English Historical Review*, vol. 87, no. 345, 1972, 717–54.

Summers, Anne, 'Militarism in Britain before the Great War', *History Workshop Journal*, vol. 2, no. 1, 1976, 104–23.

Sutton, David, 'Liberalism, State Collectivism and the Social Relations of Citizenship', in Mary Langan and Bill Schwarz (eds), *Crises in the British State, 1880–1930*, London: Hutchinson, 1985, 63–79.

Swanwick, H.M., *Builders of Peace: Being the History of the Union of Democratic Control*, London: Swathmore Press, 1924.

Swartz, Marvin, *The Union of Democratic Control in British Politics during the First World War*, Oxford: Clarendon Press, 1971.

Sweet, David, 'The Domestic Scene: Parliament and People', in Peter H. Liddle (ed.), *Home Fires and Foreign Fields: British Social and Military Experience in the First World War*, London: Brassey's Defence Publishers, 1985, 9–19.

Symons, Julian, *Horatio Bottomley*, London: House of Stratus, 2001 (1955).

Tanner, Duncan, *Political Change and the Labour Party, 1900–1918*, Cambridge: Cambridge University Press, 1990.

Taylor, A.J.P., *The Trouble Makers: Dissent over Foreign Policy, 1792–1939*, London: Hamish Hamilton, 1957.

Taylor, Miles, 'John Bull and the Iconography of Public Opinion in England, c. 1712–1929', *Past & Present*, vol. 134, 1992, 93–128.

Terwey, Susanne, 'Stereotypical Bedfellows: The Combination of Anti-Semitism with Germanophobia in Great Britain, 1914–1918', in Jenny Macleod and Pierre Purseigle (eds), *Uncovered Fields: Perspectives in First World War Studies*, Leiden: Brill, 2004, 125–41.

Thackeray, David, 'Building a Peaceable Party: Masculine Identities in British Conservative Politics, c. 1903–1924', *Historical Research*, forthcoming.

Thompson, Andrew, *The Empire Strikes Back? The Impact of Imperialism on Britain from the Mid-Nineteenth Century*, London: Pearson, 2005.

Thompson, F.M.L., 'Social Control in Victorian Britain', *The Economic History Review*, vol. 34, no. 2, 1981, 189–208.

Thomson, Basil, *The Scene Changes*, Garden City: Doubleday, Doran & Co., 1937.

Tombs, Robert and Tombs, Isabelle, *That Sweet Enemy: The French and the British from the Sun King to the Present*, London: William Heinemann, 2006.

Travers, Tim, *The Killing Ground: The British Army, the Western Front & the Emergence of Modern Warfare, 1900–1918*, Barnsley: Pen & Sword, 2003 (1987).

Turberfield, Alan, *John Scott Lidgett: Archbishop of British Methodism?*, Peterborough: Epworth Press, 2003.

Turner, John, *British Politics and the Great War: Coalition and Conflict, 1915–1918*, New Haven: Yale University Press, 1992.

Vernon, James, 'Border Crossings: Cornwall and the English (Imagi)Nation', in Geoffrey Cubitt (ed.), *Imagining Nations*, Manchester: Manchester University Press, 1998, 153–72.

Vickers, Matthew, 'Civic Image and Civic Patriotism in Liverpool 1880–1914', DPhil dissertation, University of Oxford: 2000.

Vockler, John Charles, 'Frodsham, George Horsfall (1863–1937)', *Australian Dictionary of Biography*, vol. 8, Melbourne: Melbourne University Press, 1981, 590–91.

Waites, Bernard, 'The Government of the Home Front and the "Moral Economy" of the Working Class', in Peter H. Liddle (ed.), *Home Fires and Foreign Fields: British Social and Military Experience in the First World War*, London: Brassey's Defence Publishers, 1985, 175–93.

Waites, Bernard, *A Class Society at War: England, 1914–1918*, Leamington Spa: Berg, 1987.

Wallace, Stuart, *War and the Image of Germany: British Academics, 1914–1918*, Edinburgh: John Donald, 1988.

Ward, Paul, *Red Flag and Union Jack: Englishness, Patriotism and the British Left, 1881–1924*, Woodbridge: Boydell Press, 1998.

Ward, Paul, 'Socialists and "True" Patriotism in Britain in the Late 19th and Early 20th Centuries', *National Identities*, vol. 1, no. 2, 1999, 179–94.

Ward, Paul, 'Women of Britain Say Go: Women's Patriotism in the First World War', *Twentieth Century British History*, vol. 12, no. 1, 2001, 23–45.

Ward, Paul, *Britishness since 1870*, London: Routledge, 2004.

Ward, Stephen R., 'The British Veterans' Ticket of 1918', *The Journal of British Studies*, vol. 8, no. 1, 1968, 155–69.

Warren, Allen, 'Sir Robert Baden-Powell, the Scout Movement and Citizen Training in Great Britain, 1900–1920', *English Historical Review*, vol. 101, no. 399, 1986, 376–98.

Warwick-Haller, Sally, *William O'Brien and the Irish Land War*, Dublin: Irish Academic Press, 1990.

Watson, Alexander and Porter, Patrick, 'Bereaved and Aggrieved: Combat Motivation and the Ideology of Sacrifice in the First World War', *Historical Research*, vol. 83, no. 219, 2010, 146–64.

Watson, Janet S.K., *Fighting Different Wars: Experience, Memory, and the First World War in Britain*, Cambridge: Cambridge University Press, 2004.

Weinroth, Howard, 'Norman Angell and *The Great Illusion*: An Episode in Pre-1914 Pacifism', *The Historical Journal*, vol. 17, no. 3, 1974, 551–74.

Welch, David, *Germany, Propaganda and Total War, 1914–1918: The Sins of Omission*, London: Athlone Press, 2000.

Wilkinson, Alan, *The Church of England and the First World War*, London: SPCK, 1978.

Wilkinson, Alan, *Dissent or Conform? War, Peace and the English Churches 1900–1945*, London: SCM Press, 1981.

Williams, John, *The Home Fronts: Britain, France and Germany, 1914–1918*, London: Constable, 1972.

Williams, Richard, *The Contentious Crown: Public Discussion of the British Monarchy in the Reign of Queen Victoria*, Aldershot: Ashgate, 1997.

Wilson, Keith, 'The Foreign Office and the "Education" of Public Opinion Before the First World War', *The Historical Journal*, vol. 26, no. 2, 1983, 403–11.

Wilson, Trevor, *The Downfall of the Liberal Party, 1914–1935*, London: Collins, 1966.

Wilson, Trevor, *The Myriad Faces of War: Britain and the Great War, 1914–1918*, Cambridge: Polity Press, 1986.

Winter, J.M., *The Great War and the British People*, Basingstoke: Macmillan, 1986.

Winter, Jay, 'Spiritualism and the First World War', in R.W. Davis and R.J. Helmstadter (eds), *Religion and Irreligion in Victorian Society: Essays in Honor of R.K. Webb*, London: Routledge, 1992, 185–200.

Winter, Jay, 'British National Identity and the First World War', in S.J.D. Green and R.C. Whiting (eds), *The Boundaries of the State in Modern Britain*, Cambridge: Cambridge University Press, 1996, 261–77.

Winter, Jay, 'Popular Culture in Wartime Britain', in Aviel Roshwald and Richard Stites (eds), *European Culture in the Great War: The Arts, Entertainment, and Propaganda, 1914–1918*, Cambridge: Cambridge University Press, 1999, 330–48.

Winter, Jay and Prost, Antoine, *The Great War in History: Debates and Controversies, 1914 to the Present*, Cambridge: Cambridge University Press, 2005.

Winter, Jay and Robert, Jean-Louis, 'Conclusion', in Jay Winter and Jean-Louis Robert (eds), *Capital Cities at War: Paris, London, Berlin 1914–1919*, vol. 2, *A Cultural History*, Cambridge: Cambridge University Press, 2007, 468–81.

Winter, Jay, Parker, Geoffrey and Habeck, Mary R. (eds), *The Great War and the Twentieth Century*, New Haven and London: Yale University Press, 2000.

Winter, Jay and Robert, Jean-Louis (eds), *Capital Cities at War: Paris, London, Berlin 1914–1919*, vol. 2, *A Cultural History*, Cambridge: Cambridge University Press, 2007.

Wohl, Robert, *The Generation of 1914*, London: Weidenfeld and Nicholson, 1980.

Wolffe, John, *God and Greater Britain: Religion and National Life in Britain and Ireland, 1843–1950*, London: Routledge, 1994.

Wolffe, John, *Great Deaths: Grieving, Religion and Nationhood in Victorian and Edwardian Britain*, Oxford: Oxford University Press, 2000.

Wrigley, Chris, *Changes in the Battersea Labour Movement 1914–1919* (pamphlet), Department of Economics, Loughborough University, 1979 (1977).

Wrigley, Chris, 'The State and the Challenge of Labour in Britain, 1917–20', in idem (ed.), *Challenges of Labour: Central and Western Europe, 1917–1920*, London: Routledge, 1993, 262–88.

Wrigley, Chris (ed.), *Challenges of Labour: Central and Western Europe, 1917–1920*, London: Routledge, 1993.

Yeo, Eileen Janes (ed.), *Radical Femininity: Women's Self-Representation in the Public Sphere*, Manchester: Manchester University Press, 1998.

Young, Harry F., *Prince Lichnowsky and the Great War*, Athens, GA: University of Georgia Press, 1977.

Index

Note: names of localities generally refer to parliamentary constituencies.